Theatre Masks Out Side In

Theatre Masks Out Side In examines masks from different angles and perspectives, combining the history, design, construction, and use of masks into one beautifully illustrated resource.

Each chapter includes key information about an element of mask study: history and uses, theater traditions, practical principles for directing, performing exercises, design considerations, mask-making techniques, and considering makeup as mask. Artist interviews, theater company profiles, and hundreds of images provide insight into the variety of mask styles and performance applications. Project suggestions, discussion questions, useful worksheets, creative prompts, and resources for sourcing masks are included to inspire further exploration.

Theatre Masks Out Side In is designed with the beginning theater maker in mind, as well as prop makers, costume designers and technicians, and actors learning to use masks in performance.

Wendy J. Meaden is a costume designer, maker, and educator. She currently serves as a Professor of Theater and Associate Dean of the Jordan College of the Arts at Butler University. Her freelance career includes designs for Indiana Repertory Theatre, the Children's Museum of Indianapolis, and Cardinal Stage Company. Her fascination with masks grew out of a number of design projects, international collaborations, and the insatiable curiosity of her students.

Michael A. Brown initiated his exploration of masks as a student and later as a teacher at the prestigious London International School of Performing Arts, a center for physical and devised performance grounded in the training approaches developed by Jacques Lecoq. He has appeared in and directed numerous theater productions in the United States, United Kingdom, and China and served as a movement artist and trainer for the international phenomenon *War Horse* and for the feature film *Gravity*. Currently Michael is an Associate Professor of Theater and Director of the MA/MFA Program in Acting and Contemporary Performance Making at Columbia College, Chicago.

Theatre Masks Out Side In

Perspectives on Mask History, Design, Construction, and Performance

Wendy J. Meaden with Michael A. Brown

CRC Press is an imprint of the
Taylor & Francis Group, an **informa** business

A FOCAL PRESS BOOK

Designed front cover image: Neutral Mask by Alfredo Iriarte. Photo by Michael Brown.
Center back cover image: Mask by Mike Oleon for Rough House Theatre's Invitation to a Beheading. Photo by Michael Brown.
Left back cover image: The Fool by Bernardo Rey Rengifo for Woyzeck at Butler University. Photo by Steve Nyktas.
Right back cover image: Interior of Balinese Sidakarya mask. Photo by Steve Nyktas.

First published 2023
by Routledge
605 Third Avenue, New York, NY 10158

and by Routledge
4 Park Square, Milton Park, Abingdon, Oxon, OX14 4RN

Routledge is an imprint of the Taylor & Francis Group, an informa business

© 2023 Taylor & Francis

The right of Wendy J. Meaden with Michael A. Brown to be identified as authors of this work has been asserted in accordance with sections 77 and 78 of the Copyright, Designs and Patents Act 1988.

All rights reserved. No part of this book may be reprinted or reproduced or utilised in any form or by any electronic, mechanical, or other means, now known or hereafter invented, including photocopying and recording, or in any information storage or retrieval system, without permission in writing from the publishers.

Trademark notice: Product or corporate names may be trademarks or registered trademarks, and are used only for identification and explanation without intent to infringe.

Library of Congress Cataloging-in-Publication Data
A catalog record for this title has been requested

ISBN: 978-1-138-08418-6 (hbk)
ISBN: 978-1-138-08419-3 (pbk)
ISBN: 978-1-315-14621-8 (ebk)

DOI: 10.4324/9781315146218

Typeset in Gill Sans Std
By KnowledgeWorks Global Ltd.

*To our mentors, who brought us to this place,
and to our students, who will carry on.*

CONTENTS

Acknowledgments — xi
Introduction: Face to Face — 1

CHAPTER 1 FIRST ENCOUNTERS WITH MASKS — 3

FACES FASCINATE US — 3

MASKS ENGAGE US ON MANY LEVELS — 6

MASK FUNCTIONS — 10

MASK FORMS — 22

PROJECTS FOR FURTHER STUDY — 30

SELECTED RESOURCES — 31

CHAPTER 2 FACING THE STAGE — 33

EXPECTATIONS AND CODES — 36

CHINESE BIAN LIAN — 41

JAPANESE NOH AND KYOGEN — 42

BALINESE CALONARANG AND TOPENG — 51

KOREAN HAHOE AND SANDAE GUK — 54

THAI KHON — 57

SRI LANKAN SANNI AND TOVIL — 59

ANCIENT GREEK AND ROMAN — 62

EUROPEAN MEDIEVAL THEATER AND CARNIVAL — 67

ITALIAN COMMEDIA DELL'ARTE	69
CONTEMPORARY EUROPE AND AMERICA	76
PROJECTS FOR FURTHER STUDY	78
SELECTED RESOURCES	79

CHAPTER 3   THE DIRECTOR'S PERSPECTIVE — 81

SHOULD WE USE MASKS IN PERFORMANCE?	81
COLLABORATING WITH DESIGNERS	90
IN THE REHEARSAL ROOM	95
PROJECTS FOR FURTHER STUDY	99
SELECTED RESOURCES	99

CHAPTER 4   THE ACTOR'S PERSPECTIVE — 101

MASKS AND ACTOR TRAINING	101
THE NEUTRAL MASK	102
NEUTRAL MASK EXERCISES	104
FULL-FACE MASKS	105
FULL-FACE MASK EXERCISES	111
HALF-FACE MASKS	117
HALF-FACE MASK EXERCISES	119
CONCLUSION	121
SELECTED RESOURCES	122

CHAPTER 5   MASKS BY DESIGN — 123

ASKING QUESTIONS: FUNCTION, TRADITION, WORLD, CHARACTER, AND PRACTICALITIES	123
PREPARATION: RESEARCH	124
DECISIONS: THE FORM	136
DESIGNING THE DETAILS	146
STYLES	159
PROJECTS FOR FURTHER STUDY	166
SELECTED RESOURCES	167

CHAPTER 6 MASK MAKING — 169

- WHERE DO I BEGIN? — 169
- RESOURCE ANALYSIS: TIME/TALENT/TREASURE — 174
- PROCESS: FITTING THE ACTOR — 176
- PROCESS: SCULPTING THE DESIGN, CASTING AND MODELING – CREATING THE BASE FOR THE MASK — 179
- MASK TECHNIQUES AND MATERIALS — 183
- MODELING TECHNIQUES — 198
- MOLDING AND SHAPING — 202
- CAST MATERIALS — 217
- PATTERNING AND FORMING — 221
- CARVED MATERIALS — 224
- ADVANCED MATERIALS — 225
- PROJECTS FOR FURTHER STUDY — 234
- SELECTED RESOURCES — 235

CHAPTER 7 MAKEUP, A LIVING MASK — 237

- FORM — 237
- FUNCTION — 238
- CONCLUSION — 258
- PROJECTS FOR FURTHER STUDY — 258
- SELECTED RESOURCES — 259

Appendix A: Glossary — 261
Appendix B: Project Worksheets — 266
Appendix C: Resources for Buying Masks and Supplies — 275
Appendix D: Artists and Theater Companies that Work with Masks (A Selection) — 277
Appendix E: Plays that Use Masks (A Selection) — 279
Appendix F: Museums with Mask Collections (A Selection) — 281
Appendix G: Films and Videos that Feature Masks (A Selection) — 283
Bibliography — 287
Figure Credits — 292
Index — 303

ACKNOWLEDGMENTS

Theater relies on collaboration. From the performer's need of an audience to the creative work of teams of writers, directors, designers and makers, giving and receiving are integral to the art of performance. This is also true in education as ideas flow between mentors and students. Our efforts in creating this book are the result of myriad collaborations in classrooms, theaters, museums, and studios. We are grateful to all the artists who shared their time and love of mask arts with us. We appreciate them all, and name a few of those who have been particularly instrumental in our journey.

We are indebted to our mentors. Wendy thanks Bernardo Rey – the most inspiring of all artists/teachers; Marco Luly – keeping Commedia alive and relevant and who opened doors for me in Italy, I Nyoman Sedana and Kunju Vasudevan Namboodiripad for generosity of spirit and ideal collaborative experiences, and John Green – who started me on a journey of interest in physical theater and told me I could do anything. Michael is forever grateful to Thomas Prattki, who helped me find the mask under the mask, and continues to inspire and provoke; my collaborators in mask performance projects in London, Hong Kong, and Chicago, especially the wonderful artists and humans at AFTEC and my dear friends and collaborators at Rough House Theatre.

We thank our students who continue to teach as well as learn, and who participated in many exercises and projects with us. Their questions and curiosity drive us forward.

We are grateful for our many colleagues whose friendship, intelligence, and generosity inspired terrific conversations and collaborations and provided access to images and interviews for this project. Among them, Jonathan Becker, Russell Dean, Denise Wallace-Spriggs, Dr. Courtney Elkin-Mohler, Rob Faust, Giancarlo Santelli, Hajo Schüler, Vicki Wright, Rachael Savage, Mary McClung, Candy McCleman, Mike Oleon, Rachel Pollock of La Bricoleuse, Arianne Vitale Cardoso, Mike Chase, Sandy Bonds for permission to reprint photos from *Bejing Opera Costumes*, Dr. Amy Cohen, Ada Marcantonio at Castrum di Serravalle, Hideta Kitazawa, Ron Emmert, Willie Cole, Chelsea Warren, and Jackie Penrod.

As we continue to learn and explore, we thank all the scholars and artists who create and document this fascinating world. We thank the theater companies and museums who provided access to their collections: Association Werner Strub, Mattie Feint at The Clown Museum-London, Jennifer Noffze and The Children's Museum of Indianapolis, Indianapolis Museum of Art at Newfields, Wellcome Museum London, Alexander and Bonin Gallery, and Butler University. And we thank the artists and festivals that help keep mask performance alive and well through their creativity and support, among them our wonderful friends at Familie Flöz in Berlin and the London International Mime Festival.

And of course, we are indebted to our families. From Wendy: thank you to Tom, who is always there for me, and to my mum, Jody, who has been my first and final line of review: I appreciate your unfailing support. From Michael: thank you to Shannon, for being the counterbalance and the countermask, and to Gabriel, who reminds me that what's important is to play. Finally, we each thank our co-author for so many conversations, developments, and clarifications.

Wendy and Michael

INTRODUCTION

FACE TO FACE

Imagine a moment in human history – that first time when someone intentionally covered their face with another object and perhaps distorted their body as well. What prompted them to do that? What was the effect of their transformation? Was their intention to frighten or intimidate another, perhaps in a moment of conflict or battle? Were they planning to disguise themselves? Covering their head and body with the head and hide of an animal, to be less conspicuous while hunting? Were they attempting to take on the face, and thus the character, of another person, to honor or to mock them? Were they seeking to venerate or preserve the memory of a loved one, as with the death and funeral masks of ancient cultures? Were they hoping to conjure, appease, or embody spirits, gods, or devils by replacing their faces with an image of these supernatural beings? To share a story, or to entertain? What were they doing – this first person who put on a mask?

Whenever and wherever the first use of mask occurred – one thing we can say for sure is that its effect was powerful. So powerful, in fact, that masks have been with us for as long as we can trace back human history. They occur in religious rites, in shamanic practices, in formal ceremonies, in war, in festive celebrations, and in performances of various styles, across almost all cultures and geographic regions. Masks are so powerful, in fact, and so varied in their forms and uses, that a full examination of masks would draw us into the disciplines of (at least!) art, anthropology, religion, folklore, cultural studies, identity studies, psychology, performing arts, even architecture and political history. There are thousands of publications and performances to inform mask researchers. The study of masks engages us with the religious, social, and artistic histories of diverse cultures, and can even lead to a deeper understanding of human nature.

Our goal in this book is to investigate the power and appeal of masks, and to explore the application of that power to the art of theater and performance. For us, the starting point with masks involves two essential questions, which shape our journey through this book.

First, we ask "why." Why, as theater makers, would we choose to work with masks? What happens when the human face and/or body is "covered" by a mask? What are the emotional, cultural, aesthetic, and poetic responses of both the mask wearer and the audience? What characters and worlds can masks evoke? How do we decide that a performance allows for or even requires the use of masks?

Second, our book seeks to explore the question of "how." How does a mask come to be? How do we decide what a mask should look like? How do we approach its construction, choose materials, and develop a process? And once the mask is made, how is it brought to life by the performer? How is a world defined by the creative team? In addressing the questions of why and how, we become more accomplished theater makers, by deepening our performance, design, and construction skills, and by exposing ourselves to possibilities we might never have encountered otherwise.

Theatre Masks Out Side In is structured to look at masks from multiple perspectives. We bring the reader from the historical and cultural place of masks to the specific concrete challenges of designing, making, and performing with masks. We start with a broad perspective, introducing how masks function, and explaining a variety of ways masks are used and the forms they can take across different cultures, styles, and periods of history. Then we introduce a selection of masked performance traditions and consider their traditional systems of story, character, movement, and appearance. From there, we focus on the process and perspectives of some contemporary creative teams: directors, writers, designers, and devisers who discuss when and how to incorporate masks in their productions. Next, we invite you inside the mask to explore performer training with neutral, larval, and character masks. Then we lead you to design and build a mask, offering various techniques and considerations for constructing them. Finally, we consider some ways in which makeup is – and is not – masklike. Each chapter presents information to whet your appetite, get you thinking, and encourage you to make and play with masks. We are pleased to introduce you to some vibrant mask artists, companies, and sample productions. Resources and suggestions for further study are included in each chapter and in the appendices.

Each of these areas lends itself to a lifetime of exploration and study. Our interest in masks comes from our work as theater artists and teachers, discovering and delighting in the transformational power of masks, both in performance and in the classroom. This book has evolved out of our experiences as designer, maker, actor, writer, director, and teacher. In it, we share some of our delights and discoveries and offer them as a series of starting points for theater makers. We have tried to respond to our students' need for a selection of information on why masks capture our attention, how they have been used, and when and how to implement them in performance. We hope this introductory text will allow connections to be drawn among the cultural, historical, aesthetic, and performative elements, between the why and the how, and that it will be useful for introducing students and other theater makers to this fascinating aspect of human culture and creativity. We hope you will be engaged and inspired.

As worshippers, healers, artists, performers, and revelers have known for millennia, masks are powerful, enjoyable, transformational, and beautiful. Whenever we play with masks, we marvel at the magic and power of that first moment of transformation. We hope you will be inspired to continue your own personal journey in the world of masks.

Wendy and Michael

CHAPTER 1

FIRST ENCOUNTERS WITH MASKS

FIGURE 1.1 *This Neolithic stone mask from the Judean Desert dates to about 7000 BCE; it may be the oldest surviving mask in the world. Musée Bible et Terre Sainte*

FACES FASCINATE US

Human response to faces is ingrained. From birth, we respond to them.

Humans recognize each other primarily by face, more than by smell, sound, or movement. By looking at people's faces, we gather information about gender, age, ethnicity, and health. We evaluate attractiveness and assess emotional states. Instinctively, we combine information to determine family relationships, potential partners, social interaction, and danger. We "put on" faces as part of our projected identity by mimicking the facial expressions of others. We use our faces to communicate both deliberately and subconsciously: raised brows signal feigned interest, scowls issue a challenge, pursed lips or a scrunched nose suggest dubious consideration, grins extend happy welcome. A mobile face is incredibly communicative.

FIGURE 1.2(A) *Expressive faces*

BOX 1.1 MANY OF OUR IDIOMATIC EXPRESSIONS RELATE TO FACES

Put on a brave face
Interface
Face up
Long face
Face of the earth
Bald-faced lie
Save face
Face value
Barefaced
About face
Face the truth
Get your game face on
Face off
Red-faced
Face to stop a clock
Face of things
Clock face
Get in your face
Face to face
Face the music
Poker face
Straight face
Two-faced
Lose face

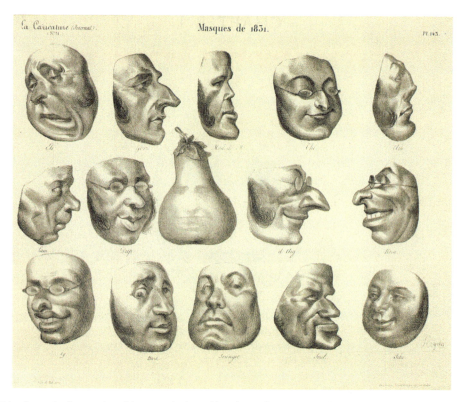

FIGURE 1.2(B) *Expressive faces are incredibly communicative and have been a favorite subject of artists throughout history. Honoré-Victorin Daumier, Masks of 1831, plate 143 from La Caricature (France)*

Our attraction to faces is so strong that we perceive them even in non-human objects. **Pareidolia** (*parr-i-DOH-lee-ə*) is the tendency to interpret a vague pattern as something known to the observer: for example, two marks above a line in a circle become a face. Typed emojis work because we quickly learn to understand this visual shorthand for interpreting emotion. This ability also allows us to see simplified shapes such as those in larval masks as representational characters. We can also interpret overly complex compositions as faces, as evidenced in the delightful portraits by Giuseppe Arcimboldo.

FIGURE 1.3(A) *Pareidolia allows us to see faces in non-human objects such as a house, emojis and emoticons, and larval masks*

FIGURE 1.3(B) *This larval mask by Jonathan Becker shows a simplified facial structure*

First Encounters with Masks 5

Masks as faces are equally fascinating. Throughout history, masks appear in virtually every region of the world, including Africa, Oceania, Mexico, Highlands of South America, Latin America, Northwest Coastal North America, Europe, and South and East Asia.

Over 30,000 years' evidence of masking includes:

- Cave paintings, leopard skins, and ivory statues in France (40,000–15,000 BCE).
- Neolithic Stone masks from the Judean Desert (9000 BCE).
- Animal-headed decoys for hunters in the Sahara (4500 BCE).
- South African animal-headed beings (elephant, deer, & more) in rock paintings (4000 BCE).
- Depictions of Egyptian priests as Anubis, the jackal-headed god of death.
- Funerary and theater artifacts from ancient Greece and Rome.
- Rock paintings of anthropomorphic figures in the Colorado Plateau, Utah, Nevada, and Wyoming (6750 BCE onward).
- Anasazi, Hopi, Zuni, and Pueblo tribes who maintain masking traditions.
- Australian aboriginal evidence.
- Ancient Japanese ritual masks, Kagura, from 10,000 BCE, and Gigaku from the 6th century AD.

FIGURE 1.4 *Sketch of Giuseppe Arcimboldo's* The Vegetable Gardener: *in one orientation, the viewer sees a bowl of vegetables; inverted, we imagine a face*

FIGURE 1.4(A) *Sole Brother Number One by Willie Cole (2007): 18 × 18 × 19 in./45.5 × 45.5 × 48 cm. Photo by Jason Mandella, courtesy of the Artist and Alexander and Bonin, New York. These engaging sculptures are part of a series of mask objects made of worn shoes, yet the artist's combinations are easily read as faces*

FIGURE 1.4(B) *Sole Brother Number Two by Willie Cole (2007): shoes, wire, washers, and screws, 19 1/2 × 16 3/4 × 18 in./49.5 × 42.5 × 45.5 cm. Photo by Jason Mandella, courtesy of the Artist and Alexander and Bonin, New York*

Nunley and McCarty assert that "Masks are the most ancient means of changing identity and assuming a new persona."[1]

Cultures use masks for different purposes. It is easy to imagine people gathered around a fire, enjoying a feast, and seeing one of the members of the group put on the skin or antlers of their prey to act out a successful hunt, acknowledge the prowess of a hunter, or celebrate the good forces of nature that led to a fruitful harvest.

People have always been drawn to masks. Not only do we respond to facial stimuli from birth, we also develop the ability to craft identities with masks and costumes from an early age. Kids love to play dress up … and the proliferation of **LARP** (Live Action Role Play), **cosplay**, and reenactors confirms that many adults do, too.

We feel different when we wear masks ourselves – safe, empowered, incognito, disassociated, mysterious, playful …. "They delight us, hide us, liberate us, protect us, scare us. They are power objects. They can transform us. And … we all seek transformation sometimes."[2] Masks are magical, often delightful. Yet to some, masks are frightening.

When others see us masked, they may treat us differently – they may exhibit distrust, amusement, fear, or intrigue. We respond to seeing masks differently from seeing faces.

The wearer can't help but become the mask, and we cannot help but to treat him differently.

This is because we perceive people by their faces, for identity, character, mood, attitude. We consistently rely on the face to read others, and we "take the faces of our fellow men as true and infallible indexes of their souls. We have such implicit trust in their correctness, and respond to them so spontaneously, that when a living face is replaced by a mask - when the false index is substituted for a true one - we still let ourselves be guided by it."[3]

Why is that? What makes us respond strongly to them? Is a mask more than an immobile face? What happens when you see a mask? When you wear one? What is it about us as humans that makes masking a ubiquitous phenomenon?

Masks have a dual nature as static objects and as animated faces. Their duality includes not only its tangible form, but also its sense of character. It is both the wearer and the character: me, but not me; you, but not you. It hides and reveals, is dead and alive, tangible and filled with its spirit. The illusion that a mask is alive and an independent entity has been observed by all who encounter them. "[The mask] has a place quite apart among things made by human hands. Looking at it, even we who pride ourselves on our realism and sophistication, are seized by a strange feeling of uncertainty whether peradventure it is not alive. When a mask is put on and enacted by someone, this uncanny quality and the mystification it creates are intensified to the point where the real personality of the masquerader is totally obliterated from our perception; we see only the creature the mask represents."[4]

MASKS ENGAGE US ON MANY LEVELS

The sense that a mask is alive provokes physical, emotional, and intellectual responses.

Physical Response

Our physical response begins in the most ancient part of our brain. Russell Dean used his puppet character, Mike, to explain how the brain responds to masks and puppets in a 2017 TEDx talk. When we see a puppet or mask, we note lifelike aspects of its appearance: facial features, skin-like surface, expression. When animated by the performer, it seems to be alive: breathing, moving, perhaps talking, an autonomous and vulnerable being. If it is still, we detect the disturbing absence of breath, a marker of death, danger, and disease. This is why lifelike puppets, dolls, robots, and masks, are so uncanny.

From the moment this encounter begins, our brains respond to the presence of something that appears to be simultaneously alive, and not alive. First, the amygdala, an ancient part of the limbic system sometimes referred to as the "lizard brain," kicks in. The amygdala works only in the present, to see danger and keep you alive. It's responsible for survival, for emotions such as fear, anger, and lust, and for creating memories. The survival brain sees the mask, perceives potential danger, triggers the release of adrenaline and cortisol (a stress hormone), and initiates a fight – freeze – or – flight scenario. It does not care that you saw your friend put the mask on two minutes ago. "Our amygdala tells us to run, or to hit and possibly eat him."[5]

But then our neocortex fires up. This part of the human brain developed later is responsible for rational thought, social thinking, and imagining projected scenarios. It works very quickly, to save us from life or death situations.

> *It calculates: What are the odds that he would be alive … attack me personally … or overwhelm a group of us? Would I be embarrassed by running out? We laugh, because we decided the odds are in our favor, then laugh because the stress factor has been lowered. The laughter of relief is an ancient group response to the passing of danger. The heart rate lowers, we get a high and a sense of social well-being; as soon as the social brain kicks in the laughter of relief, a sense of empathy is engaged, and we see it differently.*[6]

This creates the perfect situation to create an audience from a group of apprehensive individuals.

First Encounters with Masks   7

(A) "The Sorcerer" sketch based on the figure of an antelope shaman from the cave paintings in the Trois Frères, France

(B) Sketch of a bull sorcerer figure from Trois Frères, France

(D) Shell Mosaic Ritual Mask, Teotihuacan Culture, 300CE–600CE, Mexico. Stone and Spondylus shell with stucco (7 1/8 × 8 1/4 × 4 5/16 in.). This stylized portrait mask would have been displayed in a residential compound or temple and used in a commemorative ritual. Ancestors acted as intermediaries between the living and the deified forces of nature. The shell mosaic suggests both the high status of the artifact and the sacred generative power of lakes, rivers, and the sea

(C) Aztec people, Ritual Impersonator of the deity Xipe Totec, late 15th century, ceramic and pigment. The Art Institute of Chicago

(E) This gold death mask, known as the "Mask of Agamemnon," was found in a tomb in Mycenae by Heinrich Schliemann in 1876. The mask is believed to be from the 16th century BCE. Two holes near the ears indicate that the mask was tied onto the deceased's face. The authenticity of the mask has been formally questioned due to the high level of detail, such as the beard and ears. No other mask of its type has a similar amount of detail, but the use of a sheet of gold indicates the wearer was a man of means

FIGURE 1.5 Ancient mask art

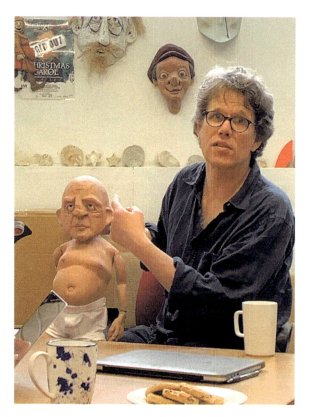

FIGURE 1.6 *Russell Dean and Mike at the office*

FIGURE 1.7 *Observers respond to masked figures at a Vamos Theatre Company walkabout*

Once our brains transition past the fight or flight response, we begin to engage on another level.

Emotional Engagement

Empathy, the ability to understand and share feelings of others, is contagious. It's a process of feeling with, not about, others. We mimic faces and masks, both when watching and wearing them. This is a normal part of engaging with others. You smile, I smile back. You cry, I take on a concerned look and may also feel weepy. When we see another face, we reflexively make micromovements that mimic the face we see; this process of taking on the facial expression of another person triggers a similar emotional feeling in us, and therefore empathy for the person we observed. The same thing happens when we see a mask. We respond to it as if it were a face, changing our expression reflexively and engaging with it as if it were alive. When wearing a mask, it is usual for the performer to take on the character's expression as well as to change their posture and voice. Neuroscientists note that 80% of our emotional communication is not through words, but facial expression, vocal intonation, and body language. *How* you say something is often more important than the choice of words.[7] So when we see another being, we interpret expression, body language, and vocal tone. We begin to mimic the message we see and become empathetic. We see ourselves in others.

Yet some people just find masks creepy. Some may dislike the feel of wearing a mask on their face or may distrust the reaction of viewers. Kids … and grownups … have been known to kick, hit, or run from masked persons. Mascots and clowns, who often appear as lone masked figures in a social setting, can be especially off-putting. Keith Johnstone observes, "Normally we keep altering our faces to reassure other people. The effect is subliminal, but when it's missing we can't understand the anxiety created in us. We continually reassure people by making unnecessary movements, we twitch, we 'get comfortable', we move the head about, and so on. When all such reassurances are removed, we experience the Mask as supernatural."[8] Many find disguise to be untrustworthy, or dangerous. We may not trust the immobile features, the inability to see eyes clearly, or the surprise of the unknown character. Scary movies that include masked characters as villains or monsters play on our fear of the unknown and half human. **Maskaphobia**, or **masklophobia**, the fear of masks, is recognized by the American Psychological Association as a diagnosable condition. It is understandable that something that hides, changes, and deceives would cause consternation.

The power of the mask has often led to prohibitions against them. **Anti-masking laws** refer to legislative or penal initiatives that seek to stop individuals from concealing their faces. These laws are usually prompted in response to people who mask in order to hide their identity and avoid identification/retribution, whether for legal or illegal acts (i.e., protest/demonstration, burglary, vandalism, crimes against persons, lewd or immoral behaviors). When the hiding of identity is perceived as a threat, laws prohibiting masking fall into a claim of protecting the public. Anti-mask laws have sometimes responded to mask use in situations where masking in the predominant cultures is less likely to

FIGURE 1.8 *EMPATIA Stocking mask created for a protest in Brazil*

be regulated by social custom or taboos. Unfortunately, this prohibition has been enforced against religious headdress without distinction of function, even when it does not pose a threat. During the Covid-19 pandemic, regulations requiring the use of masks in public were met by some with a variety of negative responses, including disbelief of medical necessity, misconceptions about hypoxia, concerns over racial profiling, association with other cultures, physical discomfort, self-consciousness, diminished communication ability, and psychological resistance linked to political allegiance, individual rights, machismo, and showing weakness.

Intellectual Understanding

In addition to understanding our physical response to and emotional engagement with masks, we should consider our intellectual reactions, whether they are consciously articulated or not. Let us continue to explore the way masks work, and what they are.

Does a mask do more than cover the face/identity of the wearer?

In *Making Faces, Playing God: Identity and the Art of Transformational Makeup*, Thomas Morawetz notes that unlike the Gods of ancient Greece, mortals are not able to transform fluidly. Yet people in every culture have pushed these limits, altering the body and craving to assume new identities. Purposes of self-change include decoration and enhancement (beauty), but "the deeper and more radical purpose is transformation."[9]

Transformation is another fundamental human concept that fascinates us.

We continue to respond to masks when they make the transition from a static to a performing object. Consciously or not, when we interpret the mask as an other being, we engage in the belief that the mask has its own identity. The skilled wearer magnifies this impression through body movement, gesture, and sometimes sound. When expertly done, it can be a magical transformation. Humans are able to use masks effectively because we can imagine the mask as both part of us and separate from us. We subscribe to many philosophical ideas, such as:

- There is a spirit world, which includes people, animals, ancestors, gods, and elements of nature (water, forest, desert, thunder, sun, etc.).
- Invisible forces can empower visible matter.
- New life can emerge from old life.
- I am not myself.
- Lack of scientific reasoning leaves space for mystical explanations.
- Human transformation (masquerade) could be a way to seek longevity for the self, the group, and progenitors from the spirit world.

Our understanding of these phenomena allows us to experience the magic of transformation.

Human transformation is an idea that we may find aspirational and empowering. When we can control it, we can engage our imaginations in positive scenarios. We could become Gods or superheroes with power to do good just by donning a mask and costume. It should be so easy! We could connect with ancestors, nature, gods, and other spirits. We can even become a "fly on the wall" when transformation is valuable to us.

When transformation is beyond our control, it becomes fearsome. In *Making Faces, Playing God,* Morawetz describes transformative scenarios as the three fantasies of identification.[10]

- One's own face changes uncontrollably and unpredictably, such as into a werewolf, Kafka's roach, a fly, or an utter stranger or alien. These are the most unnerving changes of identity, as they steal our primary sense of self as well as our control.

- One is able to change their own appearance/shape at will. Transformation is less frightening if one is in control, but "Metamorphosis at will liberates one from attribution and responsibility. It becomes the necessary means, the perfect means, for committing and getting away with illicit action." Perhaps this is initially appealing to the transformer. *The Strange Case of Dr. Jekyll and Mr. Hyde* presents this as a danger: what begins as a means to indulge one's selfish desires becomes an uncontrollable force of evil, fearsome for the victims, observers, and eventually the transformed.

- Others have power to change faces at will. Another's transformation is neither as alarming as the first scenario, nor as liberating as the second, but remains problematic because our "connections to the world, trust, and constancy are all jeopardized."[11] Recent movies have expressed that even our superheroes who do good are not always trusted by those they mask to serve.

Belief in transformation may lead us to wonder about the nature of human identity and control. When wearing the mask, do our actions belong to ourselves or the mask? Are we capable of the spiritual power of gods and spirits? Embedded with the evil of monsters and demons? Connected to the experience of animals and ancestors? Does the mask add to our identity, replace it, or bring out what may be hidden? Are we ourselves when we wear the mask? When the markers of our identity are blurred, we may get uncomfortable.

Joseph Campbell describes the phenomenon of transformation in his comparative study *Primitive Mythology, The Masks of God*. He explores the universal existence of myth in human cultures and recognizes that themes become both the basis of a society's spiritual power, and the subject of a culture's liturgy, stories, arts, song, dance, philosophy, and visions. Human propensity toward embracing mythology and our ability to imagine transitions between real and magical worlds allow us to perceive the mask as a transformative object. Campbell specifies that gods and demons can exist simultaneously in multiple times and places.

The mask in a primitive festival is revered and experienced as a veritable apparition of the mythical being that it represents - even though everyone knows that a man made the mask and that a man is wearing it. The one wearing it, furthermore, is identified with the god during the time of the ritual of which the mask is a part. He does not merely represent the god; he is the god. The literal fact that the apparition is composed of A, a mask, B, its reference to a mythical being, and C, a man, is dismissed from the mind, and the presentation is allowed to work without correction upon the sentiments of both the beholder and the actor. In other words, there has been a shift of view from the logic of the normal secular sphere, where things are understood to be distinct from one another, to a theatrical or play sphere, where they are accepted for what they are experienced as being and the logic is that of "make believe" - "as if."[12]

Most people are capable of this willing suspension of disbelief, even when scientific proof or logic conflict with our beliefs. The fun of playing is part of our human nature, and we are willing to experience symbolic acts as real events – whether the transubstantiation of a Catholic mass when a priest consecrates the host, the representation of a character by an actor, or the animation of a doll in child's play.

Like all artifacts, masks have forms and functions. **Functions** refer to how and why masks are used, and what their use allows to happen. We will look briefly at social, practical, and decorative functions here, and then expand on theatrical applications in Chapters 2–4.

Designers agree that form follows function. The **forms** of masks embody a variety of influences, including available materials, cultural aesthetics, artist preferences, community expectations, historical precedence, and traditional representations. Chapters 5 and 6 will focus on the design and construction of masks.

MASK FUNCTIONS

Masks are used for a variety of reasons. Broad functional categories include socio-cultural, religious, practical, decorative, and entertainment. Often these functions may intersect, as when a rite of passage (sociocultural) is also a time of cultural entertainment and celebration, or when a practical mask (such as a hockey goaltender's helmet or samurai armor) is embellished with symbols. This is true of proto-religious theatrical events, which often evolve from mystical to entertainment-focused traditions. Disguise can be practical for the worker, thief, or superhero … and have decorative and symbolic elements too! Mask forms are deliberately designed to function and to appeal, whether for symbolic or aesthetic reasons, or both. Sears Eldredge adds, "We can consider the Mask as a Mirror, which shows the internal fears, desires, wonder, awe, or raw emotional concerns of the society (or individual)."[13]

Socio-Cultural Masks

Socio-cultural and religious masks have a purpose that is significant to the participants beyond occupational protection, decoration, and entertainment. These masks have inherent power separate from the wearer. Eldredge describes masks

FIGURE 1.9 *A Hockey Mask for Boston Bruins' goaltender Tuukka Rask featured a snarling bear (bruin), as well as team colors and the Bruins' logo*

serving as a catalyst to stimulate change. Mack notes that in socio-cultural contexts, "the masquerade *is* the spirit and becomes so in spite of, not because of, the performer."[14] Occasions for masking include a variety of rites of passage, seasonal festivals of renewal, social control or instruction, gender reversal, and connection with intangible forces such as gods, spirits, nature, and ancestors. Because masks are usually made and controlled by men, they are part of male rituals more often than female ceremonies. The vast number of examples is beyond the scope of any one volume, but knowing some of this variety helps to demonstrate the power of masks.

Rites of passage relate to the human life cycle, including both physical transformations such as puberty, childbirth, and death, and social milestones such as marriage, successful hunting, or taking a leadership position.

- In several African cultures, the Bondo or Sande society's Nowo-masked figure instructs young women in life skills and social expectations. Chokwe people have masked figures to begin and monitor male transition to adulthood, including circumcision. Poro, a secret society of men in several West African countries, serves to educate members on conduct, magical medicine, economics, and politics. In Bulgaria, Kukeri masquerades mark young men's maturation and bring good luck to the community.[15] Dozens of cultures around the world include masked traditions for the transition to adulthood.
- Childbirth is infrequently depicted in art, possibly because of high rates of infant mortality. Nunley notes two exceptions: for the birth of a future pharaoh as pictured in the Egyptian Temple of Hatshepsut, and for the birth of twins among Bantu-speaking peoples of central Africa.[16] Janus (two-faced) masks are sometimes used to represent twins in other cultures as well.

FIGURE 1.10 *Sande Society Mask, Gola People, 20th century wood, pigment, mastic, fiber, metals, cowrie shells, claws. 16 1/8 × 8 1/2 × 9 in.* "Helmet masks of the Mende, Vai, Gola, Bassa and other peoples of the sub-region are the best documented instance of women's masking in Africa. These masks are used by the Sande association, a powerful organization with social, political and religious significance. Although worn only by women, these masks, as is the case elsewhere in Africa, are carved by men. Girls who have reached puberty are taken into a special initiation school in the bush for a number of months. During this time, they learn the secrets of the Sande association and acquire the skills and knowledge necessary for womanhood. It is primarily during this period that maskers—women who are already initiated—appear. Masks which are owned by middle-level Sande association members embody personal protective spirits. In order to attract spirits, masks are made to be ideal presentations of feminine beauty with shiny black surfaces, neck rings and elaborate hairstyles. The masker, who sees through slits in the neck or eyes, wears a garment of blackened plant fibers. The elaborate hairstyles represented in Sande masks resemble those worn by local women. They include amulets, cowrie shells and animal claws. In many areas in Africa, projections from the top of the head are believed to represent the wisdom and intelligence of an individual, and the pointed elements of some Sande masks may refer to this belief."

- A Potlatch is a cultural gathering of the indigenous people of the Pacific Northwest Coast of North America, often hosted by and to celebrate a tribal leader; the event may include masked storytelling as well as feasting and distribution of wealth.

- Masks are often used in funerary contexts. They may be placed on the dead for burial, used in effigy to represent a specific individual, or represent ancestral spirits in general. Death masks can be a static portrait, which freezes rather than transforms the identity of the wearer's face[17]; many of these were made of famous writers, philosophers, and statesmen in Europe and the United States for commemorative purposes. In ancient Rome, wax casts of patricians were worn to represent the deceased in funeral processions, served as models for portraits, and were displayed in the home to honor and remember them. In ancient Egypt, the mask functioned in many ways: to connect the Ka (soul) to the gods in the afterlife, to create an idealized representation

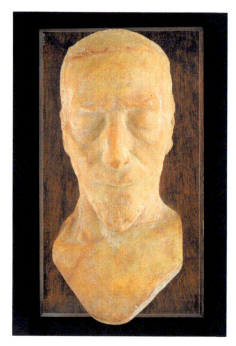

(A)   Wax Death mask of Benjamin Disraeli

(B)   Egyptian Mummy mask: 332–30 BCE., linen, plaster, papyrus, pigment, gold 14 × 10 1/2 in. The iconography of this mummy's mask is typically pharaonic: the wings and sun disc represent the scarab beetle, which Egyptians associated with the rising and setting sun and, hence, rebirth. The gold-colored face identifies the deceased with Osiris, the god of the underworld, who himself died and was reborn in the afterlife

(C)   Funeral mask for a Peruvian Ruler, Lambayeque (Sicán) culture, 10th–12th century. Gold, silver-copper overlays, cinnabar. H. 11 1/2 in. × W. 19 1/2 in. × D. 4 in. The eyes of this mask have thin, skewer-like projections emerging from the pupils, perhaps suggesting powerful or even piercing vision. In other masks, these projections include small beads of amber and emerald, which have led scholars to interpret the projections as tears. On the ears and ear ornaments can be seen restored examples of the silver-surfaced overlays (now corroded green) that would have also been originally present attached to the mask. Further surface additions include danglers on the U-shaped nose ornament. Such spangles would have caught the light of the bright sun and conveyed a sense of movement and life as a mummy bundle was conveyed to its final resting place. (Joanne Pillsbury, Andrall E. Pearson Curator)

FIGURE 1.11   Death masks

First Encounters with Masks   13

(A1)   An elaborate beaded Kuker mask

FIGURE 1.12(A)   There are many styles of Kuker masks

(A2)   A group of masked Kukeri in procession to drive out evil spirits

(A3)   Kuker masks. XIX International Festival of Masquerade Games Pernik, 2010. aladjov. CC 3.0

for eternity, and with the inclusion of appropriate symbolic information, to ensure safe passage to the afterlife. Aztec, Mycenaean, Qidan (Khitan), and other cultures also made burial masks. Many more cultures utilize masks for maintaining favorable contact with the dead.

Seasonal cycles and festivals of renewal relate to the growing season, nature, and religious calendars.

- Pre-Lenten carnivals that include masking traditions are common and may begin as early as Epiphany (12th day after Christmas, January 6th) and increase through Mardi Gras (Shrove Tuesday or Fat Tuesday). Venetian Carnivale (Italy) is one of the most famous, as are New Orleans' Mardi Gras Festivities (United States), Fasching (Germany), Fiesta de las Flores Y las Frutas (Ecuador), and carnival celebrations throughout Europe, the Caribbean Islands, South and Central Americas.

FIGURE 1.12(B)   A Halloween mask

- The autumnal equinox and other fall harvest festivals such as Halloween, Guy Fawkes, and Samhain mark the transition away from long days and fruitful growing seasons.

- The winter solstice, Christmas, and many New Year festivals include masks. A few of these are Krampus (Germany), Kukeri (Bulgaria), Jonkonnu (Jamaica), winter festival (Kwakwaka'wakwa, North America), "Festival of Dreams" (Iroquois and Huron people,[18] North America), Kagura (Japan), and the lion and dragon parade masks of China.

- Times of planting, rains, harvest, and hunting are abundantly celebrated with masked characters, such as the Bilmawn and Boudmawn of Morocco. The Hopi people (North America) and Dogon people (Mali) are just a few of those continuing these vibrant traditions.

Social control, instruction, and protest may also be occasions for masking. In some instances, the mask may be worn by the object of control. In many Islamic cultures, veiling of women is a means of social control, protecting them from the desiring male gaze, and protecting men from temptation. Social protests sometimes employ masks to protect people from retribution for speaking out against injustice; these masks can simply hide identity with a fabric covering, incorporate relevant messages, or exhibit a specific character such as David Lloyd's black and white Guy Fawkes' mask, popularized in the film *V for Vendetta*. In contrast to protective use, scold's bridles were imposed as punishment on some outspoken women in Medieval Europe. In many cultures, masks are used by those who

FIGURE 1.13(B) *Scold's bridles were sometimes used in medieval and renaissance Europe to silence and humiliate women who were judged to be disturbing the peace by excessive quarreling*

FIGURE 1.13(A) *Executioner's mask made of steel that helped to protect the wearer's identity and shield him from retribution*

choose to or are appointed to exercise control. In the United States, the Ku Klux Klan used a tall white pointed hood to create anonymity for its members, who have used that secrecy to exercise intimidation and hate crimes, and to avoid prosecution for their actions. When masks are used to mete out judgment, covering the face allows the culture and wearer to project the actions of the person wearing the mask onto the artifact. Recipients of punitive actions then attribute judgments to the society or deity, not to the wearer. This nicety protects the wearer of the mask from ill feelings or retribution. The executioner's mask is one example. Social instruction by masked characters is often incorporated into rites of passage, and presentation of myths and fables. It also exists in sharing information such as hunting practices – as a decoy tool, for ritual fortification, or in thanks and blessing.

BOX 1.2 MASKS IN ACTION

These masks were created by students in Brazil as part of a project "Costume in Action" conceived by artist, researcher, and teacher Arianne Vitale Cardoso. With this project, she and her participants explored how the body can be transformed by mask and costume into "extraordinary figures;" she posits that the process of creating and wearing costumes, adornment and masks can activate the body and mind, leading to performative acts. They used both poetic and activist approaches to place the transformed body into political and artistic spheres. The masks created for this project used recycled materials, including pantyhose, tulle, packing materials, pigments, textiles, and other found objects, and incorporated "slogans and words of action for human rights and desires and yearnings for change and struggle." They were used in political demonstrations in São Paulo as part of an Open Call Against Fascism, and in a Brazilian open scene festival. The process of designing and creating mask and costume in response to a situation prompted participants to consider the power of reinvention, questions of narrative, and examination of structure. Concurrent with the socio-political content, the eye-catching visual components adorn, transform, empower, and amplify the significance of body, moment, and place. The project made it evident that for both participants and observers, the artistic creation and representation of political ideas was an effective means to amplify their message.

 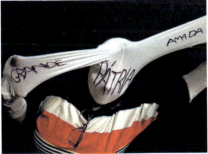  

Religious Masks

Religious/spiritual masks are those that attract, house, or represent a god, spirit, or ancestor. Eldredge describes this mask as mediator: by wearing the mask, the spirit of the supernatural (god, nature, spirit) and the social world of the wearer are acknowledged and affirmed, with the mask acting as connector to mediate and direct the flow of power within a system.[19] These relationships can include:

- Connection with or transformation to an ancestor or spirit.
- The spirit journey of an individual and their totem.
- The dual disguise and revelation of identity.

These masks also function as transformers, to unite and transform the person with the spirit of the mask.[20] The Balinese witch Rangda in the sacred ceremonial Calonarang, Japanese proto-religious Shinto mask rituals, Mesoamerican Quetzalcoatl figures fall into this group having religious/spiritual functions. There are also face coverings such as veils, burqas, and niqabs that are worn in accordance with religious practices, but these function to protect the modesty of the wearer, not to attract or represent a specific entity. While they may be included in some anti-masking statutes, they are not, by our definition, masks.

FIGURE 1.14 *Balinese Mask of Rangda*

FIGURE 1.15(A) *Practical splatter mask for a British WWI soldier*

FIGURE 1.15(B) *Practical mask for a beekeeper*

FIGURE 1.15(C) *Practical mask for an astronaut*

Practical Masks

Practical masks offer protection from physical or mystical danger, healing, and sometimes disguise. They may have offensive and defensive functions singly or in combination, and each mask has a form that includes both practical and aesthetic components.

Occupational masks typically offer physical protection from the environment or attack. They include those used in welding, firefighting, diving, medical situations, beekeeping, space exploration and by high-altitude pilots. These high-tech masks can add oxygen to the environment, or prevent germs, chemicals, and particulates such as dust, pollen, or paint from entering it. Military armor, gas masks, and war paint also serve practical purposes of offense and defense. To the extent they maintain breathable air and protection from impact, they offer physical, defensive protection. They can be spiritually protective when including talismans for protection by or from superhuman forces, and can also have an offensive function when the form frightens the enemy.

Sports masks include those used for fencing, hockey, baseball, motor sports, wrestling, and paintball. They provide both physical protection and the opportunity for displaying an aesthetic form that may reflect a combination of symbolic meanings for the wearer, the team, or the observers. The history of goalie masks in hockey stems from the need to protect

FIGURE 1.15(D) *Copy of a Plague Doctor's mask: herbs would have been placed in the nose of the mask to "protect" the doctor from harmful vapors. This style of mask has been popular since the Middle Ages, initially as a practical mask, but now for its aesthetic and historical appeal*

FIGURE 1.16(A) *Armor often includes forms that are intended to intimidate, such as this iron mask by Myōchin Muneakira (Japan, 1713)*

FIGURE 1.16(B) *Close Helmet with Mask Visor in form of a human face, attributed to Kolman Helmschmid ca. 1515, German. Steel, gold. Helmets fitted with masklike visors were a popular German and Austrian fashion from about 1510 to 1540. With their visors forged and embossed as humorous or grotesque human masks, such helmets were often worn in tournaments held during the exuberant pre-Lenten (Shrovetide) festivals, celebrations somewhat akin to the modern Mardi Gras. Substitute visors of more conventional type were often provided for everyday use*

FIGURE 1.17(A) *Sporting masks for Kendo, a Japanese martial art*

FIGURE 1.17(B) *Wrestling masks, particularly popular with Mexican Luchadores, provide a small measure of physical protection and personal disguise. More importantly, they are used to create personas, increase spectacle, and introduce a sense of mystery. They frequently include bright colors, symbols, and references to legendary figures, gods, or animals*

goaltenders from repeated injuries. Motorsports riders have also developed the art of the protective mask. Many people responded to the Covid-19 pandemic by creating a "wardrobe" of masks that blended physical protection and practicality with aesthetic variety, humor, trademarks, and slogans.

For centuries, Inuit people carved wooden or walrus ivory "sunglasses" resembling a domino mask with narrow slits for vision that protect their eyes from the glare of sun on snow and ice. Might eyeglasses or ski goggles be considered a protective mask or serve to disguise? In a plain form? Or when decorated? Imbued with mystical symbols or practices?

Spiritual protections in cultures include:

- Using a mask to represent a powerful other, where the mask is inhabited by the spirit, and the wearer is thereby protected from both the force of the spirit and the associative gaze of the spectators.
- Using symbolic materials or symbols to engage a divine intervention on behalf of the wearer.
- Invocation of a spirit who acts to the benefit of the community or targeted individual, such as by bringing favorable weather, bountiful hunt, fertile marriage, or health of an individual or group.

Healing masks are used for curative purposes as well. Some cultures, such as the Iroquois of North America, use a masked character to cleanse locations of bad spirits and drive spirits out of ill persons.[21] The Calonarang, a Balinese dance drama between the witch Rangda, and the Barong, a positive force of nature, restore spiritual balance in the community. Masks are used in behavioral therapy to help people who have difficulty with expressing particular emotions or who can learn from masked interaction, addressing emotional issues, developing empathy, and practicing socially productive behaviors. Mike Chase describes the use of masks in psychodrama that guides participants to "examine areas of concern, better understand themselves and their history, resolve loss, overcome fears, improve their relationships, express and integrate blocked thoughts and emotions, practice new skills, or prepare for the future."[22] In addition to spiritual healing, we wear specific masks to limit the transfer of germs. We use oxygen masks to help restore or maintain health in patients. Vicky Wright, a craniosacral therapist and theater artist, has investigated masks as a tool for increasing body awareness, and using that knowledge to work in better health.

Disguise can also be a practical function, or a cultural one. Simple examples of disguise are often tied to covering the face as a means to mask identity, allowing the wearer to act without retribution. Participants in Venetian Carnivale notoriously used masks to shield indulgent or immoral behavior. Burglars frequently are represented in a clichéd mask – whether a black knit ski mask, bandanna, stocking, or rubber Halloween mask. Masking identity in order to perpetrate crimes, or to protest government action, has led to anti-masking laws in many countries.

FIGURE 1.17(C)   A utilitarian catcher's mask

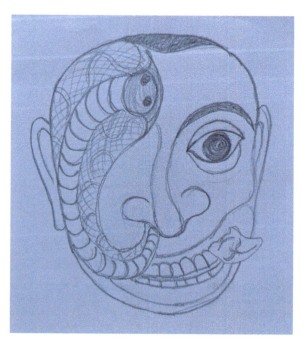

FIGURE 1.18   Gulma Sanniya, *the demon of Parasitic worms and stomach ailments. This mask is worn by an exorcist in a Sri Lankan curative ceremony*

First Encounters with Masks 19

FIGURE 1.19(A) *Zorro's black fabric mask is among the simplest iconic masks*

Christopher Agostino explains that the entire face need not be covered to achieve the function of disguise. By interrupting the normal pattern of the face, we make it difficult to identify the performer. We are willing to see the mask as other than the performer. So, a simple neckerchief over the lower face as in Western film bandits, or the black cloth over the eyes of Zorro, may not entirely cover the face, but we take it as a disguise. Similarly, with the stocking mask or dollar-store mask of a burglar, the distortion or covering of the face is key.

FIGURE 1.19(B) *Detail of Bauta masks from Pietro Longhi's Colloquy Between Masks*

Decorative Masks

Art masks are not intended for wearing as a character, but for aesthetic appreciation or personal expression of visual, tactile, symbolic, or representational pleasure. They may be created for commemorative, aesthetic, or symbolic purpose but are not intended to function in either theatrical or social contexts. We see these hung on walls, incorporated into jewelry, and displayed in galleries, museums, gardens, and architectural structures. Across the world, decorative masks are sold to tourists even when there is no local cultural history of their use.

Masks may be fashion accessories, such as the small domino masks worn over the eyes for parties. Masked balls allow the wearers to enjoy the mystery of disguise as well as the satisfaction of an aesthetic presentation. Carnivale celebrations in Venice (Italy) and Rio de Janeiro (Brazil), Mardi Gras in New Orleans (United States), Jonkonnu in Jamaica and the Caribbean Islands, and dozens of pre-Lenten and seasonal festivals around the world include people in masks for decoration as well as entertainment and symbolic functions. Body modifications such as makeup and body painting (tattoos, piercing,

FIGURE 1.20 *Decorative mask from the author's collection*

FIGURE 1.21 *Architecture often features carved forms, including this tragic mask by Carl Milles on the façade of the Royal Dramatic Theatre in Stockholm, Sweden*

implants, and scarification) are sometimes considered mask-like to some as they may alter the apparent identity of the wearer or fix a deliberately crafted representation. Permanence is usually not indicative of a mask, but permanent modification may share some intentions of defining or disguising identity.

Architectural masks include those in ancient Greek, Roman, and Japanese temples. The Maori people of New Zealand hang carved wooden masks that represent ancestors in their meeting houses: the mask includes a representation of the ancestor's *moko* (facial tattoo), and each part of the building represents a different part of the ancestor's body.[23]

Masks for Entertainment

Broadly construed, this function is apparent in communal storytelling, performing arts, and individual play. We know from prehistoric depictions that early peoples used masks. It is easy to imagine people gathering around a central area to watch and listen as people from the community dance, drum, and tell or enact stories of hunting, storms, creation myths, or other events. The oral tradition of passing on cultural history and wisdom continues to this day. Among indigenous peoples of the Pacific Northwest Coast, Potlatches are festivals of celebration and giving, which often include masked storytelling. Many performing arts utilize masks, including theater, dance, and film. Entertainment is a component of masks used for parties, festivals, parades, Halloween, and cosplay. When masks are used, there is a heightened sense of excitement, mystery, and anticipation.

Performing arts: Theater and dance are entertainment forms that use masks in several ways. Historically,

(A) *Duckbilled domino party mask by Newman*

(B) *A Helmet mask, worn for the fun of it*

FIGURE 1.22 *Masks for entertainment: cosplay, parties, and Halloween*

First Encounters with Masks 21

FIGURE 1.23 *A collection of theater masks*

the transformative property of masking was an essential element of ritual that connected the observer with their gods, nature spirits, ancestors, and community. This remains an integral part of many dance and drama traditions, both comic and poignant. Besides the transformational aspect, masks provide the practical ability to convey an unending range of characters, allow individual performers to present several characters, project to the audience at a distance or in dim light, and may show changes in a character's mood or status. The use of masks also creates an aesthetic context that, through visual choices, helps define a theatrical world. Sears Eldredge describes this concept as framing.[24] When we put a frame around something, it tells us to look at it in a different way. Using masks does the same thing: it signals us to acknowledge another reality. Cirque Du Soleil's movement-based storytelling sometimes includes masks as well as many fantastic makeups to signal its otherworldly theatrical environments. In addition to character masks, neutral, larval, and emotional masks are used in performer training to develop effective body language and communication. Masks are also used for some improvisation, devised work, and several types of street theater.

Film has employed masked characters from its beginnings with Georges Melies' *A Trip to The Moon* and Fritz Lang's *Metropolis*, through many iterations of Frankenstein's monster, Dracula, werewolves, monsters, aliens, and deformed beings. Sometimes, these are part of a large chorus of characters; other times leading characters are masked in beautifully crafted and detailed and fitted masks, such as Batman and other superheroes. Several of Dave McKean's films, including *Mirror Mask*, incorporate outstanding mask work. Some makeups are considered masklike when they achieve visual transformation for the viewer, or a sense of "other" for the performer. The Star Trek TV series and Star Wars film franchise are filled with transformative masks and makeups.

FIGURE 1.24 *Dance masks for* The Firebird *adapted by Elizabeth Snider for Butler Ballet*

FIGURE 1.25 (A AND B) *Fright masks for Halloween often copy characters from horror films and science fiction/fantasy*

Personal entertainment: Masks may be decorative, thematic, or disguising. Certainly, the above-mentioned decorative masks worn by revelers at parties, masked balls, parades, and festivals include a component of entertainment. Renaissance fairs, GenCon, Comicon, Sci-Fi, and Anime conventions draw large gatherings of cosplayers and LARP participants who often include masks as part of their character costumes. Some consider these to be performance arts and draw inspiration from comics, films, manga, anime, video games, literature, and historical figures as well as some original characters. Many museums, such as the Mascot Hall of Fame and the Children's Museum of Indianapolis offer masks and costumes for visitors to dress up in as part of interactive exhibits, as well as displaying mask artifacts from their collections. Halloween in the United States is an occasion on All Saints' Eve (October 31) to dress in disguise and go to neighbors' homes or parties requesting treats; scary, humorous, and aspirational costumes often include a mask. Día de los Muertos, or Day of the Dead, which celebrates ancestors on All Saints' Day (November 1) originated in Mexico but is celebrated widely and includes skeletally masked figures. Samhain (at end of harvest season, Celtic New Year) also incorporates masking traditions. Kids play with masks and costumes to try out different identities.

Environment is the final aspect of mask use to consider. Specifically, the gaze of an observer is required of some mask functions. Practical masks, such as protective occupational or sporting masks, do not require an observer to be effective. Decorative masks also have limited need for a continuous audience or interaction. They may have symbolic significance but primarily exist to be admired without interaction. Social, religious, and theatrical masks, however, require an audience to receive the character in order to function. For these masks, there is a transformation inherent in the donning of the mask and the creation of character by a performer for other members of the community or the watchful presence of a higher power. The talent and interpretation of the performer increase the effectiveness on the audience.

MASK FORMS

In addition to the many functions that masks have, there are many forms of masks. Their scale, style, aesthetics, and materials allow for unending variations. Masks can be worn on any part of the body, carried, or displayed. While frequently we think of masks as something that covers the face, there are times when the mask is worn on another area of the body, and the face may or may not show. In these cases, we remember that the mask embodies a character or spirit and need not be aligned with the performer's face. Puppets and masks work in similar ways; the line of distinction between them is subject to interpretation.

Scale

Scale refers to the size and fit of the mask in relation to the wearer(s).

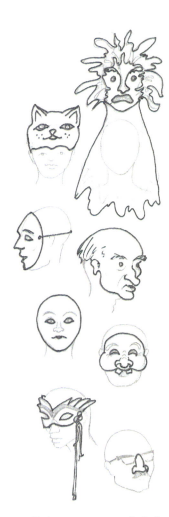

FIGURE 1.26 *Masks can cover some of, all of, or more than the face: oversized, helmet, full head, full face, half face, domino, and feature masks*

Schüler creates full head masks for the German-based company Familie Flöz.

Helmet masks are worn on top of the head, with or occasionally without face cover. Helmet masks of the Sande-Poro society add significant volume and height while shielding the wearer's face during ceremonial rites of passage. Julie Taymor designed helmet masks for an opera version of Oedipus Rex: these helmet masks deliberately show the faces of the principal opera singers while adding to the scale of the primary characters for a huge audience/space, and adding readable character in detail. Julie Taymor and Michael Curry's masks for *The Lion King on Broadway* include other examples of effective helmet masks.

Three-quarter masks fit the face fairly closely, even if some features may be exaggerated. They facilitate playing the front and side ranges, and the slightly larger scale garners attention. Russell Dean's lively masks for Vamos Theatre Company make use of this form.

Half masks leave the performer's mouth visible, allowing for clear speech and expression. Ideally, they fit the individual performer's face closely and seem to grow out of it. Some versions of *The Phantom of the Opera* use a half mask, as do various designs for Batman. They are appropriate for vocalized characters and genres such as Commedia dell'Arte.

Domino masks cover the eye area. They offer minimal disguise, so are often just suggestive of character, or used as a decorative accessory. Batman fans are familiar with Robin's domino mask, Netflix's series *The Umbrella Academy* uses them for the young siblings, tourists at carnival and Mardi Gras celebrations have many decorative options to choose from, and craft stores provide a selection of forms to decorate.

Partial masks frequently emphasize a single feature. They may be used to suggest a specific attribute of character, or to set the grotesque nature of a character. Bernardo Rey's feature masks for Stephano and Trinculo in *The Tempest* are examples; they reflect the piggish and doggish natures of the characters. Animal nose masks are readily available for purchase. Cyrano, Pinocchio, and the Wicked Witch of the West are characters who are defined by their noses. And finally, the clown nose, often referred to as the smallest mask of all, transforms in a big way.

Parade masks are often carried or worn above the head by one or more persons. They are scaled to be seen from a distance, so are larger than life. Bread and Puppet Theatre's political masks, Plank masks created by the Bwa people of Burkina Faso, the dancing dragons and lions at Chinese New Year, and the spectacular mask and puppet works of Michael Curry are just a few examples of these mask giants.

Oversized full-face masks can be used to project character over distance, as in ancient Greek and Roman amphitheaters, or for theatrical effect, by manipulating human form and scale. Mary McClung's masks for West Virginia University's production of Durrenmatt's *The Visit* show this effect. Mascots also tend to be oversized: they are designed for large venues, and because costume and mask not only cover the entire face and body, but also often extend the head and shoulders, their scale can be intimidating in close range.

Full head masks integrate hair and ears to present a seamless effect that is useful for creating more realistic characters; they are often used in voiceless theater. Hajo

Representational Style

In addition to varying scale and fit, masks' visual qualities range in style due to a number of factors. Form responds to function: parade masks must be light, and spoken masks should reveal the mouth. Available materials have impact. Cultural or personal aesthetics may prefer lifelike or abstract forms. Style also refers to historical and genre-based traditions, such as the Japanese Noh drama. Many artists such as Russell Dean and Georgio Di Marchi develop a personal style, while others, including Bernardo Rey and WT Benda, create masks in many styles.

Life masks, and some **death masks**, are cast directly from the face of the subject, using wax, alginate, or plaster. Life masks may become the basis for a totem/spiritual object, a decorative art piece, or the base for creating a fitted character mask. Death masks may create a record of the person at that time – these have been popular from the 16th to 20th century in Europe and the United States, capturing likenesses of Abraham Lincoln, George Washington, Napoleon Bonaparte, and many writers, composers, philosophers, and statesmen. Some are displayed or used as a model for sculptors. In ancient Rome, death masks were worn or carried by paid actors or professional mourners in funeral processions and might be displayed in the home as a remembrance of the deceased. The verisimilitude of the mask was important to honor the person. In other cultures, such as ancient Egypt, death masks may be idealized and rendered with less realistic detail, but more symbolic meaning. Egyptian death masks were important so that the *ka*, or soul, of the deceased would know how to return to the body. Other death masks appear to be decorative or status oriented, such as the gold death "mask of Agamemnon" from Mycenae, and metal and mosaic burial masks of the Aztec, Mayan, and Inca Civilizations. Some of these masks were placed on the dead for burial and/or used in rituals surrounding death.

Realistic masks are crafted to look like living people with a high degree of accuracy, including such details as warts, scars, wrinkles, and other imperfections.

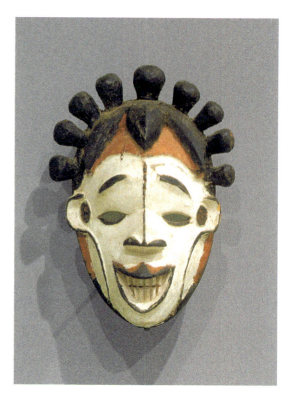

FIGURE 1.27(B) *Idealized Masks: Igbo Maiden Spirit*

Idealized masks may be very lifelike, but without the imperfections. Greek heroes are often idealized youth or mature figures. The Igbo people of Nigeria carve maiden and mother masks that reinforce cultural ideas of beauty in the essentialized features.

Caricatures exaggerate features to emphasize particular characteristics or habits of the mask. They might have an extraordinary nose, an expressive pucker, or overly hollowed cheeks. Often it is the intent to lampoon the character in some

FIGURE 1.27(A) *Many of W.T. Benda's masks had a high degree of realism and projected a lifelike effect*

FIGURE 1.27(C) *Idealized Masks: Apollo masks created to mimic a black figure vase style*

FIGURE 1.27(D) *Emotional Masks by Todd Espeland*

way, but to also keep it playable as a person. This category includes emotional masks for actor training/improvisation.

Satiric masks, like caricatures, emphasize specific attitudes or features, often in a critical way.

Grotesque masks exaggerate further, to where the emphasis seems to be an illness, monstrosity, or liability. A good grotesque mask creates a tension by attracting and

FIGURE 1.27(E) *Sketch of W.T. Benda's satiric mask, The Old Wag*

FIGURE 1.27(F1) *Grotesque mask by Werner Strub (photo by Giorgio Skory)*

FIGURE 1.27(F2) *Grotesque mask in leather with stucco by Bernardo Rey*

FIGURE 1.27(H) *Larval Masks by Craig Jacob-Brown*

repelling us in equal measure. We are not just horrified, but also intrigued, for the effect is neither wholly tragic nor comic.

Abstract masks use features and/or arrangements that are not human in some way. They are lifelike in that the arrangement of features seems human. Abstract masks may or may not be symbolic and may represent automatons, artistic styles, or concepts.

Larval masks are oversized, simplified forms, neutrally colored (usually white) that have immature personalities. Also called *emergent* or *Basel* masks.

Neutral masks are primarily used for actor training; these masks should express no emotion but be able to take on subtle changes based on the performer's ability to communicate with their body. The "blank" expression should be full of potential but is disconcerting for many.

Symbolic masks have meaning to a certain audience or maker, which may or may not be evident to those outside the group. The symbolic nature is often linked to its function but may be personal or esthetic. The mask may symbolize a god, spirit, or ancestor bringing communication, protection, or advocacy. The materials may be imbued with cultural significance, as when cut from a living tree, made from the tangible remains of an animal, or are the source of sustenance or wealth. Symbolism may be conveyed by the maker who was inspired by gods or trained and approved by his culture. Kait Lamansky's allegory of knowledge draws on her idea of how information is transmitted to and from the brain. The Janus (two-faced) mask might be used to symbolize twins, life and death, or comedy/tragedy. Sande masks include symbolic hairstyles relating to agriculture and fertility. This decorative art mask symbolizes nature in autumn.

Aesthetics

The conveying of style is achieved not only with the scale and type of mask, but also by its visual aesthetics. Artists' vocabularies define elements and principles of design; these invoke

FIGURE 1.27(G) *"Gasp" Abstract Mask designs by Rob Faust*

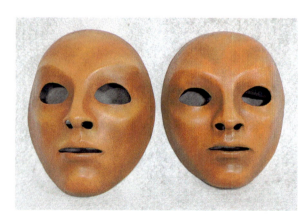

FIGURE 1.27(I) *A pair of neutral masks by David Knezz*

FIGURE 1.27(J) *Knowledge allegorical mask by student Kait Lamansky*

responses from the viewer and can be part of an established style or utilized to create a specific response in the viewer. We will consider these tools again in Chapter 5, Masks by Design.

- Line, shape, volume
- Color, value
- Texture/materials
- Balance, scale, proportion
- Rhythm
- Harmony, unity

Materials vary across the globe, from specifically harvested and prepared skins, woods, and grasses to chemically developed materials and found objects.

- Fiber is commonly used in agrarian societies across globe, including North America, Africa, Oceana, Europe. Different types of straws, grasses, reeds, corn husks, and other plant material can be dyed, twisted, braided, and formed into masks or attached to them.
- Leather can be free formed, cut and strung, stretched and hammered, or combined with other materials.
- Paper is a widely used mask material, in pulp, strip, and patterned techniques.

FIGURE 1.28 *It's useful to understand how design concepts are applied to mask work*

FIGURE 1.29(A) *Fiber helmet mask, Maninka people*

28 Theatre Masks Out Side In

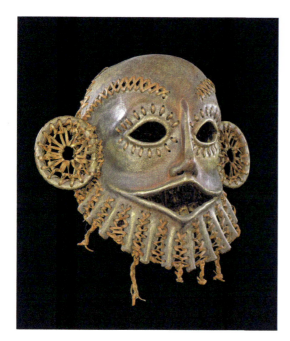

FIGURE 1.29(B) *Leather mask of Hermes by Werner Strub for La Paix by Aristophanes (photo by Giorgio Skory)*

- Wooden masks are carved in a wide range of rough and fine styles that may respond to the natural shape of the root/branch or be carved into a finely detailed object.
- Latex and neoprene are poured castings; styrene is molded over a form. These materials are available in a range of weights and flexibilities.
- Wax, clay, plaster, fabric, and cork have been used for masks.
- Found objects are frequently used as or incorporated into masks.
- Terra-cotta, stone, porcelain, and precious metals have been carved or formed into masks, often for funerary or decorative use.
- Makeup and prosthetics are sometimes used in masklike ways.

FIGURE 1.29(C) *Paper masks by the author*

FIGURE 1.29(D) *Wooden masks from Zaire, from the private collection of Richard W. Judy and Jane Lommel*

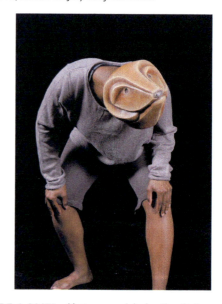

FIGURE 1.29(E) *Neoprene mask by Jonathan Becker*

FIGURE 1.29(F) *A stitched fabric mask for the Mayor in Dr. Festus by Werner Strub (photo by Giorgio Skory)*

FIGURE 1.29(G) *Found objects incorporated into a mask by the We people*

FIGURE 1.29(H) *Terra-cotta mask, ChupÃ-Cuaro*

This last group may be only temporary masks: they cease to hold their form as a mask when removed from the wearer's face. For some mask artists, this quality of impermanence disqualifies them from the category. We will explore the idea of how makeup and prosthetics can be like and unlike masks further in Chapter 7, Makeup as Mask.

Artists and influencers: Particular artists and cultures may also define or influence style.

Major influences on masks come from many cultures, as art and anthropology share global experiences. East and South Asian forms influenced each other's development; indigenous

FIGURE 1.29(I) *Tin mask from Mexico*

American people shared (or borrowed) styles of neighboring cultures, and African tribes' interactions cannot be totally free of cross-pollination. Explorers and conquerors from European and later North American cultures brought artifacts from Oceana, Africa, and Asia that impacted the work of many artists and writers, including Picasso, Poiret, Yeats, Craig, O'Neill, and many others. Within the world of performance masking, ancient Greek and Roman theater, Italian Commedia dell'Arte, Balinese Topeng, and Japanese Noh traditions have been significantly influential. Some of the many recent influential mask artists and companies are listed in the appendix.

FIGURE 1.30 *This leather mask by Werner Strub shows the influence of Japanese demon masks and armor (photo by Giorgio Skory)*

Process

Form is frequently planned in advance of creating the mask; makers usually have an idea of what they want the mask to look like. Sometimes however, the process is more important than the result. The creation may include ritual components. In cultures throughout the world, mask maskers acknowledge the spiritual components of creating masks. Some traditions have a formal process of thanking the world, the spirit of the tree and or character, and their ancestors for their contributions or blessings. The mask artist may begin with a prayer of thanks and end with a prayer of invitation to the spirit represented by the mask. For some, such as Elise Dirlam Ching and Kaleo Ching, the ritual is inseparable from the process of design and construction, and it is the process that is most important; the resulting form of the mask is a result of a self-reflective process, not a predetermined goal.[25] Even without defining a spiritual connection, it is interesting to go through the process of changing your face into another face, that of the mask, even if it is your anatomical foundation that is the beginning of form.

In drama therapy, the mask maker's process is also more important than aesthetic outcome. Some artists respond to the material, some to a voice, dream, or vision, some keep an idea smoldering for a while in their subconscious, play music or crave silence, pray, research, cook, or clean.[26] Each individual artist's process is a matter of creating and responding to the materials and aesthetics of the evolving character.

Such a disparate group of artifacts! Yet they all have some things in common. So how do we tackle such an immense topic? How do we define masks in the scope of this volume?

- By form? Or by function?
- By what it hides, or what it reveals?
- By its permanence, or the fleeting nature of performance?
- By its face, or its spirit?
- By the transformation of the wearer, or the experience of the audience?

There are so many elements to consider! These paradoxes are part of our fascination.

Given the wide parameters and examples, it may not be possible to provide a single definition that suits all uses.

The English language provides many references to faces and masks. At its simplest, we define the mask as a static object that covers something, or a verb synonymous with concealing. Broadly speaking, all face covers can be referred to as masks. John Mack's book *Masks and the Art of Expression* points out that in Western culture, we often define and refer to the mask as an object separate from character, costume, performer, or event. We focus on the act of concealment, disguise, deception, or pretense, focusing on the altered appearance of the masker, "rather than to the status of the portrayal."[27] Is a mask just the face-covering object? Or is there more to it? By contrast, in many cultures, the mask refers not just to the disguise of a person or tangible face covering, but to the creation of character. The Latin term for mask, *persona,* references this creation. Analytical psychologist Carl Jung used the word persona additionally "to denote a mental rather than physical disguise: that aspect of ourselves which we choose to present to the world."[28] If we include a sense of person – whether god, spirit, animal, allegory, or human, as a critical component, we acknowledge a more complex definition that incorporates transformative functions.

One further step in defining Mask with a capital M is the incorporation of the mask into a whole experience. This includes costume, movement, established character traits, behaviors, and performance for an audience. We understand that Mask "refers at once to the mask, the accompanying clothing and accoutrements, the character of the representation, and much else besides. Indeed, the principal reference is to the masking spectacle itself and to a whole body of cultural knowledge about its implications, not to the mask as a single and separable object. This is inevitable where the mask is an element in a style of performance rich in symbolism and occurring at critical times in the lives of individuals and of society."[29] In such theatrical or cultural performances, the entire character as performed remains with the mask object. Commedia dell'Arte, Noh Theater, and Balinese Barong all use Mask in this broader construct.

As we prepare to effectively create and perform masks, it is appropriate to acknowledge that all mask use requires effective costume. Neutral masks require neutral costumes such as black dancewear to allow the body to communicate exclusively. Larval masks work best with simple costumes related to the unformed quality of the mask and characters. Character masks crave some specific garments to suggest identity. Grotesque masks extend exaggeration to some kind of body dysmorphia or stilted movement. Parade masks frequently include puppet parts such as stilts or extended arms and body masking costumes.

The interpretation of the performer through movement is also critical to bringing a mask character alive. Their timing, rhythm, body language, and voice affect the magic of transformation. The light, space, and sound contribute to a successful mask environment. And the audience, too, must be willing to witness, accept, and be moved by the mask.

Mask, actor, and performance each contribute elements conducive to transformation. As we create mask work, we must marry form with function. The richness and variety of masks demonstrate the broad scope of human imagination and indicate our belief in the power of masks to move us as participants and spectators.

Let us look next at some of the established masking traditions.

PROJECTS FOR FURTHER STUDY

- Personal response: What are some times when have you worn a mask? How did you choose the mask? What did it look like or represent? How did you feel wearing it? How did others respond to you?

- Imagine a situation where you would want to have a mask. Describe the functions of the mask, and design an appropriate form.

- Visit a museum with a collection of masks. Choose one that intrigues you, and describe your first impressions: How did you feel? What attracted you to the mask? What are the key design features? What do you know about it? What do you imagine? Do some research, and add your discoveries about the mask's provenance, use, character, and aesthetic to your response.

- Research a masking tradition and present your findings on the history, functions, production, and aesthetics of that tradition.

- Explore how we communicate with faces. Are the Navarasas (nine emotions) used in Kathakali or Jingju expressions universal? How does the subtlety of Japanese Noh work? Emojis? How do we create and use masks to present ourselves today?

- Collect available materials and create a mask with them. Seeds, stamps, feathers, papers, buttons, flower petals, coins, fabric, leather, bits of wood, leaves or grasses, shells, candy wrappers, and other found objects will allow you to play with shape, scale, features, and texture. Why did you select these materials? How did the materials impact the design and effect of your mask?

NOTES

1. Nunley, John and Cara McCarty, *Masks: Faces of Culture* (NY: Harry Abrams, 1999), 5.
2. Faust, Rob, "Behind the Mask/Beneath the Ego," Ted[x] Reset: 2014.
3. Benda, W.T., *Masks* (NY: Watson Guptill, 1946), 2.
4. Benda, W.T., 1.
5. Dean, Russell, "Puppets and Perception." Ted[x] Guildford: April 2017.
6. Dean, Russell. Interview, May 2019.
7. Faust, Ted[x] talk.
8. Johnstone, Keith, *Improvisation and the Theatre* (New York, NY: Routledge, 1987), 191.
9. Morawetz, Thomas, *Making Faces, Playing God: Identity and the Art of Transformational Makeup* (Austin, TX: University of Texas Press, 2001), xi.
10. Morawetz, 5.
11. Morawetz, 5.
12. Campbell, Campbell, Joseph, *Primitive Mythology: The Masks of God* (NY: Viking Penguin, 1991), 21.
13. Eldredge, Sears A., *Mask Improvisation for Actor Training and Performance: The Compelling Image* (Evanston, IL: Northwestern U P, 1996).
14. Mack, John, ed., *Masks and the Art of Expression* (NY: Harry Abrams, 1994), 25.
15. Nunley, 72.
16. Nunley, 66–67.
17. Mack, 16.
18. In JG Frazer's *The Golden Bough*, 553, cited by Bradley, Doug, *Behind the Mask of the Horror Actor* (London: Tidal Books, 2004), 47.
19. Eldredge, 4.
20. Eldredge, 5.
21. The Iroquois and other indigenous cultures have a strong tradition of mask use. However, it is not my right to share objects or practices that are sacred and private to their people.
22. "Psychodrama" mikechasemasks.com, accessed June 2021.
23. "Maori Mask, New Zealand." *Object Lessons*. Islington Education Library Service. Web. N.a. 9/2/19. https://www.objectlessons.org/ceremony-and-celebration-puppets-and-masks/maori-mask-new-zealand/s81/a934/#tab1
24. Eldredge, 4.
25. Ching, *Faces of your Soul* (Berkley: North Atlantic Books, 2006).
26. Bell, Deborah, *Mask Makers and Their Craft* (North Carolina: McFarland & Co, 2010).
27. Mack, 12.
28. Bradley, 37.
29. Mack, 16.

SELECTED RESOURCES

Bell, Deborah. *Mask Makers and Their Craft: A Worldwide Study*. North Carolina: McFarland & Co, 2010.

Bell, John. *Puppets, Masks, and Performing Objects*. Cambridge, MA: NYU & MIT, 2001.

Benda, WT. *Masks*. New York: Watson Guptill, 1946.

Bradley, Doug. *Behind the Mask of the Horror Actor*. London: Titan Books, 2004.

Campbell, Joseph. *Primitive Mythology: The Masks of God*. New York: Viking Penguin, 1991.

Ching, Elise Dirlam and Kaleo Ching. *Faces of Your Soul: Rituals in Art, Maskmaking, and Guided Imagery With Ancestors, Spirit Guides, and Totem Animals*. Berkley: North Atlantic Books, 2006.

Dean, Russell. "Puppets and Perception." Ted[x] Guildford: April 2017.

———. "Mask Artistry." Interview with the author, Kent, England. May 2019.

Eldredge, Sears A. *Mask Improvisation for Actor Training and Performance: The Compelling Image*. Evanston, Illinois: Northwestern University Press, 1996.

Faust, Rob. "Behind the Mask/Beneath the Ego." Ted[x] Reset: 2014.

———. Interview with the author, Indianapolis, 2019.

Gelber, Carol. *Masks Tell Stories. Beyond Museum Walls*. Brookfield, Connecticut: Millbrook Press, 1993.

The Human Face: Emotions, Identities and Masks. Directed by Jon Silver. Produced by Dane Archer. Berkeley Media, 1995.

Mack, John, ed. *Masks and the Art of Expression*. New York : Harry Abrams, 1994.

Morawetz, Thomas. *Making Faces, Playing God: Identity and the Art of Transformational Makeup*. Austin, Texas: University of Texas Press, 2001.

Nunley, John and Cara McCarty. *Masks: Faces of Culture*. New York : Harry Abrams, 1999.

BOX 2.1 CULTURAL APPRECIATION AND APPROPRIATION

Most societies interact with outside cultures; it is natural to be influenced by their people, ideas, arts, and stories. **Cultural appreciation** encompasses learning about others, respecting their traditional ideas and behaviors, as well as deriving aesthetic pleasure from their arts. **Cultural Exchange** describes sharing where cultural appreciation is mutual, and both groups contribute and benefit equally. When one group loses its identity or power through assimilation, deprecation, or aggression, dominant and marginalized cultures result. Throughout history, societies have been marked by power differentials where a dominant culture derives disproportionate legal, monetary, educational, and status advantages. **Cultural appropriation** occurs when a person or group from the dominant culture uses something from the other culture without understanding of, permission from, or benefit to the source culture.

If you are inspired to incorporate aspects of another culture, how can you ensure you are not simply appropriating?

Understanding requires research. It is inappropriate to co-opt someone's cultural heritage just because you like it. Learn the cultural significance of your topic/item: its social, historical, personal, and religious origin, context, function, and meaning. Prioritize the perspectives of the culture you are investigating: seek and use indigenous voices in your research, and connect with people in the culture who are willing to share insights with you. Build a relationship that allows the culture both input and influence over the goals, approach, and outcomes. Work with someone who is recognized by their community as having both the knowledge and the authority to make decisions and grant permission to access, represent, or use their cultural heritage. State your goals clearly and honestly, and respect and follow indigenous preferences, including privacy. Some parts of a culture are not available to outsiders.

Clarify the purpose of borrowing from another culture and ensure that you are sensitive to the values of that culture. Do not perpetuate stereotypes, deficit assumptions, a primitive image, or something that would be offensive to the host culture. Reject interpretations that caricature, parody, sexualize, or belittle. Discard inaccurate, blended, and incomplete depictions. Do not use items in a way they were not intended (i.e., a sacred artifact such as a headdress for personal decoration). Do not use restricted symbols – including items of spiritual significance, distinct honor or status, or specific to identity (such as copying the tattoo pattern of a Maori person).

Do ensure that if you are taking inspiration or utilizing an aesthetic or artifact from another culture, that your use is appropriately sourced. Major retailers often sell caricatures or inauthentic and inaccurate native "inspired" designs that have zero connection to any actual authentic voices or artists. If purchasing an item, such as a mask, choose one legitimately made by a native artist. Especially as a member of the colonizing culture, never appropriate:

- As a symbol or demonstration of your belonging to a group that is not yours.
- For personal, artistic, or financial gain without benefit to the borrowed culture.
- As *a* **token** of diversity.
- To perpetuate the power of or benefit the dominant entity at the expense of the donor culture.

Always obtain permission, follow the wishes of the culture represented, give credit for the contribution and collaboration, and ensure reciprocity and benefit-sharing.

Understanding the difference between appreciation and appropriation is especially important when learning about different cultures and creating works from that knowledge. The issue is important because marginalized people often are not allowed control over what or how parts of their culture (language, mores, artifacts, arts) are used or represented; they are often denied the benefits of intellectual, artistic, and economic credit.

Genuine interest in other cultures, and the sharing of ideas and techniques, is important to developing artists and global citizens. Awareness of how we exchange information is worth developing.

CHAPTER 2

FACING THE STAGE

FIGURE 2.1 *The ancient Greek theater at Taormina, Italy. Photo by CH Munro*

In this chapter, we narrow our focus from the world of masks generally to the world of the stage and the use of masks in theatrical forms across the globe. In doing so, we look at what has influenced the development of masked entertainments, and at what these entertainments have in common with the influences that precede and inspire them. Scholars have pointed to evidence that numerous masked theater forms arose from religious and socio-cultural traditions, and we also know that intercultural exchange, whether through peaceful means such as trade and travel, or through war and conquest, also influences the development of these forms.

Many of these theatrical forms even now retain their religious significance or bear the mark of the folk traditions, social structures, and even politics from which they originated. Since masked traditions reflect people's relationship with their gods and their physical and social world, it is not surprising that modern theatrical forms would contain traces of the stories, themes, characters, and concerns of earlier rites and traditions.

In addition to reflecting the relationship among the individual, the social, the natural, and the supernatural, we also know that mask wearing is inherently performative: the mask is meant not only for the person who wears it, but also for another, or for an audience. In religious and cultural rites, for instance, masks embody forces outside direct human control and portray or embody divine, human, animal, ancestral, and chthonic spirits. The masked characters were used to serve and make offerings to gods, to invite spirits from the sacred to the temporal world, and to request good health and harvests. Ritual performances allowed people to exorcise demons and restore the balance of good and evil forces. Possession by the mask defined the performer as a vessel for gods/spirits and reaffirmed connections among human, divine/chthonic, animal, and ancestral beings. Another forerunner to modern masked theater forms, *Folk theater*, was created by local villager-turned-performers for seasonal festivals, religious occasions, and entertainment. It reinforced traditional beliefs about the nature of the world and created solidarity in the community by examining human behavior and commenting on social life, a staple of most theater forms.

We can see the influence of religion and socio-cultural traditions on modern masked performance, and we can meaningfully say that these traditions have commonalities across the globe. At the same time, we must admit that some cultural traditions and religious contexts have been more favorable to the development of masked theater from earlier masked forms than others. Religious contexts favorable to masked traditions include the practice of Hinduism, Buddhism, Confucianism, Daoism, and Shinto. Polytheistic and atheistic cultures often allow for multiple levels of being and reality; their complex view of life and death allows movement between those worlds. In these traditions, mind and body are celebrated as conduits for divine contact and power. Alternative modes of consciousness, including trance, possession, meditation, and ecstatic worship, are accepted ways of communing with spirits. Ancient Greek Theater developed from Dionysian worship. Shamanic exorcisms are the source of and reason for Sri Lankan *sanni* ceremonies. Balinese presentations of the battle

DOI: 10.4324/9781315146218-3

between Barong Ket and Rangda have at their source the need to restore balance to the world. Masked theater traditions flourished in Asia, supported by polytheism, ancestor focus, and the characterization of nature as a living entity.

By comparison, monotheism, binary perceptions of good and evil, objectification of the world, and the religious transfiguration of indigenous folk traditions contributed to suppression of theater in general and masks in particular in Europe. Most monotheistic religions (Christian, Jewish, and Islamic) distrust graven images and are wary of transformation, trance, and multiple consciousness. John Emigh cites monotheism as a contributing factor in the demise of masked theater forms in the West.[1] Europe saw the Christian church absorb or reassign folk traditions and seasonal festivals as religious celebrations[2] and oppose the continuation of theater. In the Middle Ages, Mystery and Morality plays used masks to indicate Death, Demons, corrupt spirits, and God, but most masking traditions were relegated to social, pageant, and parade use. Masks are still worn or used in effigy to recreate stories from the Christian bible, crusades, and historical milestones in Christianity, and to venerate the Virgin Mary and other saints. German Fastnacht, Bulgarian Kukeri, Caribbean Jonkonnu, Jouvay, Mardi Gras, and Carnivale are just a few such uses. Venetian Carnivale was notorious for licentious, gluttonous, and immoral behavior, going far beyond its original religious purpose of consuming meat before the period of Lenten discipline that includes fasting. Even the use of Halloween masks on the evening before All Saints' Day facilitated pranks, misdeeds, and bargaining for treats. Because masks were used by people who took advantage of the opportunity to behave immorally, the Law and the Church worked to ban them. Many folk traditions continued to include some forms of disguise, but with the exception of Commedia dell'Arte, Europe did not develop strong theatrical masking traditions. Their use is growing again with the influence of teachers and makers such as Jacques Lecoq, Donato and Amleto Sartori, Werner Strub, and a new generation of artists.

Socio-political systems also influenced the development of theatrical forms. In societies with royal rule and strong social class systems, royal patronage made the courts a source of developing art forms. Stories that expound on war, heroes, gods, demons, and everyday people reinforced the current political dogma and cultural standards of that same period and culture. For example, Confucianism was reflected in stories and characters that promote social harmony, value fidelity to rulers, fathers, husbands, brothers, and friends, maintain social hierarchies, and practice altruism. *Elite theater* was supported by ruling classes. It was presented to an Elite audience for state occasions and celebrations, and its content reinforced royal prerogatives, civic/political ritual, and the ideologies of the ruling class. Located in centers of political and economic power, court theater reflected a culture's highest literary and artistic standards. It was created by court functionaries, including professional

FIGURE 2.2 *Folk theater celebration of Jonkonnu in Jamaica*

Storytellers, Musicians, Dancers, and Actors. Courts were likely to document standards for the most popular traditions. For example, a detailed documentation of Korean arts was commissioned during the Yi dynasty (1392–1910), a "peak in the evolution and refinement of Korean dance and music."[3] Kings Sejong, Sejo, and Sonjong encouraged the arts and documented the dances. The treatises Ahk-Hak-Kwoe-Bum (Standards of Musical Science) include directions for performers, costumes, and musical notation, suggestions on arranging programs, and a catalogue of properties and instruments. In the 18th century, King Yong-jo issued another codification, the Shi-Yong-Mu-Bo (Scripts of Current Dances). Aristotle's *Poetics* (Greece) and Zeami's treatises on Noh theatre (Japan) are other early documents that led to clear standards for theater genres.

Countries have influenced and borrowed from each other. Genres intermixed as performers traveled to foreign countries, influenced local performers and populations, learned new forms, and brought them back home. Additionally, seafaring traders carried stories, ideas, and influences between cultures. During wars, entire performance troupes were captured as booty in China and Vietnam (11th–13th century) as well as in Cambodia, Thailand, and Burma (15th–18th century). Western cultural exchanges began in the 16th century; from the 20th century, exchanges accelerated dramatically in both directions. Western playwrights including Yeats, Brecht, and O'Neil were just a few of those significantly influenced by the traditions of Japan, Bali, India, Sri Lanka, and more in late 19th and 20th centuries. Western theater exchanges have since impacted Indian, Chinese, Japanese, and other traditions, throughout the 20th and 21st centuries. As travel and communications have become easier, the exchange of ideas and integration of cultural forms has grown.

In theatrical events, masks retain their transformational functions. On a practical level, masks present recognizable characters to the audience (Noh, Commedia, Hahoe). Masks allow the actor to play several roles. We enjoy the game of seeing one performer become many characters. Thespis was credited in ancient Greece for using masks to transform a single actor into several characters. Topeng pajegan features a master performer who uses masks to complete the transformation into different characters for successive scenes. Bian Liang is a masterful tradition in Sichuan opera, which epitomizes the quick change of masks to show a character's change in emotion or persona. Masks have been used to unify the chorus in Greek plays, as well as to blur the faces of strangers in more recent productions such as Mark Haddon's *The Curious Incident of the Dog in the Nighttime*. Masks may be designed to satirize or idealize individuals or types. They may serve as a symbol, as in August Wilson's *Gem of the Ocean*, or allow metaphorical representation as in Eugene O'Neill's *The Great God Brown*.

In traditions where mind and body are celebrated as conduits for divine contact/power, masks facilitate transformation as a spirit embodies the mask and performer. The

FIGURE 2.3(A) *Devon Painter used plain masks to blur the individual faces of people rushing by in Indiana Repertory Theatre's production of* The Curious Incident of the Dog in the Night-Time, *a play by Simon Stephens based on the novel by Mark Haddon*

FIGURE 2.3(B) *Moon mask by Kaleb Loosbrock for Lorca's* Blood Wedding; *the designer incorporated images of skulls, bulls, and the phases of the moon as visual metaphors for the themes in the play*

Dithyrambs of ancient Greece, the Calonarang of Bali, the Hopi Corn goddess – all allow the performer and spectator to connect with the divine. Although we are not studying theater as cultural anthropologists do, and we will not use masks as religious or spiritual objects, this knowledge leads us to wonder about the mask-audience and mask-actor relationships in theatrical presentations. How does an actor feel? What does the audience perceive or believe? We will look at these questions in the next two chapters.

EXPECTATIONS AND CODES

Masked theater, more than other genres of performance, creates an expectation of something special. In Nunley and McCarty's book, *Masks of Transformation*, John Emigh observes that vitality, intensity, imaginative range, precision, physical commitment, and links to ritual and myth are common to all masked theater forms.[4] They alert and engage us by stimulating not just recognition but also, more importantly, our imaginations. Sears Eldredge clearly alerts us to this fact: "Mask theater is not realism! The characters and situations are more heightened, more intensely who or what they are. They are automatically more archetypal, more mythic, more representative, and metaphorical."[5] So, just what is it that makes masked entertainment special? What particular practices support our heightened expectations? Genres of performance that use masks often develop *codes*, a framework of conventions that support the use of masks. These codes develop over time and become part of training, performance practices, and cultural consciousness. Codes often include systems of stories, characters, language, music, movement, and appearance.

Stories may or may not have a specific script written by a playwright. There certainly are written scripts with centuries of use, including Japanese Noh and ancient Greek plays. Epic literature such as the *Mahabharata* and *Ramayana* provide material for many cultures, including Thai Khon, Balinese Wayang Wong, and Kutiyattam of India. Medieval European Passion plays dramatized scenes from the *Bible*. Retellings of well-known stories or legends such as *Jataka* (tales of the birth of Buddha) are common material. Some forms, such as Commedia dell'Arte and Topeng, create a performance from loosely constructed scenes, songs, dances, and comic routines. Some forms are completely improvised, playing to local legends, events, and traditions. The content may be suited for mask work because it has mythological or divine content, animal, allegorical, representational, or other non-human characters, or some other non-realistic themes. Across cultures, theater scrutinizes the human condition. Themes include mockery of human foibles, retribution for misdeeds, reinforcement of social structures and ethics, glorifying heroism, displaying regret, criticizing extreme behavior, naming evils to be overcome, and restoring balance in the

---

BOX 2.2 SCENARIOS

Many masked theater forms use improvised scenarios. In these, the troupe or sponsors would select themes, stories, dances from an established repertoire to suit the occasion or cultural situation. Story scenarios would have listed plot elements and characters but would not have a script.

For example:

Balinese village performance begins with a cleansing prayer or rite, then an invocation to the gods and the audience, a procession and/or dance, then a selection of plays or skits on specific themes or characters, and a concluding dance or cleansing.

Hahoe performances in Korea contain a group of three plays, alternately featuring an aristocrat, a monk, and a scholar.

Commedia dell'Arte performances linked a story – often a love intrigue in three acts – with a variety of characters presenting the scenes, songs, and lazzi (comic business). The scenarios did not have written dialogue but were improvised based on the actions posted. Duchartre translates one from Flaminio Scala[6]:

Brighella enters, looks about the stage, and, seeing no one, calls.
Pantaloon, frightened, comes on.
Brighella wishes to leave his service, etc.
Pantaloon recommends himself to him.
Brighella relents and promises to aid him.
Pantaloon says (in a stage whisper) that his creditors, especially Truffaldino, insist on being paid; that the extension of credit expires that day, etc....

- At this moment -

Truffaldino (scene demanding payment).
Brighella finds a way of getting grid of him.
Pantaloon and Brighella remain.

- At this moment -

Tartaglia comes to the window and listens.
Brighella espies him. He and Pantaloon pretend to be very wealthy.
Tartaglia comes down into the street. He goes through the 'business' [lazzi] of begging for alms from Pantaloon; in the end they agree to a marriage between Tartaglia's daughter and Pantaloon's son.

Etc.

world. Masks are useful tools for presenting caricatures of human behavior.

Language may incorporate formal poetry, classic prose, colloquial language, or a combination of them depending on the genre. Many traditions include different languages or dialects for different classes of characters. In Balinese Topeng, for example, five or more languages are learned: Sanskrit prayers and chanted Kawi texts maintain part of the religious functions; while refined characters do not speak, their words are delivered in poetic middle Javanese language by mid-ranking characters; the Penasar brothers translate and comment for the audience in Indonesian or middle Balinese; and bondres (clown) characters use improvised, bawdy vernacular.[7] In Commedia dell'Arte, characters' dialects reflect stereotypical qualities that entertain audiences: Pantalone, a miser, from the trading port of Venice, Dottore, a learned fool from the university town of Bologne, and El Capitano, the cowardly braggadocio from Spain (Italy's rival). There are many forms of Dance Dramas in which the masks do not speak at all but pantomime the story, while a dalang or chorus provides sung or spoken narration. Diction, vocal tone, range, dynamic, and rhythm are specific to different forms and character groups.

Music often has a designated role in masked performance. It is more than background sound: it may set the pace and emotional tone, provide the story elements through song lyrics, emphasize a moment of action (as the slapstick of Commedia), highlight a cathartic transition, and identify characters. Readers familiar with Tchaikovsky's *Peter and the Wolf* may recall the connection of specific orchestral instruments being assigned to Peter (strings), the hunters (timpani), grandfather (bassoon), and different animals (duck – oboe, bird – flute, cat – clarinet, wolf – french horn). Similarly, particular instruments, voices, songs, rhythms, tempos, and dynamics are often associated with a specific character or action in masked theater. Performers learn to perfect these qualities, reinforcing the audience's expectation and understanding. The most formal codes (such as Noh) specify the number and type of instruments, how and when they are used in the action, and what motives are played. Gamelan orchestras in Bali vary the number and specific instruments depending on the type of performance and are flexible in accompanying action that may change depending on the performer. Some genres select from sets of song cycles while some, like Commedia, use local contemporary song selected by performers for the occasion. Whether set or improvised, or a combination of both, the sounds support the heightened world of masked performances.

Movement codes include dance, movement, posture, balance, gesture, hand, head, and even eye movements. Many dances have formal structures. Tumbling, acrobatics, and stage fighting are choreographed. Performers' movements – their walk and posture whether moving or still – are defined for different types of characters. Imagine the posture of a shy innocent girl, a seasoned warrior, a mischievous monkey,

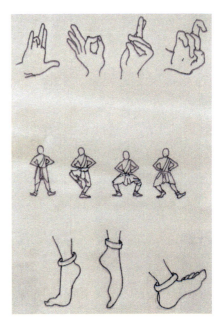

FIGURE 2.4 *Mudras indicate words and ideas through single and double hand gestures. Foot and body position is also communicative*

or a malevolent demon. How might they move? Stand? Sound? Wave? Other kinds of movement are also defined. In India, *Mudras*, which are symbolic hand/wrist/finger gestures that convey words and ideas, are part of many dance and drama forms as well as religious and spiritual practices, including meditation and yoga. *Navarasas* are specific facial expressions that portray the nine basic human emotions, and which are used in both performing and visual arts of India.

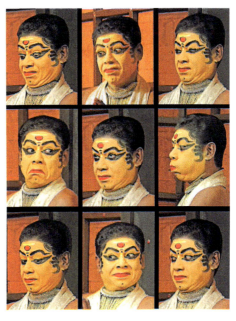

FIGURE 2.5 *Navarasas show nine basic human emotions*

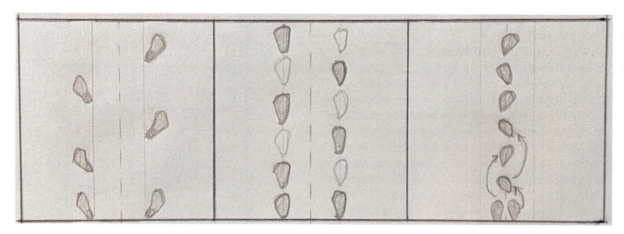

FIGURE 2.6 *Japanese patterns of footsteps for warrior, gentleman, and maiden: The Warrior moves with feet and knees turned out, arms held out, and steps forward in a wide stance landing the heel with a thud. Men move formally with a low center of gravity, knees slightly bent and feet pointing forward, silently sliding each foot directly forward, pausing briefly at the center of each step before gliding forward onto the other foot. Women move formally with shoulders back, hips forward, and the spine gracefully curved; with knees together, toes pointing in, feet follow a straight path by sliding each foot in a curve to land quietly in front of the other. This creates a slight sway in a figure eight pattern*

Actors must develop stamina for animating the mask through specific body movements and must learn to manage costumes and props such as Peking Opera water sleeves, fans, and weapons in appropriate meaningful gestures. It should also be noted that strong gender codes for movement support successful cross-gender performance. Assumptions about the right way to embody characters are as consistent in Commedia dell'Arte as they are in Topeng and Noh. Additionally, some visual compositions – such as the broad tableaux in Thai Khon drama – are consistent with architectural friezes or cultural art forms.

FIGURE 2.7 The Two Pantaloons. *Etching on paper (1616). Jacques Callot captured many images of the postures of Commedia dell'Arte characters in the early 17th century*

Characters are types first, speaking for larger classes of beings. Within types, there are variations, including specific figures from religions, literature, and history. Defining characteristics include age, occupation, and temperament. Human ages – young, mature, or old – are indicated in several cultures by the use of facial hair (its presence or absence, color, and length), representation of wrinkles, and sometimes color. Gender is frequently indicated by complexion, hair length, and expression. Male types can be as warriors, princes, aristocrats, scholars, officials, and clowns; their headdress and costume may indicate occupation, or they may be divided by character. Women's roles are also divided by ages of maidens (innocent or coquettish), matrons, and crones and often assigned as a virgin, goddess, bride, mother, princess, or witch. The complexion, arrangement of hair, and intensity of emotions give clues to their social status and emotional state. Animals, demons, and spirits make other categories, and Gods may be beneficent, wrathful, or teasing. These non-human characters often have distinguishing features such as fangs, bulging eyes, horns, coloring, or symbolic markings. The social status or emotional qualities of a character are also reflected in many mask systems. For instance, refined, just, and ethical characters are idealized, while ill-behaved people are more likely to be exaggerated and caricatured. In many forms, masked and unmasked characters perform together, such as in Noh, Commedia, and Khon Drama, where human characters of high status are often unmasked, while the highest (deities and spirits) and lowest (demons and commoners) are masked in idealized, frightening, or comic extremes. In other forms, such as the contemporary masked theater created by Familie Flöz, Strangeface Theatre, and Vamos Theatre, all characters are masked to sustain a consistent theatricality.

Appearance may be coded as well, including costume types, garments, colors, and textures as well as masks or makeup and headdress. Masks exaggerate and essentialize human forms of emotion, character, and behavior. Visual aesthetics and codes may idealize (as in Greek and Noh) or satirize the banal as in Commedia or bondres (Bali) or Kyogen comedies (Japan), they may stretch our imaginations (gods and demons) or represent emotional suffering or heroism. Typed and true, masks are instantly recognizable to local audiences.

Often the systems particular to each genre are part of a culture's zeitgeist, so audience members understand presentational conventions through overlapping experiences. For example, art, literature, and performance conventions consistently color the Hindu gods Vishnu, Krishna, Rama, and Shiva blue. For people familiar with this convention, it signifies their aura, and positive, all-inclusive qualities.[8] Some of these traditions are intuitive and easily understood by novice viewers. Imagine, for example, a performer whose mask has smooth skin, delicate features, long neat hair, a slight smile, who moves with small, gliding steps, a slight sway, and graceful circular gestures to the sound of a solo flute and high-pitched bells. Compare that to an actor with a mask who has an exaggerated grin, bulging eyes, bright contrasting colors, and wild hair, who moves with a constant up and down, high stepping gait, arms wide out, hands shaking rapidly, to a mélange of rapid drum beats, cymbals, and xylophones. Or a carefully coiffed, helmeted figure with fierce expression, dark facial hair, walking with knees turned out, arms akimbo, at an even pace to a slow bass drum. Which is male? Female? Young? Mature? Human? Supernatural? These conventions, or codes, use universally and culturally significant assumptions.

Another aspect common to masked theater traditions is the specific training required to create effective performance. Most traditions rely on a master training a new generation of performers within a family, troupe, or school. Intense performer training provides stamina for the rigorous demands of performance. Any variation or improvisation by the performer must be built upon mastery of the tradition, form, and material. We will look at some types of performance training in Chapter 4.

The phenomenal artistry of mask making and performance includes a wide range of styles from the perfected subtle emotions of Noh *onna-men* (female masks), to the humorous *bondres* characters of Balinese Topeng, distinctive hierarchies of Thai *Khon* masks, to the fantastic gods and demons of many traditions. We are learning more and more about mask traditions around the world. While there is not room here to provide generous summaries of the myriad of mask traditions, introductions to a few of the major forms of mask theater are included to whet your appetite and to illustrate many of the principles we've been discussing.

FIGURE 2.8 *Greek masks: Relief of Menander with youth, false maiden, and old man masks of the new comedy*

FIGURE 2.9(A) *Balinese and other Asian mask conventions include light skinned, composed, balanced features for Alus (high status) characters, including this royal pair*

FIGURE 2.9(B) *Conquistador mask showing European features*

FIGURE 2.10, 11, 12 *Clown masks often exaggerate physical traits: these Bondres, Hillbilly, and Flautino masks feature grinning teeth and gums*

CHINESE BIAN LIAN

Bian Lian, the Chinese art of face changing, is an aspect of Sichuan opera in which performers change their faces using silk masks to indicate changes in the character's emotional state. Each change is done in a fraction of a second, to a carefully choreographed turn, toss of the head, wave of a fan or sleeve, or distracting dance move. A performer may hide the change behind a toss of powder or pull makeup across his face to alter his appearance. Performers make their own masks and rig them to their costumes. Bian Lian methods are now taught at the opera school, but like other forms of "magic" are protected secrets. The masks follow the conventions of face painting for Chinese opera, with bright bold colors and divisions, which are easily readable and so have strong, instant impact on the audience. Unlike other mask performance styles, Bian Lian uniquely relies on the magic of the quick change. Specific trained movement is still an important part of an effective performance. Begun over 300 years ago, the art form is one of China's national treasures.[9]

FIGURE 2.13 *Bian Lian performers enact magical quick changes in seconds*

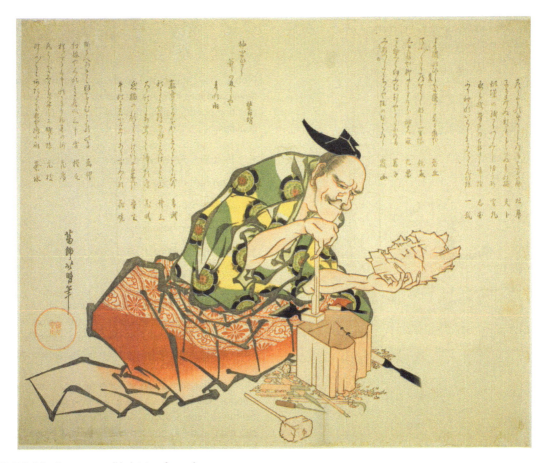

FIGURE 2.14 *Japanese woodblock print of a mask carver*

JAPANESE NOH AND KYOGEN

Noh masks are among the most famous worldwide. Known for their finesse and artistry, they developed over centuries of careful and consistent study. Much has been written about Japanese masks, from prehistoric shell and clay forms through the present development of "English Noh" such as that practiced by Theatre Nogaku. Prior to the establishment of **Noh**, **Gigaku**, **Bugaku**, and **Gyōdō** were introduced by visitors from China, Korea, and India. Japanese artists took up these imported forms, established performing troupes, developed repertoires, and mastered carving techniques.

Gigaku included a liturgical procession, staged vignettes, and musical interludes, incorporating Buddhist dogma with humorous secular elements. About 240 Gigaku masks worn for both procession and staged pieces still exist. They are quite large, covering most or all of the head. They include garish colors, tufts of horsehair for brows and facial hair, exaggerated features, and malevolent or comical expressions.

Bugaku is a collective term for a body of about 50 indigenous and foreign religious and secular dances. Twenty types of masks are named for the dances they were used in. Few of these masks remain, probably because they were more popular, and more likely to be worn out. Bugaku masks[10] are smaller, covering the face just to the ears, but the stylized features include some wonderful mechanical effects such as moveable jaws and swiveling eyeballs.

FIGURE 2.15 *Japanese Bugaku mask*

Gyōdō was a tradition of Buddhist rites and ceremonies performed by and for monks, involving an outdoor procession or pageant but no secular content. Masks represent the pantheon of Buddhist celestial beings and lesser gods, divine attendants, and superhuman guardians. Representations were copied from Buddhist statuary. Gyōdō later was applied more loosely to any religious or quasi-religious procession. This expanded definition of Gyōdō allows the inclusion of demon masks in this category.[11]

Tsuina is a temple ritual to drive out evil spirits and misfortune before New Year. Tsuina masks represent these evil demons and include fearsome but benevolent gods. Some consider Tsuina an offshoot of Gyōdō; others regard them as early folk *Kishin* masks.

Folk masks are the Indigenous forerunners of most Noh masks. Tree roots from which they were made were considered sacred or magical. They were donated as votive offerings and kept in shrines. Used in religious rituals and festivals, their functions included serving as effigies and manifestations of divine entities. Folk masks transitioned from divine representation to dramatic performance with use in quasi-religious dramatic forms of *Kagura*, *Dengaku*, *Sarugaku*, and *Ennen Furyū*. Six classes of masks are considered the forerunners of Noh masks: *Kishin*, *Okina*, *Jō*, female, young men, and *Ryō-no-Otoko*.

Noh Theater

Noh is now the best known Japanese mask tradition. It developed into its current form by the 14th century, incorporating poetic drama, music, and dance. It is known for its qualities of

- Restraint, austerity, economy of expression
- Chant-like singing
- Unadorned stage
- Minimal, symbolic props
- Deliberate pacing
- Significant gesture

Noh was favored by the ruling shogunate, and its practitioners were afforded high status as artists. Competitive family troupes, traditions, and schools were established. Beautiful masks became highly prized possessions, passed down from generation to generation.

Traditionally, a day's performance begins with ceremonial **Okina**, an ancient set of three dances that include a character, Okina, whose mask is a smiling old man with a pointed white beard[12] who performs a "dance of gratitude and prayer."[13] A sequence of nine plays follows. Five Noh plays are based on the **shite** (leading performer) role. The pattern of Noh plays is called *shin-nan-jo-kyō-ki*: gods, warriors/men, women, lunatics, and demons,[14] relating to the type of shite role in the Noh. These alternate with four **Kyogen** comic pieces featuring the **waki** (side kick).

Noh masks function to represent character and have three transformative levels. At the highest level, *Kishin* and *Jō* masks are gods, transforming the actor into a supernatural being. At the next level are gods disguised as humans: their "masks do not personify gods but depict their human form… in which they temporarily reside while on earth."[15] This level includes old men, who were venerated and believed to be close to the gods, and young innocent females who were also considered closer to the divine and sometimes used to represent goddesses. The remaining masks represent humans. Initially, human characters were not masked, but as Noh developed, female masks were useful to extend the illusion of male performers playing female roles.

Each mask has its own **kurai**: the persona, mood, details, essence unique to it. If several options for a role are available, an actor chooses a mask for a performance based on its kurai. The subtle differences from one mask to the next may resonate with the actor's mood or interpretation that day. He begins by examining the mask closely, and not just putting the mask on, but also putting himself into the mask. When the performer subjugates his natural expression, voice, posture, movement, and appearance to the traditions of Noh and the kurai of the mask, "the pure life essence of the humanity of the actor is brought to the fore."[16] In Noh performance, tradition supersedes individual interpretation. Each character has trademark looks, movements, and sounds that must be conveyed. The actor's performance is judged on his skill in presenting these specific identifiers; individual finesse is appreciated in concert with the expected context.

Mask Construction

Learning to carve Noh masks requires years of training in Noh traditions, forms, and skills. Mask carver and performer Michishige Udaka notes that the mask maker must have "insight into and understanding of the roles in which the mask is used," as well as considerable craftsmanship. He writes, "This demands more than just dexterity - the innate beauty of a Noh mask inhabits a dimension different from its perfection. When the maker approaches his task armed with a proper understanding of the themes of the play, accepting the hero's state of mind as if it were his own, the Noh mask buried in that square block of wood should clearly reveal itself. His task then is to carve it out of the wood without losing that image."[17] During his years of training, an aspiring mask maker is expected to create 90 or more **utsushi** (faithful copies of **honmen** – original masterpieces) in order to learn the nuances of creating subtle expressions as well as flawless technique.

Noh masks are carved of wood. The best hinoki cypress is over 250 years old, exposed to water for 20 years and dried for 20 more before carving.[18] While parts of the carving process[19] are similar to other traditions, a Noh carver works with templates to ensure exactly accurate proportions. When the carving is complete, the face is given from 5 to 15 undercoats of baked, ground oyster shells (*gofun*) and animal glue (*nikawa*) to create a very smooth, white surface. Three to ten coats of mineral pigments (*ganryo*) are layered to develop skin tone. The artist chooses one of six finishing textures *(uwanuri)* from granular to matte to lustrous. *Sumi* ink is applied with brushes to create shadows and to color eyes, lips, and teeth. Character continues to be defined by process of *kegaki* – the art of painting hair, including the sideburns, brow, mustaches, beards, and hairline/bangs. Finally, *koshoku-zuke*, the process of aging the mask to replicate patina of original masks,[20] is applied. Supernatural masks may have gold eyes and teeth added. Okina, Jō, and some Kishin masks have horsehair pegged/glued into small holes. A few masks include separately carved horns that may be added for particular uses or permanently attached. Okina masks that are carved in two pieces must be tied together at the jaw.

Noh masks have two distinct aesthetic styles. One shows highly emotional fixed expressions, such as the grimaces of Kishin, Onryō, Ryō no Otoko, Buddhist deity, and old warrior figures, plus the smiling Okina and Jō masks. The other style, reserved for human masks, shows subtle, refined features, sometimes described as neutral – yet with subtle asymmetry capable of showing great emotional range. This principle of beauty encompassing intensity and ambiguity is called **yugen**; it reflects the ability of a wooden mask to seem to have flexible expressions, particularly those of joy and sorrow joined together in a single mask.[21]

To capture a universal human condition, rather than an individual likeness, artists abstracted and idealized the face: for example, on young female masks, the forehead is elongated, eyes are narrow, and the mouth is small with a slightly jutting lower lip. While idealized, the mask's subtle asymmetry allows the performer to change the mask's expression with movement. When the head tilts down (**kumoru** or **kumorasu**), the face "clouds," representing sadness; when the face tilts slightly up (**teru** or **terasu**), it "brightens" and indicates a cheerful or joyous state.[22] Similarly, the left and right sides of a mask may indicate different emotions if the carver creates a gaunt or full cheek, a downcast or forward looking eye, a slight downward or upward curve of the mouth, a flared or relaxed nostril, and the actor emphasizes showing one side or the other to the audience. "The value of the mask lay in its ability to convey the essence of that condition from the stage to the audience and to project all the necessary intensity and range of emotions."[23]

The Japanese artist Master Bidou Yamagucci uses Noh carving and painting techniques to create mask sculptures of artistic likenesses. "During his training, Bidou and his teacher discussed how the neutral or indeterminate expression (*chukan hyojo*) of Noh masks of younger women like Ko-Omote and Zo-Onna recalls the beguiling smile of Leonardo's Mona Lisa, and how the Noh mask maker, like the brilliant portrait painter, is challenged to capture such nuance."[24]

Mask Categories

Noh masks include 6 categories evolved from folk masks, plus 60 or more subgroups, and over 200 distinct masks, including derivations and special masks for specific plays. Names of the masks may relate to the type, a specific character or play, a physical feature, or even a carver. Understanding Japanese characters is useful in categorizing, as the names often include indicators of the character, play, or type, plus descriptive prefixes related to strength, potency, size, age, color, gender, nature, or physical feature such as whiskered, fanged, or with bulging veins. Stephen Marvin's extensively detailed text *Heaven Has a Face, So Does Hell* expands the traditional categorization to include ten types and many subtypes.

Kishin and **Kijin** (guardian deities and demons) masks predate Noh. They include *Zen kishin*, which protect the Buddhist faith and people, and *aku kishin*, which wreak havoc and destruction. They are the opposite of yūgen.

Two primary subclasses of Kishin are *Tobide* (open mouthed guardian deities with bulging eyes) and *Beshimi* (close mouthed demons); each has many subtypes and variations. A third subclass, *Akujō*, is a powerful god who shows righteous anger or intense compassion.

Additional categories of supernatural beings include *Oni*: demons, *Onryō*: vengeful ghosts of the dead, *kami*: divine spirits, and *ryō*: ghosts.

Okina (aged deity) represents physical incarnations of gods or supernatural forces in the form of a male elder (ancestor/spirit) and is the guardian deity of troupes. Features included a hinged jaw, a completely open eye (not just the pupil), dimensional brows of horsehair, rabbit fur, cotton or hemp, highly stylized wrinkles, and darkened *kanmuri* hairline (for divine or high-ranking characters), but

FIGURE 2.16(A) *Japanese Noh mask: Asakurajo*

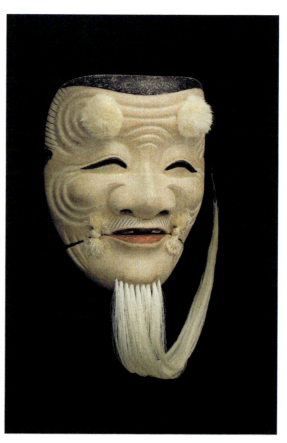

FIGURE 2.16(B) *Hakushiji-jo (Okina). Mask by Hideta Kitazawa. Photo by Sohta Kitazawa. Private collection, 2020*

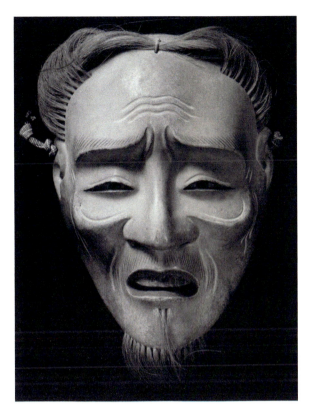

FIGURE 2.17 *Japanese Noh mask: Kojo*

no ears. Two forms are white, a third is black. This mask links to astrological beliefs also: seven holes represent the seven stars of the north pointing constellation (Ursa Major) and the seven shrines of the Lord of the Mountain, an avatar of Buddha.[25] Old men were venerated and believed to be close to the gods; the "masks do not personify gods but depict their human form…in which they temporarily reside while on earth."[26] It is significant that only this mask is donned "in full view of the audience to symbolize his transformation into a representative of the gods."[27]

Jō, or jo-men, are elderly male masks: these are a single piece, yet the open mouth allows for speech. Compared to okina masks, the age furrows and creases are fewer, smaller, and more realistic, eyebrows are painted, only the pupils are opened, and they have ears (they are worn with a wig that fills the space behind the ear of the mask and the performer's own ear). Jō masks have white or light brown hair braided across the top of the forehead and may have unbraided mustache and chin whiskers; a headpiece/crown covering the braided hairline may be used for an aged god character.[28]

Onna men (female) include goddesses, mediums, and humans. Originally based on Shinto statuary, these masks are the most idealized. Faces are nearly oval, pale, with features placed in the lower half of the mask, neat center-parted black hair, smooth forehead, narrow elongated eyes, high softly rendered brows in ancient Japanese fashion (*denjō mayu*), blackened teeth (*ohaguro*), reddened lips, without ears. There are many subtypes based on age and life experiences; they are visually distinguished by individually painted strands of hair, aging, and subtle differences in the shape of their features.

- *Ko-omote* is an iconic Noh mask and the pinnacle of yūgen, used for goddesses as well as innocents. Ko-omote is the youngest and most cherished female mask. She is recognized by two or three long parallel strands of hair along the edge of her mask, a plumper chin and cheeks (signs of youth), and larger tapered eyes, a longer jaw, more pronounced smile, very light skin, and teeth slightly out from the plane of the face.

- *Zō-onna* is a youthful goddess – removed from the world, with an immaculate, icy beauty; sparser brows, narrower eyes, sharper nose, taut cheeks, narrow jaw, minimal if any smile, and teeth flat to plane of face. Three swags of hair fall back into the body of hair.

- *Magojirō* is a sensual young wife, young widow, or child of Ko-omote[29] with two intersecting sets of hair strands.

- *Waka – onna* is a refined, graceful, attractive young woman in her 20s to early 30s, probably experienced in the world.

- *Fukai (Fukai-onna), shakumia* are mature women (aged 30–45), including mothers and women traumatized by separation from a spouse or child. They are visually thinner, with upper lids hooded over lower, rounded or half round pupils, teeth curved in slightly, shallow nasolabial folds, and a somber expression.

- *Uba, rōjō, and wa* are old women or their ghosts; age is represented by a narrow face, slack, protruding cheekbones, sunken eye sockets, slits or half-closed eye lids (rather than a pupil), wrinkles, and gray or white hairlines that show short hairs and loose wisps.

Otoko are male masks. Their style is more realistic than divine, probably because characters who are real people are not usually masked. Their appearance is a lifelike tan or light brown, without ears. The mouth is slightly open with upper or both upper and lower teeth blackened. Painted hair includes sideburns, sometimes a light moustache and chin whiskers, and at the upper edge the straight black **kanmuri** hairstyle or crown. Otoko commonly have furrowed brows, "a vague expression of sorrow, worry or

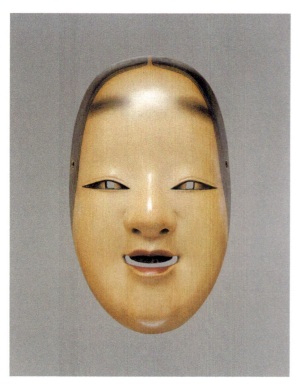

FIGURE 2.18(A) *Japanese Noh mask: two views of a Ko-Omote*

FIGURE 2.18(B) *Japanese Noh mask: two views of a Ko-Omote*

anxiety,"[30] and occasionally dimples. This category includes Chūjō, a young aristocrat who has a refined, somewhat melancholy persona and sense of yūgen.

Stephen Marvin recognizes an additional category of adolescent boys who can be either juvenile mortals or eternally youthful sprites with simple, elegant designs, in their teens-20s. The shape, dimensions, and configuration of their features are similar to young women masks.[31] The hairstyle is distinctly different: as on otoko masks, the kanmuri is depicted straight across the forehead without the meticulous long strands of hair seen on female masks.

Ryō-no-Otoko are a class of Nature and troubled spirits, minor gods, and wrathful ghosts. They can be male or female. They have features of both Otoko and Kishin masks: smooth brows, stern expressions, and flowing facial hair painted against light brown, ochre, or ruddy complexions, with widely parted lips that show teeth but no fangs. They are usually earless. Their irises have gold paint or brass rings to signal their supernatural state.

Onryō (deluded or wandering spirits) are listed by Marvin as a separate category of masks, while other scholars include them with *ryō-no-otoko* or *kishin*. They personify supernatural beings: *Yase-otoko* and *yose-onna* are male and female spirits undergoing the anguish of hell,[32] consumed by unbearable jealousy, rage, or bitterness. *Hannya*, a horned, vengeful demon woman is the most recognized. *Ikiryō* – spiritual husks of a living person and *shiryō* – the malignant ghost of a dead person are physical manifestations

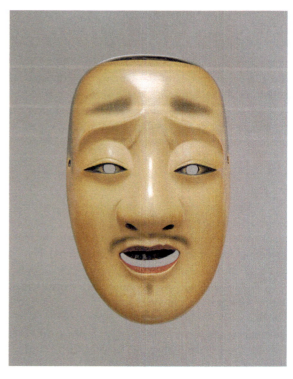

FIGURE 2.19 *Japanese Noh mask: Chūjō is a mask worn for roles of young male aristocrats, such as the tragic heroes of the Heike clan. Mask by Genkyu Michinaga 18th century. Painted wood*

Facing the Stage   47

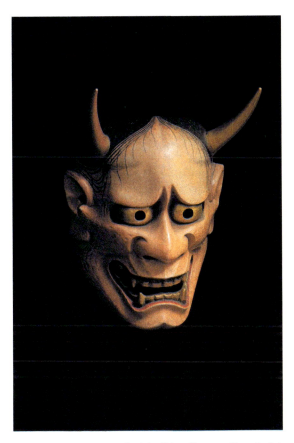

FIGURE 2.20   *Hannya. Mask by Hideta Kitazawa. Photo by Sohta Kitazawa. Private collection, 2013*

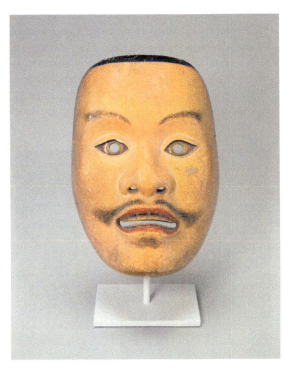

FIGURE 2.21   *Japanese Noh mask: Mikazuki, a type of Ryō-no-Otoko mask*

capable of interaction. Apparitions – ghost-like entities imagined or dreamed by another character – are usually benign, and without the metal eye rings of ryō or demons.[33]

Marvin recognizes additional categories of masks: *Heita* or *Heida* that are ghosts of mature warriors, and Buddhist deities sometimes included in the Kishin category. The Buddhist deity masks are copied from Gyōdō forms. Often blue in color, they feature long droopy earlobes, gilt eyeballs showing the right eye down, while the left eye looks up, plus fangs, carved locks, and a V-shaped furrow on the lower brow.

Kyogen

Kyogen, meaning "inspired" or "mad speech," are the interludes between Noh plays. Like other comic forms, they contain comic dances, tales of the human condition, and an auspicious prayer for longevity. They affirm the Shinto belief in the natural goodness and order of the world. Masks are used occasionally for special human characters, women, animal spirits, and insects. Their exaggerated expressions range from playful and joyful to absurd. *Usofuki* – "whistling masks," with their pursed lips, wide rounded eyes, raised brows, and asymmetrical glances are particularly delightful.

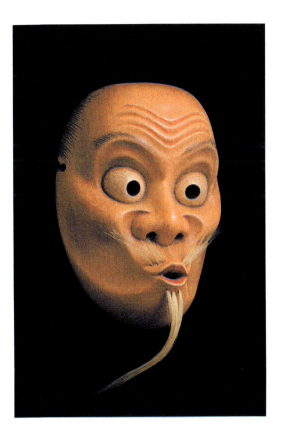

FIGURE 2.22   *Usofuki mask by Hideta Kitazawa. Photo by Sohta Kitazawa. Department of Theatre and Dance, University of Hawai'i at Mānoa. Created in 2017 for Derailed, a kyōgen-style play set in contemporary Hawai'i, which premiered in the production, Power and Folly: Japanese Satire*

BOX 2.3 CONVERSATION WITH HIDETA KITAZAWA AND RICHARD EMMERT

TB 2.3(A)   *Mask artist Hideta Kitazawa*

Hideta Kitazawa is an award winning contemporary Japanese mask maker. His masks have been commissioned and performed in productions across Asia, Europe, and the United States. In addition to carving traditional Noh and Kyogen masks, he is well known for creating contemporary masks in the Noh style, which have been commissioned for English language Noh. Kitazawa-san and Richard Emmert, a founding member of Theatre Nohgaku, graciously shared time to provide additional insights into Noh mask work. Professor Emmert noted the complex and subtle nature of Noh, and Kitazawa-san framed our conversation with this caveat: "Each Noh mask maker has his or her own way of thinking, and there is no general correct answer. Questions about making Noh masks are difficult to answer easily and can be misleading."

Training:

Hideta Kitazawa first learned carving by watching his father, Ikkyou Kitazawa, a renowned Shinto temple carver. At 23, after earning a college degree, he returned to training as a professional wood carver with his father and became a member of Tokyo's traditional woodcarving association.

WM: Kitizawa-san, how did you first come to carve masks?

HK: This Tokyo woodcarvers' association invited a professional to teach related woodcarving; I learned from him once per month for a year. Then Ito Michihiko sensei came to us and taught Noh mask making. I really enjoyed that, plus Ito sensei's personality is wonderful and respectable. I asked him if I could continue to learn mask making. He had a class for amateurs three times per month. I joined this class and went for nine years. Then Ito sensei advised me to be independent. I learned more about Noh and masks with every project.

About 25 years ago, I received a commission from the Nomura family, who are famous Kyogen actors. Nomura Mannojo the fifth asked me "Why don't you learn Kyogen plays? It must be good for your career. At that time, he was busy and did not teach amateurs. So, I started to learn Kyogen from his younger brother Nomura Manzo the ninth when I was twenty-nine years old. I really liked his play and nice personality. I have always respected him, and I learned much from him. [He chuckles, showing me a picture of himself in a shite role.] I am not a professional actor! but sometimes I play Kyogen. It is not usual to do both. I don't know other mask makers who make mask commissions and perform."

WM: Did you go to traditional theater as a young person?

HK: When I started mask making, I went to Noh theater and watched Noh because it was necessary for me to learn about it. There I saw Kyogen, too. [They are usually performed together in one program.] I still meet my teacher's friend who is also a professional mask maker, at Noh and Kyogen performances; we meet at the theater and discuss the masks and program of the day. It is very important to exchange information. I never intended to be a mask carver. But, over time, I lost interest in making other things and prefer to continue learning the ways of Noh.

WM: My research consistently notes the importance of making utsushi – copying clearly the master masks of earlier masters, using not only patterns to capture form and expression, but also matching

TB 2.3(B)   *Refining the carving of a mask in progress*

color, patina, and imperfections. Am I understanding this correctly?

HK: Yes, the student has to learn exactly what the master does – drawing the front and side, working with patterns, learning to carve and paint. As is typical in learning to carve masks, I created many utsushi while refining my skills.

WM: When making new Noh masks, how much room for interpretation is there?

HK: I still take commissions to recreate exact copies of original honmen, but often it is the essence, or atmosphere of the mask that is desired. A performer may request that the copy be slightly larger or smaller to fit their face, because the old masks may be too small for contemporary performers. Some of the old masks look very dark, and I am asked to make a lighter copy, or one that looks newer, or brighter. Other requests may be for a specific play or character, or just for a type of mask such as a ko-omote. Mainly I do that kind of work. I also make some Kyogen and English Noh masks.

WM: The Italian master mask artist Donato Sartori wrote and taught of the specificity of the mask object and placed importance on understanding that the character, story, actor, production, and location all impacted the "type" of design. It is my perception that Noh, too, is very precise about including

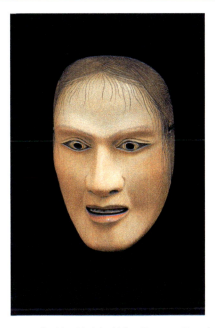

TB 2.3(D) *Cordelia. Mask by Hideta Kitazawa. Photo by Sohta Kitazawa. Property of Jubilith Moore. Created for Theatre of Yugen's 2011 production of Erik Ehn's Cordelia*

TB 2.3(C) *Crazy Jane. Mask by Hideta Kitazawa. Photo by Sohta Kitazawa. Property of David Crandall. Created for Theatre Nohgaku's 2010 production of Crazy Jane*

all these qualities in each mask. Are Noh masks this specific?

RE: Sometimes, but not usually. Plays are not done exactly the same way each time. There are classical plays that have a mask made just for that play: actually, there are a bunch of masks that were made just for that play, and they are different from each other. There are many more masks that are suitable for use in many different plays. Professional actors are very discerning about everything, including how to make the mask expressive. The choice of which mask, costume, performers, and interpretation for a Noh presentation is very specific, but the design of the mask can be either narrowly specific or broadly used.

WM: Would you speak about what influences your designs?

HK: I begin not only with research, a knowledge of traditional forms, the play, and character, yes, but also reading and discussing with the performer what aspects of the character, story, and mood are important. This discussion informs the kurai of the mask. I look at images for reference, especially for Western faces, whose profiles and features have different proportions than traditional Japanese forms.

WM: Professor Emmert, when you are creating English Noh, how are masks chosen? Do you use some standard stock or always work with new?

RE: In Noh tradition, the actors choose costumes and masks and are limited to what is available or what they can afford to have made. Sometimes we commission a new mask, and sometimes we use a mask again for another character.

WM: When creating new masks, what's the collaborative process like?

RE: When we did the Elvis mask for Theatre Nohgaku, John Ogilvie (a company member) looked up lots of images of Elvis. There could have been different kinds of masks. We discussed what parts of his character were most important. When I work with Kitazawa-san, he sketches his idea then sculpts a full-sized model in clay; these become tools for discussion. During our meeting, Kitazawa may adjust the sculpt in response to our conversation, perhaps brightening the countenance, chiseling the features, or adjusting the emotion. When the model is satisfactory, he begins the carving process to make the mask.

WM: When selecting and designing characters for English Noh, does either the story or the character come first, or do they develop in tandem?

RE: We usually start with a play and choose a most appropriate mask [style] in response to the character – though the mask may take on an influential aspect to the production. In 2006, Kitazawa-san created masks for *The Pine Barrens*. He came to where we were performing it, and in the process of seeing it, he realized he could have done it in a slightly different way. If we do *Blue Moon Over Memphis* again, would we use the same Elvis mask or decide to do something slightly different, or older or younger? I don't know.

HK: It takes a long history and long trial to make a traditional Noh; if Theatre Nohgaku will continue into the future, maybe that will make Elvis a standard, too.

RE: This makes me wonder, when you design English Noh masks, do you have a classical mask in mind and then make adjustments to it for Western faces?

HK: I always try to make the attitude of one of the classical Noh masks, but it depends on each case.

WM: What appeals to you about new forms – specifically the English Noh you have carved?

HK: It's important that the mask looks like Western people but is constructed like a Noh mask. The placement of where the eyes are in the mask is very precise, and the features of Western characters are not the same proportion as Asian masks. I have to adjust inside and out, so it has balance. I make sure the mask can still play like Noh, so when the mask turns up or down the shadows can make the mask take on different emotions. I am pleased that the creators and performers have very good Noh training and use masks exactly the same way as Noh actors.

RE: Your ability to get the same effect of Noh mask on a non-east Asian face is amazing.

WM: What are your thoughts about other kinds of masks – have you been tempted to try carving "for fun" in the topeng or Commedia style, or Korean Hahoe, or Native American peoples?

HK: Of course! I am interested in the masked cultures of the world. I have exchanges with mask artists from Italy, South Korea, China, Canada, Slovenia, etc., and I would definitely like to visit the mask festivals in Portugal and West Africa.

WM: What does the future look like for mask makers in Japan? Is traditional craft being taught?

HK: There are some options for national learning, and others for commercial craft. There is no paper [certificate, diploma, or license] for mask makers, but there are many programs to help keep people making masks.

Workshops offered by the government, cities, and cultural or educational organizations show people how to carve masks: these are for very amateur

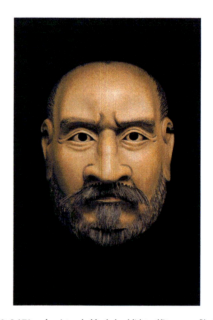

TB 2.3(E) *Armistead. Mask by Hideta Kitazawa. Photo by Sohta Kitazawa. Property of Elizabeth Dowd. Created for Theatre Nohgaku's 2017 production of Gettysburg*

students. While a few of these students may continue to take classes or even study with a teacher, they do not rise to the level of master carvers who can provide the quality of mask needed to perform at a high level.

Long ago, a mask maker would be part of a school/group of artists and travel with them, so would know the performers and stories and provide masks for the group. He learned because he was always carving and learning; his livelihood depended on it.

Now, there are just a few makers whose work is used on stage, and they are commissioned to make masks by particular artists. A mask artist may make several masks for a performer and have a good relationship, but the performer may also commission other artists.

There is not enough need for masks artists for it to be worth making a whole school to train artisans. We need just a few really good high-level makers. To reach that level, the artist must keep studying and learning. Even I have not learned enough. If I want to keep working with the highest level Noh performers, I need to keep training every day.

WM: What else would you like to tell us?

HK: Go to the theater! We have many more chances to see Noh performances on You Tube or the internet now. Once you see that, go to the theater. Watching from the screen, the information is very limited. Noh is very special. Please see it directly. Noh is difficult for new audiences to understand at first, it needs imagination and sometimes patience to get to the exciting scenes. It does not move at our contemporary pace. But Noh has a most important philosophy for human beings.

BALINESE CALONARANG AND TOPENG

Bali shares performance traditions with the many cultures that make up Indonesia. Ancient and modern, sacred and secular, public and private, these arts co-exist in public and private temples, villages, family compounds, and theater spaces. Most of us are familiar with concepts of balance, including yin and yang, good and evil, high and low, left and right. The concept of balance is essential in Balinese culture and is evident in each aspect of performance.

The Balinese perceive that "the spirit world is a living force that must be recognized and appeased through rituals and offerings."[34] Processions, rites, dances, and dramas are offered to appease and delight supernatural beings as well as to instruct and entertain. In villages, the stories presented are often chosen to highlight current events and to provide relevant moral or social instruction,[35] just as artistic directors in Western theaters select a season that is deemed relevant to their audience. Both comic and serious stories "served as reminders of their principles as they attempted to rebalance the harmony between good and evil."[36]

Training begins with young children learning dances in the village. When they have mastered the traditions, the accomplished performer becomes "married" to his masks in a *mewinten* ceremony by a Brahmin priest.[37] Performers pray to their ancestors that **taksu**, spiritual charisma, will come down into their souls so their performances will engage the mortal and divine audience.[38]

Balinese dance drama movement flows back and forth across the figure to embody the balance of forces in the universe.[39] This movement style alternates between static poses (**agum**) and fluid transitions (**angsel**).

Characters fill a spectrum of high and low personalities, and their masks portray those qualities. However, designations are not quite parallel to Western ideas of good and evil. It should be noted that "demon" is a Western appellation for witches and low spirits – who may be impetuous, mischievous, or destructive, but who also serve to protect the village and can do good acts.

Tapel means mask. Because they are magically charged, masks are treated with respect through formal rituals for their creation, use, and storage. With an effective mask, a spirit may decide to enter the mask, possess the dancer, and be part of the performance; this is evident when a performer or spectator falls into a trance. At other times, a spirit may choose to just watch and enjoy the performance without possessing the mask.

Undagi tapel are mask makers. It is a hereditary profession, learned by copying the masks of master carvers. The process is generously shared with mask makers from other places. While anyone may make masks for the tourist trade, a dedicated undagi tapel must understand the rituals connected with sacred masks and experience a purification ceremony.[40] Of these, only a few master carvers are allowed to carve sacred Rangda and Barong Ket masks. Performance masks for Balinese use undergo several rituals, beginning with a prayer to harvest pule wood from a living tree, three purification ceremonies (four for Barong and Rangda), and an invocation. Judy Slattum's *Balinese Masks* provides a good introduction to mask rituals.

Performance Traditions

The best known Balinese masks belong to the Barong, Rangda, Topeng, and Wayang Wong.

Barong is a sacred dance. **Barong Ket** is the Lord of the forest and a Buddhist protective figure; he signifies good, right, white magic, and maleness. As the village guardian, he wards off evil as part of a procession, by performing in a dance drama, or by accepting offerings on the temple altar. His mask is a sacred object. It is made only by specialist artisans, using sacred wood. It must be ritually purified and worn by trained performers. It is stored in the local temple, where prayers and rites observed in the making and wearing of the mask ensure that he will bestow blessings on the community.

Barong masks take varied animal forms. He is frequently a lion but can also be an elephant, boar, tiger, cow, deer, bear, or a composite of animals. They display many intricate details of expression: prominent tusks, bulging eyes, a beard and mane of hair, ornate tooled leather extensions, and adornments of mirrors, glass, flowers, and gilt. With the costume, the Barong may weigh 100 lbs. It is worn by two men of the community working together. When the spirit inhabits the mask, an audience or performance member(s) falls into trance. Many notice the similarity of the Barong to Chinese lion and Japanese Dragon masks.

Calonarang is one of a collection of ritual ceremonies, dances, and stories about powerful demonesses, including Rangda, Durga, and Calonarang. Her masks represent the opposite forces from the Barong and are necessary for balance in the world. Initially a sacred dance performed at a village temple to exorcise evil spirits, it is now also a popular tourist attraction. The best known performances feature a battle between Rangda and Barong. The ceremony begins with the priests' blessing of the masks with holy water and prayers. **Durga**, the Goddess of Death, appears as the witch **Rangda** or the medieval sorceress **Calonarang**. Her mask is very large, with bulging eyes, fierce fangs, a long tongue, and a mass of long hair. She has long fingernails and carries a white cloth with magic symbols. The villagers attempt to drive her away, but she wields power over the dancers, forcing them to turn their swords (*Kris*) on themselves in a frenzied trance. The Barong appears and casts a counter spell that protects the bewitched villagers from injury. Together, the Barong and the men of village cast out the evil Rangda, restoring the balance of good and evil.

Wayang Wong presents tales from the Ramayana, dramatizing the triumph of virtue over vice and reinforcing moral codes of behavior. In addition to demon and human masks, Wayang Wong includes animal masks that are relics of mythical protective spirits, and part of older rites incorporated into Ramayana stories. The masks are different from topeng but have similar conventions.

Topeng Mask Drama has many forms based on old Balinese and Javanese myths and history. Its performance simultaneously worships, celebrates, honors, and requests blessing from common ancestors.[41] The oldest form is *topeng pajegan*, a sacred temple performance that includes four introductory masked dances, followed by a masterful solo performer who alternates a series of noble and clown masks to tell a story. The presentation ends with an old man mask, **Sidha Karya**, who

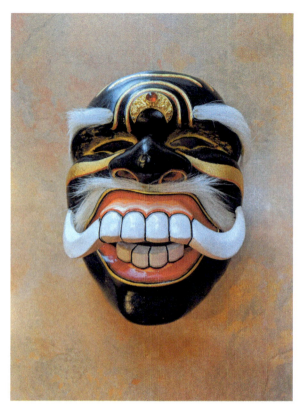

FIGURE 2.23 *Balinese Topeng mask of Sidha Karya*

performs sacred rituals of purification. Finally, the performers enact a dance ritual to bring desired blessings to the people of the village.

Topeng panca is a popular ceremonial 19th century offshoot of topeng pajegan. It means five-person topeng, though modern performances may have as few as three or as many as ten dancers presenting the traditional repertoire. It is characterized by faster action and more clown scenes: it rarely includes Sidha Karya. Topeng panca includes two Penasar brothers always onstage as interpreters and commenters.

Mask Categories

Wildly imaginative demon (**Butha**) and animal masks have five small horns that are symbols of magical power: three on the center of their forehead and one at each temple. Male earlobes have a large ring, and a **cuda manik** sits between the brows on the forehead.

Animal masks are not realistic and may be mythological. They share some demon features such as gaping mouths, protruding fangs, and protuberant eyes, plus elaborate crowns and earrings.

Human characters' appearance relates to their status and personality. **Alus** heroes and heroines wear "attractive,

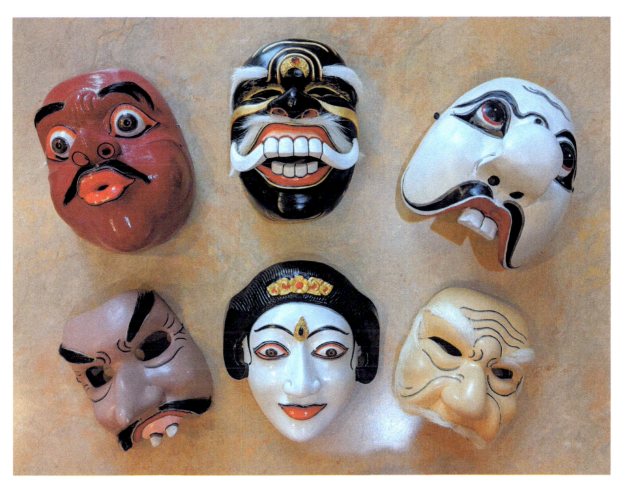

FIGURE 2.24 *Balinese Topeng masks*

refined" full-face masks described below. Coarser characters wear ¾ masks that may have a moveable jaw and exaggerated features: bulging eyes, thicker mouths and noses, imperfect teeth. Alus characters look straight ahead or slightly down as a sign of humility; **Keras** characters look up, indicating arrogance and self-importance.[42] Color is also character specific: white, a symbol of purity, is often used for alus (refined) characters, and darker colors for keras (low).

Topeng masks include (in order of appearance in topeng pajegan):

Patih is the king's assistant or a prime minister – may be foolish, pompous, or humorous, arrogant, prideful, or ambitious. Wide eyes, smooth brows, and a range of natural skin tones are the norm.[43]

Topeng Tua is worn for a variety of respected elder men, who have pathos, dignity, strength, tenderness, sadness, and humor. A slight smile sits on his aged features, which include jowls, hollowed cheeks, wrinkles, and white hair.

Dalem masks are worn by Raja (King) and Putrah (Prince) characters. He is a handsome hero and/or ruler, with the ideal characteristics of intelligence, nobility, and a forceful, positive disposition. As a romantic lead, he shows inner and outer beauty: white complexion, even mother of pearl teeth, almond eyes,[44] sleek hair, gold headdress/crown, and a gold or jeweled cuda manik (symbol of knowledge and wisdom) that sits like a third eye between the groomed brows. These full-faced masks are non-speaking and paired with formal, stylized movement.

Raja Putri (topeng putri) masks are for female noblewomen or Sita in Ramayana. They are the visual partner to Dalem, with thin painted brows (vs. hair), and downcast eyes as sign of subservient demeanor.[45] This mask was originally for a male dancer performing a female role; it is rarely used now but continues to be available for the export market.

Penasar brothers are usually servants to the lead character. Always on stage, they act like emcees, translating or speaking for voiceless masks, and commenting on the action. Both are half masks to allow speaking. The older (Kelihan) has bulging eyes and a more serious expression than his jovial younger sibling.

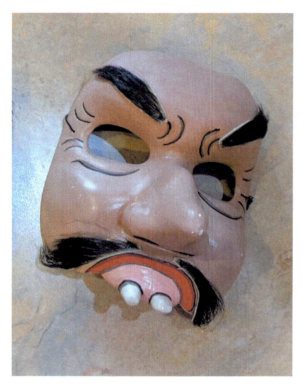

FIGURE 2.25 *Balinese Topeng bondres mask*

Bondres are the villagers. Each dancer has his own collection of these clown masks; there are many varieties, often bordering on the grotesque with contorted expressions, bad teeth, hare lips, or other disfigurements. Sometimes aged and toothless, bondres may be lusty, drunken, deaf, disabled, or unfortunate in some other way (such as spinsterhood), often through their own actions. Eyes are usually open to allow more of the performer's expression to show. Half masks allow speaking, often in vernacular directly to the audience, with a more realistic and interactive acting style.

Sida karya is a symbol of Buddhism used to frighten away low spirits. He has two versions: *Selem* (black) or *Putih* (white). Described as frightening, rowdy, and powerful,[46] he has an engaging wide, demon-like grin, squinting slitted eyes, and wild white hair. He performs sacred ritual as part of the topeng and represents powers of both good and evil simultaneously.[47] He is considered spiritually dangerous, so is never touched out of context, but stored in a special container in the house.[48]

Some other forms of Balinese masked arts are:

- *Telek*, a refined masked dance.
- *Wayang (orang) parwa*, in which unmasked dancers and masked clowns enact scenes form the Mahabharata.
- *Jauk* – masked dance dramas of the 18th century, where both Ramayana and Mahabharata stories are presented.

KOREAN HAHOE AND SANDAE GUK

Korean mask traditions date back over 2000 years. Philip Freund describes the extensive body of evidence for them in his book *Oriental Theatre*. ***T'al***, a Korean word for mask, holds dual meanings. It comes from Chinese character meaning to shed stress or grief. In Korea, it has not only taken on the general meaning mask, but it also means misfortune, illness, and difficulty. This connotation supports the idea that there is some residual negative force in the masks. These beliefs are why most (gourd and paper) masks are burned following their use in a performance, and why durable wooden performance masks are stored in village temples, where offerings are made to ensure safe and effective use.

The general terms **t'al nori** (masked play) and **t'al chum** (masked dance) refer to a variety of genres. Masked dance-plays developed in two forms: Court Dramas *sandae-togam-guk* and Village festivals *purakje*.[49] Some specific regional performance traditions include:

- *Sandae guk* and *sandae nori* are regional dance dramas.
- *Pyolsandae*, meaning "separate stage performance," features masks made from painted gourds, with exaggerated features attached.
- *Ogwangdae* features five performers (clowns), in five scenes, to the five directions.
- *Yaryu*, "field plays," include a procession with singing, dancing, and exorcism followed by four or five scenes with 11 masks.

Plays vary regionally but have similar characters and themes, which satirize authority to the amusement of locals: monks incurring punishment for misbehaving, women shaming men, servants fooling arrogant or foolish noblemen, and villagers getting the best of shrewd, incompetent, corrupt, or insensitive officials. Plays often satirize male authority figures who stray from accepted social mores or Confucian ethical principles. Stories are transmitted orally and spontaneously improvised from rough synopses. The stories emphasize the villagers' point of view, reinforcing social mores and dispersing social tension by satirizing and criticizing people who do not live up to expectations. An event usually includes at least one aristocrat, one monk, and one domestic play. Dialogue ranges from poetic verse to bawdy vernacular; both plays and dances feature witty dialogue and puns.

Music and movement styles vary by region. Music features singing with a combination of fifes, a flute, two drums, a fiddle, and gong, sourced from folk tunes and shamanistic chants.[50] Movement in court theater and Confucian social dances is solemn and stately. Folk Dances allow more improvisatory, freer movement.[51] Freund also notes that Korean Dance is performed on the heels, citing Dong-wa

FIGURE 2.26 (A, B, C, D)   *Korean Painted masks for old woman, man and maidens*

Cho: "The Korean dancer steps forward with his or her toes up. Such steps undoubtedly run counter to the natural movement of the body, but it is an important attribute to the introverted spiritualism of the Korean dance in that it holds body movement in check."[52]

One distinctly Korean mask style is made from dried gourds and/or paper. They are painted with symbolic colors: black for old characters, red for male, and white for female. Distinctive features include the use of large oval forms, tear shaped eyes, dotted decorations, the addition of exaggerated features, and a strong graphic design quality. A dark cloth (***t'alpo***) conceals the back of the head. These masks are usually burned at the end of ceremonies to dispel any lingering negative energy or spirits.

FIGURE 2.27 *Korean Hahoe masks of Kaksi, Yangban, and Sonpi, carved of wood for sale in the Hahoe Folk Village in Andong, Gyeongsangbuk-do, South Korea. (©~mers)*

Another distinct Korean mask form is the Hahoe Tradition, traditionally performed during a new year's festival or in celebration of Buddha's birthday. Students might compare Hahoe to Commedia dell'Arte.

Hahoe masks[53] are carved from alder wood, partially painted, and lacquered. Deliberate subtle asymmetry and the hinged jaws on men's masks increase the variety and mobility of their facial expressions. As is true with masks of many cultures, the ability to create animation in a static face is testament to the skill of both the carver and the performer. This style of carved mask first appeared in the mid-12th century, carved by the artist Huh Doryong. Legend has it that a young man was told in a dream to carve 14 character masks typically represented in dance dramas and instructed by his village deity to do so in isolation. Unfortunately, a girl who was in love with the carver peeked in at him, at which time he instantly perished. These masks include:

- *Imae*, a jolly fool, is often servant to the scholar Sonbi. His drooping wrinkled eyes express foolishness and naivete; his crooked nose suggests a physical deformity and he moves with faltering steps. Unlike the other male masks, Imae has no chin. This relates to the origin story of the masks – Huh Doryong was working on this mask when he died, so Imae went unfinished.
- *Ch'oraengi*, a wise fool and the aristocrat's servant, provides comedy by mocking and fooling his master. Ch'oraengi is described as a hasty, scatterbrained meddler; he has a mischievous, crooked mouth, with sharp or buck teeth, a thin face (he's hungry), bulging eyes (sees much), and solid brows (stubborn). Discontented, he takes "frivolous" steps.
- *Paekchong*, or *Paekjung*, the Butcher, is considered an unfavorable, cruel character, who enjoys his job of killing animals. His expression alternates between maniacal laughter and an evil leer, featuring coarse wrinkles, narrow eyes, and slanted (ill-tempered) brows. His movement is described as "perverse."
- *Chung*, or *Jung*, is a depraved Buddhist monk. His character had power and influence, but through time the plays responded to increasing corruption, greed, lechery, and drunkenness with negative caricatures. Chung is often middle aged, with a bump on his forehead, narrow crescent eyes, and "deceitful" steps.
- *Sonbi*, or *Sonpi*, the Scholar, enjoys some social status but does not hold a government appointment and may be characterized as a fraud. A wide forehead indicates his intellect but contrasts with his narrow jaw and sharp cheekbones that indicate conceit and disdain. Protuberant eyeballs suggest he reads too much. He takes long, pompous strides.
- *Yangban*, the Aristocrat, is the most powerful character and the most mocked. His narrowly closed eyes, thin smile, and hinged jaw make him appear laughingly generous, arrogant, and angry. Yangban

is often bested by his servant, prompting the village audience to delight in repercussions for his faults. He may have a long dignified black beard. Yangban swaggers.

- *Kaksi*, the Bride, embodies visual and character traits desirable in young maidens. She is young, pale skinned, lightly blushed, with long black hair that seems to sway because it is twisted in opposite directions on each side of her face. Her small, closed mouth and small downcast eyes suggest she is modest, shy, and quiet; one forward looking eye indicates her ability to face her fate. In the opening procession, Kaksi represents a local goddess, so the performer is carried in standing on the shoulders of another performer. Later, as the Bride, she walks with soft steps.

- *Halmi*, the widow, shows a small brown wizened face appropriate to her age. She has wide round eyes and open mouth (to complain and to take food); her narrow forehead and chin suggest poverty and a lack of blessings. She moves in a "hip dance."

- *Punae*, or *Bune*, the flirtatious young woman is sometimes a concubine of Yangban or Sonpi. Her mask is a symmetrical oval, with a small mouth, high nose, crescent brows, red lips, rouged cheeks, and tinted forehead, all considered elements of beauty. She has closed eyes and a general air of happiness and good humor. Her hair is piled on top of her head, while two cords hang at the sides of her mask. She sings, dances, and moves elegantly.

- *Chuji*, the Lion – these two masks represent two Buddhist winged lions, although they are imagined, not realistic representations. They are shaped of wide ovals, often red, with large eyes and a protruding snout. They are held not worn and given a fluttering movement to protect the playing space and performers from evil spirits. One is male, the other female; the ceremony includes a fight between them, and the victory of the female signifies productivity for the upcoming year.

Three other characters' masks have been lost:

- *Ttoktari* – the old man.
- *Pyolch'ae* – a civil servant or tax collector.
- *Ch'ongkak* – the bachelor.

Hahoe carved masks take considerable time and skill to make. These are not burned but stored in the village temple when not in use. The 11 existing originals are now kept in the Korean National Museum (Seoul) as National Treasure No. 121.

FIGURE 2.28 *Thai Khon mask*

THAI KHON

Thai masked dance dramas have their origins in religious dance dramas and festivals as far back as 1431, when Khmer musicians and harem wives were captured as booty.[54]

Khon includes five forms of masked dance dramas. The stories are adapted from Ramakien, the Thai version of India's epic Ramayana. Battles, journeys, abductions, genealogies, origin stories, love stories, treachery, and magic are conveyed with two literary styles: *kampak* (descriptive poetic verses) and *Ceraca* (rhythmic prose dialogue). One or more *Khon pak* (narrator) chant the story to the accompaniment of an offstage chorus and a *Piphat* orchestra. Musical passages are rigidly fixed and symbolize specific events.

Dancers' movements mime the action with athletic, masculine movement and square, flat-footed stances. Specific hand, head, and foot gestures express emotions and responses. Visual friezes correlate with puppet forms and other artistic representations.

Khon dance dramas use full-head masks that follow a strict iconography of color, expression, and headdress. While many masks appear identical except for a few small details, over 200 distinct mask/headdress combinations exist.[55]

Demons comprise the largest category of masks, with specific colors, expressions, and headdress for over 100 male and female characters. Demons may have bulging (open) or crocodile (half open) eyes. Mouths show teeth and fangs, either straight or curved, clamping or snarling. Dominant features are not only painted but are also given dimension by the addition of strips of lak (sumac tree resin), which can be softened to take fluid shapes. Other features specific to characters include ear flaps and trunks. Demons have 14 types of crowns/headdresses with up to three tiers[56] in peaked and bald styles. More important characters wear more elaborate styles. Multiple faces or body parts indicate power. Tosakanth is the most important demon:

> Tosakanth's green face is highlighted with blue and gold lines and bright red lips. He has bulging eyes with a snarling mouth and curving, tusk-like canine teeth. His crown is his most distinguishing feature. He is the only character with a three tiered … Crown of Victory. The first level is a gold leaf cap complete with jewels and flower designs. The second level contains a face identical to the mask proper. This face is repeated on all four sides and represents Tosakanth's ten faces. The top level of the crown is the face of a celestial being.[57]

Monkey masks are the second most numerous type, with 30–40 individual characters. Their masks all have bulging eyes; their mouths may be open or closed.

FIGURE 2.29(A) *Thai Khon mask*

Crowns and headdresses for the monkeys include seven types.[58] Bald masks, divided into four types based on military rank, are more common. Hanuman is by far the most important monkey.

> [Hanuman's] white mask is highlighted in green and pink. He wears only a coronet so red and gold markings are evident on the top of his head. Hanuman's gaping mouth displays his canine teeth which are usually just features of the demons. His gaping mouth also makes visible the jewel in the roof of his mouth. The jewel is a symbol of his special powers. Hanuman is the son of the God of Wind and can thus fly through the air. Also, when Hanuman yawns, he exhales suns, moons, and stars. This is the magical power by which people recognize Hanuman, the jewel is sometimes referred to as a "glass canine" thus, Hanuman has five canines. Another symbol of Hanuman's special power is the jewel between his eyebrows. This symbol appears on statues of the Buddha and represents inner energy. Possibly it means the same with regards to Hanuman.[59]

Celestial and human mask faces are simpler and considered more refined in appearance. The painting follows color symbolism, but the line quality is lighter and more realistic. Mouths are closed; eyes are open but not bulging. Expressions are clearly painted but do not have the dimensional reinforcement of lak strips around their features. Important gods display a painted jewel between their eyebrows and wear more elaborate crowns. Celestial and human masks are still used at the beginning of Khon performances in a ceremony recognizing the gods and ensuring the performers' safety. While many of these roles no longer use masks, the performers still wear the variety of prescribed headdresses adorned with flowers.[60]

Aesthetically, Khon masks are distinctive in their shape, detail, and painting style.

The process of making a Khon mask begins with a clay sculpture.[61] After sculpting, either the clay is hardened or a plaster mold is made of the form. *Sa* or *Koi* paper (the same type that Buddha's teachings were written on for temple manuscripts) and rice flour glue are used to form 15 layers of paper mache. Once dry, the mask is cut off the mold, stitched together, and additional layers of paper mache are added to cover the cut. The surfaces are smoothed, and strips of *lac* are formed into the mouth, ears, and brows then covered with another layer of paper mache. Additional features such as tiaras and earflaps made of buffalo skins may be added. Finally, gold leaf, colored glass jewels, and mirrors are applied to the headdress and facial details are painted on. Part of Khon masks' distinctive style is the finely painted details: thick lines that form the mouth, eyes, and brow ridge are often textured and reinforced with a

FIGURE 2.29(B) *Thai Khon mask*

pattern of dashed lines and/or contrasting colors. Groups of three narrow lines together create crisp highlights and shadows. Finer sets of lines indicate expression and age on human and celestial characters. Additional fine details decorate teeth, devotional marks, and the jawline. On demon masks, mother of pearl fangs are applied. Often, the masks are made by several artists in a workshop. Master craftsmen have been recognized as national treasures by the Thai government.

Zat Pwe of Burma (Myanmar) and *Lakon Khol* of Cambodia are similar to Thai Khon forms.

SRI LANKAN SANNI AND TOVIL

Sri Lankan mask traditions include many sizes and forms, from small partial masks through colossal processional masks. The most developed are those face masks with elaborate headdresses used in Tovil, Sanni, and Kolam. Their scale and complexity are impressive, and the complex forms tell stories to a knowledgeable viewer.

Tovil religious rituals can be staged to propitiate gods, to appease demons or deceased persons, to protect a person or community from negative forces, or to cure illness or possession.[62] Many tovil ceremonies include figures wearing half masks fitted with leather straps, or open-mouthed masks showing two pairs of teeth fitted with string.

Sanni, which means disease, are a specific group of curative rites. There are 18 types of Sanni masks, including blindness, vomiting, bleeding, fever, insanity, boils, paralysis, even flatulence.[63] Each affliction is related to a different demon. The masks reflect the physical ailments they represent,[64] such as closed eyes for blindness, boils for skin diseases, flames for fever, and asymmetry for paralysis. Before a Sanni ceremony, a shaman examines the patient to determine which demons might be responsible for their illnesses and selects an auspicious time for the ceremonies. At the appointed time, the shaman (*yakadura*), who is the lead performer, prepares offerings for the patient to give to the demons. Dancers wear the demon masks associated with a person's afflictions and perform a series of specific dances. The masks are intended to create fear in the diseased person, but the ensuing witty impromptu banter between the masked demon and the drummer balances the fear and humiliates the demons, who agree to stop afflicting the patient. The rites end with the appearance of *Maha Kola* (the terrific or all-encompassing one), whose mask and headdress incorporate miniature representations of the other 18 demons surrounded by snakes.

Dance dramas are also created for entertainment. They have roots in fertility rites, reinforce cultural norms, and satirize social mores. Sokari Folk operas, in which just a few characters are masked, are connected with cult worship of the goddess Pattini and fertility rituals.[65] They dramatize the misadventures of an itinerant trader and his young wife, for whom they are named. Themes of marital relations, conception, and deception are common. In addition to offering devotion to Pattini, the stories allow locals to lampoon foreigners, chastise infidelity, caution inattentive husbands, and satirize social foibles.[66] Popular in rural villages, they were performed as a post-harvest play, originally outdoors or on a threshing floor; now they are presented in a variety of venues at different times of year. Sokari still delights audiences.

Kolam is a cycle of dance dramas and masked dances, with over 100 different masked characters, and a more consistent, intricate iconography. Kolam performances include one or more evenings of dance, gesture, mime, song, and dialogue. Dialogue is mostly verse, with occasional impromptu prose conversation[67] among the narrator, drummers, and actor/dancers.

FIGURE 2.30(A) *Sri Lankan Maha Kola mask, encompassing the 18 sanni demons*

Kolam stories are based on a themed series of episodes, with human and superhuman characters. The production begins with an invocation and retelling of the origins of Kolam: a pregnant queen of the primeval world craved seeing a masked dance drama; when King Maha Sammata's ministers and subjects were unable to solve the problem, the gods arranged for the Divine Artisan Visvakarma to carve the masks from sandalwood for the royal couple. The second section

FIGURE 2.30(B) *Naga Raksha Demon mask from Sri Lanka*

FIGURE 2.30(C) *Demon mask from Sri Lanka*

FIGURE 2.31(A) *Sri Lankan theatre mask*

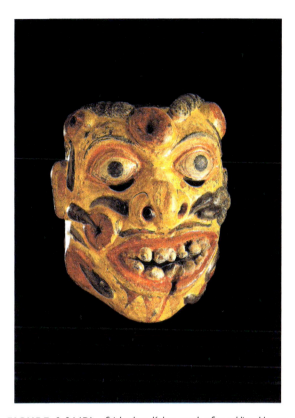

FIGURE 2.31(B) *Sri Lankan Kolam mask of a soldier, Heraya, showing cuts, sores, and leeches*

includes songs and dances by specific characters or groups to entertain royal patrons and the audience. The third section is a dance drama: often based on Jataka (Buddhist birth stories) with religious, social, or moral significance. The performance ends with the dance of the Gara demons, to exorcise negative elements and to spread a positive effect and prosperity among the audience and the performers.[68]

Mask-Making traditions are passed down through families orally and through practice.

There are verses that detail characteristic colors and decorative motifs of some masks,[69] but these manuscripts do not specify size, angles, or proportions, so exposure to traditional forms is important. Most are made of *kaduru* wood that is plentiful and soft to carve. Earlobes, headdresses, tusks, tongues, and other protrusions may be cut separately and eventually joined to the main face of the mask with dowels or tabs; some are permanently set, others may be detached for storage. Hair, beards, and whiskers can be carved or added with fibers. Additional materials occasionally include leaves, bark, animal hide, leather, paper, and fibers; these materials are more often used in minor traditions and tourist souvenirs. Headdresses help define characters, especially demons. The headdresses of heavenly beings have female figures, royalties have crowns, and a variety of hats and hairstyles are assigned to other characters.

FIGURE 2.31(C) *Sri Lankan theatre mask*

Human masks are scaled to human size and follow conventions that idealize higher classes and parody lower classes with exaggerated emotions and distorted features.

Animal masks include recognizable key features but are not photorealistic. They have deeper dimensions to accommodate snouts, beaks, and mouths. Some are used to represent demons and may share realistic or featured teeth, open mouths, tongues, and protruding eyes.

The masks of supernatural characters are impressive in size (up to 24" wide by 30" tall) and complexity. Gods, demons, and spirits include legendary figures from literature and mythology, and demonic characters. The former have naturalistic faces in light green or blue and elaborate compound headdresses with anthropomorphic components (people, gods, and animals). The demon group have red or reddish-brown skin, fangs, open mouths, protruding eyes, and large earpieces and hoods of one or more cobras and other decorations, both figurative and geometric. Benevolent demons may be pink or yellow faced rather than red.

In Sri Lanka, masks are considered inauspicious at best and malignant or evil at worst: people do not hang them in their houses for fear of inviting demons into the house at night.[70]

ANCIENT GREEK AND ROMAN

If we look to the Western hemisphere, we also find many instances of masked religious and socio-cultural practice. In the Americas, there are the wonderful examples of Aztec, Incan, and Mayan cultures, Northwest Pacific Coastal peoples, Hopi, Iroquois, and many others. A few of the African peoples with masked religious and socio-cultural traditions include, among others, the Baule, Chokwe, Dogon, Igbo, Makonde, We, and Yoruba. Proto-European cultures were also incorporating mask and makeup in various types of guising and ritual.

One of these cultures, in ancient Greece, gave rise to one of the most influential forms in the history of Western theater. Greek theater evolved from ritual celebrations of Dionysus, the god of wine, fertility, and transformation. Cult initiations included ecstatic possession, drinking, singing, and dancing. These celebratory practices developed into presentations of satyr plays and tragedies. In Athens, performances were offered as part of the annual spring City Festival of Dionysus.[71] They probably arose out of some combination of two main influences: the dithyramb, a danced and sung ritual in celebration of Dionysus; and the tradition of wandering epic poets, who would dramatically recite the ancient myths and tales of humans and gods. Tragedy developed as a form of drama in the 6th century BCE, came fully into its creative heyday and the form we recognize in the 5th century BCE, and remained tremendously popular for hundreds of years. By the time of Alexander the Great, professional guilds of actors, playwrights, musicians, costumers, and mask makers had begun to form.

The subject matter of Greek tragedies was largely drawn from traditional heroic myths and featured humans of high status struggling against a supernatural element of Fate or the gods. Tragedies contained a combination of sung and danced

BOX 2.4 GREEK MASK CONVENTIONS IN NEW COMEDY

Visual expectations for male, female, and slave masks of different ages, in Greece and Rome from the 4th century BCE.

Greek and Roman Terms	Age	Gender	Occupation	Skin	Hair	Expression
Geron, senex	Old	Male	9 types, grandfather, leading player, pimp	Dark	White or bald	Bearded
Aner	Mature	Male	4 types, fathers, citizens, soldiers, husbands	Dark	Dark	Bearded
Ephebos, adulescens	Young	Male	4 types, sons	Dark	Dark	Beardless
Doulos, servus	Varied	Male	7 types, slaves	Reddish	Red	Wide mouth, with or without beard
Doula, ancilla	Varied	Female	2 maidservants	Light		
Kore	Young	Female	5 types, virginal daughters, maidens, young wives	Pale	Dark curly hair	Youthful, laughing open mouth
Gune, matrona	Mature	Female	Matrons	Pale	Dark hair	Mature
Graus, anus	Old	Female	3 types for widows, crones	Pale	White	Aged, lined
Hataera, meretrix	Varied	Female	7 types of prostitutes	Light	Yellow	
	Varied	Mostly male	Rustics, foreigners, soldiers, flatterers, parasites, special characters			

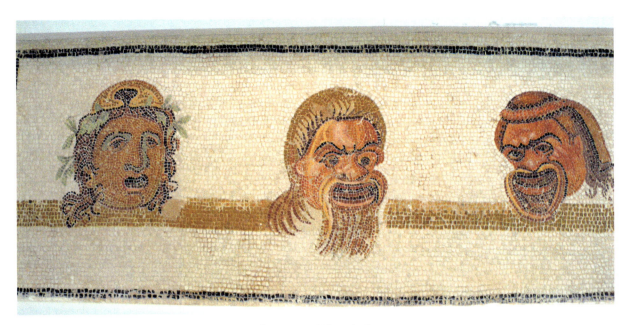

FIGURE 2.32 *A mosaic depicting Ancient Greek masks. ©Ad Meskens/Wikimedia Commons*

passages presented by a chorus, usually 15 male member of the citizenry (who participated in theater as consistently as they did democracy and religion.) The chorus members were identically costumed and masked and could represent human society or supernatural beings such as the Furies. In the early tragedies, the chorus was counterbalanced by the presence of one narrator/actor, who was also masked according to the character or characters he portrayed. As tragedy evolved, plays for the single actor (an innovation credited to Thespis) grew to two actors (as credited to Aeschylus) and eventually to three actors (credited to Sophocles), who through the use of mask and costume would each play several different characters through the course of the play.

The earliest Greek comedies were the satyr plays, which probably originated in fertility rites. By the time tragedy had established itself, satyr plays written by the tragic dramatists were also a featured part of the Festival of Dionysus. Satyr plays also featured stories from heroic mythology, and – most notably – a chorus of satyrs, a male nature-spirit who is part human and part horse (or goat). These satyr choruses were costumed with a tail like a horse, mask that was part human, part beast, horse ears, and an exaggerated fake phallus in perpetual erection. They were, in other words, comically grotesque, and their lewd dancing, ribald songs, and references to basic bodily functions and parts certainly added to this effect.

Old Comedy grew out of the satyr plays, with such playwrights as Aristophanes. These early comedies also drew their stories from the heroic myths, tales of gods and supernatural beings, and parodies of tragic plays, as well as becoming a rich source of political satire, and therefore influence over public opinion. We can also see in the masks of the Old Comedy the early emergence of still-recognizable comic types, such as the old man and the clever servant.

The evidence that we have of the masks in Greek tragedy and comedy comes from depictions of theater in

FIGURE 2.33(A) *Ancient Greek actor statuette in comic mask. Photo courtesy of The Metropolitan Museum of Art*

FIGURE 2.33(B) *Ancient Greek actor statuette in comic mask. Photo courtesy of The Metropolitan Museum of Art*

other contemporaneous art, including vase paintings, frescoes, and sculpture, and from writings about the theater by authors of the time. None of the actual masks from Greek or Roman theater survive, though we can draw conclusions about them from the evidence we have. We hypothesize that they were made of shaped and hardened linen or leather or possibly carved from cork or wood. All of the masks covered the actor's entire face, usually in the form of a "helmet," meaning they fit over the actor's entire head, with a headband to hold them in place. The mask could include hair or a headpiece to complete the image. The mouths were wide open, allowing for speech, and in many depictions the mouth had a slightly funneled shape, which may have provided for a slight amplification of the actor's voice. Extant plays and other commentary laud actors for the power and expressiveness of their voices, and certainly mask makers would have done all they could to magnify the resonance of the actor's voice.

Beyond the material and shape, the scale and level of naturalism in the masks is the subject of some dispute, based on the visual evidence mentioned above. Archaic masks had more neutral expressions, perhaps using the body to indicate expression through the tilt of the head, physical stance (*schêmata*), and gestures (*cheironomia*). Some depictions show masks proportional to the actor's body – thus in a realistic scale – and painted or detailed with naturalistic, even refined and beautiful, features. Other images show realistically scaled masks with strong emotion or characterization, though still in a naturalistic vein. And then we have evidence of large-scale masks with exaggerated and even grotesque features. Within these styles, there were conventions to indicate age, gender,

FIGURE 2.33(C) *Satyr with mask of Silenos. Photo courtesy of The Art Institute of Chicago*

FIGURE 2.34(A) *Ancient Greek vase depicting actor with mask. Photo courtesy of The Metropolitan Museum of Art*

and social status, including skin tone, beards, expression, and hair color. One practical theory about the change in scale suggests that as theater spaces were built in increasing size, the oversized and exaggerated masks were easier to see from the back rows. By the 3rd century BCE, New Comedy was primarily a social commentary: new masks were introduced to present young men and their fathers as respectable citizens, with longer tunics.[72] There is also evidence that some masks were made as recognizable caricatures of real people. Moreover, those lampooned and insulted by such masks may have escalated tensions to the point of danger, and masks may have transitioned to stereotyped figures partly in response to political and social pressure.

We certainly know that comedies and their masks did – and still do – traffic in exaggeration and grotesquerie. We also know that there were developments in tragedy that led to the masks becoming larger in scale and more exaggerated in their features. The top of the mask, for instance – the hair or headpiece of the character (onkos) – had become larger and more pronounced, especially by the time the Romans had adopted the tragic form. In addition, the features of the face became more exaggerated, though not on the level of grotesquerie that we see in the masks of comedy. Gregory McCart's essay "Masks in Greek and Roman Theatre" notes that, concurrently, Roman theater moved actors to a high stage behind the central orchestra, and that "the nature of performance no longer relied on athletic and choreographed movement but on a towering presence and vocal delivery."[73] Whether these changes in scale and exaggeration in the masks of tragedy were an evolution of the form over time or were present at the beginning or indeed were an innovation of the Romans as they adopted tragedy is still a matter of uncertainty.

As we have indicated, another notable change in Greek theater was the shift from what came to be known as the Old Comedy to the New Comedy. In the early days of Athenian comedy, as previously noted, the subject matter of the plays was heroic mythology, the gods, and parodies of tragedies. Over time, however, the comedies came to focus more and more on domestic themes, especially those of the conventional citizenry. These plots involved the very recognizable tropes of young lovers in distress, greedy old men, stupid and clever slaves, overbearing or braggart soldiers, pretentious doctors or teachers, and so forth. As in other genres, the masks of young lovers retained the more refined and beautiful appearance of tragic masks. The remaining masks of the New Comedy began to reflect clearly the comic types they represented, without losing the exaggeration and grotesquerie.

Ancient Rome

Theater, both tragic and comic, was an activity the Romans associated with the Greeks. Consistent with their treatment of most of Greek culture, the Romans were very free in their appropriation but did little to change the forms from those they had adopted from Greece. Roman tragedies retained almost all of the conventions of their Greek precursors and in fact were often directly lifted from the Greek playwrights, translated into Latin but still set in Greek locales. Roman actors wore masks and costumes in the Greek style, with the possible evolutions in tragic masks that we mentioned previously.

Roman comedies were similarly deeply beholden to the Greek forms. Prior to its invasion by Rome in the 3rd century BCE, the southern portion of Italy comprised a number of Greek city-states. As we mentioned, the New Comedy in Greece utilized fixed character types and standardized plot elements. The Greek comedy in the southern portion of Italy had developed to include established costumes and masks for these New Comedy character types. These comedies, usually short, improvised sketches or curtain-raisers for other plays would come to be known as Atellan farces (after the town of Atella, near Naples).

The stock character types of the Atellan farces, which we will see echoed in our later discussion of Commedia dell'Arte, included an old man (Pappus), a comic slave (Centunculus), a braggart soldier (Manducus), a crafty, pompous Doctor (Dosennus), a gluttonous fool (Buccus), and a hunchbacked, beak-nosed fool (Maccus), the latter of which came to be extremely popular in the Atellan-inspired Roman comedies. Each of these characters had their own distinct mask and costume, and there were likely conventions for physicality and voice in the playing of each mask. Pollux alludes to an established vocabulary of gesture used by actors in 2nd century Rome.[74]

FIGURE 2.34(B) *Silver Denarius (coin) depicting a mask of Pan. Roman, 48 BCE. During the 1st century BCE, powerful Roman families issued their own coinage, which often bore a personal icon. In this case, the moneyer, a member of the Pansa family, used a mask of Pan in reference to the family's name. Photo courtesy of The Art Institute of Chicago*

FIGURE 2.35(A)   *A female Roman tragic mask. Photo courtesy of The Metropolitan Museum of Art*

FIGURE 2.35(B)   *Masks from the Paris Opera collection. Photo courtesy of The Art Institute of Chicago*

Atellan farce had a huge influence on Roman comedy – especially the plays of Plautus – and even the comedy that came long after the Roman Republic and Empire had passed. As Kate Meehan writes, "Whether these comedic styles directly influenced Commedia dell'Arte or not, they established a formula for 'Italian' comedy rooted in domestic and social stereotypes."[75]

Two other masked performance traditions from Greece and Rome are important to mention here: mime and pantomime. In the original use of the word, mime was an ancient form of theater representing (mimicking) scenes from everyday life, often in a comical, vulgar, or ridiculous way. It featured a single performer telling a story using multiple masks and spoken word and influenced the development of other forms of comedy, including the work of Aristophanes and the later development of the Atellan farces. Mime was very popular in Roman society and was incorporated as interludes in other performances, as part of festivals and celebrations, and mimes were likely regular features of entertainment on the streets and in the houses of the wealthy and influential. Roman pantomime originated out of mime, as a form that drew its stories from myth, legend, and even the comedic material of the mime. In difference to the traditional mime, it was non-verbal, though still performed by a single male actor, who relied on masks, dance, skillful physicality and gesture, and music to convey the story. The masks used by the performer were similar to those used in tragedy and comedy, with the exception that the mouth was closed, since the performer did not speak. Pantomime was hugely popular throughout the Roman world and very likely continued in various forms right up through the Middle Ages, influencing such later forms as Mummer's plays and the Commedia dell'Arte.

EUROPEAN MEDIEVAL THEATER AND CARNIVAL

The Roman Empire collapsed in the 6th century AD, leaving an artistic and cultural void.

In the Eastern Empire (Byzantium), theater continued to include Greek and Roman-influenced tragic and comic forms, along with popular entertainment inspired by the masked traditions of mime and Roman pantomime. It is unclear if liturgical dramas were part of Byzantine culture. Despite church bans and prohibitions against actors and theater, theater survived until the 8th century when Islamic rulers also forbade it. Nonetheless, it was through Byzantine culture that Greek and Roman plays were preserved and reintroduced to Europe in the 15th century.[76]

The Christian church, growing in strength, had opposed Roman theater because of its roots in pagan festivals, cross-dressed characters, licentious and violent themes, and because Roman entertainments often ridiculed Christian practices and sacraments. For roughly 500 years, there is little record of European theatrical activities or dramatic texts. However, we know that remnants of theater were seen in bands of performers that included Roman-influenced mimes, storytellers, jesters, jugglers, acrobats, animal trainers, and minstrels. In *Crossing the Borderlines: Guising, Masking, and Ritual Animal Disguises in the European Tradition,* Nigel Pennick catalogues many folk traditions, festivals, and seasonal rites that began in pre-Christian Europe, adapted through the centuries, and continue to be performed today. Many of them involve mask wearing or mask performance. Guild records document some guising activity, but the clearest evidence of mask uses may be the church's continued prohibitions against them!

FIGURE 2.36 *Masked mummers in a tradition dating to medieval times. Note the performative elements in a domestic setting, and the masked character in the center as well as at the far right, in this depiction by Robert Seymour (1798–1836)*

Ironically, it was also through the Christian Church that theater was revived in Europe. By the 10th century, liturgical services and holy days included theatrical elements, including processions, symbolic props and attire, and responsive readings between individuals or groups. From the 11th century, liturgical plays began to be presented to the public in larger churches throughout Europe. Most liturgical plays enacted scenes from the Bible, especially stories of the Easter and Christmas Seasons. Since medieval services were held in Latin, a language of educated people, a visual retelling would have had greater impact than the language of the church. Some Christmas festivals, however, developed elements of buffoonery. The Feast of Fools particularly leveraged an opportunity for ridiculing church life and leaders and is thought to have influenced the development of comedy in religious and secular plays of the later Middle Ages. As some of these feast days became more outrageous – and popular – they were moved out of the church proper.

Once plays moved outside the church, Liturgical theater began a transition to vernacular languages, spoken rather than chanted verse, secular presentation, and experimentation (possibly competitive!) by guilds and groups presenting stories. From the 14th through 17th centuries, there were several forms of dramas. **Mystery plays** developed from liturgical dramas. Mystery plays were often performed in cycles, telling a series of Bible stories, sometimes beginning with creation and ending with the final judgment and departure of the damned into hell. The series of stories were performed on multiple platforms, built onto wagons, and wheeled into the town or city in an elaborate procession. Some of the Mystery play cycles were so elaborate and expensive – the entire cycle would sometimes take days or even weeks – that they were only offered every few years. **Miracle plays** presented the lives of the saints. **Morality plays** taught Christian ethical behavior by presenting an "everyman" who faces a journey of moral corruption in daily life, faces death and damnation, and must seek spiritual redemption. Morality plays often used the seven deadly sins and four cardinal virtues as allegorical characters interacting with an Everyman.

In addition to religious plays, there were secular dramas and farces, and a wide variety of secular entertainments and folk traditions that used masks. **Disguisings** were social events where men and women wore decorative masks, creating "a deliberate tension between the wearer and the mask, a flirtation with concealed identity and a tacit invitation to penetrate the disguise."[77] **Masques** were lavish court spectacles, including music, dancing, and allegorical presentations. **Mummings** are a folk tradition of disguising as characters and processing from house to house as entertainment and seasonal celebration. While we expect that folk masks were made locally, we know from guild records[78] and household accounts that masks were being carved, molded, painted, and decorated for theater and private use; people could buy a variety of face masks individually or in bulk, custom or premade, from leather, wood, or fabric and plaster.

Medieval theater used masks in two ways. One was to show extremely good and bad characters. God, Christ, and sometimes angels and archangels would be portrayed in beautiful and ornate golden masks or makeup and white robes. Angels have also been noted as having red faces, or red veils, though such masks are not evident. Devils and demons were described as horrible and black, for they "were charred when they fell from

FIGURE 2.37(A) *A medieval farce played on a booth stage, easily dissasembled for movement to another performance location, and with a curtained "backstage" area*

heaven."[79] They were represented by grotesque masks with very imaginative designs: bestial horns, sharp teeth, large animal ears, wild hair, large red tongues, large misshapen noses, warts, sometimes a snapping jaw, even apparatus to emit smoke and fire. Death usually wore a skeletal mask. Many examples of these in carved wood and painted leather can still be seen in European museums. The other use of masks was symbolic and allegorical, showing the inner state of a character, or demonstrating its duplicity. For example, Treason might wear a fair-faced mask while carrying a knife behind her back.[80] To represent his spiritual corruption, a human character might add a mask showing physical deformity such as leprosy, or an animal head such as a pig-like mask, and then remove the mask when he is redeemed.

Religious plays were banned in 1558 by Elizabeth I, in an attempt to calm the ongoing religious conflict in which "drama was used as a weapon to attack or defend particular dogmas."[81] Similar restrictions on dramatizing religious subjects in other parts of Europe led to the growth of secular drama, revival of Greek and Roman works, and the rise of national styles. Concurrently, the loss of church and state support for theater began the transition to private patronage and then independent professional status.

The masks of devils and demonic creatures are intrinsically connected to earlier pagan rites of fertility, seasonal change, and symbolic struggles between life and death. Nigel Pennick's *Crossing the Borderlines: Guising, Masking, and Ritual Animal Disguises in the European Tradition* documents many of these ongoing traditions. In the bestial qualities of the masks, the seasonal representation of death and rebirth, and the bacchanalian traditions that carnival embodies, we can see a line straight back to the birth of theater in the Dionysian dithyrambs, even if the historical links are intermittent. Such devil and demon masks and the vestiges of liturgical drama can still be seen in carnival processions in Europe, the Caribbean islands, and South America.

ITALIAN COMMEDIA DELL'ARTE

Commedia dell'Arte is a form of unscripted, highly physical, mostly **improvised**, masked theater, which developed in 16th century Italy and eventually spread throughout much of Europe. Commedia was hugely popular for the next 150 plus years and has seen a resurgence of interest since the 20th century. Scholars are still searching for evidence to expand what we know of Commedia's origins.

In the late 15th century, a renewed access to, study of, and fascination with the plays of classical antiquity led to a revival of Greek and Roman comedies. While it is not clear if there is a direct link between the Commedia and the Roman **Atellan farces** or the plays of Plautus, the similarities in plots and characters are far too strong to simply dismiss. The synchronous revival of interest in these ancient playwrights and the arrival of the Commedia dell'Arte is reflected in artistic renderings of scenes from Commedia showing visual similarity with representations of characters from Greek and Roman theater.

There may also be links between Commedia and **Carnivale**, the pre-Lenten loosening of societal restrictions; there are 16th and 17th century depictions of Carnivale in which revelers are disguised in masks in the style of the Commedia. While there are no direct links that we know of between the annual rites and the farcical comedic form, Commedia's spirit of anarchic rebellion and subversion of authority was apropos of the spirit of Carnivale and undeniably part of the long-lasting appeal of the Commedia dell'Arte.

In this period, farmers, artisans, charlatans, traveling minstrels, and actors plied their trades in urban squares and market spaces. These market days were both economic and social cornerstones, as they coincided with agricultural seasons and religious holy days. The **trestle stages** of early Commedia performances were surely influenced by the platform stages of medieval theater; they also addressed the necessity of being seen above outdoor crowds, and when on wagons were the practical means of moving an itinerant company's goods from town to town. Documentation in the form of illustrations and paintings, household accounts, and references in sermons,

FIGURE 2.37(B) *Devil mask made for a Carnivale celebration, a tradition that dates back to pagan rites. Photo by Alejandro Linares Garcia*

FIGURE 2.38 *Commedia dell'Arte performance*

FIGURE 2.39 *Pulcinella and a musician on a simple platform stage. Cooper Hewitt, Smithsonian Design Museum*

letters, and public records points to the unmistakable place of Commedia dell'Arte as a popular entertainment. Many troupes gained notoriety and eventually patronage; the most famous Commedia companies such as the Gelosi were invited to perform at the weddings of the Medici family or at the courts of France and Spain.

Commedia performances were improvised from a basic structure, or **scenario** (a scene-by-scene summary of the play). The stories were variations of time-honored themes, such as young lovers who were destined to be together but foiled by their powerful and self-interested fathers, or servants trying to trick their masters. Of course, being a comedy, the lovers would wind up together, and everyone else would get what they deserved as well. And boy, did they deserve it! Scenes were interspersed with recitation of poetry or songs by the lovers, and with comic business (**lazzi**) such as a scene where a servant eats lots of cherries, spitting the pits at another actor, and then gets sick, or he performs a complicated routine of tripping, falling, or hiding from his master or is torn between enjoying a meal or seducing a lady. These basic structures featured stock characters instantly recognizable to the audience. Each character (mask) had their own comedic and recognizably human excesses: there was the miserly, lustful old man (Pantalone); the braggart soldier (Il Capitano); the gluttonous pedantic "doctor" (Il Dottore); the scheming, clever or not-so-clever male and female servants (among the most famous are Colombina, Arlecchino, Pulcinella, Scapino, and Brighella), and many others who developed as the Commedia evolved and spread throughout the continent. The naïve and immature lovers (Innamorati) did not have a character mask but might have a fashionable one to facilitate mistaken identity. The masks themselves are half-face, leaving the mouth and jaw free to speak clearly, but exaggerating the features and expressions associated with their characters. Each character developed specific attributes of posture, movement, voice, and appearance.

BOX 2.5 THE STOCK CHARACTERS OF THE COMMEDIA DELL'ARTE

There are many different characters within the world of Commedia dell'Arte, and even a huge range of variations of each major character type. However, we can identify some enduring and central "types" or "stock characters" that have survived through the ages. Below is a list of what are generally considered the major stock characters, along with an indication of the function they serve within the comic narrative, and the traditional physical, vocal, and mask qualities for each character.

One of, if not the, most famous of the stock Commedia characters is the servant **ARLECCHINO** (or Harlequin, as the character is often known in English). The servant to Pantalone, Capitano or Dottore, and therefore also to the Young Lovers, the character is always on the edge of survival, i.e., always hungry, tired, or urgently avoiding the consequences of whatever trouble they have stirred up. And they stir up a lot of trouble: hatching schemes to help one of the Lovers (which never work out as planned); misunderstanding directions; getting sidetracked by food or the possibility of an amorous encounter, and generally failing to consider the consequences of their actions or learn from their experience. This latter quality, a certain innocence coupled with an agile body and – later in the development of the character – a quick wit, is a big part of what makes the character so attractive for audiences. Some of the physical and vocal traditions that have developed for portraying Arlecchino include: a nimbleness – often highly acrobatic – in movement; a light, high voice; rapid speech; the tendency to overreact and then quickly forget all provocations, including love, hunger, and danger; and a tendency to embellish movements – Arlecchino never simply reaches for an object without adding a twist, a leap, or a somersault to emphasize the thought and emotion of the character. The mask usually has a pug nose, feline or monkey-like eyes, innocent with a certain mischievousness, and quality of being "surprised." There is a signature bump on the forehead, of debatable origin but possibly the remnant of "devil horns" from early versions of the character. The costume features ragged pants and shirt, which later included colorful patches that became synonymous with the character, and the iconic slapstick, used for multiple purposes, including slapping others and getting beaten themselves!

Perhaps second in renown to Arlecchino is the character of **PANTALONE**, the miserly, authoritarian, often lecherous old merchant. This character is usually the highest in prestige among the Commedia characters, because they either have or are pretending to still have, a lot of money. Which they dearly love. For its own sake, not for what it can do for them or – perish the thought – for anyone else. They part with money only when there is no other option, and usually after faking their own death to avoid doing so. Pantalone is often the parent (traditionally the father) of one of the Young Lovers, and their desire to marry off their child for financial advantage forms the basis of many Commedia plots. These schemes inevitably lead to Pantalone getting their "just desserts." Some of the traditions for portraying this character include: a tendency to sudden and extreme emotional outbursts; an upper class accent, coupled with a shrill, high-pitched tendency when angry or amorously excited; and a quickness and sharpness in movement, though by no means as nimble and acrobatic as Arlecchino. The mask includes a large, hooked nose, prominent eyebrows and moustache, and qualities of authority, coupled with the downward movement of age. The costume would include fine fabric and textures, multiple layers, and a prominent moneybag.

Usually the foil to Pantalone, **DOTTORE** (the Doctor) is also an authority figure in the Commedia plays, and often the parent of one of the Young Lovers. The Doctor is either a real doctor or, more comically, a pretender. Thus, the need to hide their actual ignorance in a cascade of "expert" assertions, pronouncements, and generally interminable speeches, which would be full of mispronunciations, malapropisms, bad puns, and terrible logic. As with Pantalone, the Doctor normally is brought down to size by the events of the play, but with every indication that they will be up to the same mischief soon. Traditions for portraying Dottore include a pretentious voice full of "hot air," the ability to speak extemporaneously at great length, ponderous and deliberate movements, and large, sweeping gestures. The mask features a bulbous nose, large "pretentious" eyebrows, a large moustache, and has the interesting quality of not covering the face below the actor's eyes, allowing for distinct gestures such as "looking down the nose" affectedly while discoursing.

CAPITANO is a parody of the braggart. Usually a soldier from a foreign land (or at least pretending to be), this gives Capitano permission to lay claim to extraordinary feats and accomplishments. Which they do, at great length, especially to impress the object of their desire or a potential rival. While Capitano is most certainly a liar and pretender, there are multiple ways to play this. For instance, they may be a total coward, who runs at the slightest hint of real danger. Alternatively,

they may be truly courageous, but only a danger to themselves as their fighting "skills" are less than advertised. Capitano's goal is to land in a comfortable setup, married and with money. The events of the play usually lead to the revelation of the truth about the character and, at least momentarily, they get their comeuppance. The mask inspires many of the traditions for portraying Capitano, as it includes a long, straight, and prominent nose, an impressive moustache, and an aggressive shape around the eyes (with hints of retreat or fear in the sculpting). Actors often adopt a wide stance, long strides, a certain peacock quality in the chest and movement, and the tendency to rest in heroic poses when still. The voice is loud, commanding, and pitched low, turning into a high-pitched squeal when frightened. The costume is a bright, ostentatious uniform of questionable origin and usually includes a sword or weapon that has been impressively named.

The **YOUNG LOVERS** are the closest to realistic characters in the Commedia, and the plot usually revolves around their attempts to be together, despite the obstacles thrown their way by the older generation. The children of Pantalone, Dottore, or Capitano, they start the play vain, immature, more in love with themselves than with the other, fickle, and petulant. They cannot solve their own problems, and so rely on undependable (or malicious) servants and others for help. However, they are not cruel. Their failings are the failings of youth, and by the end of the play they will have matured and seem capable of real love. The lovers were unmasked in the Commedia but would wear beautiful makeup and be clothed in the best fashions of the day. They speak well, with eloquence and poetry, their voices always musical and pleasurable to hear, even in the deepest despair (which, after all, is never quite real anyway). Their posture features an upward movement in the chest, exposing the heart, and a graceful, balletic stance. Their movement is composed and lyrical, as they are always aware of being "on display."

COLOMBINA, another unmasked character, is a female servant and often a partner or lover to Arlec-

chino. There is a wonderful mischievousness coupled with an earthy intelligence about the character. Colombina seems to always know what's really going on, to see through the ruses and lies of the other characters. Despite the status of the character as a servant, Colombina is also frequently able to speak truth to power, for instance calling out Pantalone or exposing Dottore. Actors portraying Colombina would frequently opt for a country dialect, or a streetwise city dialect, and either an earthy, knowing, maternal voice or a light, laughing, charming, and quick-witted delivery. Movements can be earthy and slow as well, with unexpected displays of speed in the feet and hands, and acrobatic skills. The costume is usually plain, with similarly colorful patches to Arlecchino's. Though unmasked, Colombina would be made up heavily around the eyes to call attention to this part of the face (and possibly to move the character visually closer to the masked characters).

with a short and sharply hooked nose, wiry moustache and small fox-like eyes. The costume was a servant's or, later, a hotel manager or bar owner, sometimes with a cloak (to hide the dagger they were not afraid to use). The voice was seductive and smooth, but with the edge of a blade. Movements are unhurried, cat-like, and with sudden and shocking agility.

PULCINELLA, also a member of the lower status characters, can be either a servant or a low-status "independent" character. They are earthy, crass, boisterous, and have a very special intelligence (or luck) that allows them to always come out on top, no matter what their intentions are and no matter how poor their actions. Audiences love Pulcinella, because the character does the things we would love to, but we fear the consequences. They represent a form of freedom. Pulcinella can be played either as a stupid person trying to be clever, or a clever person pretending to be stupid. The movement is top heavy – originally, Pulcinella had a large hump on his back and a pot belly, though the hump disappeared over time. The voice is a chicken squawk, and the character is highly talkative – to other characters, to the audience, or to themselves. The costume is usually baggy white pants and a white shirt that buttons down the middle, with a belt that sits below the large belly, and which can hold Pulcinella's cudgel. The mask is black or dark brown, with a very large, downward sloping nose, hooking over the mouth. The eyes have a bird-like quality, frequently also incorporating furrowed eyebrows.

BRIGHELLA is often the other half of a comic duo of servants that includes Arlecchino. In difference to Arlecchino, Brighella is clever, cunning, sharp, and cruel. This is the character we love to hate, as Brighella is a ruffian, a lout and a gangster, but with charm and often with a fine musical ability that would be exploited as part of the performance. Their ability to be unscrupulous and charming, to be quicker on the draw than their social superiors, and to still seem willing to do whatever it takes to get what they want, was a pleasure for audiences – as the knave always is. Brighella's mask is either green or brown,

Each of these characters is represented by (or more appropriately, *is*) a mask. Put differently, the mask is the character. We are not talking here about the complex characters of psychological realism; these are distilled and essentialized **types**. "In *Commedia dell'Arte* the isolation of, say, avarice in Pantalone or of intellectual pretension in Dottore is completely crystalized in their masks…Actors must 'live up' to the mask."[82] You don't act in a mask – you play the mask (we will have more to say about the art and craft of mask performance in Chapter 4). Actors in the troupes who performed Commedia plays specialized in one mask, often apprenticing for a considerable time before they were allowed to perform.

Commedia is often called the "actor's theatre." This is for a number of reasons. First, the troupes that traveled performing Commedia were all actors, who also took on the roles needed to run the company, build the stages, marshal the resources, and so on. Commedia was also one of the first theatrical forms in Europe to feature female performers on stage. Moreover, Commedia actors were not only actors – but they also were exceptionally skilled *performers*: acrobats, dancers, singers, musicians, and even fast-thinking escape artists, since the troupes were often running just on the wrong side of the local authorities and getting out of town fast was a good skill to have!

As Commedia developed, the best theater troupes enjoyed the patronage of wealthy lords. As troupes moved indoors to theater houses with permanent stages, scripted plays replaced improvisation, and **market theater** traditions faded. Remnants of outdoor Commedia dell'Arte can be seen in **Punch and Judy** puppet shows.

Although its heyday had come and gone by the middle of the 18th century, Commedia continues to hold a fascination for theater makers, due in no small part to the powerful tradition of mask making and mask performance that it inspired. Donato Sartori notes that Commedia's resurrection after the Second World War was part of a general urge to reclaim their own Italian identity and heritage. "Perhaps the very festivity of the Commedia dell'Arte, its naughty pranks, its rustic tit-for-tat, its mischievousness, its derision of everyday authority figures is the reason for its return – the desire to laugh and to make fun of everyone."[83]

The contemporary revival of fascination with Commedia stems also from a movement in the early 20th century to enhance the creativity and physical expressiveness of the actor. This movement included actors, directors, and teachers (among them Jacques Copeau, Vsevolod Meyerhold, Jacques Lecoq, Giorgio Strehler, and Dario Fo), and the revival of Commedia techniques and mask performance seemed to offer an approach to a new kind of actor training. At the same time, mask-making

FIGURE 2.40 *Commedia player sketch by Jacque Callot. Photo courtesy of The Art Institute of Chicago*

luminaries like Amleto Sartori, his son Donato Sartori, and Antonio Fava have revived a strong interest in the tradition of crafting Commedia masks and have led a new generation to continue their experiments. The Commedia dell'Arte lives on.

CONTEMPORARY EUROPE AND AMERICA

It is safe to say that masks have been a continuous part of European traditions that bridge Christian and seasonal folk celebrations. However, the popularity of masks in theater has waxed and waned depending on the tastes of audiences and even the artistic intentions of theater makers in various historical moments. A similar waxing and waning can even be seen if we look out across the last 100 years in Europe and the United States.

In the early part of the 20th century, there was a definite revival of interest in the mask as a performative instrument. This was true for several reasons. First was a late 19th and early 20th century break from realism and naturalistic theater, and a desire for a restoration to theatricality, ritual, and myth. Edward Gordon Craig, for example, sought a return to more abstract, ritual, and spiritually significant forms.[84] Bertolt Brecht experimented with using masks to jar the audience from being passive observers to active thinkers. William Butler Yeats sought to elevate Gaelic folk heroes into mythic stature. Tyrone Guthrie's famous Stratford, Ontario production of *Oedipus Rex*, based on an adaptation of the play by Yeats, sought to restore a ritual essence to the ancient Greek tragedy. Meanwhile, Eugene O'Neill used masks as metaphor in his non-realistic play *The Great God Brown*, and WT Benda created masks for satirical plays as well as for decoration. In Europe, notable directors such as Vsevolod Meyerhold in Russia and Giorgio Strehler in Italy experimented with reviving the tradition of the Commedia dell'Arte. In France, the renowned director Jacques Copeau experimented with masks as a tool for training his company of actors.

Directly and indirectly, Copeau influenced a generation of acting teachers and theoreticians, most notably Jacques Lecoq and Michel St Denis, both of whom would go on to found influential schools that used mime and mask work as a central element of their training. These schools, especially Lecoq's (and the many schools he inspired, both in Europe and the United States), would guide many theater makers to an interest in the possibilities of mask as a performance form. Similarly, the Commedia dell'Arte tradition kept alive in such spectacular form by Antonio Fava and many others has meant that this indelible form has never lost its ability to inspire.

In Europe, companies such as the Trestle Theatre Company, Vamos Theatre, and Familie Floz continue to explore the possibilities of non-spoken plays in full-face masks. The traditions of mime and mask performance come together in a fascinating way in the work of Mummenshanz, the Swiss company formed in 1972 that continues its work with full-body

FIGURE 2.41 *Masks made for* Four Plays for Dancers, *adaptations of Japanese Noh plays by W. B. Yeats. Yeats had been introduced to Noh masks in 1913. Photo by Davy Ellis. Reprinted with permission, all rights reserved*

FIGURE 2.42 *The Bread and Puppet Theatre performing in Vermont in the mid-1980s. Photographed by Walter S. Wantman*

FIGURE 2.43 *El Teatro Campesino's production of the mythic play Bernabe. Photo courtesy of El Teatro Campesino*

masks of many different forms. The Rude Mechanical Theatre Company in England is inspired by the traditional Commedia but has resolved in the end to create an aesthetic that draws on the traditional types and techniques while utilizing makeup, wigs, and headpieces to achieve the effects that masks have traditionally had. Ariane Mnouchkine's renowned company Theatre du Soleil has used masks as both training devices for the company and as a theatrical form.

In the United States, the 1960s saw a relative explosion of mask performance, much of it in service of satire and social commentary and rooted in the desire to encourage social change. Companies like Teatro Campesino, Bread and Puppet Theatre, and the San Francisco Mime Troupe found much value in the popular traditions of mask performance and the Commedia dell'Arte. Peter Schumann's Bread and Puppet theatre brought pageant and processional masks to the forefront. This hugely influential company would inspire others, like Minneapolis' In the Heart of the Beast Puppet and Mask Theatre. Mask traditions served several purposes important to each of these companies: they allowed for the stereotyping of characters who were the subject of ridicule or critique; such performance was more effective outdoors, where these companies often performed; and the spectacle of masks removed the audience from an interpretation of the play that was simply about the characters and situation, achieving a similar alienation to that which Brecht desired in his experiments with masks. More recently, Julie Taymor's landmark production of *The Lion King* has created renewed interest in theatrical masks and puppetry.

It is impossible to ignore the influence of mask on the film industry, especially in science fiction and fantasy. How might comic book characters or movie versions of them fit into a discussion of mask work? Are they our folk heroes? From Zorro in the 1920s through contemporary characters such as Deadpool, many of them don masks. As in theater, the mask brings disguise for the wearer (often a common person or a deformed or alien individual); the mask provides recognizable character information (with the caped, colorful, or camouflaged body-emphasizing costume); it offers transformation including superpowers, and it frames the action for us. While we have moved to a time when digital technology has in many instances (though not all) replaced the actual mask worn by an actor, the skills required of a mask performer are still highly in demand, and we can even see the benefits of mask training on the work done by performers in motion capture technology.

Beyond theater and film, professional wrestling is another contemporary popular entertainment that makes extensive uses of masks as performance tools. While it is probably true that the use of masks is partially driven by a need for protection of the head and face, for many wrestlers, the mask and the persona have become one thing. Many wrestlers have turned to mask makers steeped in theatrical traditions, such as Stanley Allan Sherman, for their ability to sculpt a compelling characterization into a leather mask. Across the world, interest in masks is also growing through cosplay and live action role play. It is clear to us that as humans, our fascination with masks continues.

PROJECTS FOR FURTHER STUDY

- Choose an established theater tradition and research it; suggested points to investigate are listed in Appendix B
- Watch a performance in one of these traditions and write a response to it, following the prompts in Appendix B
- Research, watch, and compare two performances such as
    - Noh and Kabuki
    - Topeng and Khon
    - Ancient Greek and Noh
    - Kathakali and Jingju
- Watch an Asian inspired production of a Western play and discuss how it incorporated the two cultures: such as
    - Kathakali *King Lear*
    - *Gettysburg*, an American Noh
- Research and compare/contrast variations of a specific character or story across cultures, such as
    - Hanuman the Monkey King
    - Comic, Prince, or Demoness Masks in different traditions
    - A story of Rama and Sita
    - Korean Hahoe and European Commedia dell'Arte genres

NOTES

1. Emigh, in Nunley, *Masks: Faces of Culture* (NY: Harry Abrams, 1999), 209–210.
2. Nunley, 132.
3. Freund, *Stage by Stage. Oriental Theatre* (London: Peter Owen, 2005), 254.
4. Emigh in Nunley, 229.
5. Eldredge, *Mask Improvisation for Actor Training and Performance* (Evanston, IL: Northwestern UP, 1996), 160.
6. Duchartre, Pierre Louis, *The Italian Comedy* (NY: Dover, 1966), 51–52.
7. Slattum, *Balinese Masks: Spirits of an Ancient Drama* (Hong Kong: Periplus Editions, 2003), 17.
8. "Why is Krishna Blue?" Isha Institute of Inner Sciences. https://isha.sadhguru.org/us/en/wisdom/article/why-is-krishna-blue, 8/7/21.
9. *The King of Masks*, directed by Wu Tianming, Hong Kong: Shaw Bros, 1996 includes scenes showing this art form.
10. Marvin, *Heaven Has a Face, So Does Hell* (Warren, Connecticut: Floating World Editions, 2010), 5.
11. Marvin, 8.
12. Cavaye, Griffith, and Senda, *A Guide to the Japanese Stage* (Tokyo: Kodansha, 2004), 168.
13. Marvin, 153.

14 Cavaye, Griffith, and Senda, 168.
15 Marvin, 14.
16 Hisao Kanze in Marvin, 90.
17 Udaka, *The Secrets of Noh Masks* (Tokyo: Kodansha, 2010), 157.
18 Udaka, 155.
19 Marvin includes a detailed description of the carving, coating, and painting processes.
20 Brown, *Traditions Transfigured: The Noh Masks of Bidou Yamaguchi* (Long Beach, CA: University Art Museum, 2014), 11.
21 Udaka, 7.
22 Udaka, 155.
23 Marvin, 26.
24 Brown, 8.
25 Mark Nearman in Marvin, 153.
26 Marvin, 14.
27 Marvin, 154.
28 Marvin, 158. Marvin specifies three subclasses:

- gods in human form (Kojō and Akobujō)
- aged gods in true form (Maijō, Shiwajō, and Ishiōjō)
- ordinary old men (Asakurajō, Sankōjō, Waraijō)

29 Marvin, 186.
30 Marvin, 18.
31 Marvin, 237.
32 Cavaye et al., 178.
33 Marvin, 105–106.
34 Slattum, 11.
35 Slattum, 32.
36 Rubin and Sedana, *Performance in Bali* (NY: Routledge, 2007), 3.
37 Slattum, 32.
38 Dibia and Ballinger, *Balinese Dance, Drama and Music* (North Clarendon, VT: Tuttle, 2004), 11.
39 Rubin and Sedana, 4.
40 Slattum, 23.
41 Rubin and Sedana, 102.
42 Dibia and Ballinger, 47.
43 see Rubin and Sedana for subgroups, 112–113.
44 Dibia and Ballinger, 47.
45 Slattum, 46.
46 Dibia and Ballinger, 66.
47 Rubin and Sedana, 109.
48 Rubin and Sedana, 108.
49 Freund, 264.
50 Freund, 258.
51 Freund, 262.
52 Freund, 253.
53 Kim, Dong Pyo, *Hahoe Masks on Phrenological Viewpoint; Analysis on the Basis of Physiognomy* (Hahoe Mask Museum). http://www.mask.kr/coding/english/sub02.asp
   Hahoe 10 Masks & Byengsan 2 Masks (Korean National Treasure-Intangible Cultural Asset No. 121, Andong.net). http://anu.andong.ac.kr/~hyun/andong/norital.html)
54 Brandon, *Cambridge Guide to Asian Theatre* (Cambridge, MA: Cambridge UP, 2009), 234.
55 Robertson, *Khon Masks of Thailand* (Seasite.niu.edu, n.d.), accessed 4/23/19.
56 Yupho, in Robertson
57 Robertson
58 Yupho, in Robertson
59 Robertson
60 Chandavij and Pramualratana, *Thai Puppets and Khon Masks* (Bangkok, Thailand: River Books, 1998), 108.
61 Chandavij and Pramualratana illustrate this process, 114–115.
62 "Tovil and Sanni, Powerful Exorcism Rituals," *Asian Traditional Theater & Dance* (Theatre Academy, University of the Arts Helsinki. #71, 2018), accessed 1/4/21.
63 Bailey and de Silva, "Sri Lankan *sanni* masks: an ancient classification of disease," (*BMJ* 333(7582), 2006), 1327–1328.
64 Bailey and de Silva, 1327–1328.
65 Goonatilleka, 15.
66 Goonatilleka, *Masks and Mask Systems of Sri Lanka* (Sri Lanka: Tamarind, 1978), 82.
67 Goonatilleka, 47.
68 "Kolam, Masked Folk Theatre" *Asian Traditional Theatre and Dance* (Theatre Academy, University of the Arts, Helsinki. #71, 2018), accessed 1/4/21.
69 Goonatilleka, 16.
70 Goonatilleka, Masks of Sri Lanka (Columbo, Sri Lanka: Department of Cultural Affairs, 1976), 19.
71 City Festivals honoring various gods and holidays were part of Greek and Roman culture. Athletic and musical contests, feasting, and local traditions were part of these festivals. Tragedy and Comedy developed in the city of Athens, and spread to other Dionysian festivals, including in Rome and other cities. Graf, in McDonald and Walton, *Cambridge Companion to Greek and Roman Theatre* (Cambridge, UK: Cambridge UP, 2007), 55.
72 Trendall and Webster, *Illustrations of Greek Drama* (London, UK: Phaidon, 1971), 10.
73 McCart, in McDonald and Walton, 264.
74 McCart, 252.
75 Chaffee and Crick, *The Routledge Companion to Commedia dell'Arte* (London: Routledge, 2017), 207.
76 Brockett, *History of the Theatre, Fourth Edition* (Boston, MA: Allyn & Bacon, 1982), 92.
77 Twycross and Carpenter, *Studies in Performance and Early Modern Drama* (Burlington, VT: Ashgate, 2002), 277.
78 Twycross and Carpenter compile documentation for further reference.
79 Twycross and Carpenter, 202.
80 Twycross and Carpenter, 234.
81 Brockett, 148–149.
82 Rudlin, *Commedia dell'Arte: An Actor's Handbook* (London, UK: Routledge, 1994), 35.
83 Sartori in Marcia, *The Commedia dell'Arte and the Masks of Amleto and Donato Sartori* (Florence, Italy: Casa Usher, 1980), n.p.
84 Nunley, 243.

SELECTED RESOURCES

Bailey, Mark S. and H Janaka de Silva. "Sri Lankan *Sanni* Masks: An Ancient Classification of Disease," *BMJ: British Medical Journal*. Vol. 333, No. 7582 (2006), 1327–1328.

Brandon, James R. *The Cambridge Guide to Asian Theatre*. Cambridge, Massachusetts: Cambridge University Press, 2009.

———. *Theatre in Southeast Asia*. Cambridge, Massachusetts: Harvard University Press, 1967.

Brockett, Oscar. *History of the Theatre, Fourth Edition*. Boston, Massachusetts: Allyn & Bacon, 1982.

Brown, Kendall H., ed. *Traditions Transfigured: The Noh Masks of Bidou Yamaguchi*. Long Beach, CA: University Art Museum, 2014.

Cavaye, Ronald, Paul Griffith and Akihiko Senda. *A Guide to the Japanese Stage: From Traditional to Cutting Edge*. Tokyo, Japan: Kodansha International, 2004.

Chaffee, Judith and Olly Crick, eds. *The Routledge Companion to Commedia dell'Arte*. Routledge Companions, 2017: 4. London: Routledge, Taylor and Francis Group, 2017.

Chandavij, Natthapatra and Prompom Pramualratana. *Thai Puppets and Khon Masks*. London, United Kingdom: Thames and Hudson, 1998.

Dibia, Wayan I. and Rucina Ballinger. *Balinese Dance, Drama and Music*. North Clarendon, Vermont: Tuttle Publishing, 2004.

Duchartre, Pierre Louis. *The Italian Comedy*. New York, NY: Dover Publications, 1966.

Eldredge, Sears A. *Mask Improvisation for Actor Training and Performance: The Compelling Image*. Evanston, Illinois: Northwestern University Press, 1996.

Emigh, John. *Masked Performance: The Play of Self and Other in Ritual and Theatre*. Philadelphia, Pennsylvania: University of Pennsylvania Press, 1996.

Freund, Philip. *Stage by Stage. Oriental Theatre: Drama, Opera, Dance and Puppetry in the Far East*. London, UK: Peter Owen, 2005.

Goonatilleka, M.H. *Masks and Mask Systems of Sri Lanka*. Colombo, Sri Lanka: Tamarind Books, 1978.

——— *Masks of Sri Lanka*. Colombo, Sri Lanka: Department of Cultural Affairs, 1976.

Marcia, Alberto and Centro Maschere e Strutture Gestuali. *The Commedia dell'Arte and the Masks of Amleto and Donato Sartori: Centro Maschere E Strutture Gestuali*. Florence, Italy: Casa Usher, 1980.

Marvin, Stephen E. *Heaven Has a Face, So Does Hell*. Warren, Connecticut: Floating World Editions, 2010.

McDonald, Marianne and J. Michael Walton. *The Cambridge Companion to Greek and Roman Theatre*. Cambridge, UK: Cambridge University Press, 2007.

Nunley, John and Cara McCarty. *Masks: Faces of Culture*. New York, New York: Harry Abrams, 1999.

Pennick, Nigel. *Crossing the Borderlines: Guising, Masking, and Ritual Animal Disguises in the European Tradition*. Berks, United Kingdom: Capall Bann Publishing, 1998.

Robertson, Mary Lou. *Khon Masks of Thailand*. Seasite.niu.edu, n.d. Accessed 23 April 2019. http://www.seasite.niu.edu/Thai/literature/ramakian/khonmasksofthailand/khonkhon.htm

Rudlin, John. *Commedia dell'Arte: An Actor's Handbook*. London, UK: Routledge, 1994.

Rubin, Leon and I. Nyoman Sedana. *Performance in Bali*. New York, New York: Routledge, 2007.

Slattum, Judy and Paul Schraub. *Balinese Masks: Spirits of an Ancient Drama*. Hong Kong: Periplus Editions, 2003.

Trendall, A.D. and T.B.L. Webster. *Illustrations of Greek Drama*. London, UK: Phaidon, 1971.

Twycross, Meg and Sarah Carpenter. "Mask and Masking in Medieval and Early Tudor England," in *Studies in Performance and Early Modern Drama*. Burlington, Vermont: Ashgate Publishing Co., 2002.

Udaka, Michishige. *The Secrets of Noh Masks*. Tokyo, Japan: Kodansha International, 2010.

CHAPTER 3

THE DIRECTOR'S PERSPECTIVE

FIGURE 3.1 *Theatre Temoin's production of* The Marked. *Photo by Idil Sukan*

Why use masks in performance? How does their use affect the audience? How is the meaning of a play, story, character, or design aesthetic affected by the use of masks? What is the relationship between a performer and their mask? How does the use of masks affect the writing process, the collaboration with designers, and the rehearsal process?

These are some of the essential questions that must be asked by a director when the use of masks is contemplated in a theatrical production. Our goal in this chapter is not to provide the final, definitive answers to these questions (as if one ever could). Rather, our aim is to address a series of important questions that help to illuminate the issues that must be faced when a group of theater makers decides to use masks as a performance tool. Rules are made to be broken, precedents to be overturned, and principles to be tested. So, we encourage you to engage with these issues, and as all mask artists have done, to find your own creative answers.

As we examine these questions, we will consider the work of several mask performance artists and companies. We hope these profiles of mask types and their different creative applications will elaborate the questions a director must address when deciding whether and how to use masks in performance. And while our discussions will focus on mask theater that is primarily concerned with human characters, the principles we are exploring are applicable across a wide range of mask performance. Indeed, some contemporary companies like Punchdrunk, famous for their immersive theater experiences, even turn the question of mask use "on its head" by having the audience wear masks. In a similar spirit, we encourage you to test the principles we examine and explore the questions that are raised, as you discover even more ways to use masks in performance.

SHOULD WE USE MASKS IN PERFORMANCE?

There are many very good reasons to use masks in a theatrical production, and their revival as a theatrical tool in the 20th and 21st centuries has been influenced in part by their ability to affect an audience in ways that realistic performances cannot. Having said this, it is also very possible for masks to be misused, or employed poorly or as an untruthful gimmick, even with the best of intentions. Therefore, an understanding of the function and effects of masks, and some basic considerations of types of masks, is an important place for a director to begin when contemplating whether and how to use them.

What Do Masks Do?

Let's begin with this very essential question. To help us think about why we might use masks in a theatrical performance, it helps to think about the functions of masks – in other words, what a mask is used for, or what it does – for an audience, for

FIGURE 3.2 *El Teatro Campesino's 2018 production of* La Carpa de los Rasquachis. *Photo by Robert Eliason*

the performers, and for the story being told. As we discuss these functions, it is important to bear in mind that while we can talk about them as if they are separate and discrete from each other, in reality the different functions are often in operation simultaneously, with some functions being more prominent at times than others.

First, and most basically, the presence of a mask declares that the event of the performance is "an activity that is set apart from the normal and the everyday."[1] This is what Sears Eldredge calls the **framing** effect of masks. As a frame around a picture or painting might do, the presence of a mask sets apart the event, or performance, from the world around it. Of course, in many ways the theatrical event itself already serves this function – it happens in a special location, with a particular relationship between audience and performers, and the stage itself is a reminder that this is not "real life."

The mask, however, has the ability to take this framing effect a step further. The presence of masks in theater removes us from the world of **naturalism** or **realism**. This must be understood by directors, whether or not they hope to use the masks to portray recognizable characters and real situations. As Eldredge says, "Mask theatre is not realism! The characters and situations are more heightened, more intensely who or what they are. They are automatically more archetypal, more mythic, more representative, and metaphorical."[2] Directors who understand the way that masks shift an audience reception of the performance event will be much more successful in taking advantage of the mask's expressive potential.

Masks can also be used to create a "frame within a frame," for instance, when the mask sets apart an event or persona within the world of the play. This effect has been employed, for example, in service of a memory, dream, or supernatural sequence in a play where performers are otherwise unmasked.

Beyond creating a "frame" for the performance and shifting the audience's expectations away from the realistic, the mask has another very important function. It acts as a catalyst, or stimulus to the audience member. The mask provokes the viewer or audience member in a number of ways. It might engender a sense of awe, strangeness, or fear. Alternatively, it might provoke laughter, or even empathy. These responses to the mask are grounded in a very complex relationship that has evolved in humans and our relationship to the face. This is far too broad a topic to fully engage here but suffice to say that we are deeply programmed to look

FIGURE 3.3 *Three characters from* Dead Good, *by Vamos Theatre. Courtesy of Vamos Theatre and Graeme Braidwood Photography*

at other faces as primary means of social communication and information. This programming is so innate that, presented with the image of a human face – even a static and clearly artificial mask – we immediately scan it for information. This explains why the mask has the power to affect us emotionally.

It also explains why theater makers can employ the mask for another, related purpose, which is to engage our imagination. In the hands (or, more precisely, on the head) of a skilled performer, the mask engages the emotions and imagination of the audience, as they begin to "fill in the blanks" or "complete the thoughts" of the character. This is certainly one of the most important functions of the mask for performance – it asks the audience to become co-creators, to engage in the making of the performance in a much more interesting way than as passive recipients of information. Simultaneously, this engagement of the individual imagination creates the space for a multiplicity of "readings," in which audience members create their own subtext, inner life, etc. for the characters.

Because this function is so important for theater makers, let's illustrate how it works with an example. A performer enters the stage wearing a mask – for instance, the mask depicted above. Audience members have an immediate reaction to the mask, perceiving it as friendly, a threat, familiar, etc. This first impression will be largely the result of the attitude or primary characteristics that are inherent in the mask's design, along with the information conveyed by the performer's body. After this first impression, another process begins. The audience members ask themselves, "What is that character thinking? What are their intentions? What do they want or need? What are they going to do?" These questions of course will not be that explicit in the audience member's mind, but we can be sure that the audience is scanning the mask for more information about these things. The mask, however, does not change. It is a fixed object. So, the next thing that happens, after the mask has appeared, is that the performer does something – a movement, a gesture, an action. When this is accomplished skillfully (see Chapter 4), it starts another process. The audience begins to interpret the action or movement as an expression of the thoughts/emotions/intentions of the character. Another way of saying this is that the audience has begun to project, using their imaginations, onto the mask.

In this way, the mask has activated the fundamental dynamic of the theatrical event. An audience agrees to join a game, to be complicit in the creation of a world that they simultaneously know to be false and at the same time accept as "real" – what we often refer to as the **suspension of disbelief**. Thus, in the moment of imagining the mask to be a living, breathing, thinking, feeling entity, the audience has entered the fundamental event of theater. This helps explain why the mask has been such an exciting tool for so many theater makers. It cuts straight through to the central event of our art form. A performer/director/writer/designer offers a proposal. An audience member takes up that proposal and, through their own complicit imagination, turns it into something that does not actually physically exist.

As it provokes and stimulates the audience member's imagination, the mask can also serve another function, that of being a mirror. In this sense, the mask presents an image to the audience that can be both recognizable (i.e., a social **type**, an animal, a fantastical creature) and that can also be an externalization of an "inner" image (emotions like fear or anger, or a sense of awe, achieved through techniques in the mask and performance like **exaggeration** or **distortion**). The mask can be an immediately recognizable social type, or even a particular famous personality. This may allow the theater makers and audience to move more efficiently to another level of communication. In this way, the mask works on the audience member both as an individual and as a member of a particular culture. For instance, we might all recognize, as members of the same culture, the social type of a miserly old man (Commedia's Pantalone), but our individual experiences might mean that the mask has further ambiguities of meaning or emotional connotation.

Another function of the mask is as a conduit of communication between the audience and the performer. In this function, which we will explore further in the chapter on acting in masks, the mask allows the audience to give clues to the mask performer through their responses to the mask and allows the performer to affect and move the audience through their use of the mask.

Another word we could use for the functions of the mask we have described is **transformation**. The mask transforms – the actor's face and appearance, the observer's reading of the event, the imagination and projection of the audience, the power relationships within a society, the relationship with gods and the transcendent. This transformative aspect of masks is, according to Eldredge, "the most recognized and discussed aspect of masks" in the scholarly literature about them.[3] And the transformative effect of masks is not limited to the audience. The performer may also undergo a very powerful process of transformation. Throughout the history of mask use in the theater, actors have celebrated (and at times shunned) this transformative effect. We will have more to say about this in the chapter on performance but suffice to say that the mask can be a very powerful tool for the actor, releasing new levels of play and creative openness, connection to the character, immediacy with the audience, and sense of freedom from their personal inhibitions.

When Should We Use Masks?

So, when should the director use masks in a theatrical production? One very practical reason, at least from the director's perspective, may be that the play itself calls for masks. Since the beginning of the 20th century, well over 200 plays written for the Western theater have called for the use of masks, including plays from such notable playwrights as Eugene O'Neill, Bertolt Brecht, Luigi Pirandello, Jean Genet, and Eugene Ionesco. There are also surviving plays of the Commedia dell'Arte or Greek and Roman plays in which the playwright imagined a style that required the use of masks. For an excellent listing of plays that call for mask performance, from the late 19th to the late 20th century, see the appendix in *Masks in Modern Drama* (1984). In addition to plays that already call for masks, many directors have made the decision to use masks in an existing play that did not call for them. There are many good reasons to do this, though the principles of mask performance discussed above and elsewhere in this book must be kept in mind, if the director is to avoid confusing the audience or creating a situation where the masks feel like an unnecessary device.

Whether the existing play calls for them, or the director and creative team have made the decision to use them for other reasons, there is another aspect of when to use masks that must be considered. Sometimes a writer, director, or company will choose to mask some characters and not others. This can serve a number of creative purposes and can be very exciting for an audience. For instance, masked characters in a play with unmasked characters may represent a memory, a dream/fantasy, or even supernatural characters. However, the use of masked and unmasked characters side by side may also be confusing, if certain principles are not adequately acknowledged and accounted for. The audience will in most cases immediately "read" the masked characters as existing in a different reality, or as a different order of being, from the unmasked characters. As Eldredge succinctly puts it "if we say the mask is the reality, then what is the unmasked face? If the face is the reality, then what does the mask represent? If masked and unmasked characters are employed … the effect is frequently that of otherworldly characters (the masked characters) appearing as visitors from another reality. Two orders of beings are on stage together."[4] If the director recognizes this effect on the audience and is intentional in its use, masked and unmasked performers in the same play can be a wonderful tool.

Finally, there are of course instances where a director and a creative team have decided to make a play specifically for mask performance. Trestle Theatre, Vamos Theatre, Bread and Puppet, Familie Flöez, Mummenschanz, Antonio Fava, Julie Taymor, and Marco Luly are only a few examples from the contemporary and recent history of companies and artists who create plays specifically for styles of mask performance. In the section on rehearsal process, we will discuss the advantages and challenges of creating work specifically for mask performance.

FIGURE 3.4 *The goddess Hera, depicted in a mask, with the human characters in the background unmasked. From a production of* Jason and the Argonauts *at The Absolutely Fabulous Theatre Connection, Hong Kong, China*

FIGURE 3.5 *A Vamos Theatre character interacts with a bystander at a performance of their Walkabout experience. Courtesy of Vamos Theatre and Graeme Braidwood Photography*

BOX 3.1 PROFILE: RACHAEL SAVAGE AND VAMOS THEATRE

In recent years, the United Kingdom's Vamos Theatre, led by their Artistic Director Rachael Savage, has taken full-face mask performance into some very interesting and creatively rich directions.

Giving Voice to the Voiceless

Using the inherent ability of full mask theater to "tap directly into the power of empathy and encourage awareness of our shared human experiences," Vamos Theatre creates stories that intentionally engage issues of social relevance. In doing so, they consult and collaborate with members of their community, base their work on real-life stories, and engage in extensive research and listening so that their stories can effectively capture the many aspects of the issues they are addressing.

These stories are meant to serve as a vehicle for exploring unspeakable human truths, and for giving voice to individuals who cannot effectively speak for themselves. This ability of a wordless theater to give voice to the voiceless is evidenced in shows such as the award-winning *Finding Joy*, an emotionally insightful production that approaches the subject of dementia from the point of view of people living with it and those who care for them. *A Brave Face*, the compassionate and very moving story of a soldier returning home from the war in Afghanistan, was created following two years of research with current and former soldiers, their families, and health professionals who deal with issues of post-traumatic stress. And *The Best Thing* explores the changing morals of the sexual revolution in the 1960s, based on extensive research with women who had experienced forced adoptions because of becoming pregnant outside of marriage. Because of the human themes and the universal language of mask theater, these shows have played to audiences worldwide.

As Rachael Savage shared with us, "Full mask theatre is so engaging - you have to watch and interpret and meet the performance half way. The performers give clarity and detail to the work, and the audience must use their brain, which gives us access to their heart - when they feel, they think."

Inclusive Theater

In addition to the productions themselves, Vamos Theatre is also pioneering ways to make theater accessible and enjoyable for those who might otherwise be excluded. For instance, the company has created what they call relaxed or "chilled" shows. These performances are geared to audience members who may have learning disabilities, or mothers with young children, or individuals living with dementia or post-traumatic stress. The performances incorporate house lighting that allows for free movement in and out of the theater during the show; audiences are encouraged to speak, clap, laugh, or otherwise make sound during the performance; strong stage effects such as harsh lights or loud sound effects are subdued; and the company even takes care to prepare the audience by introducing the actors before the show and allowing the audience to see them don their character masks. In addition, they have prepared character and story guides for some of their shows such as a visual guide to *Finding Joy* for those on the autistic spectrum or with sensory or communication disorders or learning disabilities.

Out and About

Another direction Rachael Savage and Vamos Theatre have taken their work is literally out into the streets. And the parks. Even to people's houses; this is street theater with a twist. Through their programs under the heading Walkabout Theatre, Vamos Theatre sends their full mask performers to festivals, private parties, weddings, and corporate events. Mask actors portray "nurses," on call in case of emergencies, bumbling "caterers," and even two hilarious old ladies who are available to lightheartedly enforce moral codes, encourage social distancing during the COVID-19 pandemic, and occasionally break into some surprising and very humorous disco moves.

Care Homes

Rachael Savage shared with us that one of the most important aspects of Vamos Theatre's current work are the shows they create to be performed in care homes and other locations where they can reach the people they were created for. *Sharing Joy*, for instance, was created for people living with life-shortening conditions such as dementia, cancer, heart disease, and other neurological conditions, plus their families and caregivers. The show employs dance, music, masks, and lots of laughter to encourage pleasure, participation, empathy, and skill building. It's "a huge celebration of life and all its joys." The show was created to be performed in a variety of locations, including theaters, care homes, hospitals, and community centers. Vamos Theatre's latest production, *Love Through Double Glazing*, was made as a response to the coronavirus pandemic. The show combines masks, clowning, music, food fights, bubbles, and ballet – even a real-life dog – and is staged entirely outside (with windows closed), but viewed from the inside, "where it's warm, cozy and, most importantly, safe."

For more wonderful advice and resources on creating mask theater, as well as mask sets and exercises, we recommend a visit to Vamos Theatre's website: www.vamostheatre.co.uk.

FIGURE 3.6 *"Gasp," by Rob Faust. The masks are not recognizable human characters, but still require a high degree of physicality. Courtesy of Rob Faust/Faustworks*

What Types of Masks?

Having answered questions of why and when to use masks, the director and mask designer must now explore the question of what type of masks. We have addressed aspects of this question in our chapters on design, so we will address it here from the director's perspective. The first question is whether the masks are human or non-human. Are they meant to represent people as we know them, or an exaggerated/**grotesque** version of human beings? Social types? Recognizable famous individuals? On the other hand, are the masks meant to represent something non-human, for instance, gods or supernatural creatures? Or, on another level, are the masks an abstraction of an emotion, a dynamic, or an event?

If the masks are to portray particular characters, whether human, god, or mythical creature, the director and designer must come to an understanding of what primary characteristics the mask is meant to express. Effective masks make a very clear impression from the moment they appear. The major trait(s) of the character are sculpted into the mask. Of course, a skilled actor and director can find and express nuances and even oppositional qualities, so that the mask becomes a more complex character. But the mask will operate at its most effective if the first impression is clear, and consistent with the mask's role or function in the development of the story. To achieve this, the director will need to make sure the designer has access to as much information as possible about the character. The script (if there is one) will need to be shared, of course, along with an aesthetic contextualization for the visual production as a whole, what is often referred to as the **production concept**.

Once rehearsals have begun, the director may invite the mask designer into rehearsal to see what the actors are doing, how the characters are developing, and even how the style of the play is clarifying and evolving through the performances. Directors may also write up clear descriptions of the characters and their functions in the play, to be shared with the mask designer and others on the creative team. The more

FIGURE 3.7 *A picnic scene from the production* Finding Joy *by Vamos Theatre. Courtesy of Vamos Theatre and Graeme Braidwood Photography*

FIGURE 3.8 *A nightmare vision from Grafted Cede and Theatre Temoin's Nobody's Home. Masks by Will Pinchin and Dorie Pinchin, photo by Jet Sun*

information such a description contains – both factual and imaginative – the better a designer will be able to do their job.

Finally, the decision about the type of mask includes the question of whether the mask is speaking or non-speaking. Does the performer need to be able to use their voice? If so, is it important that the audience understand what they are saying? The general rule, agreed to by most contemporary Western theater makers, is that **full-face** masks are used if the role is non-speaking. If the actor is required to speak, it is generally agreed that a **half-mask** or **three-quarters** mask is preferable. As with all other mask "rules," however, there are exceptions. For instance, ancient Greek theater used full-face masks for speaking roles, though they were specially designed to allow the actors' voices to be projected and the text understood. Full-face masks are also used by Japanese Noh and other Asian forms, though again mask makers pay special attention to ensuring that actors can be heard and understood.

FIGURE 3.9 *Two fantasy characters represented by masks in the author's production of* Invitation to a Beheading. *Courtesy Rough House Theatre, photo by Evan Barr Photography*

BOX 3.2 CASE STUDY: INVITATION TO A BEHEADING

For a 2019 adaptation of Vladimir Nabokov's surreal novel *Invitation to a Beheading*, we made the decision to use puppetry and masks in the production as a means of maintaining the question for the audience of what is real and what isn't in the world of the play. Since the masks were designed and made specifically for the production, this involved a process of communicating with the project's mask and puppet designer, Mike Oleon of Chicago's Rough House Theatre. What follows is a brief description of the process that Mike and I went through to arrive at the masks we used in the performance.

The first set of questions we had to answer concerned the overall concept of the masks. We had to consider questions such as the realism (or lack thereof) of scale, facial features, and color of the masks. We also had to consider how the actors would use the masks, such as their ability to speak and move, and how the masks would interact with other design concepts in the show. Based on both the demands of performance and the effect we wanted the masks to have on the audience, we decided on masks that had the following characteristics:

- Those representing principal characters would be half-mask, thus allowing the actors to speak. Other masks would be stylistically similar full-face masks.
- The masks would be "larger than life," or out of scale with the human head and face.
- The features of the mask – particularly nose, eyes, mouth, and the shape of the face – would be exaggerated and even cartoonish.
- The masks would be white in color, but with necessary shading so that the features would "read" from a distance.

This process was aided, according to Mike Oleon, by the clarity we had already achieved in our vision for the project. As Mike says, "it works well when the director has a strong perspective on the text or the performance style. This makes it possible for the prompts in a designer's brief to be pretty open. If the director has a looser interpretation, or is less clear, then the designer needs to ask more specific or guiding questions."

The next challenge we faced was finding a design for each mask that captured the essential qualities of the characters from the novel. As the writer/director, I created a description of each character as a reference for the designer. I included descriptions of the character from the novel, as well as other things I knew about the character from our initial explorations with performers, such as the character's physicality, voice, temperament, and particular mannerisms and gestures. To further inspire the designer's imagination (although not for literal incorporation into the mask), I included descriptions of the character as an animal, an instrument, an element, and so forth. I wanted to give Mike both clarity about the character and room for his own imagination and creativity. As he puts it, "Finding what you are personally excited by within the director's vision is hugely important. Design discussions should be geared at spurring both the designer's and director's imagination, so you find the place in the middle where the two perspectives can be playing

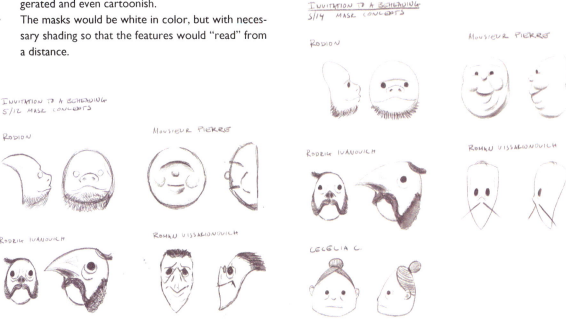

TB 3.2(A) *Courtesy of Mike Oleon and Rough House Theatre*

TB 3.2(B) *Courtesy of Mike Oleon and Rough House Theatre*

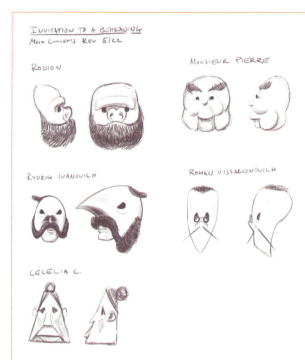

TB 3.2(C)   *Courtesy of Mike Oleon and Rough House Theatre*

half, more details mean less space for the audience to project their own imaginations."

Here is a portion of the description I sent for Monsieur Pierre, one of the pivotal antagonists in the story. The first set of descriptions are drawn from the novel, while the remaining descriptions are from our theatrical work on the character.

a beardless little fat man … sitting with one stubby leg crossed over the other and clasped his shin with his plump hands … his long eyelashes cast shadows on his cherubic cheek …. Calm and composed …. Melodious, high-pitched voice coming from the throat … dignity and that particular grace with which nature endows a few select little fat men … Charming tact.

Graceful, Light, Effete, Smooth, Round, Undefinable.

His rhythm is that of one who is either a "lifer" or a trust fund baby. He is never in a hurry.

Age: Ageless. He could claim any age between 25 and 60, and be believed.

Element/Material: Smooth as silk; Glowing warmth of a hearth in winter.

Animals: Big cat, Bird of prey.

Instrument: Violin, Oboe.

Head Shape: Round.

Facial Hair: None.

Based on this description, Mike created a series of sketches. Between each round of sketches, discussions were held between the director, actors, and designers regarding the character and the developing mask design. The above images are a series of sketches showing how the design evolved, which can be compared to the completed mask in performance, shown on the previous page.

together. What animal, what do they eat for breakfast, even thinking about the musicality of the character was very helpful. Broad descriptions allow me to find my way of imagining the characters. And at the same time, it is necessary to focus on the qualities and details that were important to this particular production. Masks for performance work in broad strokes. We should think in terms of creating something archetypical. When a mask performer has the challenge of commanding the audience's attention for an hour and a

COLLABORATING WITH DESIGNERS

Because masks by their very nature free all theatrical gestures to expand beyond the realistic, they offer exciting opportunities for designers as well as performers. However, they also come with a strong set of demands that must be understood and incorporated into all design and performance decisions. We will discuss the performer's work in more detail in the next chapter but let us briefly discuss some of the ways in which the decision to use masks in a production will impact the work a director does with designers.

Whatever the reasons for using masks, and whether they will be employed for some or for all the characters in a play, it is essential that the **production concept** be articulated and that the use of masks sits comfortably within this concept. Since the masks need to live within the world of the play, the development of the production concept is ideally the result of discussions among the entire design team at the same time. These discussions are a very exciting part of the production process, since no matter how well formed the director's vision may be, designers will often have ideas that dramatically affect the production concept's visual style. Thus, establishing the world of the play is an important step that must take place alongside the development of the mask designs. In addition, each of the designers will need to recognize certain demands placed on their work by the use of masks.

Scenic designers, for example, need to understand that masks work best when seen primarily from the front. Many mask companies, like Familie Floz, go to great lengths to "complete" the mask from behind, with hair, hats, etc., and some even go so far as to use makeup on exposed skin like the neck and hands in order to join the body and mask in one image. However, the mask will still be at its most

FIGURE 3.10 Infinita, by Familie Flöz. Note how the scale of the set adds to the impression that the mask character is a child. Courtesy of Familie Flöz

expressive when viewed from a limited range and mostly from the front. Just as mask actors need to learn the limits of "play" of the mask they are wearing – its range of horizontal and vertical movement – scenic designers need to pay careful attention to the sight lines of the audience, so that the mask has the best chance of being visible. This will impact decisions about set design such as entrances, exits, playing areas, and so forth. The scenic designer will want to take into consideration such issues as the sculptural qualities of the mask – its three-dimensionality or relative frontality. Entrances and exits will want to allow for the mask to be present as much as possible for the audience at the moment of entering and at the moment of exiting. Finally, consideration must be given to the restricted vision that is imposed on the actor by many masks, and this must be taken into account when constructing scenic elements that must be negotiated by actors. **Rakes** and other changes in playing levels, edges of furniture and other set pieces, even the size and placement of entrances and exits, all require additional thought when dealing with masks.

Costumes will need to complement the style of the masks, and costume designers will need to make some specific decisions, as mentioned above, about how to treat other parts of the body. One direction these decisions can take is to bring the whole image of the character into harmony with the mask, through such means as makeup, hair, head coverings, etc. Another direction that is often taken is to highlight the duality of the image – actor and mask are both present, and the audience is constantly aware of this dual presence, even on a subconscious level – by not matching the color of the skin to the color of the mask, or even at times not completing the back of the mask, so that the actor's head and the attachment mechanism remain visible when the mask turns away from the audience. Again, these are important stylistic and design decisions, and must be reached with intentionality and a careful understanding of the desired effect on the audience.

Lighting designers also have a specific set of challenges presented by mask theater. The style of mask – specifically the texture, color, and sculptural choices the mask maker has taken – will impact the effectiveness of certain kinds of lighting. Lights that work well on the unmasked human face may be less effective on certain styles of masks, especially those that are on the darker or lighter ends of the spectrum.

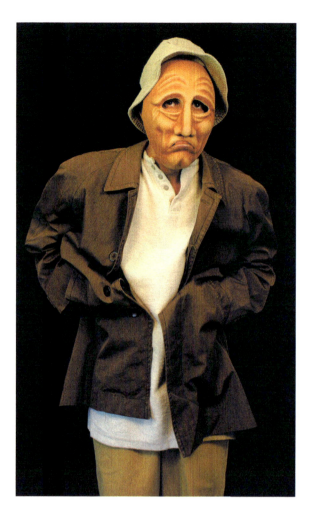 

FIGURE 3.11 (A AND B) *A character mask by Jonathan Becker. Note how the change in costume and physicality changes the gender, age, status, and even attitude of the mask, although the mask does not change*

Directional lighting might be less effective with masks, which often benefit from a more generalized wash, and **uplighting** may be more necessary than normal, to fill in the lower half of the face, especially when half-masks are in use. Take care, though – too much light, and there will be no shadow, and so the form of the mask will not be visible. Due to the restrictions imposed on their senses by most masks, actors may also need more time and outside help in finding and utilizing their light when masked. Since the masked actor can't "feel" their light in the way they may be accustomed to, it might be necessary to develop strategies such as finding their position relative to aspects of the set or the seating, depending on the sight restrictions of the mask.

Sound designers also face a unique set of challenges and opportunities. In a production utilizing full-face masks, sound can be an extraordinarily important, even essential, means of expressing the experiences of the characters. Music, for example, can support, punctuate, frame, and even reveal aspects of the character that might otherwise remain unexpressed. Strongly rhythmic music can support actors in a discovery period, as they create the character, relationships, and sequence of actions. Sound effects for movements and actions are frequently incorporated in performance for half-mask styles like Commedia – again, an example of how the presence of the mask frees the theater maker to go beyond the realistic. At the same time, sound designers face certain challenges specific to mask theater. As expressed by Corey Smith, a sound designer and composer, "performers can struggle to hear in the mask, so important sound cues that trigger action on stage have to either be A) Mixed loud enough for the performers to hear it OR B) Subtly equalized to be particularly legible onstage (cutting mids, bumping the highs and the lows)."[5] Masks can also impact sound in the way that they affect a performer's relationship to their own voice. For instance, they can "block nasal resonance, forcing a performer to use more chest voice to project, in both speech and song. Masks may also catch a bit of the sound and make a small echo chamber in the performer's head, making it harder for them to hear how loud/soft they are, thus affecting their dynamic range."[6]

The Director's Perspective 93

FIGURE 3.12 *A production of Woyzeck at Butler University. Notice how makeup is used to give the impression that the mask and lower face are the same image*

FIGURE 3.13 *The Familie Flöz production of Dr. Nest. The lighting does an excellent job of illuminating the mask while still allowing shadow so the sculptural features can "read." Courtesy of Familie Flöz*

BOX 3.3 PROFILE: FAMILIE FLÖZ

Creating Theater with Masks

Familie Flöz, a group of more than 30 international theater artists based in Berlin, has been creating full-face mask performances without spoken text since 1994. During this time, they have made 14 original shows, which have toured and performed in over 40 countries. Hajo Schüler, an actor, director, author, and mask maker, is a Co-Founder and Artistic Director of Familie Flöz. He spoke with us about some of the important lessons the company have learned as their work has evolved over the years.

Why mask theater? What do the masks allow?

"Once the audience is connected to a mask, there is a huge amount of imagination happening for the audience. And there is a huge amount of personal material the audience uses in imagining the character, whether they realize this or not. They are drawing on their own experiences. When you start to speak, it is a different area of the brain that is engaged. It is much more specific and defined. Even when the words do echo with our own experience, it is much more defined and limited than the first process."

"The way we work is to give the actor all the power, to put the emphasis on transformation. The audience knows it's a mask, but I take your hand and I invite you to imagine. All the cards are on the table, the audience knows that it is an actor wearing a piece of paper mache, and so forth."

Your shows are all original works. How do you begin your process?

"We always start with an image or a basic idea. At the same time, we ask an important question: is this a theme which can be explored without language, is it a theme that is useful to play with masks? The mask is in a way simplifying, but at the same time 'condensing' a story. The cast and team do research, read books, share images. Then we begin to work with improvisation, looking for constellations and images. We call it 'material.' By developing and arranging that material we slowly create a story."

"When we started working together, we worked on simple relationships that you recognize immediately, say the boss and two workers. In the way, say, in a classical clown situation, you have the two clowns, you know who is the stupid one and who will lose, and you want this one to fall from the ladder, and so forth. And then, as we learned more about masks, we began to experiment more and more with situations that were not archetypal, where we were not sure if the mask would work, and we began to avoid more and more those classic archetypal situations, to see if there is the possibility with the mask to tell more psychological, multilayered stories. But still keep a level of mask playing, which was difficult in the beginning."

"As we work on a show, the early improvisations use language. People who work with us for many years know what they are looking for as they improvise with text. It's a kind of perversion in a way. They know that while they are improvising, playing, they are looking for those moments where suddenly the body, the posture, a certain conflict is everything. This is the track that they try to follow. The actors who are not used to this can get lost. They produce a lot of material, they invent text, and they create a skeleton for the character based on text. Then they have a lot of difficulty to find the inner text later on."

Do the characters and masks arise from these improvisations?

"Yes, as the actors are exploring the characters, the director and mask maker are also looking for the inspiration that will lead to the masks. Sometimes in an improvisation, there are a couple of seconds that confirm that the character will survive in the story, and that help us know who they are."

"There are also characters that appear and seem that they will end up in the show, but never quite make it. For instance, in the case of Dr. Nest (a production from 2019), I designed and made 8 or 9 masks that never made it into the show, because the characters did not survive the rehearsal process. Sometimes I make a mask for a character, and it doesn't really help, or the character changes, so I make another. And of course, this takes time since a mask can take several days to make."

What are some challenges that actors face when they perform in mask?

"One challenging thing is to realize the level of tension or energy that is required in the body. It is demanding physically, and the actor must become comfortable with this. In addition, there is the clarity of thought that the mask needs. This clarity leads the performer to a clarity in the body. It's a misunderstanding, in my opinion, that the form itself is enabling the mask to come to life."

"The second thing that is tricky is to understand what the mask can do for you as a performer, and what you have to do for the mask. The more difficult part of this is to understand what the mask can do. This is the ego part. It is difficult to stop 'acting,' and to allow the mask to do its work. To feel what the mask is doing in this moment with the audience, to hear and feel this, and not to interfere. That is the tricky part. To let the mask do. You have to develop a confidence when you are inside the mask that the mask from time to time is doing magical things!"

What are the important things for a director to keep in mind as they shape the moment-to-moment work with mask performers?

"It is very much linked to the breathing. In a way, you could say that we compose the breathing of a character through the scene. It doesn't mean that we set it, but these are the questions I am putting to the performer. When do you breathe in, or breathe out? When do you want the audience to breathe out?"

"And then of course it's guiding the focus, which is tricky when you work without words. We must think about the eye of the audience. When does one mask look at another to give focus, or when is there a movement over there and I must be still so that the audience's focus goes to the other mask?"

What would you say to designers when working with masks?

"We discovered that there must be the possibility that the mask character can get into contact, to touch, the things that the audience sees. It needs certain objects and materials. In my experience, it is difficult to put a mask into a reduced or abstract context. We tried this, and it didn't go well! For the design to work, it must be clear and simplified, like a mask itself. It is usually a process to reduce it to one clear idea or material."

What is an example from your recent work of something that only a masked performance can achieve?

"The first simple example is the ability to have two masks that are the same character, where the character faces themselves. The audience knows right away that this is a poetic image, that the character is looking at themselves, at their past, or future, or soul, or whatever. If you would do this with makeup, or other tools, it would always have a different meaning than the poetry of doing it with masks."

"Another thing that masks do, which is a miracle that masks can do, is that within two or three seconds, the audience can feel they know exactly who a character is, even though they don't know anything about her – they don't know her story, but they can imagine it through the mask. And then what they see is like a confirmation of what they already know. You feel, in a way, that the character is beyond words."

When you are constructing a mask, do you look for these types, or archetypes?

"The difference between the way we work and, for instance, Commedia, is that when I am making a mask I am looking only for the character. In some forms of mask theatre, the form is 'written,' it is an existing form of archetype or hierarchy. When I do a mask for a character, it does not have a form yet, but there is a content, a story to tell. I know how the character should feel in the end, based on a concentration of all the material I have witnessed in the improvisations and rehearsals. Then in the process of modeling, I stop when I think 'this is someone that everybody knows.' But it is not about consciously making 'the boss.' I just care about the story of the character."

IN THE REHEARSAL ROOM

We will now consider how the decision to use masks affects the actual rehearsal process. What are the challenges likely to be faced by the director, actors, writer, and **stage managers**? Some of these challenges, for example creating believable characters, building truthful relationships, rehearsing and refining **blocking**, finding the right pacing and rhythm, are similar to the challenges faced by any creative team staging an existing or new play. However, we will find that the use of masks adds another dimension to many of these issues, which alters – slightly or substantially – the approach that must be taken to the rehearsal process.

Working with Limitations

One challenge that becomes immediately clear and has a tremendous impact on the rehearsal process is the restricted vision (and to a lesser extent hearing) caused by many masks. These restrictions affect an actor's rehearsal process by creating problems with their relationship to the space around them and to their scene partners. Let's take a look at some strategies for dealing with these challenges.

In the first place, actors find that the restricted vision of the mask causes them to spend a great deal of energy and concentration avoiding running into the furniture or the set (or, even worse, time spent recovering from actually doing so).

This problem has two immediate impacts on the performance. First, and obviously, it means the actor is inhibited and distracted, leading to an unsatisfactory level of performance. Second, it means that, consciously or not, the actor is signaling information with the mask that is not pertinent to the story. If an actor looks down to check where the edge of the stage is, or to verify that their shin is not about to contact the sharp edge of a chair, then the mask has directed its focus to a specific place, which for the audience means it has offered valuable information about the intentions/thoughts/actions of the character. If this information is regularly misleading or confusing, eventually the audience will begin to tune out – the worst possible outcome of mask theater! Alternatively, the information provided by the focus of the mask may be less of a problem than the simple fact that the mask must turn away from the audience so that the actor can orient themself in space, thus making the mask "dead" to the audience – remember, masks are effective when they spend most of their time seen from the front.

So, how to avoid this problem? First, many directors will request to have the set, or a very close facsimile, available as early as possible in rehearsals. This means, obviously, furniture and other movable pieces. However, even the structures through which actors will enter and exit, or the levels/rake of the floor, will also need to be approximated as closely as possible. It is fine to tape out exits on the floor for an actor who has use of their full peripheral vision. But actors in masks need more to go on, other ways to navigate their way through space. They may need to navigate using structures that are at eye level, since they can't see the floor without pointing the mask's focus at it. Additionally, thinking about "markers" for actors that are in the space around them, and that help them orient themselves, is important. For instance, in a recent production using masks we encouraged an actor to use an offstage "marker" – an exit sign – that happened to be dead center. If he aligned himself with that marker, he knew he could make a full cross from USC to DSC without breaking the focus of the mask, all the while threading his way through three pieces of furniture as if he could see them perfectly (which of course he could not). This brings up a final point regarding staging and the sight restrictions of masks. Masked actors may need wider lanes between set pieces, and clearer paths, than actors do without masks. Depending on the size of the performance space, this may impose certain restrictions on the set design, as mentioned above.

FIGURE 3.14 Soldier's Song, *by Strangeface Theatre. Photo by Mark Dean*

Masks also affect an actor's relationship with their scene partners. Because of the demands of keeping the mask visible to the audience, along with the inherent sight and hearing restrictions of many masks, actors find that they are less able to maintain eye contact with their partners. Many actors, especially those less experienced with masks, find that their sense of relationships, actions, and intentions are affected by the mask, since they are less capable (while wearing the mask) of perceiving what their partner is doing and how they are affected.

A useful approach to this issue – and to the previous one as well – is to build in rehearsal time for actors to work without masks, as well as with them. This gives them time to build relationships and sequences of discovery/reaction/decision/action, to clarify gestures by linking them to inner monologues, to speak their inner monologues so that the sequences of actions and events become clear for everyone, and to become attuned to their partners and surroundings so that the sensory restrictions of the mask are less intrusive on the actual performance.

Shaping the Performance

The director guiding a mask theater rehearsal process must always be asking such basic questions as "Do I understand what the mask is thinking/feeling/doing? Do I believe it? Is it interesting? Am I bored, confused, overwhelmed with information?" Indeed, the first line of defense against an audience being disengaged, confused, or frustrated by the masks is the director's ability to observe with a keen eye whether the masks are communicating effectively, and to analyze what is amiss when they are not. Of course, this is essentially true of the director's job in any rehearsal process. However, the demands on an audience of mask theater are considerable, especially when the masks are full-face or otherwise non-speaking.

Very often the novice director of a mask performance will find themselves losing interest or growing confused by what they are seeing but will not necessarily know why. Here are some helpful guidelines for the director, essentially a list of what to look for when it feels that something is wrong with the performance. With these guidelines in mind, the director should be better equipped to help the actor shape their performance, by letting them know when things are clear for the audience, and when the actor's choices aren't legible, are not believable, are confusing, or are inconsistent with the story being told.

First, let's remind ourselves of the process that is initiated in the audience's imagination by the appearance of a masked performer. As we mentioned, the audience must "complete the thoughts" of the mask, by interpreting the movements of the mask and the actor's body, and the changes in rhythm, energy, and spatial dynamics. Once the audience has engaged with the masks imaginatively, they are constantly undergoing this process – observing the actions of the performer, turning those into the thoughts/emotions/intentions of the mask (character), and articulating those thoughts and emotions for themselves. "Audiences read the movement by adding their own commentary, filling in the thought process with their own words … they are listening to their own voice, their own vocabulary, based on their own experience of life."[7] With this process in mind, let's have a look at some of the most common things that interfere with an audience's ability to engage with the masks.

The first problem that quite often detracts from the effectiveness of a performance is gestures or actions which are unclear, repetitive, or not linked to an inner monologue. Unclear or illegible actions are an obvious problem but may require more attention from the director than normal, since the actor may be less aware of what they and their partners are doing while in the mask. Unnecessary repetition usually occurs when an actor does not trust that a thought or intention has been communicated. They begin to embellish unnecessarily. As Toby Wilshire explains it, "When the audience have thought your thoughts, it is boring for them being made to think them again."[8] The director must therefore be attuned to this in rehearsal. Has the actor made the character's thought clear, and is the next gesture therefore unnecessary? Gestures which are not linked to an **inner monologue** are another reason that performances may go off track. These are gestures or movements that "come across as either irrelevant or meaningless and are confusing and irritating for the audience."[9] Here again, working without masks can be extremely helpful. Get the actors to go through their performance, saying out loud the thoughts and intentions of the character. They will discover, and so will you, where those thoughts are unclear, or repetitive, or extraneous to the story.

Even if the gestures and actions are clear, believable, and linked to the character's inner life, they may still be ineffective for the simple reason that the audience may miss them, in whole or in part. This happens when the mask is "speaking" without having focus. An actor gestures or commits to an action, but because the audience's focus is somewhere else, the thought which is linked to that movement is lost. As with all theater, directors must remain vigilant about where the audience focus is at any given moment. The audience needs to know where to look, and so do the masks. A general guideline is that a mask only moves when it is "speaking," and that masks "throw" focus to the next "speaker" at the end of a thought. Of course, there are exceptions to this, and masks moving simultaneously can have rich dramatic implications. However, more than one mask in motion usually means that more than one set of thoughts is being revealed to the audience, which requires attention and discernment from the

FIGURE 3.15 Nursing Lives by Vamos Theatre. The inner monologue must be clear for each actor so that the individual physicality comes fully to life. Courtesy of Vamos Theatre and Graeme Braidwood Photography

director and the actors, or it risks becoming confusing for the audience.

Mask performance also requires a different sense of timing and rhythm. Since the audience is undergoing a constant process of interpreting the mask character's actions, gestures, and other expressions into thoughts that they imagine and then articulate for themselves, a space is needed for this translation to occur. This is sometimes described as the space around the mask character's thoughts, which is different than the space around our thoughts or articulations in normal life. Additionally, "some of the more important realizations and decisions need to be expanded moments, the speed and rhythm of the moment pulled apart as if it were happening at a slightly slower speed."[10] There is a very fine line here, and of course if the element of time is overemphasized the performance will begin to feel labored and mechanical. Again, the sensitivity of the director to time and rhythm will help the actors know when they are clear enough in what they are doing but are not allowing the audience time to receive it.

Poor construction of the physical space is another reason mask performance can be ineffective. Can the masks be seen? Are they too close together (masks need space around them to communicate effectively)? Is the physical space inhibiting or distracting the performer from the work of expressing the inner life of the mask for the audience (are we watching the actor stumble, not the character)? Is the placement of scenes and characters allowing for clear shifts of focus, and does it support the timing/rhythm issues discussed above? Are the masks lit? Are they hidden by features of the set? Again, the actors will be less aware of these issues than they normally are, since the masks will restrict their peripheral awareness. The director must therefore be more aware.

Finally, when all else fails, the director, writer, and actor can ask themselves if they are trying to say things that cannot be said in masks. As we've mentioned, the mask is a tool that clarifies, simplifies, and **essentializes**. This allows the theater maker to cut through to certain fundamental themes and human situations. However, it also means that there are things that cannot be "said" in masks. A great question for the director is whether the mask is trying to express something that would be better expressed in another form.

BOX 3.4 DIRECTING MASKS

Principles to Guide you in Rehearsal

1. Remember that the mask engages the emotions and imagination of the audience, as they "fill in the blanks" or "complete the thoughts" of the character. Audience members create their own subtext, inner life, etc. for the characters.
2. As you watch the performance, ask yourself: Do I understand what the mask is thinking/feeling/doing? Do I believe it? Is it interesting? Am I bored, confused, overwhelmed with information?
3. Look out for gestures or actions that are unclear, repetitive, or not linked to an inner monologue.
4. Work without masks at times, so that you can clarify the actor's inner monologue, actions, and intentions by letting them speak these out loud.
5. Time without masks will also help actors clarify their relationships with scene partners and build the moments they will need to play in masks.
6. Watch out for moments when a mask character is engaged in an action without having the focus of the audience. Look for ways to guide the audience's focus where it is needed.
7. In rehearsal, build in time for actors to find strategies to navigate their way through entrances, exits, around set pieces, etc., as they work with the sight limitations of the mask.
8. Is the timing of actions, discoveries, reactions, allowing the audience time to process and interpret the mask character's thoughts? Perhaps there needs to be a bit more space around moments.
9. Masks need a little more space around them to be fully effective. Make sure actors aren't positioning themselves too closely, and that the physical space allows for effective separation.
10. As always, but more importantly with masks, pay attention to the spatial placement of scenes, the visibility of the masks, the ability of the actors to find their light (harder in masks), and the clarity of sight lines, since the masks must be clearly seen by the audience.

PROJECTS FOR FURTHER STUDY

Choose an existing play that calls for the use of masks, or a story that you would like to use as a starting point for a **devised** project using masks. You may also choose to use a play that does not explicitly call for masks, for which you have decided to use masks as an element of performance.

- Read the text, asking questions from the first section of this chapter about the function(s) of masks within the story. Are all characters masked, or only some? How does the use of masks "frame" the theatrical event, or specific events within the play? What do the masks represent? How do you expect the audience to respond to, and "read" the masks? Are the masks speaking or non-speaking? Full face or partial? How will you approach conversations with your mask designer about the style, function, and effects of the masks?

- Using the same text, and drawing on the information in the second section of this chapter, create a list of questions/conversation points to guide your initial discussions with each member of the design team.

- Based on what you learned in the third section of the chapter, create a plan for 3–5 rehearsals of the story you have chosen, taking into account the needs of the actors and the requirements of the piece you are developing. Do you begin with masks, or without? What will your actors need in order to orient themselves to the world, the character, and the work of the mask?

These are steps to get a director thinking more clearly about the use of masks in performance. Assuming you will want to use masks, we would also refer directors to the discussion and exercises in the chapter entitled "The Actor's Perspective." The exercises in that chapter can be especially useful in rehearsals or when generating original material for masks.

NOTES

1. Eldredge, Sears A. *Mask Improvisation for Actor Training and Performance: The Compelling Image* (Evanston, Illinois: Northwestern University Press, 1996), 4.
2. Eldredge, 160.
3. Eldredge, 7.
4. Eldredge, 160.
5. Corey Smith, interviewed by author July, 2019.
6. Corey Smith, interviewed by author July, 2019.
7. Wilsher, Toby. *The Mask Handbook* (New York: Routledge, 2007), 32.
8. Wilshire, 125.
9. Wilshire, 125.
10. Wilshire, 126.

SELECTED RESOURCES

Barba, Eugenio and Nicola Savarese. *A Dictionary of Theatre Anthropology: The Secret Art of the Performer.* Translated by Richard Fowler. New York: Routledge, 2006.

Bell, John, ed. *Puppets, Masks, and Performing Objects.* Cambridge, Massachusetts: MIT Press, 2001.

Blumenthal, Eileen and Julie Taymor. *Julie Taymor, Playing with Fire: Theater, Opera, Film*. New York: H.N. Abrams, 1995.

Brecht, Stefan. *Peter Schumann's Bread and Puppet Theater*. London: Methuen, 1988.

Chase, Mike. *Mask: Making, Using and Performing*. Gloucestershire: Hawthorn Press, 2017.

Craig, Edward Gordon. *The Art of the Theatre*. New York: Theatre Arts Books, 1956.

Eldredge, Sears A. *Mask Improvisation for Actor Training and Performance: The Compelling Image*. Evanston, Illinois: Northwestern University Press, 1996.

Emigh, John. *Masked Performance: The Play of Self and Other in Ritual and Theatre*. Philadelphia, Pennsylvania: University of Pennsylvania Press, 1996.

O'Neill, Eugene. *Preface to The Great God Brown*. New Haven, Connecticut: Yale University. 24–29.

Raymond, Dave. *The Power of Fun*. West Grove, Pennsylvania: SDR Consulting, 2019.

Saint-Denis, Michel. *Theatre: The Rediscovery of Style and Other Writings*. London: Routledge, 2009.

Shevtsova, Maria. "Robert Wilson," in *Designers' Shakespeare*. John Russell Brown and Stephen Di Benedetto, eds. New York: Routledge, 2016. 118–136.

Taplin, Oliver. *Greek Tragedy in Action*. London: Routledge, 2003.

Wilsher, Toby. *The Mask Handbook*. New York: Routledge, 2007.

Wyles, Rosie. *Costume in Greek Tragedy*. London: Bloomsbury, 2011.

CHAPTER 4

THE ACTOR'S PERSPECTIVE

FIGURE 4.1 The actress Claire Saxe in the production of Rough House Theatre's Invitation to a Beheading. Mask created by Mike Oleon, photo by Evan Barr Photography

Masks work a certain kind of magic in performance. In fact, as we've pointed out elsewhere in this book, that magical alchemy that exists among performer, mask, and spectator is a big part of the reason that masks have been around – in ritual, religious, and performative settings – for as long as humans have tried to find ways to express the inexpressible. Let's take a moment to remind ourselves of what makes masks special in a performative context, so that the necessary work the actor must do can be seen in its proper light.

The moment an actor enters the performing area in a mask, a series of events happens in the audience member's mind. First, there is the recognition of one obvious but essential fact about the mask: its artifice. The mask is an inanimate object placed (usually) on the head of an animate being (the actor wearing it). This contradiction – the presence of the real and the unreal, the organic and the artificial – places the audience in a very interesting position. They might choose to see only the artificial nature of the mask: "Oh, it's just a mask. I wonder why they're wearing it?" Or something else might happen: the audience might choose to suspend their disbelief and accept the mask as a human character, an animal, a spirit, or a supernatural being.

We are accustomed to this suspension of disbelief – the fundamental act of theater relies on it. But the suspension of disbelief with masks is substantially different than when it happens with an actor in a naturalistic or realistic performance. With masks, we *never* forget that the actor and the mask are separate, and that the mask is artificial. However, if the conditions are right, the audience can be coaxed into playing an imaginative game, in which they experience the mask as the face of a living person or being. What are the right conditions? First, there is the mask itself, which exploits our instinct to read faces, and to assume that character, history, and intention are written into the face. Instinctively, the audience looks at the mask/face for information about the character. As they do this, the actor begins to supply them with information through a movement, a gesture, or a change of tension in the body. The audience begins to perceive a link between the information they are getting from the "face," and the information they are getting from the actor's body. The two things have become one image, an illusion, which the performer then sustains for the course of the scene or the entire play!

MASKS AND ACTOR TRAINING

From the actor's point of view, however, the mask *in* performance is only one of its values. The mask is also a great preparation *for* performance. As Michel Saint-Denis points out in his book *Theatre: The Rediscovery of Style*,[1] mask work helps the actor build concentration, diminishes self-consciousness, strengthens inner feelings, and develops an actor's physical expressiveness. In working with masks, actors can move toward this greater awareness and expressivity in a number of ways. They can enhance body awareness; develop greater specificity in their physical and vocal work; discover more imaginative and expressive freedom; become more sensitive to the possibilities in movement and stillness; cultivate an openness to the audience; fine-tune the ability to live "one moment at a time"; and find a greater ability to express character and tell a story with the body. In addition, masks can reveal aspects of an actor's personality that are normally not as visible in your "social" mask, as anyone who has ever experienced Halloween or cosplay knows. Masks thus enhance the actor's expressive range and their capacity for **transformation**.

Of course, all of these magical effects of the mask in performance and as a tool for performance training are possible only insofar as the actors and directors working with the masks understand what is necessary to bring these effects to life. In the following sections, we will look at several broad categories of mask (**neutral mask**, **full-face mask**, and **half-face mask**), exploring the distinctive qualities of each type of mask, and laying out the foundational work that actors must do in order to benefit from the mask as a training tool and to make it come to life effectively for an audience.

While much of the discussion and images in this chapter will focus on masks that depict human characters, it is worth noting that this is because these masks are an accessible reference point and therefore allow for specific examples that can aid our discussion of the general principles of mask performance, even when the masks are not meant to depict human characters. It is our hope that this specificity grounds the discussion, and that our readers are encouraged to test these principles with a wide range of mask styles.

It is also important to note that while we are working in this chapter with masks that demand specificity in gesture, movement, and voice, we are not working with masks that have a clear and **codified** language of movement, such as we would find in the Noh tradition. Nor are we working with masks that have a specific cultural and/or spiritual significance, as with many of the masks we have discussed from traditions like those in Indonesia or Africa. Even Western traditions like the more clarified traditions of the Commedia dell'Arte, in which a particular physical expression was assigned to each mask, are beyond the scope of this book. There are wonderful resources for many of these traditions that we refer to later in the text.

THE NEUTRAL MASK

History and Description

The idea of a "neutral" mask as part of modern acting training began to emerge in the early part of the 20th century, through the work of a French theater artist named Jacques Copeau. In reaction to the excessive performance conventions of his time, Copeau envisioned a theater that returned to simpler forms of expression. He realized that in order to have actors capable of fulfilling his vision, he would need to find new ways of training them. Through experimentation, Copeau (and the influential teachers who followed him) began to realize the value of masks in actor training. In particular, Copeau became interested in the possibility of a mask that would allow the actor to experience a state of simplicity, calmness, and efficiency and that might allow the actor to step away from their ingrained physical habits.

Copeau's ideas would influence the development of theater in the next century, primarily through the artists and teachers he inspired. Chief among them for our purposes are Jacques Lecoq and Michel Saint-Denis, both of whom made their mark by founding important actor training programs in Europe and the United States. More than any other teacher, Jacques Lecoq has been responsible for the popularity of the neutral mask in actor training. Inspired by the aims Copeau had articulated, Lecoq formed a partnership with the mask maker Amleto Sartori, and the two began a series of experiments in the 1950s. The result of these experiments was a mask design that has become iconic and has influenced many other mask makers. Over the years, Lecoq came to regard training with the neutral mask as a central element of his training of the "actor-creator."

BOX 4.1 NEUTRAL MASKS

If we look at several neutral masks – made by Donato Sartori and by two contemporary makers who were influenced by the Sartoris – we can see some of the features that are particular to this style of mask. One of the first things actors typically notice about the mask is its symmetry. There is no obvious distortion of the features or any notable expression – the mask, or face, seems to be at rest, or in a state of calm. Another quality that gets mentioned early on is that the lips are slightly parted, as if the mask were breathing, or perhaps on the edge of speech. Sometimes it is even said that the mask is about to smile! This, combined with the wide-open quality of the eyes, seems to express a particular kind of calmness. It is an energized calm, alert and prepared. As Sears Eldredge says, "The starting point was to be not an attitude but a silence serving as a resting state, a condition without motion but filled with energy, like the condition of a runner in the moment before his race. All impulses were to arise from that state and return to it."[2]

This state is so important to the performer that we can find it echoed in many different traditions. Eugenio Barba, in works such as his landmark *Dictionary of Theatre Anthropology*, describes it as the "pre-expressive" state, an energetic state sought by many performance traditions, and with a number of practices that have been developed to train and cultivate the "pre-expressive" presence of the performer. As many authors have noted, the neutral mask is very likely influenced by the Ko-omote (young girl) mask of the Noh Theater and almost certainly is influenced by the aesthetics of the Noh tradition, "where there are various roles which require the actors to perform neutrality."[3] Neutrality, or the pre-expressive state, is understood to be a state full of dramatic presence and potential. It is a state of awareness, economy, readiness; a state that is neither the performer in their everyday mode of action and behavior, nor an actor fully inhabiting a character and a dramatic action or conflict.

TB 4.1(A–C) *Neutral masks by Alfredo Iriarte, Donato Sartori, and Russell Dean*

Benefits of the Mask

As many teachers and authors point out, the state of neutrality is a nearly impossible state to achieve. So why try? Let's look more closely at some of the benefits of working with a neutral mask. In the first place, work with a neutral mask reveals the actor's habitual movement patterns. By "removing" the face, the attention of both the actor and the spectator shifts to the body. This brings a direct awareness of habits, ingrained patterns of movement, and personal stories that impose themselves on simple actions. While this level of exposure of one's habits can be initially uncomfortable, it is also a hugely helpful calibration for the actor. The difference between the "neutrality" proposed by the mask and the habits of the actor – posture, gesture, **tempo-rhythm**, gaze, relationship to audience and space, and so forth – is an initial and crucial step toward the actor's desire for transformation.

In a sense, the mask offers the actor an opportunity to participate in a "game," albeit a serious one with profound implications. The mask is an image, and wearing it invites the actor to participate in that image. It is at once a heightened state (the mask is not "everyday," and therefore the body cannot be either if it is to serve the image). At the same time, we are not dealing with a state that is somehow an exaggeration or grotesquerie, as we shall see with other masks. In attempting to embody the image that the mask proposes, the actor must come face to face (pun intended) with their ingrained habits that depart from neutral.

Early exercises in the mask usually include simple tasks such as stillness, entering the space, walking, sitting, or discovering an object. As Eldredge says "Under the mask, *how* becomes more important that *what*."[4] Stillness gives the opportunity for much to be seen by the spectator and, after a few repetitions in the mask, sensed by the actor themselves. The teacher and actor begin to look for what many have described as "parasitic" movements, movements that are unnecessary to the action and that therefore depart from neutrality. We notice places of resistance in the body, places of excess tension or effort. Arms that swing excessively while walking, a bobbing of the head, a protrusion of the chest or pelvis, shoulders that are off-balance, all of these and more provide simple but profound opportunities for the actor to confront their own habits, and to begin, lightly and with a sense of curiosity and discovery, to choose when to move away from these habits. Along the way, actors become comfortable in stillness and in activity and can commit equally to both. This brings us toward that elusive quality that we often call "presence."

How to Use the Mask

Since perfect neutrality is impossible, the question often arises, especially early in work with the neutral mask, of what we should pay attention to, as an actor and as a spectator. Here are some helpful guideposts that can then be applied to the exercises that follow.

In stillness, the actor should search for a state of being that is relaxed but alert and poised for action, whether mental, verbal, or physical. It is quite often helpful to "toggle" between the everyday body and the neutral mask body, as a way of experiencing this difference more fully. This also allows us to look for physical attitudes that are imposed on both stillness and action and that therefore give us a sense of a character with prior experiences or expectations. In the neutral mask, everything happens for the first time.

In action, we also look for an economy of movement, thought, and emotion, as evidenced in the body. We are seeking to engage an action, even a simple one like walking, looking, or waving with only the energy that is needed, and with the movements and rhythm that are precisely what the action requires. Departures from the neutral include movements that are not necessary to the action; extraneous tension or effort; or a tempo-rhythm that invites the audience to imbue the action with story, meaning, or character – for instance, if the actor hesitates before touching an object, or grabs it too quickly. The actor's work in the neutral mask is to find the action without the inessential elements.

The healthy struggle with this demanding mask begins over time (but more quickly than you might expect) to bring an awareness to the actor of all the ways that character can be expressed in the *how*. A hesitation, or rush, or lingering over a moment too long, or excessive tension, each creates the image for the audience of both a past and a potential future. Of character. Of conflict. Of story. Confronting each of these digressions from "neutrality" broadens and deepens the actor's awareness of the immense range of expressive choices available to them. At the same time, the experience with the mask brings their attention to the clarity of their movements, their ability to command rhythm, space, time, and stillness, their generosity of sharing the action with the audience, their openness to the moment, their ability to move with presence from one moment to the next, and their ability to be simply present while being observed by others.

Bearing in mind that most teachers and artists agree that the neutral mask is not a performative mask, we have articulated here a few foundational exercises to help explore the opportunities of the mask as a training tool.

NEUTRAL MASK EXERCISES

Discovering the Mask

"The first lesson is the discovery of the mask as object."[5] At the Lecoq school, and other schools based on the Lecoq pedagogy such as ArtHaus Berlin, students first spend time contemplating the mask as a sculptural object. What do we notice, for instance, about the texture, the shape, the eyes, and mouth? This is a very useful first step with any mask, as it allows the mask to work on our imagination and alter our physical expression in subtle ways.

After a discussion of the mask features, students should take turns holding the mask. Look directly at it, paying particular attention to the shape of the mouth and the expression in the eyes. Slowly begin to mirror those qualities of the mask in your own face. Each time you do this, with any style of mask, resist forcing the expression or working hard to hold it on your own face. This will defeat the desired effect. Mirror the expression lightly, and notice how it begins to affect your body, breath, and internal state. Spend some time on this step, allowing the mask to work on your imagination.

Discovering the Body

As with most exercises in this chapter, the benefits of the neutral mask exercises will be as great for the observer as they are for the actor in the mask. Observers will see very clearly where the body departs from neutral and will begin to take those lessons into their own work in the mask, so that you can see a group progress quite rapidly if the quality of attention is high.

One actor at a time, position yourself so that you are as centered in the space as possible. The space should be open and free of clutter. Take the mask and hold it, with your body turned away from the audience. Give yourself a moment to look at the mask, mirroring it lightly in your own expression. As you feel the mask begin to affect your body and your inner state, place the mask over your face. Take a breath, then turn and face the audience.

To begin with, simply stand there. Don't try to stand perfectly – whatever that is – just be curious about how you are standing. What is the contact of your feet with the floor? The position of your hands and arms? The position of your hips? Shoulders? Head and neck? Let your sense of how you are standing deepen. If you need to reposition, do so. Breathe.

Now turn away from the audience. Take the mask off, breathe, then turn and face the audience as yourself. We like to give the actor a moment at this stage to process their experience wearing the mask for the first time, if they want to. There is no pressure, and no response is usually offered by the teacher. This is NOT a time for the observers to begin offering feedback. We want this process to be organic and driven by the lived experience of the actor in the mask. Each actor takes a turn with this first step.

The next step is to repeat the process, but this time to see what the actor's body has learned from their first experience, and from observing other actors in the mask. Now we can deepen our quest for the body of the neutral mask, by going in search of the most economical, or efficient, way of standing. Here are some tips: place your feet at about the width of your hips, and let the weight be equally distributed between your feet, so that you can sense a vertical line running down through the spine, and then down both legs. Place the feet more or less in parallel. See what adjustments you might make in the position of the hips, and the shoulders. Place your eyes on the horizon. You are looking for the sensation that the body is ready to move, in any direction, with equal ease and no extra preparation. Try it – move to the right, to the left, up, down, backward, forward, returning to the neutral center between each. Check your feet, hips, the balance of your weight, your shoulders, head, and neck.

Now turn and go. As you face away from the audience, and without removing the mask, let the body come back to your own normal way of standing. Then find the body of the neutral mask again. Turn, face the audience, and take a step or two into the space. Stand, finding neutral. Facing the audience, and with the mask still on, let the body again come back to your own normal way of standing. Relax for a moment. Now, once more, discover the body of the neutral mask. Turn, and go.

This is a good moment for the actor to reflect on what they experienced, and for the observers to begin offering constructive observations on what they saw. Where did we experience that the body and mask were one – that they were the same image? Where did the body depart from the proposal of the mask? Keep these observations short and constructive.

The next stage is to take the neutral body for a walk through the space. This can be done one at a time in the mask or, after everyone has experienced the previous steps, it can be done with the entire group, as if they were wearing the mask. Find the body of the neutral mask, then take it for a walk. Not a stiff or robotic walk, and it can be fairly short. Come to a stop. Notice what happens, how the body is arranged as you move and as you come to stillness. Do you retain the state of calm readiness that the mask proposes? Are you aware of excess tension or unnecessary movement? Do you hesitate, or start too quickly? Continue moving from walking to stillness, and now begin a simple inner monologue. I walk. I stop. I look. I walk. I stop. I look. I discover. I decide to go. I arrange myself to go. I go. I walk. I stop. Note: when you look with the neutral mask (or any mask), imagine that you look with the entire face, not just the eyes. This means your head will turn, which allows the audience to see what you see.

Again, we are looking for ease, lightness, calmness, and efficiency. Only what is necessary, no more and no less. Each actor should have a chance to experience this, with and without the mask, and everyone should also have a chance to observe others. There is so much that will be learned by observing. As actors explore moving in the mask while being observed by others, they should start as before, by putting the mask on, then taking a moment to find the body of the mask. Turn, and discover something on the horizon that draws you into the space, so that your body follows into the space as a result of the discovery. I like to give actors an image – for instance, you turn your head and see the ocean. You are drawn to it, so your body follows. You take two steps and find yourself on the edge of the sea.

This is the moment that actors will really start to notice a shift in their own and others' "presence." It is very powerful.

Discovering the World

Now we are ready to explore the mask in action. Start, as before, with your back to the audience, looking at the mask. Put it on, find the body, then turn and enter the space. Some teachers will use imaginary landscapes at this stage, and some will use real objects. Either choice will give ample opportunity for discovery and deepening of the sense of neutrality. The important thing is that the prompts provide the actor with the necessity to engage with the world around them.

For instance, you might place a series of objects in the space, which the mask must discover "for the first time." In seeing, moving toward, and manipulating the objects, there will be many opportunities to note where story, character, and conflict arise. For instance, does the actor seem surprised to find an umbrella? Surprise connotes expectation and a past. Does the actor hesitate, or rush the action? These bring a sense of character and conflict. The neutral action, so elusive but so important, will tell only one story: I see the object, I pick up the object, I look at the object, I replace the object, I see another object. No more and no less.

The same can be true of imaginary landscapes or mimed actions. The neutral mask finds itself on the edge of the forest, and enters, traveling through the landscape. Can the actor be open to discovery and action that contains only what is necessary? An often-used exercise – incredibly simple and effective – is to allow the mask to discover the ocean, come to stand at the edge of the ocean, find a stone near its foot, pick up the stone, and then throw the stone into the sea. Once the action is complete, the mask turns and departs. This exercise gives rise to multiple opportunities to experience pure discovery, unadorned action, clear decision-making, and satisfying completion of an action. Each of these levels of awareness will serve later when it comes to crafting character, objective, conflict, and story.

FULL-FACE MASKS

If you look at the masks pictured in this section, you will notice that, while they are all different in style, they share two important characteristics. One, they cover the entire face, which means that – as with the neutral mask – they heighten the importance of the physical expression of the actor. The second characteristic

FIGURE 4.2 *A scene from* Dr. Nest, *by the international mask theater company Familie Flöz*

these masks share is that they all offer a strong proposal; they express a clear character or emotional state or provoke the audience's imagination in an interesting way. In other words, the mask provides a strong impulse for both the actor and the audience. And, it must be noted that the impulse or provocation is often (though not always, as for instance with abstract masks) a recognizable one – the expression of the mask is one the audience will identify and understand.

How the Mask Works

This identification with the mask as a recognizable personality or emotional quality means that the mask will engage the emotions and imagination of the audience, as they begin to "fill in the blanks" or "think the thoughts" of the character. Once the audience is engaged, the actions of the actor are interpreted to be the actions of the character or the being that the mask represents. Simultaneously, this engagement of the individual audience member's imagination, combined with the slight ambiguity that the full-face mask introduces through its restriction of speech and text, creates the space for a multiplicity of "readings," in which audience members create their own subtext, inner life, intentions, and so on, for the character.

This complex game – in which the audience, actor, and mask participate – is vitally important for the actor to recognize, because it follows from this recognition that everything the actor does must be in service of keeping the game alive.

In other words, the actor's work is to inspire and maintain the illusion that the mask is in fact the face of a living being. If the actor is successful, and the game is working well, the illusion can be strong enough that the audience will be moved to laughter, tears, or even terror! Let's examine the stages of the actor's work with a mask, followed by exercises to support these stages.

The Actor's Role

The first work for the actor is to become accustomed to wearing the mask and to become acquainted with some of the essential technique that is involved in mask performance. Mask is essentially a **presentational** form, insofar as we must always be aware of the audience and their ability to perceive the mask, whether the actor establishes a direct relationship with the audience or not. This has implications for **blocking**, **entrances**, **exits**, positioning the body while onstage, even how far the actor can turn their head from side to side or up and down. Of course, this does not mean the actor can never turn the mask in such a way that the audience cannot see it. But the audience will feel cheated if the mask is not visible for too long, or if they cannot see it in important moments of discovery, decision, and action.

Wearing a mask for the first time, the actor will find their eyesight is at least somewhat limited, and their movements consequently slow down. This is not necessarily a bad thing – too much movement in the mask does not allow the audience

FIGURE 4.3 Teatro Delusio *by Familie Flöz. Notice how the actors keep the masks and gestures open to the audience. Courtesy of Familie Flöz and Simona Boccedi, photographer*

time to experience the mask's "inner life." Each discovery, reaction, or resonance of action needs space in a mask for the audience to read it. This is often referred to as "**framing** the moment" but is really about a sense of clarity and specificity to each lived moment on stage. It requires the actor to "break down" the life onstage into its constituent parts. If the mask is a human character, for instance, this means identifying the steps of "I discover, I realize, I decide, I take action, my action leads to a new discovery," and so on. To live each of these moments truthfully, without over-embellishing them but also without short-circuiting them – while also offering them generously to the audience – is the true art of mask performance.

As many mask teachers and performers have pointed out, it is useful to think of the mask as the eye, meaning that the entire head must turn to "see" something. This helps direct the audience's focus, letting them know what the mask is seeing. If the face of the mask is the eye, the body becomes the face, which reacts to what it has discovered. This can mean a change in posture, gesture, position of the head and neck, or even a change in tension or breathing. The art, as always, is to do just enough, with a sense of truth, and not too much or too little. Movement or gesture that seems excessive (beyond the believable and truthful action of the character), or movement that reminds us of the lack of text, such as indicative pointing or excessive miming, will remove the audience from the moment and break the illusion of the mask.

There are other ways to break the illusion of the mask, and they are worth mentioning here, since this is perhaps the worst thing we can do to an audience once we have established the illusion. Touching the mask during performance immediately reminds us that it is an artificial object and pulls the audience out of the shared dream, even more so if the mask is a hard material that makes a sound. If the actor wants a gesture or action that involves touching the face – such as covering the mouth in shock or blowing the nose – a good technique is to keep a bit of space between the hand and the mask. This allows the gesture to be clear without breaking the illusion. This touching of the mask also includes adjusting it during performance, which we see a lot with young actors. Of course, proper fit is important and must be ensured during the rehearsal process, so that onstage adjustments are not necessary.

Another way the illusion gets broken is if we hear the performer trying to speak or breathe behind a full-face mask (unless the mask has been specifically designed to allow speech, for instance **chorus** masks made for **Greek tragedies**). The sound will remind us that the mask is present, and that there is a face beneath it – the actual face of the performer, which we had forgotten about. One other way to break the illusion of the mask is to show the audience the separation between the mask and the head or neck. This can be minimized by first learning through experimentation how far you can tilt your head up and down or side to side before the audience stops seeing the face and

FIGURE 4.4 *Tonight We Fly by Trestle Theatre Company*

becomes aware of the mask as an object. Another way to minimize this issue is the use of wigs, hats, and other costume items to conceal the edges of the mask and keep the illusion alive.

Once the actor has begun to master some of the basic technique, we can embark on the work of connecting to the "character" of the mask, and the further work of filling that character out physically, rhythmically, and where appropriate vocally. First, the actor must look for an understanding and connection to what the mask proposes. The architecture of the mask – the shape of the eyes, the nose, the curve of the mouth, the position of the chin – will all work together to form an impression of a character. The actor does well to discover and follow this initial impulse! We want to connect with the character of the mask so that it begins to provoke an "inner" and an "outer" life. This will include thoughts, intentions, patterns of movement, idiosyncratic gestures or a particular tempo-rhythm, and a way of relating to the external world and to other characters. We are aiming for a state of transformation, where the mask takes over, where our imagination, emotions, thoughts, and physical expression are in service of the mask.

As the actor begins to experience this transformation, as the mask begins to work on their imagination, they may begin to develop an **inner monologue**, thinking thoughts perhaps, or holding intentions and needs, or committing to actions on behalf of the mask or the quality that the mask embodies. This inner monologue gives shape to the actor's movement and specificity to their actions and reactions. It is usually most helpful – especially when working with human characters – for the actor to have this inner monologue occur in the first person "I see a cake. Oooh, that looks good. I really want a bite. Is anyone looking? I'd better take it now. Wait, should I? Oh, why not!" As you can see, each of these sentences involves a simple, clear internal or external "discovery," and each discovery will need to be articulated in a clear and believable physical change – of attitude, gesture, tempo-rhythm, etc. Of course, if this is accomplished skillfully, the audience is at the same time creating the story – and the character's inner monologue – in their own imaginations. "Oh, they want that cake. Ha, they're worried someone may see them. Ohh, they're having doubts. They're worried about their diet. Ooh, they can't help themself, they're going to do it anyway!"

In expressing this inner monologue to the audience, the actor will want to avoid demonstrative or indicative over-acting, looking instead for truthful and clear movement, posture, gesture, changes of tempo-rhythm. Simplicity is the key here. It's the moments of change that often convey a new thought for the character and provoke a new thought for the audience. A change in the angle of the head and neck, a shift in tension in the shoulders, a new gesture, a change of rhythm; if these are connected to discoveries, decisions, and actions in the inner monologue, they will feel truthful to the audience. This process

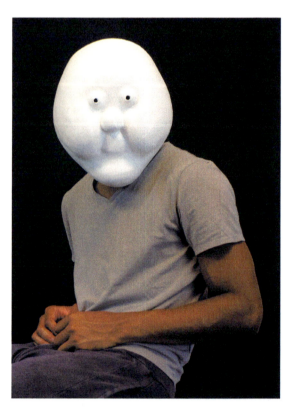

FIGURE 4.5 *An actor in a larval mask that was created by Jonathan Becker*

of discovering what is necessary, and eliminating what is not, is the place where our previous work on neutrality becomes extremely valuable.

It is worth noting here that although the process described thus far is true for all full-face masks, the level of nuance and psychological complexity of the character will vary from one style of mask to another. Take, for instance, the **larval** mask pictured on the preceding page. While these masks will require a clear idea from the actor of their essential "character," and an articulation of this character in the body, we will not expect the same level of psychological nuance from that character as we would in the more complex character masks. Indeed, the larval masks are often used in actor training as an in-between stage, moving from neutral masks into the more complex and nuanced character masks. Larval masks are especially useful for finding large movements, clear and exaggerated gestures, fully articulated tempo-rhythms, and for a level of cartoonish play married with clarity and specificity, which can be playfully liberating while still cultivating greater awareness of expression through movement. With masks that represent spirits, animals, or supernatural beings, the "character" the actor is in search of will be quite different than the more recognizably human masks, and the more symbolic, abstract, or even grotesque a mask is, the further the physical language will depart from the normal human gestures and movements.

As the "character" or physical life of the mask begins to take shape, the actor will want to place the character in situations and relationships. This will deepen the connection to the mask through the discovery of their responses to events and to other characters or beings. These initial **improvisations**, which should start as simple and clear as possible, will later allow for the construction of performances, including scenes and even entire plays. This is a very exciting step in the work with masks and allows us to discuss a further set of skills the actor must cultivate.

BOX 4.2 COUNTERMASK

The more complex a mask is, the more it allows for a fuller development of the character, and for the expression of what we often refer to as moments of **countermask**. Countermask refers to those expressions of emotion, intention, and action that diverge from the mask's apparent fixed expression. We say apparent, because in fact a well-made mask, such as the ones pictured above, will allow for multiple expressions. These masks – which Russell Dean, the mask maker, calls "Grouchy" and "Tense" – have an initial and clear proposal for the character's fundamental personality. However, if held at a certain angle, or accompanied by a particular gesture or physical attitude, the mask can suddenly appear shy, or frightened, or strangely hopeful, or even in love. A well-sculpted mask will contain multiple countermask possibilities, while still presenting a clear and strong "first impression." Discovering the countermask(s) helps actors resist the temptation to "restrict" the character to only one thing and thus makes the character more interesting, believable, and more human.

TB 4.2(A)   *Mask by Russell Dean and Strangeface*

TB 4.2(B)   *Mask by Russell Dean and Strangeface*

As we've mentioned, blocking takes on a special significance in mask performance. Since the mask must be visible to the audience most of the time, there are implications for how actors place themselves in relation to other actors, how they enter and exit the space, how they give and take **focus**, and their relationship with the audience. Since addressing these challenges will often depend on the presence of an "outside eye," we have discussed many of these issues in the chapter on directing mask theater. But let's have a look here at some specific aspects of staging that will help the actor in their work with the mask.

The first entrance is very important. This is the moment the audience meets the mask/character, and the moment needs a bit of framing. We often refer to it as "presenting the mask." We frequently advise actors to step into the space, in character of course, taking one or two steps so that the mask and the actor's body are visible to the entire audience, then "discover" something in the space that allows them to pause in reaction. This pause allows the audience to engage with the mask and begin to scan it for information (as we described earlier). Having given the audience a brief moment to register the mask, the actor begins to react to whatever they have discovered, engaging in a clear and specific action, which allows the audience to interpret the action as the action of the character. They begin to tell the story in their own minds; the illusion has been built, and the audience is along for the ride!

Of course, the more specific and clear the actions, the more the audience will be invited to "read" the thoughts, emotions, and intentions – the inner life – of the character. But no matter how specific the actor's movement is, it must include moments of stillness, space for the audience to register the discoveries the character is making. We refer to these moments of stillness as "framing the thoughts" or "framing the moments," which helps call attention to the fact that the audience must be invited to observe, to read, each discovery, decision, and action. In addition to framing moments with stillness, actors in masks also frequently employ the technique of **clocking**, or looking directly out at the audience. This technique is extremely useful in allowing the audience to read the character's thoughts and reactions and is a very good technique to practice early on in your work with the mask. Be careful, though – this is definitely a technique that can become tiresome if overused!

The next set of skills has to do with relating to other characters. While working in masks, actors must be especially sensitive not to **upstage** one another. The first remedy for this is to have interactions with another actor taking place on the same plane in relation to the audience. This works for much of the time. However, it can lead to some boring restrictions in blocking, so you also want to cultivate the technique of looking toward your partner, even when you can't actually see them. Turning the mask in the direction of the other character, even when the mask doesn't

FIGURE 4.6 Vamos Theatre's production of A Brave Face. Courtesy of Vamos Theatre and Graeme Braidwood Photography

turn fully toward them, can create the illusion that the mask is looking at the other character, which allows for more dynamic staging. It is also essential – since the audience can only perceive the thoughts of one mask at a time – that actors in masks get very good at giving and taking focus, often by looking toward the mask that is meant to have focus, and by taking focus when it is thrown to them through engaged movement.

Finally, as you work on crafting material and begin building a story and interactions with other characters, it is a very good idea to move between working with and without the mask. We often have actors move between working with the mask and running through the same scene without it, while speaking their inner monologue out loud. This gives actors, director, and writer the chance to see where the actions are supported by a clear inner monologue, and where there is physical action that is not supported by an inner truth. It is also a good way to check that the actor is working in the first person, which helps to make the action clearer and more truthful.

Before embarking on our exercises, it is worth noting that there are strong disagreements among actors and teachers about the usefulness of mirrors in the exploration of masks. Some excellent teachers and authors, such as Libby Appel and Eli Simon, advocate the use of mirrors from an early stage of exploration. Others – equally excellent – such as John Wright and Jacques Lecoq – advocate strongly against the use of mirrors. We have found over the years that introducing mirrors in the early stages creates artificiality in some actors, leading them to try to reproduce what they see, rather than going in search of the lived, embodied experience of the mask. However, we have also found that mirrors at a later stage of development can be very helpful in refining, fine-tuning, and solidifying the character, and in seeing the further possibilities of techniques like using the lower half of the face in half-masks, which we will discuss further below.

As you work your way through the following exercises, choose those that are most appropriate for the style of mask you are working with. For example, taking on the expression of a symbolic or abstract mask will have little use for the actor, who may wish to invest more time in playing with the articulations of the mask in the upper body and the possibilities for the overall physicality, tempo-rhythm, and gestures and may also wish to use a mirror in their work at an earlier stage than someone working with a more realistic human mask.

FULL-FACE MASK EXERCISES

We always recommend a thorough warm-up before working with masks, and even with full-face masks, we would include a vocal warm-up, since some of the work in the following exercises will include discovering the voice of the mask.

First Encounters

We like to make our first contact with the masks a light and fun one. If the group is big enough, we will divide them into groups of 2–5 and give each group a mask or two. One at a time, actors will put on the mask, either with their back to the rest of their group or while behind a screen or other visual obstruction.

With the mask on, the actor either turns fully to face the audience or appears from behind the screen. This allows the audience to perceive the mask and body together at the same time and helps create the illusion that the mask is a face. Keep a distance from the audience that is sufficient for them to be able to see both the body of the actor and the mask – too close and the illusion is broken, and the mask collapses back into an inanimate object. Otherwise, we encourage actors at this stage to follow any impulses they may have, so long as they keep the mask playing toward the audience. Do they fall in love with a member of the audience? Are they shy about being there? Proud? Aggressive? Initial impulses will arise in the body, provoking moments of laughter and pleasure from the audience. At the same time, the actors will receive a great deal of information from having the mask on, even for just a minute or two.

After a brief moment, we signal the actor to turn away or make their exit, and the first encounter is finished. We always make time after each brief encounter to let the observers reflect on what they learned and what they were beginning to enjoy about the character. This exercise works best if the encounters are brief (1–2 minutes max), if multiple actors have encounters with the same mask, and if each actor has

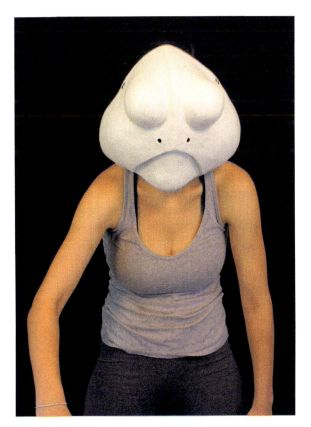

FIGURE 4.7 *An actor in a larval mask that was created by Jonathan Becker*

encounters with multiple masks over the course of the exercise. Working in small groups spread throughout the room also helps to keep an energy alive in these early investigations.

Articulations and Isolations

After these first encounters, actors are ready to begin experimenting with **articulating** thoughts, emotions, and actions with the masks. This next exercise allows the actor in the mask to experience – and the actors who are watching to see – how much can be communicated with simple, clear, specific movements.

Working with any full-face mask, put on the mask and turn to face the audience, standing with the body in neutral. Your head should be angled so that the mask is looking at the horizon. Depending on the mask, this may mean that your own head is angled differently than if *you* were looking at the horizon. Use a mirror or an outside eye to find the appropriate angle of your head so that the mask looks out over the horizon.

Keeping the rest of the body in neutral, change the angle of your head so that the mask is looking slightly up, above the horizon. Use feedback from your spectators to register any change of expression. With some masks, this will already express a strong change. Return to the mask looking over the horizon. Now repeat this, looking slightly down, then to the left, and then to the right. Return to the horizon between each of these articulations of your head and neck. Take a moment to let the audience register any changes of expression in each new articulation. Does the mask become angry? Shy? Curious? Proud?

Without moving too quickly – and returning to the neutral horizon between each new articulation – explore various articulations of the head and neck, registering how they change the expression of the mask. Let your movements be clear, simple, and framed by stillness at the beginning and the end. This allows the new expression to register for the audience.

After a round in which each actor explores changes in the head/neck relationship, and how that can express different thoughts and emotions of the mask/character, do the same again, but now start to add simple changes in the body. So, for instance, with the mask looking at the horizon, the head and neck might come forward, the head tilted slightly to one side, the shoulders might pull back, and the hands come to rest on the hips, elbows out. After framing this attitude with a moment of stillness, change to something else. Begin to look for the impulse for the next gesture or attitude in the moment of stillness, so that the changes begin to connect organically.

Once actors are getting comfortable with more complex gestures and attitudes, they can begin to play with **isolations**. For instance, only the head moves, followed by the shoulders pulling back, and then finally the hands come to the hips. Isolating each of these movements begins to articulate a complex series of thoughts, as opposed to the one thought that is articulated by making all of the movements at the same time. Once actors get the hang of articulating, isolating, and framing with stillness, they will be excited by all the expressive possibilities at their disposal.

BOX 4.3 ARTICULATING THE MASK

In mask work, much can be communicated with simple, specific movements, especially in the position of the head and neck. Here, the performer Richie Schiraldi demonstrates how changes in the head/neck relationship can express different thoughts and emotions of Russell Dean's "Tense" character mask. As you explore this, look for clear, simple changes, framed by stillness at the beginning and the end. This allows the new expression to register for the audience. Use a mirror or an outside eye to guide your explorations and confirm what is working.

TB 4.3(A)   *Photo by Jenni Carroll*

TB 4.3(B)   *Photo by Jenni Carroll*

TB 4.3(C)   *Photo by Jenni Carroll*

TB 4.3(D)   *Photo by Jenni Carroll*

TB 4.3(E)   *Photo by Jenni Carroll*

Finding the Body of the Mask

Now we begin to explore building individual characters, working from the impulses of the mask as they work on the actor's imagination and emotional life, allowing and encouraging these impulses to come to life in the body. Each actor chooses a particular mask, one that excites them or stimulates their imagination. Take the mask and place yourself somewhere in the room with some space around you, so you can work alone. Holding the mask by the side or the top, so that your hand covers as little of the face as possible, keep the mask in your hand and let your arm hang to your side.

Close your eyes and allow your body to relax into a neutral state, an energized and open place that feels ready to receive. With your eyes still closed, lift the mask so that it is in front of you, looking at your face. Open your eyes, looking directly at the mask. Notice your first impression of the mask. What does it seem to express? Is it saying anything (in your imagination, of course!)? Are there particular features that jump out at you?

Now begin to turn the mask slowly and slightly from side to side, then tilting the head up and down, then angling the face slightly from one diagonal to the other, etc. Notice how the features change, how the expression might be different if the mask is held at even a slightly different angle. As you do this, you may begin to notice certain impulses in your body. Your shoulders may begin to round, or your chest may collapse or come forward. Notice these impulses, follow them if you choose. Breath is a powerful conveyer of thought and emotion. Notice any impulses in your breath as you look at the mask.

Now allow yourself to take on the expression of the mask in your own face. Try to reproduce it as if you were looking in a mirror. If you find yourself tensing in the face or neck, relax the features a bit, so that you have a sense that you are mirroring the expression in a sustainable way that will not cause injury or fatigue. When you have the expression, set the mask lightly aside somewhere safe, and take a walk around the room, allowing the impulses in your body that arise from holding that expression to come to life. Pay special attention to the way you walk – the contact of your feet with the ground, the length of your stride, the placement of your hips and shoulders, and any impulse toward a tempo-rhythm that starts to emerge.

As you walk around the room, discovering this first draft of the character's body, check back in with the mask every now and then. Refresh the expression on your own face and start to let it be a bit more mobile, without losing the sense that your face is a mask. This slightly increased mobility will allow you to continue exploring any impulses in the breath, and now in sound. What sounds does the character make as they walk around the room? As they have brief encounters with objects or other characters? Avoid text for now, just let yourself be curious about the quality of voice and sounds the character might make.

As you walk, remember the lessons of stillness. Let something in the room bring you to a stop as you discover it. React with a gesture in the arms and hands. Do this a few times, until you feel that the arms and hands are now part of the expression of the thoughts and emotions of the character. You now have a first draft – a way of walking, a tempo-rhythm, a voice (that you can hear in your own head, and that is different than yours), and perhaps even a characteristic gesture or two.

At this stage, we like to set up a little promenade, so that there is audience on two sides and each of the actors can take their character/mask for a walk down the street. One at a time, put on the mask, and take the character for a walk. The mask's debut!

Interacting with the World

After these initial exercises that expose actors to the wonderful state of transformation that masks allow, we usually put them into interactions with objects and tasks. This allows the mask to more fully express itself and allows actors to find opportunities to play the countermask and begin to build a full inner life. Here is a series of steps that works regardless of the style of mask, from the more cartoonish "larval" masks to the finely detailed character masks.

Take an object, such as a broom or mop that can be easily handled and is used for a simple, repeatable task. Tasks that involve repetitive action, even something as simple as walking, give a wide scope of opportunities for expressing changes of thought, discoveries, decisions, and actions.

Make an initial decision about the character's relationship to this action. Are you excited to be sweeping? Would you much prefer to be anywhere else in the world? Are you resentfully cleaning up someone else's mess, or are you clearing up from a wonderful party the night before, which has left you feeling happy and light? Begin the activity, building an inner monologue that suits the action and emotional state you have chosen. Notice how the choices you've made already affect the quality of your action – the tempo-rhythm, the force, whether the action is sustained or staccato, etc. Clarify these physical expressions, so that the character's attitude becomes even more visible to the audience.

Now make a discovery in the space around you. An object someone left behind, an extra level of messiness in one corner of the room, or perhaps a $50 bill you did not expect to find. Explore how you can express the discovery through the action. For instance, you might stop in response to the discovery, then resume with a different tempo-rhythm, or a different level of tension, or a new attitude in the shoulders or chest. Taking full advantage of the simple object and repetitive task, how much can you reveal about the character's inner life and journey through the scene?

FIGURE 4.8 *A creature mask created by Rob Faust/Faustworks*

BOX 4.4 WORKING WITH OBJECTS

Objects, and the relationship an actor can build with them, provide wonderful opportunities to express character in a full-face mask. Observe how, by playing the various reactions to reading a shocking passage in a book, or the simple act of opening an umbrella, the performers Brittany Price Anderson and Richie Schiraldi find emotional nuances in these character masks made by Russell Dean.

TB 4.4(A) *Photo by Jenni Carroll*

TB 4.4(C) *Photo by Jenni Carroll*

TB 4.4(B) *Photo by Jenni Carroll*

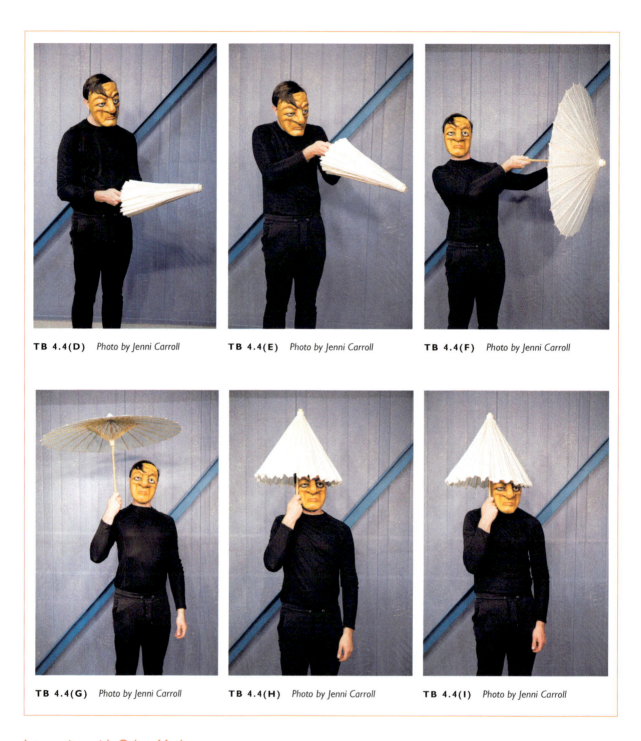

TB 4.4(D)   Photo by Jenni Carroll

TB 4.4(E)   Photo by Jenni Carroll

TB 4.4(F)   Photo by Jenni Carroll

TB 4.4(G)   Photo by Jenni Carroll

TB 4.4(H)   Photo by Jenni Carroll

TB 4.4(I)   Photo by Jenni Carroll

Interacting with Other Masks

When actors have developed a mask character to a sufficient level and have begun to clearly articulate discoveries, decisions, and actions, it is great to start building relationships and exploring the ability to tell a story one moment at a time. It is best to start with only two masks on stage. This makes it easier to give and take focus, avoid upstaging each other, and create simple improvisations that lead to satisfying stories. Here's one we love to play, inspired by Thomas Prattki, the founder of Arthaus Berlin.

Set up a café, with several tables and chairs, and perhaps even a buffet area or coffee counter (this allows for movement within the scene). The first mask enters and takes a seat at a table. They begin a simple activity, such as reading or drinking a cup of coffee. Real objects, though not too many, are useful for the performers at this stage. The first mask settles into their activity, having established whatever atmosphere or state of mind the performer has chosen or discovered.

The second mask then enters. Without seeing the first, they take a seat at another table. They establish an activity, and a state of mind. At the right moment, the two mask characters discover each other. Or perhaps one discovers the other first. In any event, it is love at first sight.

There follows a sequence of glances, expressions of shyness or doubt, attempts to improve one's appearance, ploys designed to get attention, aborted attempts at introductions, crosses to the buffet or counter, and so forth and so on. Eventually, the two find themselves seated at the same table, and the story of falling in love is complete.

Obviously, this simple theme of falling in love can be played in many different situations – a grocery store, boarding an airplane, etc. The focus of the exercise should be on establishing the characters, expressing the inner life, giving and taking focus, and finding a satisfying escalation of the crisis to a point of resolution.

Playing Multiple Characters

One of the great joys of working with masks is the ability for the same actor to play multiple characters. We also like to use this as a training tool, to sharpen the actor's ability to drop in and out of clearly articulated characters. It can be great fun to construct scenes – often but not always comical ones – in which the actors are asked to play multiple characters. Here is an exercise we frequently use with both full-face masks and half-masks.

Without the mask, bring the first character to life in the body and voice. Then drop it, returning to neutral. And back to the character. And drop. What is the key, or trigger, the place in your body or voice that allows immediate access, connection, and credibility?

Now do the same with a second character. Then begin to play between the two characters, dropping back to neutral in between. Continue until you feel a sense of play and fluidity in the changes.

Set up a screen or visual obstruction, with entrances on either side. Place both masks to be used behind the screen. Go behind the screen, put on one of the masks, and drop into character. Appear from behind the screen, cross the space, and then disappear behind the screen. As quickly as possible, change masks, drop into the second character, and reappear. Cross the space, disappear, and repeat. Continue for a few rounds, looking for efficiency in your changes.

After a few passes, begin to "justify" your exits. For instance, you're looking for the other character. Then justify the second character's entrance and exit. Perhaps they're looking for the first character. Let this game develop a bit.

Now start to keep the space alive even when you are offstage. This is easiest in half-mask, since the voice can continue even when the body is offstage, but there are very clever strategies actors have found to do this in full-face mask as well. As this develops and a theme or story begins to emerge, see if multiple actors can begin to play together. A total of four actors, eight characters, and suddenly an entire play is possible!

HALF-FACE MASKS

Many of the observations we've made about full-face masks are also applicable to half-face masks (we will refer to this type of mask as a half-mask). The defining difference between a full-face mask and a half-mask is obvious from the name. A half-mask covers only part of the face, intentionally leaving some of it exposed. The most typical construction of a half-mask is one that covers the area between the forehead and the top of the mouth. However, this is by no means the only way to

FIGURE 4.9   A Rake's Progress *by Strangeface Theatre. Photo by Mark Dean, masks by Strangeface Masks*

construct a half-mask. It is possible to have a mask, for instance, that covers the lower half of the face, leaving the eyes and forehead of the actor exposed. It is also possible to construct a mask that splits the face vertically, so that one side of the face is the actor's and the other side is a mask. There are masks that cover a portion of the center of the face, or the ears and chin, or…. One can even think of the famous Groucho Marx glasses and eyebrows as a form of half-mask, and of course the clown nose is, after all, a partial mask – Lecoq called it the "world's smallest mask." However, we will restrict our discussion here to the form of half-mask that covers the area between the forehead and the top of the mouth. There are two reasons for restricting our discussion to this type of mask: first, it is by far the most common form of half-mask, thanks largely to the influence of the Commedia dell'Arte; second, this half-mask has the distinctive quality of allowing speech and allowing the actor's mouth and chin to be visible.

As with many full-face masks, half-masks often take recognizable human features and emotions and exaggerate them to a greater or lesser degree. Half-masks, however, aim to create the illusion of a living human face by combining the actor's face with the mask to create a whole face. In most half-masks, this is accomplished by including the upper lip, which is meant to align with and cover the actor's upper lip. As John Wright points out in *Playing the Mask*, "the game is to find the most effective and the most comfortable configuration to complete the face with this new upper lip."[6] The resulting illusion of a face, which is partially the inanimate mask, and partially the actor's actual mouth, chin, lips, teeth, tongue, has a wonderfully destabilizing effect on the audience. On the one hand, the mask works on the audience as we have previously described, inviting them to an imaginative game in which they perceive the mask as a human face and read the performer's actions as the actions of the character. On the other hand, that lower part of the face is a constant reminder that the performer is present, thus creating an inherent distortion in the image, a **grotesquerie** of the human face. It is this effect that gives the half-mask, whether one in the Commedia tradition or one from a more contemporary maker like Russell Dean, a sense of exciting and dangerous possibility. Its distortion makes it unpredictable. The grotesqueness of mask and human face combined also means that half-masks tend to inspire ridicule, and therefore comedy – often at an exaggerated, amplified, even cartoon-like level. As you will find, however, half-masks can inspire many other feelings as well.

It is also important to note the aesthetic choice that must be made in working with half-masks. On the one hand, we can use makeup and even facial hair on the lower part of the face so that it integrates with the color and style of the mask, thus strengthening the illusion of a full face. On the other hand, many theater artists, such as Marco Luly, actually use techniques like white face makeup to heighten the discrepancy between the mask and the performer's face.

That the half-mask allows, in fact requires, the voice as part of the expression of the character means the mask offers challenges and opportunities that go beyond those we have discussed with full-face masks. The mouth becomes more than just a means of breathing and speaking; its shape and movement become an articulation of thought and emotion. Lips, teeth, chin, even tongue are all part of the expressive potential of the half-mask performer, whether or not their movements are accompanied by sound. At the same time, half-masks, and the comic characterizations they inspire, can allow actors to find greater expressiveness and transformation in their voice, speech, and use of text. This makes half-masks another great tool for actor training as well as a thoroughly enjoyable performance style. And be aware: there is a permission that comes in the half-mask to say things we wouldn't normally say!

Another important distinction between half-masks and full-face masks can be found in the energy and movement that the mask inspires. The amplified level of play that the mask requires means that half-mask characters will tend to be much more mobile – anarchically active, in fact. This energy is usually born out of the urgent situations that characters find themselves in, as they actively pursue their needs, which are always for concrete things like money, love (sex), or food. If this puts you in mind of a farce, it is worth remembering that farcical comedies are in many ways the modern inheritors of the Commedia half-mask tradition.

This need for greater mobility, along with the fact that the masks are meant to combine with the actor's face into a single image, has certain effects on the half-mask design. These masks tend to be smaller and closer to the actual size of the performer's face – indeed, some are based on casts of the performer's face and head. For the half-masks in *Invitation to a Beheading*, we chose to go with a larger size, in keeping with the theme that these characters were grotesque expressions of a fevered dream state. However, to allow as comfortable a fit as possible, as well as maximum mobility – one of the actors does handstands and cart-wheels in the mask – the masks were created from molds of the actors' heads, and adjusted for maximum sight and mobility.

One more aspect of half-mask performance worth mentioning here is the frequent use of social types (or stereotypes). Masks – especially those used in the service of a comedy – often employ social **stereotypes**, represented visually through the mask and physically and vocally by the actor. This convention is true in both full-face and half-face masks and is probably best represented by the conventions of the Commedia dell'Arte. Commedia employed **stock characters**, who would have been widely recognized by audiences, not as particular individuals but as types – the lecherous and miserly old man, the innocent and naïve young lovers, the braggart soldier, the pompous know-it-all "doctor," the trickster servant, and so forth. The beauty of character types for mask performance is that there is much less need for **exposition**. Divas will do what divas do, as will aggressive businessmen, pedantic professors, clumsy or forgetful butlers, etc. We don't need a justification for the personality of a type; we simply recognize them and are ready to get on with the comedy or the drama. The actor's work is to acknowledge the type and articulate it

The Actor's Perspective 119

FIGURE 4.10 *Acrobatics in a mask, in the author's production of* Invitation to a Beheading. *Mask created by Mike Oleon, photo by Evan Barr Photography*

in a way that is clear to the audience. Of course, once this is accomplished, there is ample room to play the countermask, so that the character is as complex and interesting as possible.

HALF-FACE MASK EXERCISES

These exercises build on those for full-face masks, most of which are useful for half-masks as well. As always, we recommend a thorough physical and vocal warm-up.

Find the Face, Find the Body

After spending some time looking at the mask, as we've done in previous exercises, begin to explore the lower half of the mask – your face. As you mirror the expression of the mask in your own face, explore the position of your chin, lips, teeth, even your tongue. Notice that, in difference to a full-face mask, this expression in the lower half of the face does not have to remain fixed. It can move! This can be one of the most exciting qualities of working in half-masks, as it allows for a greater range of plasticity in the expressions and can enhance the changeability of the mask itself. At first, do this exercise with the mask held

where you can see it. Then do it with the mask on, preferably with an observer to respond to the mask and to offer feedback on what is working. After some experiential exploration, this can also be a good time to add working with a mirror.

As before, allow this exploration of the mask to lead you to discoveries about the body, such as particular gestures, the tempo-rhythm of the walk, the placement of the shoulders and pelvis, and so forth. In all your movements, you are looking for a quality that is amplified but truthful, so that even in its exaggeration, the character remains recognizably human.

Once you've begun to find a body, voice, and even perhaps a social type that the mask expresses, begin to add bits of clothing – wig and hats (as with full-face masks) help complete the image that this is your head. Add bits of clothing that enhance the comic social type you are exploring.

Finding the Voice

Now you're ready to add the element that really sets the half-mask apart: the use of the actor's voice. Along with the visibility of the lower part of the face, this is definitely the greatest change from the previous masks we have explored. These masks actually speak!

As you experiment with the shape of the jaw, lips, teeth, and tongue and follow the impulses that are arising in the body, allow yourself also to follow any impulses that arise in your breath, and in simple sounds. Resist actual text at this stage, but be bold in experimenting with the different ways you can use your voice: change your pitch, rhythm of sounds, the placement of your voice, and so forth.

Through experimentation, the response of your audience, and your own innate sense of truthfulness, you will start to discover things about the mask character's voice, including where it lives in your body, whether it prefers long or short sounds, whether it is verbose or laconic, how much it likes to enunciate, and so forth. Continue to work from impulse and in movement – the body will often inform the voice (and vice versa). Let the breath be free, and in response to the discoveries and actions you are finding. As you feel the impulse, allow the breath to release simple sounds (no words yet).

Allow these discoveries to start to lead you into more complex utterances, words, and even sentences. However, for now, keep these utterances in gibberish. This will allow you to continue your intuitive and organic exploration of the voice, without the potential pitfalls of making "sense" that come along with actual text. Having said this, you may well find that your utterances, gibberish as they may be to the rest of us, make total sense to you as the character. This is a good sign that you are connecting with something truthful in the mask.

In fact, this "gibberish" can be used in performance, with wonderful effects that link to the role the audience

BOX 4.5 FINDING THE FACE

One of the exciting things about working with half-masks is how the lower part of your face becomes part of the mask, thus allowing for a greater range of expression in the face, as demonstrated here by Brittany Price Anderson, wearing an Arlecchino mask made by Antonio Fava. Notice that the exaggerated qualities of the mask allow for – even require – a greater level of expressiveness in the performer's jaw, lips, tongue, cheeks, even head and neck (as we've discussed previously). As you explore the lower part of your face in a half-mask, experiment with the full range of expressions and allow this to lead you to discoveries about the body, the gestures, and the different vocal qualities of the mask character.

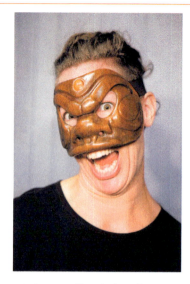

TB 4.5(A)   *Photo by Jenni Carroll*

TB 4.5(B)   *Photo by Jenni Carroll*

TB 4.5(C)   *Photo by Jenni Carroll*

plays in imagining and interpreting the meaning of movement and sound. If the action is clear, and the tone of voice is clear, the actual spoken sounds can leave a space for the audience to complete the work by "interpreting" what they mean. We have seen half-mask scenes make complete sense even though they were played in an imaginary language.

If and when you start to work with actual text, keep it simple at first, so that you can continue to discover the qualities and muscularity of the mask character's voice. A classic exercise is to take a phrase, such as "My wife/husband/lover is here." Say it in as many ways as possible. Have someone on the outside provoke the masked actor with commands like "change the rhythm," "more passion," "calm down," "lie to us," and so forth. The idea is to provoke the actor to find as many different ways as possible to say the phrase. As they do, the body will become more engaged, and the voice will become more alive and animated. Work fast, without time to process each new command before you speak.

FIGURE 4.11 A Rake's Progress by Strangeface Theatre. Notice how the masks invite an articulation of the lower half of the face. Photo by Mark Dean, masks by Strangeface Masks

Developing Material

In classic Commedia, the scenes were often divided into pairs of masks, or perhaps trios. This makes the masks easier to work with, the characters easier to develop in opposition to each other, and the staging can be cleaner without having to worry about upstaging other masks. Put two masks together, in a situation with some urgency. Let the needs of the characters be immediate and concrete. For instance, they are hungry and have come to steal food. Or they are illicit lovers who have only a brief time to find a hiding place before they are discovered by a jealous partner.

Introduce one mask at a time, even if they enter together, so that the actors continue to work on clarity and focus. The beginning of the improvisation should look to establish place, relationship, **status**, and the character's **objective** – their urgent need.

As you continue to improvise around the theme, look for the opportunities to find a game – what Commedia performers call the **lazzi**. This is a bit of comic business that gets developed, usually by finding and escalating a problem (**obstacle**) related to the character's urgent need. This might be something as simple as trying to get in a window or hide under a bed. Nothing is simple for these characters, and the joy for the actor is in finding a problem, making it worse, then resolving it only to find yourself in another problem. Ah, life!

CONCLUSION

Now that we have a good idea of how the masks work, and a series of starting points to begin bringing the different types of masks to life, we're going to need some masks! At the end of this book, we have provided a list of mask makers who create masks that can be ordered individually or in sets. This may be especially useful for those interested in working with the neutral mask, a notoriously difficult mask to design. However, we also believe that the best way to get to know a mask is to make it yourself, so in the following chapters we will look more closely at mask design and techniques for making masks.

NOTES

1. Saint-Denis, Michel, *Theatre: The Rediscovery of Style and Other Writings*. London: Routledge, 2009.
2. Eldredge, Sears A. and Huston, Hollis W., "Actor Training in the Neutral Mask." *The Drama Review*. Vol. 22, No. 4 (1978), p. 20.
3. Arrighi, Gillian, *The Neutral Mask: Its Origins and Its Applications to the Creative Processes of the Actor* (Saarbrucken, Germany: Verlag Dr. Muller, 2010), p. 29.
4. Eldredge and Huston, p. 20; emphases added.
5. Lecoq, Jacques, Jean-Gabriel Carasso and Jean-Claude Lallais, *The Moving Body: Teaching Creative Theatre* (NY: Routledge, 2001), p. 38.
6. Wright, John, *Playing the Mask: Acting Without Bullshit* (London: Nick Hern Books, 2017), p. 128.

SELECTED RESOURCES

Appel, Libby. *Mask Characterization: An Acting Process*. Carbondale, Illinois: Southern Illinois Press, 1982.

Arrighi, Gillian. *The Neutral Mask: Its Origins and Its Applications to the Creative Processes of the Actor*. Saarbrucken, Germany: Verlag Dr. Muller, 2010.

Chaffee, Judith and Crick Olly, eds. *The Routledge Companion to Commedia dell'Arte*. Routledge Companions, 2017: 4. London: Routledge, Taylor and Francis Group, 2017.

Eldredge, Sears A. *Mask Improvisation for Actor Training and Performance: The Compelling Image*. Evanston, Illinois: Northwestern University Press, 1996.

Evans, Mark and Rick Kemp. *The Routledge Companion to Jacques Lecoq*. London: Routledge, Taylor & Francis Group, 2016.

Fava, Antonio. *Commedia by Fava: The Commedia dell'Arte, Step by Step – Part 1*. Fremantle, Australia: Contemporary Arts Media, 2006. https://search.alexanderstreet.com/view/work/bibliographic_entity%7Cvideo_work%7C3925215

———Thomas Simpson, ed. *The Comic Mask in the Commedia dell'Arte: Actor Training, Improvisation, and the Poetics of Survival*. Evanston, Illinois: Northwestern University Press, 2007.

Grantham, Barry. *Playing Commedia: A Training Guide to Commedia Techniques*. Portsmouth, New Hampshire: Heinemann, 2000.

John, Rudlin and Crick Olly. *Commedia dell'Arte: A Handbook for Troupes*. London: Routledge, 2001.

Johnstone, Keith. *Improvisation and the Theatre*. New York: Routledge, 1987.

Johnstone, Keith. *IMPRO*. New York: Routledge, 1992.

Lecoq, Jacques, Jean-Gabriel Carasso and Jean-Claude Lallais. *The Moving Body: Teaching Creative Theatre*. Translated by David Bradby. New York: Routledge, 2001.

Rudlin, John. *Commedia dell'Arte: An Actor's Handbook*. London: Routledge, 1994.

Saint-Denis, Michel. *Theatre: The Rediscovery of Style and Other Writings*. London: Routledge, 2009.

Simon, Eli. *Masking Unmasked: Four Approaches to Basic Acting*. New York: Palgrave Macmillan, 2004.

Wilsher, Toby. *The Mask Handbook*. New York: Routledge, 2007.

Wright, John. *Why Is That So Funny? A Practical Exploration of Physical Comedy*. New York: Limelight Editions, 2007.

———. *Playing the Mask: Acting Without Bullshit*. London: Nick Hern Books, 2017.

CHAPTER 5

MASKS BY DESIGN

FIGURE 5.1 *Mask designers Giancarlo Santelli, Jonathan Becker, and Bernardo Rey Rengifo at work*

So many choices! Where do you begin? The design process includes identifying the function of the mask, conducting research, sketching, creating a **maquette**, and often sculpting the form from which the mask will be made. Design and construction skills take years to master; serious mask artists in many cultures train with an established artist to hone their craft. For now, the best way to learn is to get started. With time and practice, you will develop skills and a critical eye. In this chapter, we will see how to establish a character and design concept by:

- Asking questions to determine function.
- Following the design process.
- Selecting the form of the mask.

Several professional mask artists offer insights into their own process. While most artists design and make their masks, sometimes an assistant will do some or all of the construction. The casting of faces and actual making of masks will be covered in Chapter 6.

ASKING QUESTIONS: FUNCTION, TRADITION, WORLD, CHARACTER, AND PRACTICALITIES

Designers begin with understanding the *function* of the mask: What is its purpose or use? Is it a fine art object? Decorative accessory? Protective device? Does it have a social or cultural function? Is it intended for therapy, or as a training tool for actors? Or is it a performance mask which defines a character in a play?

Next, is it part of an established *tradition* with specific visual expectations such as Noh or Commedia dell'Arte? Does the tradition utilize specific materials or processes? What is the *world* of the masks? What environment will it be seen in? What production *style* will it support? Is it part of a group of masks that define the world of the performance, or does it stand out in contrast to other characters? Does it define a specific scripted *character*, or create a new persona? Human, divine, animal, or allegory? Where does it exist on a spectrum from ideal to realistic to abstracted or symbolic representation? What kind of *movement* will the mask's character have? What *practical* resources are available to create the mask?

Understanding the function is important in selecting the type and style of mask.

Art objects, decorative accessories, and some conceptual masks may be inspired by a particular material, form, or theme, or be created to satisfy a personal artistic impulse. Protective masks such as a hockey goalie's helmet require specific forms and materials, which may also be decorated. Some mask makers focus on a ritual process of creating instead of a predetermined aesthetic outcome.[1] In drama therapy, depicting particular attitudes and emotions may be important, or the mask maker's process may be more important than aesthetic outcome. In this case and in some educational environments, the form may be determined by the availability and ease of using materials. For theatrical performance, the designer creates in response to a collective need. As presented in Chapter 3, designs must serve the production, including the script, director, performers, audience, fellow designers, and makers. A combination of formal script/character analysis and conversations with the director, designers, and performers is useful in defining the world of the production. In any of these situations, the designer will "give visual form to abstract ideas."[2] The designer chooses how to present information to the audience. *Form* follows function: the size, expression, aesthetics, and style all come from a need to effectively communicate character in a particular world.

PREPARATION: RESEARCH

As the functions are defined, the designer conducts research to answer questions, clarify details, and provide inspiration.

BOX 5.1 BALI DREAMS CASE STUDY

This production based on *A Midsummer Night's Dream* by William Shakespeare was directed by scholar I Nyoman Sedana. He trained students in Balinese performance styles and traditions during his semester as artist-in-residence at Butler University. For the production, we adopted the movement, costume, and mask styles of several Balinese performance traditions. The cast divided easily into character groups: court, lovers, fairies, and mechanicals.

The court characters adopted movement and wore costumes from Topeng, a formal masked drama, and Legong, a formal dance drama in which *alus* (high status) characters wear full face masks, while their words are spoken by assistants (in *Patih* masks). The royal masks (*Dalem and Raja Putri*) follow idealized notions of serene beauty, while Egeus' *Topeng Tua* mask was more expressive.

The lovers' costumes and performances modeled Drama Gong, a contemporary performance style that incorporates both secular dress (in the forest) and performance costume (for the court wedding). Rather than masks, the lovers applied stylized makeup, which brought

TB 5.1(A) *Bondres Masks for Villagers*

TB 5.1(B) *Rendering of Bottom's Barong Mask by the author*

TB 5.1(C) *Court Viewing the Death of Pyramus*

them into a theatrical world, while allowing the full expressivity of the face and connection to the audience.

The fairies, with their elements of nature and magic, drew on several traditional dances. Queen Titania wore the full-skirted costume of the Cendrawasih bird dance. Her court wore the half wings and headdress of another bird dance, the Manipura. King Oberon's Baris warrior costume featured many tabs that paralleled the movement of Titania's costume. His entourage wore simpler tabbed costumes based on the Wirayuda spear dance. The fairies' brightly dyed batik costumes provide a sense of a tropical environment. The fairy masks for Oberon, Titania, and Puck were selected from non-human characters: Oberon wore a white *Sidakarya* mask, while Puck wore the black version of this powerful mask.

The villagers are the mechanicals or clowns of the play. In many Balinese performance traditions villager characters and clowns wear *poleng*, a black and white plaid fabric symbolic of the balance of good and evil in the world. As lower status characters, they wore a combination of western and Balinese dress, and the comical *bondres* half masks. Bottom's magical transformation to an ass was inspired by a *Barong* style mask and costume.

TB 5.1(D) *Fairy, Puck, and Oberon*

TB 5.1(E) *Alus masks for Theseus and Hippolyta*

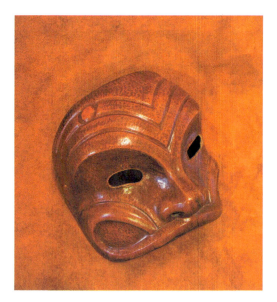

FIGURE 5.2(A) *Arlecchino Mask by Bernardo Rey*

FIGURE 5.2(B) *Arlecchino Mask by Giancarlo Santelli*

Research: Tradition and Innovation

Some traditions have expectations for aesthetic form, materials, and processes. Familiarity with masks of different cultures and makers may influence key elements or style. Designers and makers often learn by copying traditional designs under tutelage of a master artist (as in Bali and Japan), but accomplished designers may expand beyond copy work. Which traditions should you follow? What can you change? When will you innovate or synthesize? Remember that function must still be the motivating factor in design. For example,

- Commedia dell'Arte requires the mouth to be free for the characters to talk and to express with the lower half of their face. Half masks are the right choice – full masks can't be substituted as they would not function effectively. The ideal material is leather, but if your resources are limited, choosing neoprene or paper mache could still work well. Each character has some specific features, such as Pantalone's age and long arched nose or Arlecchino's wart, but there is room for artistic license as well. For instance, Arlecchino can be young or mature, clever or lucky.

- Mascots are oversized and cover the whole head – they don't work if skin shows, so incorporate screens to see through and appropriate costumes. They have to be lightweight and anchored to the head so that exuberant movement does not dislodge the mask. However, the designer will want each new character to have its own distinct look.

FIGURE 5.2(C) *Arlecchino Mask by Antonio Fava*

Masks by Design 127

FIGURE 5.2(D) *Arlecchino Mask by Benjamin Gould*

FIGURE 5.2(E) *Arlecchino Mask by Jonathan Becker*

- Noh masks are smaller than the face. Changing this scale would deprive the production of its delicacy. But some new English Noh plays are incorporating western characters and stories within the structure and style of traditional dramas.

Many designers make beautiful connections between styles or cultures.

Theatre Nohgaku collaborated with American playwright Deborah Brevoort to produce *Blue Moon Over Memphis*. It follows a traditional Noh structure and was danced and sung by

FIGURE 5.3(A) *Mascot Statues outside the Mascot Hall of Fame*

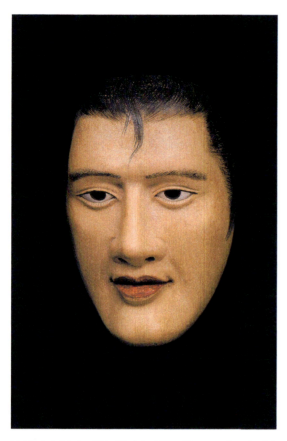

FIGURE 5.3(B) *Elvis. Mask by Hideta Kitazawa. Photo by Sohta Kitazawa. Property of Theater Nohgaku. Created for Theater Nohgaku's 2014 production of Blue Moon over Memphis*

Noh-trained actors but featured American characters, including Hideta Kitazawa's mask of Elvis in the traditional Noh style for the primary role.[3]

Julie Taymor's work frequently incorporates elements of the Balinese mask and puppet traditions which she trained in. *Oedipus Rex* (Saito Kinen Festival Matsumoto, Tokyo, 1992) bridged Greek and Japanese cultures with design elements: Japanese Haniwa tomb ceramics and pre-Greek Cycladic Sculpture suited the larger than life essential simplicity of form for tragedy. Similarly, the clay on the chorus recalled both Japanese Butoh mores and the texture of Greek cliffs.[4] As designers, we are frequently inspired by the work of other people. Some projects and productions are created in an authentic response to or collaboration with others and the resulting synthesis of ideas can speak to common elements of our humanity. Be sensitive to issues of **cultural appropriation**: include thorough research and original voices in your preparation, but know that copying others' work is not appropriate.

Research: World

Understanding the world or context of the mask informs design also. It may be as simple as knowing the available space for it to be displayed: on a wall in a home? A museum gallery? A public garden? Will it be subject to heat, moisture, weather? How close will viewers be – can they see fine details, or do large features need to carry across a stadium? Both? The world of the mask may also be connected to a playscript and discovered through reading and analyzing the text and discussing the production team's ideas. Will the world the mask inhabits be realistic or symbolic? Well-lit or shadowed? Colorful or neutral? Humorous and farcical, poetic, or tragic? Do the masks dominate the space or scene or express a struggle to find a place in the world? If working on a devised piece, it is usual to attend rehearsals to keep abreast of developments to character, script, and environment.

Research: Character

Creating a character is the most essential function of most masks. The questions answered in script analysis and discussions with the creative team, or your own project research, will lead you to find images that reflect the characters you are designing. They may be real people, or artistic interpretations of people. Character research may include images of people that are similar in age, gender, health, occupation, or ethnicity, and specific script references, as well as emotional characteristics. It may extend to animal species, plants, archetypes, elements, or other inspiration related to character, such as a particular patina or texture. It might include moving around to get the "feel" of the character, and to understand the relationship between mask and body.

FIGURE 5.4 *Dionysus by Georgio de Marchi*

FIGURE 5.5(B) *Indonesian Frog Mask*

FIGURE 5.5(A) *Animal-inspired mask by Werner Strub (photo by Giorgio Skory)*

In any mask, the essential features will develop from its function. Donato Sartori rightly insisted the maker must know all about the mask, its history, traditions, and universal components, as well as its individual variations. The nature of the performer, the style and preferences of the director, and the character's role in the production – these details are important and show up as variations among the masks.

FIGURE 5.5(C) *Bird masks for a production of William Butler Yeats'* Dreaming of the Bones

BOX 5.2 DONATO SARTORI ON DESIGN

Amleto Sartori and his son Donato worked with directors and performers to reinvigorate the art of functional mask work in Western Theatre. Amleto worked to create a perfectly neutral mask for Jacques Lecoq's school and developed character masks that helped reinvigorate the Commedia dell'Arte in the mid-20th century, as well as other masks. The Sartoris became known worldwide for their expertise and trained a generation of new mask artists in their studio near Padua, Italy. Famed Italian director, Giorgio Strehler, correctly asserted that directly or indirectly, contemporary western mask artists are indebted to them for the rediscovery and perfection of leather mask making. Of their profession, Donato Satori said, "It is also a matter of time spent every day with your tools in hand, until they become instinctive……if our studio is considered superior to others it is because we continue to produce masks every day…. I feel the imperative need for a rigorous and restless professionality through which I earn my daily bread, not just a casual or part-time activity. Otherwise, the results will not be right. That a mask maker knows how to make a functional and esthetically pleasing mask is fine by me, but that is only the first part of his job as an artist, … He must know everything about that mask - its character, its history, how it will be used."

Sartori believed it necessary for mask designers/makers to fully understand and synthesize key information about:

- The actor, his emotional and professional characteristics, his particular physicality
- The role, its character, history, aesthetic, age, temperament, emotion
- The director, his style, methods, aesthetic
- The space, light, and conditions of performance
- The play
- The historical moment, day, zeitgeist
- The precise lines, planes, angles, shapes, light and shadow

He must know all this, without error. **"The mask is an exact object."**[5]

FIGURE 5.5(D) *Ancestor Mask by Bernardo Rey*

Research: Anatomy and Expression

Because we are so attuned to human features, we read them with great subtlety. A designer needs an eye for the anatomy of the face, whether human or not. Study of the bones, muscles, proportions and aging is useful. "What makes a strong design is the feeling that the mask has both flesh and bones. The bones are solid and unchanging, creating a base upon which the flesh and the muscles of expression can have substance."[6] Prepared with knowledge of facial structure, a designer is free to choose how to simplify, replicate, or exaggerate the features.

Understanding aesthetics of beauty in the target audience also is relevant as it relates to character design. Successful masks are not necessarily beautiful, but they must capture the biological structure of the creature in order to convey the potential for movement. Expressions are key to showing character and require careful crafting to allow the mask to appear alive. A "live" mask incorporates some asymmetry, fine-tuning the emotional presentation to capture more than one emotion as it moves with the performer. This ability to show and play more than one emotion is called countermask.

Caveat on design: We are accustomed to reading identity and expression on faces. We continuously assess people and respond to what we see. We have a store of cultural and personal images to draw on, as well as our response to aesthetic qualities. **Physiognomy**, the practice of ascribing character traits to physical features, was a popular subject in the 19th and early 20th century. Physiognomists made assumptions about personality and emotion based on physical and racial traits, such as a "Roman" nose indicating a cultured person, a square face being "brutish," or a strongly arched brow as untrustworthy. Proponents falsely projected our understanding of the brain to interpret a slanted forehead as less intelligent than a protruding one. Resemblance to animals was also considered a reliable personality indicator. Leonine features were powerful, a raven-like countenance suggested cruelty, pig-like features greedy, cat-like faces delicate and aloof. **Zoomorphism**, attributing animal features to humans, plays on this assumption that our physical and personal characteristics go hand in hand. There is no scientific basis for these assumptions, yet we are given to "reading" people's character on their faces, based on both physical structure and mobile expression. Big, open eyes seem astonished. Curved heavy faces seem docile, angled ones critical, square ones stolid, powerful, or aggressive. **Prototypes** and **archetypes** also affect our cultural ideas about how to represent character. We described classical Greek statues as heroic. **Stereotypes**, too, are used to help us recognize and interpret character. Imagine what traits you expect on a boxer, a witch, a schoolboy, or dictator. Often, we do think in stereotypes. It's not politically correct, and not a way to judge people in your life. However, part of what makes a good design is balancing how we read faces and emotions with the capacity to play beyond a narrow stereotype. In mask making, we mediate the stereotype with the creation of a **countermask**.

BOX 5.3 CHARACTER VOCABULARY

Physiognomy – ascribing characteristics of personality or nature based on physical traits. This drawing of "honest" and "deceitful" features from Vaught's Practical Character Reader (1902) is just one of many problematic false equivalencies.

Prototype – the first model, from which others are copied. This Greek figurine from the early 2nd century B.C.E is assumed to be a mime, and possibly a caricature of an Alexandrian pedant (Metropolitan Museum of Art); its features are evident in old man characters in Greek, Roman, and Commedia masks.

Archetype – a quintessential example. This leather "Pantalone" by Santelli includes the long nose, droopy eyes, and prominent brows typical of representations of Pantalone.

Stereotype – portrayal using oversimplified and exaggerated but commonly ascribed assumptions or characteristics. These nurses by Russell Dean for Vamos Theatre Company pair typical costumes, facial features, and expressions to denote a severe matron, her blasé associate, and their nervous novice. (Graeme Braidwood photography.)

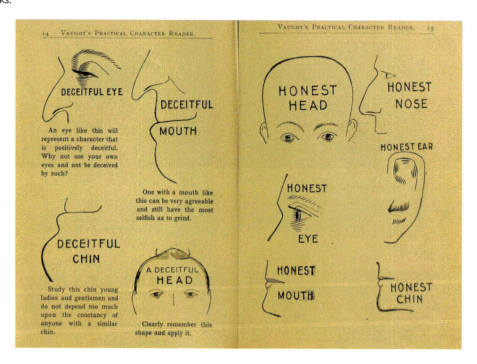

Stock character – stereotyped character that has particular repeated use in a genre, such as an old man, clever servant, or bragging soldier.

Parody – imitation of a style or person with intent to satirize or lampoon. "Elvis at Large" helmet mask by Rob Faust captures the pompadour hairstyle of "The King of Rock and Roll," while the artist takes on his facial expression and movement. (Photo by Timothy Latta.)

Caricature – representation with exaggerated features for comic effect. Sketch of W.T. Benda's "The Old Wag," which bears a striking resemblance to playwright George Bernard Shaw.

Allegory – visual representation of an abstract idea. "Knowledge" by Kait Lamansky visualizes the brain's branched and twisting connections, divisions, and pathways in a white "table rasa" form and neutral (or thoughtful) expression.

Live mask – one which seems animated in performance, creating the illusion of multiple expressions.

Counter mask – alternate personality captured in the design or performance of a mask. Habbe und Meik's masks play a terrific range of emotions with the asymmetrical combination of features and expressions. (Courtesy of Michael Aufenfehn.)

Grotesque – a figure with extremely exaggerated or distorted features, creating tension between attractive and repellent qualities. "The Captain" by Bernardo Rey for *Woyzeck*.

Beauty, Ugliness – aesthetic concepts/qualities as defined by individuals or cultures. W.T. Benda created many masks for stage, print, and entertainment, including this one of an idealized female beauty.

Rhythmic coordination – Benda's term for a design process that utilizes repeated shapes and forms to direct the eye and unify the whole.

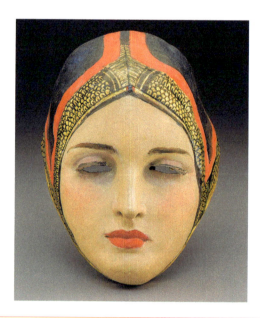

Research: Methods and Materials

Many masks, especially half masks, are best created on a life mask of the performer in order to create an effective transition between the face and the mask. The designer's research may include images, measurements, and a cast of the actor's face.

A good designer will often research or have ideas about and experience in working with different materials to share with the mask maker. It is critical to know what techniques best support the design and function of the mask, as well as what resources (time, talent, and treasure) are available. More about this is in Chapter 6.

FIGURE 5.6 (A–C)   *Zoomorphic faces by LeBrun*

DECISIONS: THE FORM

The form of the mask includes all the visual choices made by the designer. The choices develop from understanding function, digesting research, then selecting and synthesizing ideas into an appropriate aesthetic form. Many of these decisions, including size and materials, are practical.

Form: Practicalities

Begin by asking practical questions about the mask's form.

- What kind of mask is it? Helmet? Parade? Domino? Three quarter? Full face? Feature?
- Will it be worn by more than one person? Either together or in sequence?
- How does the mask integrate with the performer's face and body? Does it need to fit the face exactly? If so, will you start with a life cast? Use flexible material?
- How will it integrate into the face/head – on glasses? As helmet/hat? Elastic strap? Held in teeth? On a rod? In hand?
- How big does it need to be?
- How heavy can it be, or how light must it be? How is it balanced?
- Does it need to be flexible? Does it move (such as a hinged jaw? Wiggling ears? Rolling eyes?)
- Is it donned offstage, or is there a transition seen by the audience?
- Will it be covered with something sturdy, paint, or fabric?
- How durable does it have to be (a few shows, several years, a lifetime? One wearer or many?)
- Will it be seen up close or from a distance?

There's not just one right answer! It's important that you ask the right questions and discover how to create the right masks for your project. See Appendix B for a useful construction worksheet.

Form: Aesthetics

Form also includes aesthetic choices. It is helpful in designing masks to understand some basic visual vocabulary. The **Elements of design**, which are line, shape, volume, value, color, and texture, are the building blocks of design. The **Principles of composition**, including balance, symmetry, proportion/scale, emphasis, rhythm, and harmony suggest ways to combine them. Elements and principles of design provoke inherent responses in the viewer.

FIGURE 5.7 *Drawing of mask forms*

Consider how a line might express calm, power, humor, or craziness. How might shape do the same? And three-dimensional forms? We tend to perceive strong vertical and horizontal, rectilinear and cylindrical shapes as powerful and stable. We often ascribe romance and calmness to gradual curves, while tight spirals and circles

BOX 5.4 ELEMENTS OF DESIGN AND PRINCIPLES OF COMPOSITION

The **elements of design** are the building blocks of design. The **principles of composition** suggest ways to combine them. Elements and principles of design provoke inherent responses in the viewer.

Elements of Design

Line – a connection of two or more points that draw the eye from one place to another. Line has properties of length, orientation, path, width, porosity, and continuity.

Shape – a two-dimensional surface made of a connected line/lines such as a circle or square. Shapes can be rectilinear, curvilinear, geometric, biomorphic, or symbolic.

Form – a three-dimensional space, also referred to as Mass (suggests weight) and Volume (empty space). Three dimensional forms have weight, volume, and the properties of line and shape.

Value – inherent lightness or darkness, measured from white to black in tints, tones, and shades. Value is a scale of light/dark from white to black.

Color – the hue or name by which we identify it, such as red, rose, brick, and maroon.

Texture – dimensional or representational surface qualities, such as smooth, rough, sticky, and spotted. Textures are dimensional or apparent surface properties.

Principles of Design

Balance – an arrangement of elements that has equal visual distribution of weight; it may or may not be symmetrical. Balance may be achieved with symmetry along an axis, or by contrasting elements asymmetrically, radially, or in a grid.

Symmetry – an even distribution of elements along a plane or line; Bilateral symmetry (like a mirror image) is common in faces.

Proportion/Scale – relative size of elements to each other or a whole. Proportion is based on both what is familiar and what is aesthetically pleasing and can be manipulated for effect.

Emphasis – visual dominance, focus. Emphasis is achieved through placement, or by contrasting elements such as size, value, color, or shape.

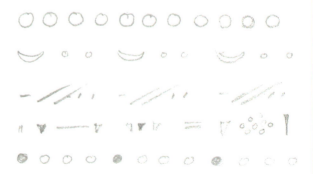

> *Rhythm* – a discernable pattern of elements. Rhythms can be regular or syncopated, simple or complex.
>
> *Harmony* – the principle of using elements in an aesthetically pleasing or effective way. Harmony is achieved when the visual impact effectively conveys meaning.

are often humorous, and irregular, tight, changing figures may be unsettling. Angular lines and forms are dramatic, unpredictable, holding tension. Note how even the simple lines and forms of larval masks prompt an emotional response.

We respond to texture emotionally also – such as considering soft, smooth surfaces to be soothing, slimy or slick to be uneasy, metallic to be impenetrable, and rough, prickly, or gritty ones to be irritating. Color also evokes a strong response, both physically (human physiology responds to red by increasing pulse and respiration and dilating pupils) and culturally (by ascribing symbolic meaning to color). How we arrange elements also creates a response. Bilateral symmetry is stable and predictable, while extreme asymmetry or disproportion in a mask can be unsettling. The scale of the head to the body can suggest age, species, and grace, and the proportion of the features also may suggest character and a

FIGURE 5.9(A AND B) *Color comparison of neutral masks by the author (paper) and David Knezz (neoprene)*

sense of normalcy, wonder, or the grotesque. The rhythm of the features helps direct our eyes to a focal point. In good design, the harmony of elements, and their corollary, variety, create a unified image.

Form: Rhythmic Coordination

Artist W.T. Benda offered both practical and aesthetic guidance to making effective masks. He maintained that the meaning of the mask is most important and recognized

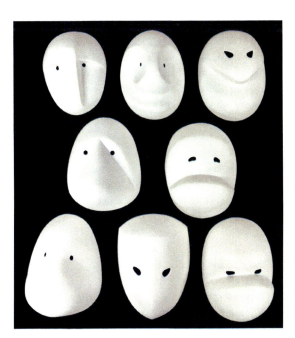

FIGURE 5.8 *Larval masks by Strangeface Masks. Photo by Russell Dean*

never-ending sources of inspiration, including exaggerated anatomy, extravagant fantasy, feminine beauty, tremendous satire, and animal species. Whatever the choice of subject or style, symbolic or direct, he stressed that design must begin with persistent and introspective study of nature. To be impressive and stir the soul, he advised that one must intensify the quality of the mask. "The simplest and most usual [masks] are ... derived from observation and comparison of human faces, which just need to be intensified, simplified, and stylized to become masks."[7] This goal could be achieved by applying the principles of design, which he referred to as **rhythmic coordination**. He wrote:

> *If a single feature or peculiarity is the theme, "the rest of the face shall be logically developed according to all the principles of rhythm and coordination. Its lines must find support and balance in their rhythmic continuity through all parts of the face in order to achieve harmonious ensemble and semblance of life."* [8]

FIGURE 5.10 Benda's rhythmic coordination as illustrated in *Masks* (1944)

BOX 5.5 WLADYSLAW TEODOR BENDA

Wladyslaw T. Benda (1873–1948) emigrated from Poland to the United States at the age of 25. Trained in engineering and fine arts, he soon secured work as a scenic painter and props artist in California[9] with the help of his aunt, Helena Modjeska, a noted Shakespearean actress. This theatrical beginning remained influential. In 1905, he relocated to New York City to continue his education and to begin work as an illustrator for a variety of popular magazines. While he made his living as a prolific artist and illustrator, his remarkably diverse skill set included mask making. He created beautiful paper mache masks for entertainment, performance, and personal artistic pleasure.

Benda recalls his own interest in making things of paper, and jumping in blind to create his first "false face" for a masquerade party in 1914.[10] He later told the *Ladies Home Journal*, "I made one by gluing together variously shaped pieces of heavy wrapping paper."[11] Benda threw the mask away at the end of night but recovered it the next morning and reconstructed it over "30 odd evenings" to become the Blue Demon wall hanging. Hooked, he created a dozen more masks over the next four years and was on his way.

Initially the masks were worn for his own delight, then at parties in his apartment by his wife, friends, and daughters. His masks were eventually photographed and exhibited in *Vanity Fair* magazine. Their display was followed by a private club performance, and eventually dance and theatre events, including commissioned pieces by playwrights Noel Coward and Eugene O'Neill.[12] His exotic beauties masks were worn by models in fashion spreads. Benda developed a reputation as a mask expert and published a book on mask making in 1944. In it, Benda expressed delight over the common attributes of all masks, including "the element of mystery wherewith they are endowed; the illusions they can produce; and the psychological effect they have on the human soul."[13]

Benda describes mask making as an "arduous task" that requires choosing an impressive subject, visualizing it clearly, planning how to make it, and the laborious and complicated work of doing it. The artist must attend not only to inspirational research, but also to:

- Esthetic and practical considerations
- Exterior and interior surfaces
- Expressing the Character and fitting the wearer
- Choosing materials that are not only thin and light but also strong and durable

He expresses a preference for "hard, unbleached paper, glued in tightly compressed layers, reinforced with stout and stiff brass wire, protected from atmospheric action by coats of impermeable varnishes, and painted with oil colors."[14] Over time, he developed four techniques for constructing paper masks; each took weeks or months to create.

1. *Direct freehand method*: constructed with paper without a mold: he built a paper framework shape, wired it, and then built up about 15 layers to form the basic structure. Then he carved out depressions (reinforcing those areas from the reverse) and added layers to increase the topography of the face. When finished, he added layers inside to reach a total of 25.
2. *Mold Method*: he sculpted a clay model, poured a plaster of Paris negative mold, and made sections of paper mache, which he then joined together: he noted that the paper mache shrinks as it dries, creating distortion, so needed to be done in sections, then combined to still fit the mold.
3. *Armature Method*: a bamboo or wire frame was constructed, then covered with "walls" of paper to form the planes of the mask. This technique was often used for larger masks.
4. *Pattern Method*: complex patterns were drafted, cut of Bristol board (like heavy cardstock), and joined together with paper strips.

For all the masks, when the form was sturdy enough and showed no weak spots, the layers of paper were sanded, painted, lacquered, and powdered. Benda also finished the insides with gold leaf and lacquer to protect

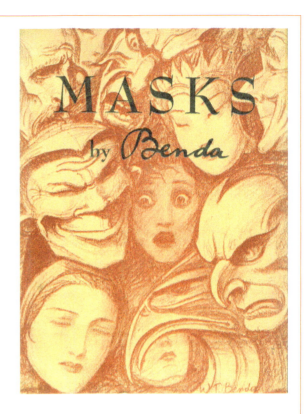

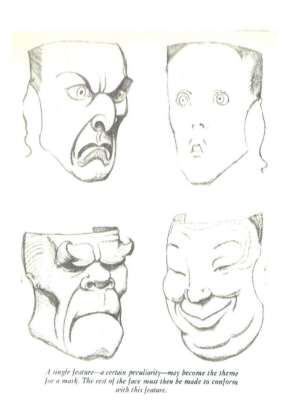

A single feature—a certain peculiarity—may become the theme for a mask. The rest of the face must then be made to conform with this feature.

Pattern for cut-out parts for a mask made of cardboard.

the mask from moisture, facial oils, and makeup. Often he decorated the inside as well.

Benda's work inspired performers and artists of his age and continues to impress generations of mask makers a century later. Benda died of a heart attack at age 75, surrounded by his masks while backstage preparing to give a mask demonstration.[15] His observation of our fascination with masks holds true today.

> I have not yet met any people, old or young, simple or cultured, serious or frivolous, artist or laymen, who are not keenly interested in masks if they have the opportunity to get acquainted with them. They may be impressed in various ways; some of them seeing masks in action may derive purely esthetic satisfaction. To others, masks give peculiar thrills which they are unable to explain even to themselves. Still others, with super-sensitive nerves, either fall in ecstasy or are frightened out of their wits; but none of them can remain indifferent.[16]

This process of distillation and analysis allows us to see characters more clearly and poignantly.

When designing masks, understanding how elements and principles of design work helps the designer create effective characters.

Remember that the mask will ultimately be connected to a body. These innate responses to form are felt both by the audience viewing the mask and the performer wearing it. You may have already experienced this in putting on a mask and feeling the urge to stand or move in a specific way. Keith Johnstone observed:

> Physical traits of the masks provoke similar responses in multiple users. For example, [a] flat forehead and wide spaced eyes trigger parental feelings in observers and a sense of wonder in the mask. Eyes which are not level convey a lopsided feeling which extends into a characteristic twisting movement in her gait. Executioner masks of soft black leather with small eye holes consistently provoke aggressive behavior. Long pointy red- nosed half masks with fluffy wigs or hats inevitably inspired happy, jabbering, quick, independent characters. And using little "men" masks with small moustaches, round eyes and noses, paired with overalls and hats led to a lot of vertical hat lifts, arms tight to body, small rocking steps, and grinning.[17]

Similarly, Sartori asserted: for the actor, "I must tune my body to the faces of the sullen old man until it becomes the body of that sour old soul. It can't be any other way. Every mask is a tyrannical master, constraining the actor to shape himself in its image. Only in this way can the mask come to life on the stage."[18]

Process: Sketching

Having established the functions of the mask, completed research, and decided on the practical aspects of the form, the designer begins to sketch or model the design. I often have in mind how the elements and principles will apply to the look of the mask. It's also important to have a sense of how the character will move. Imagine yourself as the character: stand up, make your face like the mask you imagine, move around a bit. How is your body positioned? Where is

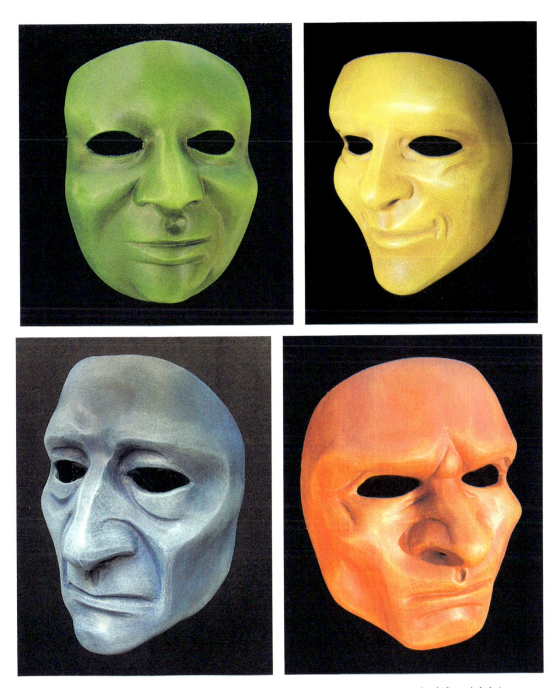

FIGURE 5.11 (A–D) *Masks based on the four temperaments by Mike Chase: phlegmatic, sanguine, melancholic, and choleric*

the energy coming from? How is your spine shaped? Your weight balanced? What is leading as you move? Your hips? Gut? Chest? How is your head positioned? Looking up or down? Tilted to side? What expression are you wearing? What emotions do you feel as you make the mask's face?

Begin to sketch the body position – try to capture in gesture the positions of the spine, shoulders, hips, and limbs, and the angle of the head. Keep the drawing loose; strengthen the parts you like, but don't bother to erase.

Then focus on drawing the head – capturing the angle and tilt, overall shape and line, size and shape of features. Again, strengthen lines you like, ignore ones that are unsatisfying. Be sure to consider where the mask meets the face. Sketch profile view(s) also, and from above or below if you can. Some designers use colored sketches to communicate what the mask will look like, and sculpt the prototype from the rendering. Others go on to create a maquette.

FIGURE 5.12(A) *Rosie, who cheerfully leads with her nose*

FIGURE 5.12(B) *Energetic yellow mask which often plays in a monkey- or cat-like manner*

FIGURE 5.12(C) *The mouth breather*

FIGURE 5.13(A) *Mask sketch by Bernardo Rey for Puntilla (Brecht)*

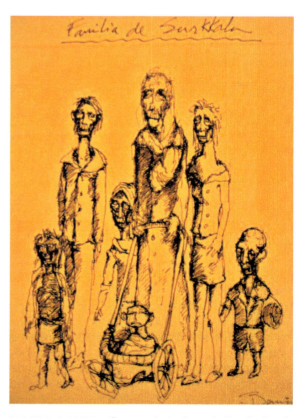

FIGURE 5.13(B) *Group study by Bernardo Rey for Puntilla (Brecht)*

FIGURE 5.13(C) *Clay sculpt for Puntilla (Brecht) by Bernardo Rey*

Process: Maquette

A ***maquette*** is a three-dimensional sketch – in this case from clay. It allows you to put your sketched ideas into a form which you can maneuver to see how it is reading as a character. It is best to work quickly without overthinking it. Your research will help guide you. This is how Russell Dean of Strangeface Theatre Company approaches making the maquette:

- Begin with a fist sized ball of clay.
- Set the essential shape of the head/face (Squared? Heart shaped? Round? Pear shaped?).
- Press eye sockets into the ball of clay, just above the horizontal center.
- Add a nose – big enough to create a profile.
- Add and quickly join two small spheres for eyeballs.
- Poke a pupil into each eyeball (Eieeuwww).
- Cut a slit for the mouth, a little below halfway between the eyes and chin (Taadaaaa! It's a face!).
- Add brows – a little higher than in the real world. And eyelids.
- Add ears – not too far forward. Include a hairstyle. It doesn't need precise details.

- Don't worry too much about perfection. That's later.
- Play with lifting, lowering, curving, angling, and straightening the lines of the face.
- Perhaps include nasolabial folds from the nose toward the sides of the mouth, adding jowls, forehead wrinkles, or adding to or hollowing the cheeks.
- Rotate the maquette in your hands as you work, looking at the expression from different angles.
- If you want to change something, do. When you are content that there are expressive qualities, and the character is a person with a story, stop!

The maquette is not intended as a final model, but as a dimensional form of the research and gesture sketches. Remain playful! It will help you transition to the next step, sculpting a full-scale model.

BOX 5.6 PROFILE: RUSSELL DEAN

Russell Dean is a freelance mask designer and creator, as well as a writer, director, performer, project manager, and facilitator. Russell is the Artistic Director of Strangeface Theatre Company, and he designs and makes commissions and box sets of masks for schools, groups, and other artists, including Vamos Theatre Company, Bootworks, and Mick Barnfather. He has developed a reputation for being one of England's leading mask makers and is regularly invited to lead workshops in mask making and performance.

Russell is dynamic in exploring the psychology of masks. His TEDx talk on Puppets and Perception, referred to in Chapter 1, explains our own brain's response to puppets and masks. As a designer, he describes the value of being able to "play against the mask" (play the countermask). He loves to put in the different qualities of a character's temperament and experiences and brings asymmetry to allow a variety of expressions in his character masks. Just as real people have complex identities, his characters are capable of amazing breadth.

Also, he notes, masks are big! Larger than life! Making masks is something like fathering a child: you give it life, tend to it, care for it – then it goes off and does its own thing!

FIGURE 5.14 *Maquettes by Russell Dean*

Process: Sculpting the Form in Clay

This is the transitional point to making the mask. It is included here because it incorporates design principles. Here are some general guidelines for getting started. Begin with a life cast of the actor if possible to ensure proper eyehole placement, nose size, depth of skull, etc. This is especially important for half masks such as in Commedia dell'Arte, where the face must fit the mask at the eyes and edges. If you don't have the means to do a life cast of the performer, work with a similar sized form and use calipers to measure relative size and placement of features. Build up the form to match key face points. Chapter 6 offers some options to working from a life cast.

A caveat here – while you can make a mask directly from a facial cast, it is important to understand that this can be difficult to play and less than satisfying to see. Toby Wilsher specifically cautions

> *Under no circumstances should this cast be itself used as the template for a mask. The mask is required to be larger - or smaller as in Noh theatre - than the actor's face. An exact representation of the actor's own face would render the mask dead. There is no breathing space, no transforming space.*[19]

Choose the clay: plasticine is oil based and does not dry out so is suitable for a longer working period and many changes. Water-based clay must be kept moist, misted occasionally, and covered w/damp paper towel or cloth and plastic between sessions. Avoid sulfur-based clays, especially if planning to use silicon, as it interferes with the curing process.

Anchor the face form to a board with clay, ensuring there's enough depth to go at least an inch beyond the edge

FIGURE 5.15 *Rough sculpt in clay by Bernardo Rey*

FIGURE 5.16 *Mask sculpt prepared for casting*

of your finished mask. This helps you to see it from multiple angles while working and gives a margin for finishing.

Work the overall shape and planes, then clarify the features and finally details. You may work with your hands for larger areas, but include tools for smoothing areas and creating detail too fine for fingers. Use calipers to check symmetry as needed both during sculpting and drawing finish lines. A damp sponge is useful for wiping away tool marks.

Look at the mask from all sides, including from some distance. Masks rarely work well in spaces where the audience is closer than eight feet, so it is good to make sure the mask reads from the distance and lighting conditions expected in performance.

DESIGNING THE DETAILS

We introduced the concepts of a live mask and of countermask. How do you achieve that? Practice. Sorry, there is no foolproof formula. It's a combination of shape, planes, detail, anatomy, expressions, fit, and a less quantifiable element of mystery, luck, and experience. Below are some ideas to pay attention to as you work.

First of all, the design must apply understanding of the anatomy of the person/animal/character. For half and partial masks, which should move with the face, they are most effective when they grow from the performer's face. The more speaking required and the more natural the style, the more important is a custom fit. To catch the light and be alive, Bernardo Rey emphasizes the precision of clear planes. We will invest time in looking at proportion, shape, facial features, and expression, as well as considering symmetry, rhythmic coordination, countermask, and styles.

Stature and Proportion

W.T. Benda noted that masks create illusion, not only of identity and expression, but also of stature and proportion. As human heads are relatively consistent in size, proportion is innately judged by it: tall people are eight heads tall, short adults may be just seven heads tall, tweens six heads, children five heads, etc.[20] A designer can create the illusion of youth with an oversized head and trigger our innate empathy toward smaller beings. This can be subtle or have a grotesque effect. In contrast, a smaller scale mask can lend elements of grace to a figure by seeming to elongate the limbs. A mask that is identical to the face in scale is harder to make come alive – it struggles to capture the magic of transformation. Changing the placement of the mask on the body can also create an arresting effect.

Size also affects movement. The performer should be able to turn their head left and right, up and down, to move and look in all directions. The designer plans how to balance the mask, and whether the mask's eyes are aligned with the performer's, or if the performer will see through the sides of the nose, mouth, or neck.

FIGURE 5.17 *Rob Faust performs with an alternate mask placement*

Shape

The overall shape of the face and features, including the silhouette, profile, and other angled views, begins to set the anatomy. Be deliberate about where the mask edges are:

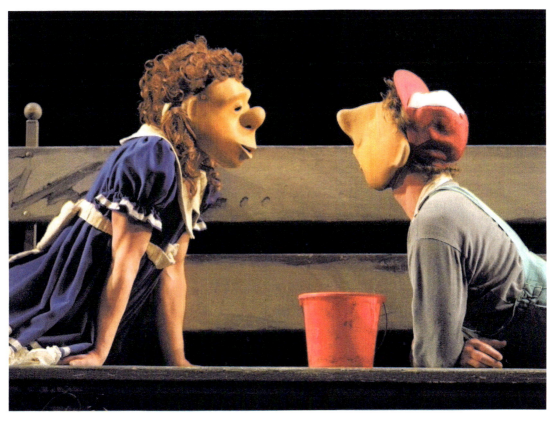

FIGURE 5.18 *Strong children's profiles by Mike Aufenfehld for Habbe & Meik's* Pipifaxen, *performed by Hartmut Ehrenfeld and Michael Aufenfehn*

FAMILIE FLÖZ HOTEL PARADISO FOTO: MICHAEL VOGEL

FIGURE 5.19 *These character masks from* Hotel Paradiso *by Familie Flöz show different face shapes*

how much around the jaw, how close to the ear, and relative to the hairline. Create a convincing and attractive place for the resolution of the cheek line against the face. It is important to maintain (or exaggerate) the depth of the face. A distinctive profile is important because it allows the figure to be recognized from different perspectives.[21] One mistake some beginners make is to flatten the face. Besides failing to fit the actor's face well, it does not read well in different positions or from different viewpoints. Viewing the mask from all directions as you build it will help avoid this problem. Eye sockets recess from the cheeks, and forehead, but eyeballs project from the sockets. Noses are made of a wedge shape with rounded nares, all of which projects from the plane of the skull. Chins may project or recede from the curve of the face. Lips have volume. Learn to see these shapes and relationships. Creating clear planes helps the mask read at a distance.

In addition to setting the anatomy of the mask, the shape sets our overall emotional response. We begin to interpret character through our response to visual elements – rectilinear conveying power, while curves are feminine, youthful, sensual, and so forth. Shapes of features also provoke reactions – angled or heavy or rounded features convey meaning and may support or contrast the overall shape of the mask.

Features

Eyes bring life to the mask. Since we perceive eyes as a critical area of communication and life, it is an interesting paradox that the hole through which the wearer can actually see does not disturb the life-like appearance. Benda addresses this paradox. In reality, Benda reminds us that the human brain fills in what it expects to see. "It is the framing of the eyes that gives them character and expression, while the eyeballs by themselves have neither, for they are all alike; they can therefore be omitted from the mask without being missed."[22] Benda believed that a fixed eye on a mask is more difficult, for its stare does not cooperate with performance.[23] In actuality, many masks include a fixed eye (rendering the lids and whites of the eye, and sometimes the pupil also) and are still effective in performance because of the quality of expression in the mask and the performance.

For practical purposes, they must clear the lashes and allow sight. Design wise, there are many choices. Eyes may or may not

- align with or show the performer's eyes
- use an almond-shaped opening to incorporate the actor's eye in a more realistic way

Masks by Design 149

FIGURE 5.20(A) *Blind "Tiresius aux antennae" by Werner Strub with gauze eyes (photo by Giorgio Skory)*

FIGURE 5.20(B) *Apollo masks with eyes screened to provide the illusion of a vase figure come to life*

- leave a small hole or slit with a fixed eye sculpted into the mask to emphasize theatricality and/or expression
- screen the opening with a sheer fabric, either to minimize the visual discrepancy between mask and skin (typical if the eye holes are very large, or not aligned with the performer's) or to maintain an illusion, such as a statue come to life, or create a sense of mystery by hiding the eyes

Larger eyes pull more focus and call for larger physical response in performance. Russell Dean's character masks, which are often for comic characters, include rendered eyes that pop out, connecting to the nose and projecting the face forward, demanding our attention. Looking at the Vamos ones, note how the eyes have focus and are reinforced by the brows and other dimensional lines – similar to Benda's principles of rhythmic coordination.

FIGURE 5.21 *Mask set by Russell Dean and Strangeface Masks for Vamos Theatre*

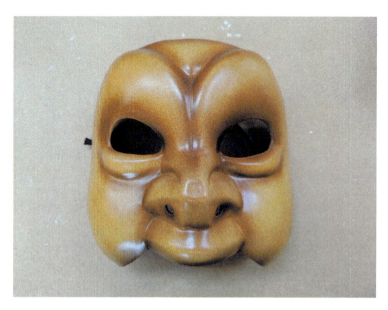

FIGURE 5.22(A)   *Round-cheeked Columbina mask by Russell Dean*

Eyebrows are incredibly expressive. Normally the mask will include a distinct change of plane at the brow to frame the eye socket. The angle, size, shape, and texture of the brows complement the line, depth, and plane of the forehead. They frame the size, shape, angle, and depth of the eyes. The texture may be painted or dimensional.

Cheeks express age, humor, and health. They complete the frame of the eye and connect the nose with the edge of the mask. Where do the cheeks lay and end? Droopy jowls? Or high and tight? Upward or downward curve? Full or hollow?

Mouths are directly related to the function of the mask. First, and most importantly, will it speak? Be barely open and poised to speak? or closed and silent? Toby Wilsher cautions designers to avoid the sense of the mask making noise, as by an open mouth, especially if the audience will not hear it.[24] However, a small opening can help

FIGURE 5.22(B)   *A hollow-cheeked Streha by Russell Dean*

FIGURE 5.23(A)   *Half smirk by Rob Faust*

FIGURE 5.23(B)   *Commedia dell'Arte half mask by Giancarlo Santelli*

FIGURE 5.23(C)   *Greek Comic Slave by David Knezz*

with respiration. If the mouth is gaping as in some Greek masks, should it remain open to hear better and see the mouth within, or be screened? Some full masks are designed with space between the head of the wearer and the mask to create a resonance chamber. On half masks, the properly aligned upper lip is part of the gestural expression, which can be very expressive, pouting, grinning, or grimacing. Neutral masks need balance, while characters require some asymmetry. The expressive potential of the mouth is fantastic, whether open or closed.

Noses provide a superb opportunity for defining character. They are in a dominant position, come in many shapes, and have great potential for exaggeration. Is the line of the nose straight or crooked? Long or short, wide or narrow? Its profile curved, straight, or angled? Its movement scrunched or flared? The line of the nose leads the movement of our eye, and of the character's movement.

Deborah Hunt notes that "The noses of the half masks are very important. Because the mask itself is relatively small, the nose is predominant and its profile important."[25] Russell Dean likes to make masks with big noses that pull attention to the face and help distinguish the masks in profile. The protruding proboscis gives them a better playing range, both by contrasting other masks, and by allowing them to play more to the side as well as to the front.[26] On a practical level, leaving some internal space around the performer's nose allows for better respiration and resonance.

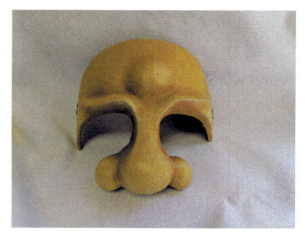
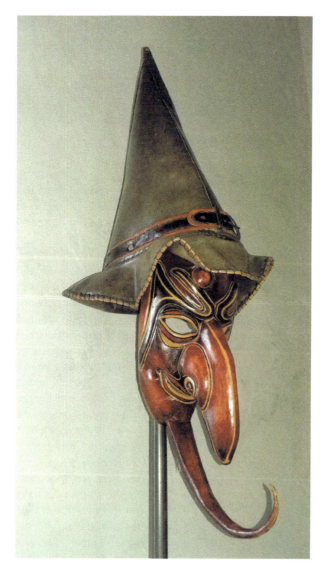

FIGURE 5.24 (A–C) *Prominent nosed masks by Rey, Becker, and DeMarchi*

Masks by Design 153

FIGURE 5.25 *Profile of a mask by Russell Dean*

Ears. You may need ears, usually two, halfway back on head – just in front of the performer's ears for humanesque masks. They usually align with the eye from the top to the base of the nose. Ears help extend the range of motions for the audience to read the mask, support the scale of the mask, which is usually bigger than face (smaller, such as Noh, don't have ears added), and bridge the real and magical by removing a real/not real divide.

Chins and Jaws usually form the shape of the lower mask and profile. Their shape is an effective part of the overall design effect, as well as offering interesting possibilities for expressing age and character.

Details are added to the planes and features of the face. These may include lines to indicate the change of a plane – such as a nasolabial fold, crow's feet, or forehead wrinkles to indicate age or expression – or to add character features such as a scar or Arlecchino's wart. Details may also include the addition of textures – smoothing youthful skin, scaling a dragon, or adding peeled flesh to a zombie. Color and value, added later, also support the complete design by adding realistic or emotional coloring, using highlight and shadow to emphasize the features, and sometimes imitating makeup or other decorative elements.

FIGURE 5.26(A) *Ears added to leather helmet mask for Karl in Woyzeck, designed by Bernardo Rey*

FIGURE 5.26(B) *Phra Ram mask from Khon drama of Thailand*

FIGURE 5.27(B) *Hahoe mask of Yangban with hinged jaw*

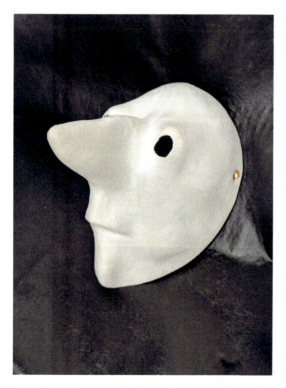

FIGURE 5.27(A) *A receding chin on "Charles" by Craig Jacob-Brown*

FIGURE 5.27(C) *Mexican Day of the Dead Mask; carved and painted wood*

FIGURE 5.28(A) *Dimensional texture carved into the sculpt*

FIGURE 5.28(B) *Painted texture on a clown mask*

Symmetry: We perceive faces as being evenly divided along a vertical plane down the center of the face. When sculpting, use calipers to check symmetry especially if important to the mask's neutrality, youth, or concept of beauty. In reality, people's faces and bodies are not perfectly symmetrical. In fact, studies have shown that while we are attracted to symmetry, the faces that we find most beautiful and interesting are not actually the most symmetrical. Also, despite our youth focused culture, faces and masks are often more interesting when they reflect some age. We are certainly prone to asymmetrical expressions as well: the dubious cocking of one eyebrow, the flirtatious wink, a slight smirk of amusement, or the flared nare of a sneer. Russell Dean emphasizes the importance of multiple things going on. As you work, include some slight asymmetry. Whether subtle or exaggerated, it is more interesting.

A little of this asymmetry is not unwelcome in presenting character. It is important to balance the mask's features, but it is not always the intent to make them bilaterally symmetrical (a mirror image). Symmetry can help them seem realistic, and a little asymmetry can help them develop a more alive, playable character. Too much, however, can backfire. "A grossly asymmetrical mask will portray different expressions at different angles. This greatly complicates character portrayal, limiting the actor and confusing the audience."[27]

Expression is the goal and result of careful sculpting. Expression provides emotional and physical context for character: "The facial expression can determine the kind of breath, rhythm, sound, gesture, and body architecture that arises."[28] Ideally, the mask will be capable of more than one expression. There is a magical moment in performance where a static mask may seem to change expressions, both because a mask is "endowed with delicate nuance and subtle complexes of expressions"[29] and because the wearer's body language gives us information which we translate to the mask. This duality is expressed by the idea of countermask.

Countermask literally means against the mask. The term refers to the potential multiplicity of expression both in the design of the mask and the performance with it by the actor. We understand this is a natural part of our identities: we may present one "face" to the world but feel or act differently underneath. Feigned interest in someone's saga, apparent calm (or bravery) in the face of danger, and the fine art of faux praise are examples of this. A good mask can take on the body language of the performer and appear to change expression. This duality/paradox is a key to its effectiveness. The countermask must be played by the actor, but to be successful the mask must have the potential to be perceived in more than one way. This is a part of what we

FIGURE 5.28(C–F) *The creative artist at threadstories uses traditional knitting, crochet, and knot work to create masks. They are meticulously crafted to be used in performance; as they move, we, as spectators, are delighted by their animation, seeing the changing expressions of the masks, and at times the wearer underneath. Threadstories uses both video and photographs to capture nuanced expressions and to explore how we present ourselves within the erosion of privacy in our digital age. (c) Breath, textile object, 2020, video still; (d) persona 1, threadstories, 2021; (e) the Watchers and the Watched, textile object, 2020; (f) persona 9, threadstories, 2021*

FIGURE 5.28(G) *A stitched fabric mask for Faustus by Werner Strub (photo by Giorgio Skory)*

define as a "live mask." Many mask artists and performers address this concept.

Lecoq articulated that masks need the countermask to allow possibilities within each mask for multiple interpretations by different people. Rolfe explains, "A mask, or an individual, makes a certain impression on sight. When subsequent events or closer acquaintance give lie to that impression, when we learn that things are not always what they seem, we are in the presence of mask and countermask." [30] Wilsher adds "if it can be seen to communicate a positive and a negative thought, the chances are it will be able to show the ambiguities which lie between. A good mask will be brought to life differently by every wearer." [31]

Mike Chase suggests giving masks a title with a dichotomy, such as timid butcher, devious saint, sadistic doctor, defeated

FIGURE 5.29 *Toby Wilsher's starter set is deceptively simple, each mask is designed to have more than one aspect in performance*

devil, or saintly assassin.³² This practice is useful for both the designer and the performer who want to explore the depths of countermask.

A strong dichotomy in the mask allows for a wider playable range and surprise when the expression "changes" and the audience perceives that the mask is actually animated.

Libby Appel's emotional masks were designed with this principle in mind, giving actors freedom to respond and grow in training. A caveat to the counter mask, however: because the actor must respond to what is captured and expressed in the mask, too much variation can be difficult to synthesize into a wholistic character and performance.

A note on **undercuts**: this is when an area of the mask curves back on itself – such as a strongly hooked, beaky nose. These can be difficult to cast and release. If your design features undercuts, it may be better to use a two-piece (or more) casting.

Directions for creating masks are provided in Chapter 6. It is wise to do a quick mask mockup to check your work before investing time and materials into a finished product. A few layers of paper mache can be done quickly over the clay form and tried on the actor to check for effective design and fit. Be prepared to do revisions to your

FIGURE 5.30 *Hartmut Ehrenfeld and Michael Aufenfehn play the strong countermasks as* Habbe und Meik

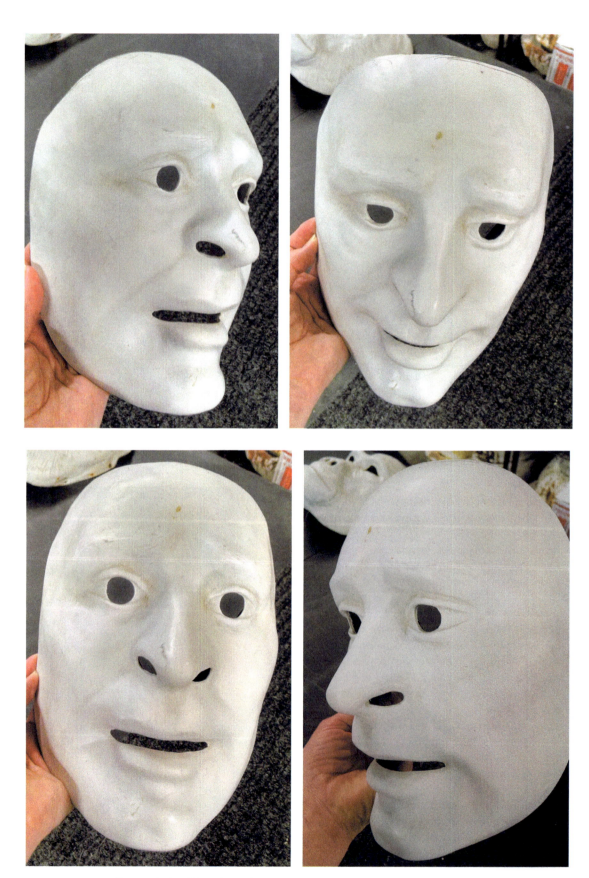

FIGURE 5.31 (A–D) *This mask by David Knezz has a subtle but effective countermask*

STYLES

As a designer, you will be called on to create different styles of masks. Understanding the mask's function is absolutely necessary to create effectively within any style. Below are some reminders of some style expectations. You may limit the design to essential elements, or work in realistic detail, deliberate exaggeration, or subconscious metaphor. Within a production, you will probably want some homogeneity of style so none stands apart from the "family." There are exceptions of course, as in Dave McKean's and Neil Gaiman's film *MirrorMask* where a variety of styles and forms elucidate the different worlds and forces at work in the story.

Neutral/Universal

For the neutral mask, the principle of "less is more" applies equally to design and to movement work: both strive to be efficient, necessary, and essential. The neutral mask strives to present what is universally and internally human, without exhibiting any reaction or attitude.

Greek sculptors strove to capture the essence of humanity and beauty by removing all traces of resemblance to any individual: his experience, personal physical attributes, and ingrained expressions. They aimed "to purge from the individual all that belongs only to him. In this way their works came to be like some subtle extract or essence, almost like pure thought or ideas, and hence the breadth of humanity in them."[34]

FIGURE 5.32 *Strong curves, such as the one under this nose, create undercuts which may be difficult to release from a rigid cast*

sculpt if the mask is not working, either because of a fit/comfort issue, the style/face isn't reading, or you can't see it in given environment/light. When creating new masks for new characters, it is important to have time to respond to the development of the character and piece by creating a working mask.

BOX 5.7 PROFILE: ROB FAUST

Rob Faust is a stand-up physical theatre performer and mask artist who brings insight to audiences of all ages through joy and humor.

THE POWER OF MASKS

Over the years I have become increasingly interested in sculpting ambiguity into the features of my masks. Although masks often have a dominant expression, one mask can project different attitudes and emotions, shifting with changes of the spine and gestures of the wearer. The effect on audiences of these metamorphoses is often pre-conscious, bypassing the brain and going straight to the heart…or to the funny bone. Having grown up in the carnival culture of New Orleans, fun and play are important components of my work.

I make masks that emphasize attitude and emotion rather than form, color, symbolism or ritual. A mask's potential to come alive is always paramount, whether it's serious, humorous, or bizarre. Masks are pregnant with potential while hanging passively on the wall, but it's when they're off the wall and on the body that their transformative power is fully revealed.[33]

Rob Faust

Amleto Sartori labored to create such a mask, which has been prized in Euro-American culture as an ideal representation of these qualities. Sartori asserted that creating the neutral mask was "the most difficult task I have ever undertaken."[35] He explained: "The neutral mask is the exact opposite of the expressive mask. It expresses absolutely nothing. It may be masculine or feminine, but its unique characteristic is the absence of connotated emotion. … Creating an emotional vacuum in a mask is not an easy task for the artist who must shape it, since he himself is subject to conditioning stemming from common experience. [like actors, mask makers are accustomed to being expressive] …A small stroke of the finger in the wrong way, a line cut a little too deeply, the cheek bones a little sharper than necessary, a light striking the mask in an unforeseen way - any one of these seemingly small details is enough to deprive the mask of its neutrality. It immediately assumes a character."[36]

Within the range of universal masks are variations of gender, scale, color, and ethnicity. Other neutral masks, including those of Argentinian Alfredo Iriarte create equally effective neutral masks in a more structurally diverse appearance. Common features of the neutral mask include open eyes, a relaxed mouth (as if poised to speak but not speaking), and ideally proportioned features. These qualities present a face ready for whatever comes next. Rolfe notes that performers in neutral masks hold themselves with a slightly elevated energy to distinguish from ordinary life.[37] That tension, energy, and potential are also necessary in design, as exhibited in balance and proportion.

The idea of capturing essential qualities is not limited to the universal mask. In addition to neutral masks used for training, many cultures employ their aesthetic form of essential beauty in masks. The female ko-omote masks of Noh theatre have this quality of neutrality and beauty.

Native North American traditions carve to an aesthetic of essential beauty rather than a realistic representation of life; in this way, their masks carry meaning through generations.

Larval, Emergent, or Basel masks focus on a simplified representation of eyes, nose, and sometimes a mouth. The characters tend to be primitive, young, simple, ready for development but not realistic or even necessarily human. Expected visual qualities include oversized scale, generalized, exaggerated features, and sometimes unrealistic placements. Some Basel masks are reduced to rounded forms with eyeholes. They usually have a flat, white texture suited to their simplicity and magic. Vicky Wright's Evolution Project used Basel style masks effectively to study the evolution of movement. She created anatomically proportioned larval masks for water-based and four-legged creatures and then explored how pre-human forms changed participants' body awareness, alignment, and movement.

FIGURE 5.33 *Neutral masks by Donato Sartori (leather)*

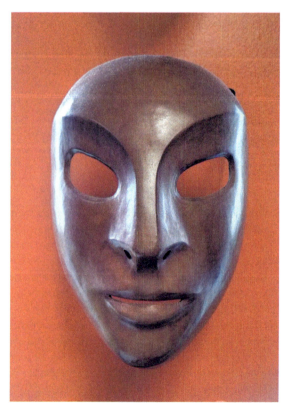

FIGURE 5.34 *Neutral mask by Alfredo Iriarte (leather)*

Masks by Design 161

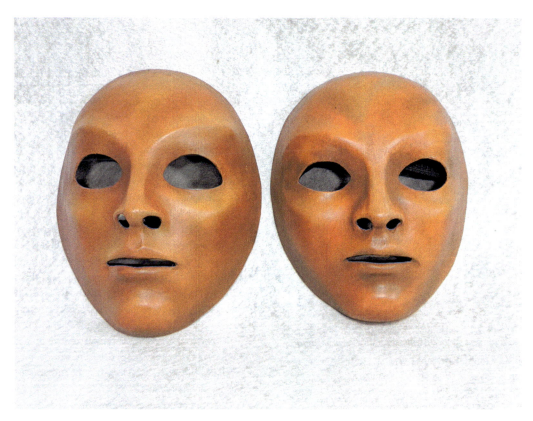

FIGURE 5.35 *Universal masks by David Knezz (Neoprene)*

FIGURE 5.36 *A set of Larval masks by Craig Jacob Brown*

BOX 5.8 PROFILE: VICKY WRIGHT

Vicky Wright is a mask maker, performer, educator, and a craniosacral and postural therapist working in London, England. As a physical therapist, she has studied a wide variety of body-based approaches to learning, including martial arts, acrobatics, yoga, breath work, Ayurveda, Structural Integration, and body energetics. Alongside physical learning, she trained at Helikos International School of Theatre Creation, Italy led by pedagogue Giovanni Fusetti training in Lecoq-based theatre movement, voice, devising, and in mask making with Matteo Destro. She is the founder of Making Faces Theatre, a company which uses science, mask, and theatre to study and teach embodied movement.

She likes the joy of surprise that masks bring, never knowing exactly what will happen. She is particularly interested in the intersection of body movement analysis with how masks can reveal information about the body and become a learning tool for the wearer. She explains that each of our bodies has within us different experiences that are part of our tissue structure as well as our energy and posture. Each mask will reflect the current sum of the wearer's body experience, health, energy, and emotion, and so unlock a deeper understanding of the body. For performers, this understanding can be used to create effective non-verbal communication.

> *The exploration of physical theatre through the medium of mask had shown me what transformative power they hold. Masks are an incredible tool for developing characters and telling a story, and the act of putting a mask on can transform an individual, a performer and an observer.*[38]

Vicky makes a variety of styles of masks, some from specific inspirations or commissioned characters, and others as a tool for research.

Curious about evolution of movement, Vicky Wright integrated several disciplines in her Evolution Project. Beginning with ten species from fish to man, she created a series of masks, accurately proportioned to fossil data and scaled to fit on a human head. These forms supported the impetus to discover water-based and quadrupedal movement. Participants explored different ways of moving, became aware of shifts in their senses, and discovered ways to bring the masks alive. By interweaving physical theatre with paleontology and the study of human movement, the masks enabled her group to embody, experience, and meet the animals in a new way. One clear observation was that as bipedal humans, we rely primarily on our eyes for information, so lead with our heads which can create postural stress. Practicing the earlier patterns of evolutionary movement brought a fuller body awareness and the potential to balance our movement better. Through the movement research, these masks not only opened an artistic doorway into our past but also provided an experiential tool in movement analysis enabling participants to really feel and find these subtler layers of movement within us all.

Going forward, she continues to develop new areas of mask research across the modalities of evolution, biological anthropology, anatomy, health, and vocality in exploring our humanness.

"Actors and dancers explore non-pedal, bipedal, and quadrupedal movement in a workshop with masks designed and created by Vicky Wright of Making Faces Theatre."

FIGURE 5.37 *Emotional masks in the Libby Appel style*

Libby Appel describes the **emotional** masks that she used as a teacher. They have more distinctly human features, but textures, colors, and proportions, which are life-like, but not realistic. Libby Appel discusses this duality of their appearance and function in *Mask Characterization, an Acting Process*.[39] She taught with a set of 25 unique, non-gendered celastic masks made by Paul Appel. She expresses the required qualities for this type of training mask: "The fundamental characteristic of these masks is their contrary and ambivalent qualities. They do not express any one type of person or emotion. The features are purposely contradictory (one side of the mouth may droop, while the other moves upward, the brow is worried and the chin is defiant, etc.). This allows great width in interpretation for the actor and prevents the development of character "types" or stereotypes. The masks provide maximum inspiration while imposing few limitations."[40] They had these attributes:

- Larger than life size
- Mouth opening covered with black gauze, to hide the actor's features
- Mouth large enough to permit sound and clear articulation
- Painted to give a highly textured effect with a rich but subtle mix of colors
- Primitive in style and expression
- Slightly grotesque and large

She continues, "In some ways, the mask may be likened to a script. It is designed by an artist (as a script is created by a playwright) who developed the faces out of his personal imagination. Like a script, the mask provides some boundaries and definitions, although it is a great deal more flexible. It is a reference point for the actor. It is far more comprehensive than a neutral mask and yet far less rigid than a preconceived character mask such as those used for Commedia dell'Arte."[41] The qualities of these masks are less suited for character work onstage, but help the performer find ways of working that can be applied to character development.

Character Masks bring additional specificity to the mask, capturing an individual persona. They present an individual, whether nearly realistic and subtle, an exaggerated stereotype, or grotesque buffoon. They bring all the expected human features in an artistic arrangement born out of selection and emphasis. Just like the playwright selects and arranges the parts of the story, the actor shows facets of the person in the role, and the designer selects appropriate costumes, the mask artist selects critical features to present. Bari Rolfe notes these additional components of a good character mask:[42]

- Features represent habitual expressions made of tensed and slack muscles.
- They can be ambiguous in sex, state of being, kind of person, and emotion.

- Characters have a sense of the world, some past experience, and expectations, plus a rhythm, stance, gesture, image, etc.

- When the wearer's features follow the expression of the mask, then the body follows the face.

Half Masks and partial masks are most effective when created to extend from the performer's face. This is easier when sculpting from a face cast of the performer and using a somewhat flexible material such as leather. Pay attention to how and where the edges of the mask meet the face, as well as the mask's eyes. In discussing Commedia dell'Arte masks, Amleto Sartori noted that Commedia looks at specifics of human characters, and requires the fit and features to be more closely related to real humanity. His experience showed that the best form is a soft, stable leather mask that "must fit like a glove."[43]

FIGURE 5.38(C)   *Character mask old man falling by Rob Faust*

FIGURE 5.38(A)   *Character masks by Jonathan Becker*

FIGURE 5.38(B)   *Character masks by Russell Dean for Vamos Theatre*

Grotesque: One strength of the performance mask is providing distance to address difficult or offensive topics. Humor is present in most mask work, even where characters are sympathetic – and where they are not. Mask design should match the level of humor. John Wright's book *Why is That Funny?* explores this question. He defines a spectrum of humor from parody to caricature to burlesque to buffoon. These steps take us from a gentle imitative rebuke to the unapologetic condemnation of the **grotesque**. At this extreme end of the humor scale, we find that the grotesque is too inhuman to be taken seriously. We are not only just horrified but also intrigued; there is something that creates a tension, attracting and repelling us in equal measure. The effect is neither tragic nor comic: when you find the grotesque, you must ask both what is horrible and what is beautiful about it.

Julie Taymor's *Fool's Fire* utilized immense masked characters – including body mask – to emphasize the grotesque in contrast to human characteristics, embodied in the characters of Hop-Frog and Tripetta, played by actors who have dwarfism.

Omar Porras incorporated prosthetic and static masks and makeup in many productions with Teatro Malandro. The range of character masks includes sublime and grotesque, often half masks, partial masks such as noses or chins, and body masks. Often the masks were added to scripted productions,

FIGURE 5.39 *Marco Luly in half mask of Arlecchino by Santelli (photo by kalyedoscope)*

such as *Don Quixote*, *The Visit*, and *Ubu Roi*. In each, the masks and costumes expanded both the humor and pathos of the characters.

One last thing: masks are theatrical. They require an expanded level of play by the actor. In addition, the mask must work with the costume. Full head and face masks generally have hair that completes the design of the head. For face masks, the transition from the edge of the mask to the face or hair calls attention to the artificial face, interrupting the illusion of one character. The designer should enable the full transition to masked character. How do you resolve this? Korean masks include a *t'alpo* (cloth) on the back to cover the performer's head, creating a neutral theatrical background. In Commedia, traditionally there is the little black hood called a *camauro*. Hats, wigs, and headdress are often part of the costume and serve to bridge the real and the mask. Big masks make the neck look absurdly skinny. A costume with a good collar, hood, or scarf improves the transition. For classwork, the performer's hair may be dressed to hide the edge of the mask. For performance, however, either a neutral cloth or a theatrical wig will be better at matching the scale and artificiality of the mask.

FIGURE 5.40 *Grotesque Mask of Leather with a stucco texture*

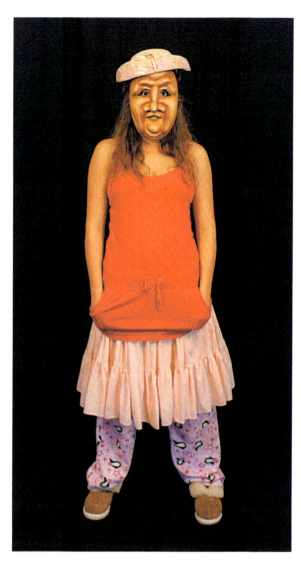

FIGURE 5.41 *Masks' characters are supported by wigs, hats, and costumes*

Remember to consider how a mask integrates with the character's body. Costume also must match function and style of mask, movement, character, and production. Neutral clothing allows the body to communicate freely with a neutral mask. Realistic clothing provides character clues for connecting with our world. Extreme costumes – such as the padded body mask – prepare us for the outlandish behavior of the grotesque.

Observe! Think! Practice! Learn from your mistakes.

Personal style is something that you develop as a result of thoughtful work. Don't worry about it. Do the best work you can. You got this.

PROJECTS FOR FURTHER STUDY

- Research a mask tradition, such as Topeng, Noh, or Commedia, or a mask artist/group, such as Family Flöz, Donato Sartori, Wladyslaw Benda, or Theatre Nogaku. What are/were the purposes of the masks? How did the material choice relate to the design? Describe the similarities between that artist's or genre's masks using visual vocabulary.

- Design a mask for a particular character of your choosing. (Do not copy an existing mask – but design one.) What is the appropriate size, form, and material? What other aesthetic decisions are necessary or optional? What research informs your design?
    - Superhero or arch villain
    - Element of nature (wind, water, fire, air, smoke, earth)
    - Season
    - Characterization from 7 Deadly Sins or 7 Cardinal Virtues

- Draw or sculpt a training mask for improvisation
    - A neutral face; try to eliminate racial preference and expression
    - An emergent mask in the Basel style
    - An emotional mask that incorporates more than one potential emotion

- Select a mask-making material and create a mask without preplanning, letting the material inspire you.

- Research and Design (on paper – over a headshot) a mask for a production, animal, allegory, or character that is integrated into the human face. Include a profile view.

- Note in examining the pictures closely, that there are many evolutions of the different Commedia characters – a clear demonstration of Donato Sartori's principles of knowing each mask before beginning and being precise to the character of that particular mask. Research a character from Commedia, and his roles in different productions. How do they differ? What should be the same to identify the character? Design a mask for a specific production/character/performer – incorporating design over images of the actor from different views.

- Research some expressive masks and diagram and describe the aesthetics in detail, including use of elements and principles of design, and biology/anatomy.

NOTES

1. Ching and Ching, *Faces of Your Soul*.
2. Corey, *The Mask of Reality*, 3.
3. Theatre Nohgaku website: Active Repertory. https://www.theatrenohgaku.org/
4. Blumenthal, Julie Taymor, *Playing With Fire*, 41.

5 The Commedia dell'Arte and the Masks of Amleto and Donato Sartori. Centro Maschere e Strutture Gestuali. Florence, Italy: La Casa Usher, 1980. Intro by Giorgio Strehler. Text by Alberto Marcia. Translated by Cynthia Baker, Anne Marie Speno, Brenda Porster, n.p.
6 Chase, Mike, *Mask: Making, Using and Performing the Four Temperaments*, 30.
7 Benda, *Masks*, 23.
8 Benda, 22–23.
9 Naversen, Ronald. "The Benda Mask." *TD&T* vol.46 No. 4 (Fall 2010) NY: USITT, 2010, 35.
10 Benda, Masks. 53.
11 Naversen, 36.
12 Naversen, 38.
13 Benda, Masks, fwd.
14 Benda, Masks, 31.
15 Naversen, 39.
16 Benda, Masks, 62
17 Keith Johnstone, *Improv*, 176–177.
18 Marcia, *The Commedia dell'Arte and the Masks of Amleto and Donato Sartori*, 1980, n.p.
19 Wilsher, *The Mask Handbook*, 163.
20 Benda, 3.
21 Dean, Russell, *Interview* May 24, 2019 Kent, England.
22 Benda, 5.
23 Benda, 5.
24 Wilsher, 164.
25 Hunt, Deborah, *Masks and Masked Faces*, 133.
26 Dean, Russell. *Interview*.
27 Mike Chase, 32.
28 Mike Chase, 91.
29 Benda, 4.
30 Rolfe, *Behind the Mask*, 33.
31 Wilsher, 164.
32 Chase, Mike, xiii.
33 Rob Faust, Artistic statement. Faustwork. https://faustwork.com/mask-art-for-sale/
Image courtesy of Rob Faust Masks
34 Walter Pater in Rolfe, 22.
35 Marcia/Sartori, n.p.
36 Marcia/Sartori n.p.
37 Rolfe, 20.
38 Wright, Vicky. https://makingfacestheatre.co.uk/2019/04/05/the-journey-so-far/
39 Appel, *Mask Characterization*, 4–5.
40 Appel, 4.
41 Appel, 5.
42 Rolfe, 28–30.
43 Sartori in Marcia, n.p.

SELECTED RESOURCES

Appel, Libby. *Mask Characterization: An Acting Process*. Carbondale, Illinois: Southern Illinois University Press, 1982.

Bell, Deborah. *Mask Makers and Their Craft: A Worldwide Study*. Jefferson, North Carolina: McFarland & Co, 2010.

Benda, Wladyslaw Teodor. *Masks*. New York: Watson Guptill, 1944.

Blumenthal, Eileen and Julie Taymor. *Julie Taymor: Playing with Fire*. New York: Harry N Abrams, 1995.

Chase, Mike. *Mask: Making, Using and Performing the Four Temperaments*. Gloucestershire: Hawthorn Press, 2017.

Corey, Irene. *The Mask of Reality: An Approach to Design for Theatre*. Anchorage, Kentucky: Anchorage Press, 1968.

Dean, Russell. Interview with the author, Kent, England. May 2019.

Hunt, Deborah. *Masks and Masked Faces: A Manual for the Construction of 22 Masks and Their Variations*. San Juan, Puerto Rico: Maskhunt Motions, 2013.

Johnstone, Keith. *Improvisation and the Theatre*. New York: Routledge, 1981. 1987 printing.

Marcia, Alberto. *The Commedia dell'Arte and the Masks of Amleto and Donato Sartori. Centro Maschere e Strutture Gestuali*. Florence, Italy: La Casa Usher, 1980. Intro by Giorgio Strehler. Translated by Cynthia Baker, Anne Marie Speno, Brenda Porster.

Rolfe, Bari. *Behind the Mask*. Berkeley, California: Persona Books, 1977. 1992 printing.

Wilsher, Toby. *The Mask Handbook, A Practical Guide*. New York: Routledge, 2007.

Wright, John. *Why Is That So Funny? A Practical Exploration of Physical Comedy*. New York: Limelight Editions, 2007.

Wright, Vicky. Interview with the author, London, England. 25 April 2019.

CHAPTER 6

MASK MAKING

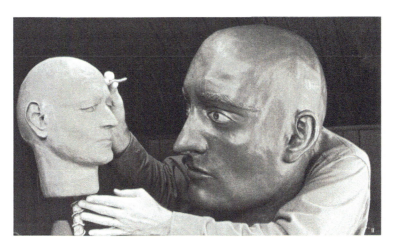

FIGURE 6.1 *Big head sculpts Rob*

To make a mask, an artist needs to know not only what it will look like, but also how it will be used, and what resources are best suited to its purpose. There are more methods and materials than we can present here, but we will consider resources, including materials, skills, time, and cost. The artist starts with questions about both aesthetic expectations and practical needs (form and function, as discussed in the design chapter), then considers the best options available for their schedule, abilities, materials, and budget (time, talent, and treasure). This chapter provides guidelines for asking preparatory questions, selecting methods and materials, learning entry-level construction techniques, and gaining inspiration for further practice.

WHERE DO I BEGIN?

Design and construction marry form to function, combining the aesthetic choices of the designer with the practical implementation by the maker. Form includes both the appearance and the materials the mask is made from. The function includes the way the mask integrates with the face and body, as well as defining character and production style. Key considerations include tradition vs. experimentation, custom vs. generic fit, and examination of the three Ts: time, talent, and treasure. An experienced designer will have considered these already.

At first, this process appears to be a linear sequence: research, analyze and develop the character, design something, then make it, right? If you are making another designer's work, or creating a custom piece for a client, the materials, form and function may be decided already. In other situations, you as maker may be called upon to advise or make decisions about construction. Like writing, performing, and other creative processes, the work of making masks is often circular, requiring research, editing and revision to be most successful. Professional mask artists know that the life of a mask as a dynamic performing object is critical to its success, so incorporate time to work with the mask or prototypes of it in the creation and rehearsal process.

Commedia dell'Arte master and scholar Antonio Fava addresses this process: he begins with a caveat about understanding the history and aesthetics of form and emphasizes commitment to the functionality of the mask over personal creative impulse before engaging in the process of sketching a design from various angles, casting or measuring the performer's face, carving a matrix in wood, and then creating the mask in leather.[1] Some artists make a quick paper mache prototype from their clay sculpt and work with it in the rehearsal studio before going on to make it in leather or neoprene, so they can adjust the scale, fit, or design as needed. For your own work, these considerations of design, liveliness, fit, flexibility, balance, durability, and materials should be examined within the context of your available resources **(see Appendix B: Mask Construction Worksheet)**.

As you begin, ask whether the mask style has a traditional method or material that is expected and necessary. If so, are you able to follow the tradition, or will you choose for aesthetic or practical reasons to break with tradition? The designer may have chosen to experiment with one or the other (or both).

170 Theatre Masks Out Side In

FIGURE 6.2 (A–C)   *Commedia masks in leather (Santelli), neoprene (Becker), and paper mache*

(A)   *Werner Strub's mask for Oedipus reflects the city in the distress of war and plague (photo by Giorgio Skory)*

(B)   *Amy Cohen's Linen mask was created with a focus on sonic resonance for an outdoor performance and on recreating a process which many scholars believe was used in Ancient Greece*

(C)   *Leather masks by Giancarlo Santelli focused on character*

(D)   *Neoprene mask for a college production of* Hecuba *by Jonathan Becker reads well in stage lighting and is an easily cleaned and reused investment*

FIGURE 6.3   *Greek mask images*

Mask Making 171

FIGURE 6.4(A) *For a custom fit, sculpt the clay character on a cast of the performer's face*

FIGURE 6.4(B) *This fantastic Mouse Queen is based on the fittings from a bicycle helmet; it is adjustable to each performer. Made by Elizabeth Flauto for Butler Ballet's production of* The Nutcracker *(2020)*

For example, Commedia dell'Arte masks are traditionally made of leather, which fits the face well and has a beautiful liveliness. However, not all productions have the resources to purchase or skills to make these, so a company might choose to purchase neoprene ones, or create their own out of paper mache. Greek masks are thought by some scholars to have been made of linen and animal hide glue, to cover all of the face, and in some periods to be oversized. But perhaps your goal in restaging a Greek play is not to recreate that aesthetic or method, but to infuse a production with a particular emotion: Perhaps, large foam masks, or thermoplastic half masks, are a better solution in your circumstances.

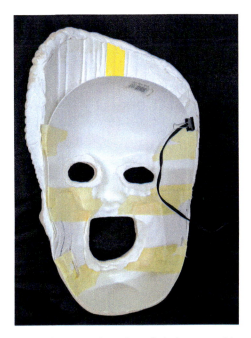

FIGURE 6.4(C1–2) *A purchased mask served as the base for this Greek-inspired class project: the student split the lower part of the mask to open the mouth, increased/aligned the eyeholes, and extended the onkos (top) with cardboard (c2). Then she sculpted the character and painted additional tone, highlight, and shadow (c1). She also replaced the thin cord elastic with a stronger 1/4" band*

FIGURE 6.4(D) *Some masks are designed to be worn by a variety of people so may have adjustable straps and interior padding*

FIGURE 6.5 *This skull mask with a moveable jaw by Jonathan Becker has two completely separate parts, each with an elastic strap to hold the mask part to the head*

FIGURE 6.6 *Mask with undercuts*

Will the mask be custom fit for the actor? If so, does it require the original sculpt to be done over a life cast? If so, additional time and materials are needed. Or will the performer's measurements be sufficient **(see Appendix B: Mask Performer Measurement Sheet)**? Does the mask have an adapted fit that will work for several performers, such as a neutral mask for actor training? In this case, perhaps the generous size and spacing of the eyeholes, interior padding, and adjustable straps will accommodate multiple users. Or is a generic fit sufficient, like a flexible domino mask for a party, or an oversized parade mask that is carried? How many will you make? Can those copies be adapted to individual fit?

In addition to the fit, assess the mask's physical attributes of weight, flexibility, balance, and durability. A large-scale mask needs to be of lighter weight material. A closely fit custom mask benefits from some flexibility and breathability. In addition to weight, balance is important: masks with exaggerated scale, horns, decorations, or wigs need attention. Are there moving parts? How are those engineered? With springs? Weights? Levers or strings?

If there are deep details and undercuts, you may be better served by a flexible medium such as latex to make the mask of – otherwise it can be really difficult to get the mask off the form, or the form must be sacrificed (i.e. a negative waste mold of plaster that allows you to make a detailed positive Hydrocal form for a leather sculpt). In general, a flexible (soft) mask can be made on a hard form, and a hard mask requires a soft form such as clay or silicone.

What conditions will the mask be subject to? What conditions are the performers working in? Mascot and Theme Park workers may need special accommodation to offset high temperatures such as extra air space, a place to include a cold pack, fan, or circulatory system. How long will it be on? Need it be easily

TABLE 6.1 *Materials Selection*

Material	Cost	Skill Level	Cast	Carved	Formed	Weight	Flexibility	Time for 1*	Multiples Faster	Durability	Specialty Tools	Other
Purchased base	$	B				V	V	Q	N	varies	N	
Direct cast on face		B	X			L	V	Q	N	F-M	N	
Cast performer (negative cast and positive mold)		I	X					Q	N	M		
Sculpt positive character		I			X			Q-WE	N	F-M		
Cast negative character		I	X					Q	N	D		
Cast positive character		I	X					D	N	D		
Paper pulp	$	B	X		X	L-M	R-M	D	N	F-M	N	
Paper mache strips (five layers)	$	B			X	L	M-S	Q-WE	N	varies	N	
Model Magic	$	B			X	L-M	R-M	Q-WE	N	M	N	
Foam, EVA	$	B			X	L	SF	WE	N	F	N	
Foam, insulation	$$	I		X		L	SF	D-W	N	M	N	
Foam, closed cell	$$	I			X	L	R	WE	N	M	M	
Fosshape	$$	I			X	L	V	D-WE	M	VM	M	
Wonderflex	$$	I			X	L-M	RM	Q-D	M	D	M	
Friendly Plastic	$$	I	X	X	X	M	R	Q-D	N	D	M	
Worbla		I		X	X	M	R	Q-D	M	D	M	
Sintra		A			X	L	R	Q-D	N	D	M	
Leather	$$	A			X	L	F	W-M	N	D	Y	
Celastic		A			X	L-M	R	D	N	D	Y	Toxicity Limited availability
Aquaform		A	X		X	V	V	Q-WE	N	VD	N	Limited availability
Vacuform	$	I			X	L	M	Q	Y	F	Y	Special equipment
Epoxy		A	X		X	H	R	WE+	N	D	M	Long cure
Sheet metal		A			X	M	RM		N	MD	Y	
Latex		I	X			L	F	WE	Y	F	N	Long cure allergen
Neoprene	$$	I	X			M-H	R	WE	Y	D	N	Long cure
Wood		A		X		M-H	R	M	N	D	Y	
3D printing	$$$	A	X			M-H	R	WE	Y	D	Y	Special equipment

Casts are assuming the use of alginate, plaster bandage, and plaster. Silicon casting is considerably more expensive both for materials and gun. Plaster is most economical and purchased in bulk rather than in craft stores, so initial outlay may be similar but you would get more casts from a bulk purchase. Character casts are assumed done in Hydrocal or other harder cement.
Materials are based on the estimated cost of producing a single full-face mask. Extensions, extra layers, or different sizes would of course impact the cost. These estimates are for comparative purposes.
Paper assumes the use of readily available paper such as newsprint and brown craft paper, lunch bags, etc. specialty papers cost more.
Thermoplastics are priced by a single layer/single face – about 9 × 12″, or a 1/8th cut. Purchasing a full sheet is more economical.
Celastic and Aquaform are not available for general purchase.
Vacuform is based on the cost of a single sheet of styrene and does not include equipment costs.
Cost: $0–10. $$10–20. $$$20–35. $$$$35–50. $$$$$50+ each.
Skill: B I A – all of us start as beginners and can develop advanced skills through practice; there are appropriate projects in each area for beginners, intermediate, and advanced artists, but these categories suggest a relative level of difficulty.
Beginner – easily acquired materials, easy to learn, no special equipment 1.
Intermediate – few specific tools, order materials, accessible to all skill levels, takes some practice to achieve consistent results.
Advanced – requires specific tools and equipment, higher learning curve/instruction needed, complex process 5.
Weight: light, medium, heavy, varies LMHV.
Flexibility: rigid, malleable (can be re-shaped to face), semi-flexible, flexible. 1 RMSF 5.
Durability: considering humidity, heat, possible pressure from crowding in storage, wear: 1 Fragile, Moderate, Durable 5/FMD.
Multiples: same time (other than increased speed with expertise) or Faster (removes set up time, can be done assembly line style).
Specialty tools: specific equipment normally needed for production, such as heat gun, chisels, horn hammer, vacuform table, or protective gear.
*Time: this is a very general guide. The experience of the maker, available tools and workspace, complexity and detail of the mask vary tremendously. Our designations do not include design time or creating a foundation such as a life cast of the actor.
Q – quick, in a few hours. D – a day's work. WE – a few days, possibly including dry or cure times; W – week, solid work; M – more. Start early.

removable between scenes, worn for several hours of a performance, or for a full day's filming? How much use will the mask get? How durable must it be? And of course, what materials are best to convey the aesthetic needs? For the scale of the mask and venue, how will the surface treatment and decoration be accomplished effectively? Will the textures be dimensional or visual?

Choosing a method and material considers both what materials are best suited and what resources (Time, Talent, Treasure) are available. There's not just one right answer! It's important that you ask good questions and discover how to create the right masks for your project.

RESOURCE ANALYSIS: TIME/TALENT/ TREASURE

Making masks can be a fun creative activity accomplished in an hour, or an intricate engineering and artistic process that takes weeks or months to complete. Some projects are great for beginners, others require years of practice to master. If you are working to a deadline and within a budget (and most of us are!), it will be necessary to calculate your resources of time, talent, and treasure. Some of this begins with the design process, and the three Ts may dictate some of your construction options. Ask:

- Are there acceptable masks for purchase? Can you buy basic forms and adapt them? Could you commission a professional mask artist to design and/or create them?

- How much time do you have to commission or build them? Expect to work months in advance.

- What materials are familiar and/or available to you?

- Do you have space and equipment to address health, safety, and practical questions?

- What experience do you and your team have in making masks?

- How much rehearsal time is available to work with, and potentially change the masks? Are the director and performers used to working with masks?

Masks can be made directly on the face, developed on an existing purchased base, or can be sculpted in clay on a life cast or generic face and made from that design. Some terminologies are helpful here: a **cast**, or to cast, is to take an impression of something – in our case, a face (either human or mask). A **positive cast** is a three-dimensional convex form: it reads forward, like your actual face. A **negative cast**, or impression, is concave – it is like the inside of a bowl, with a nose. You can make a mask on either a positive or negative surface. When we cast an actor's face, it results in a negative cast; we fill that with plaster to get a positive cast (which is a 3D copy of the actor's face, or **life cast**). Next, we sculpt a character in clay on top of the positive cast to make a new positive of the mask design, then make either a mask directly

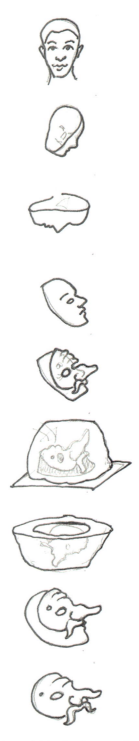

FIGURE 6.7 *Sequential drawing: face, negative cast, positive cast, clay sculpt, negative cast, positive cast, mask*

on it, or cast another negative which we can make a mask inside of, and can also make a third positive form in stronger material such as gypsum cement if we hope to make many masks on it. Got it? Okay, back to the three Ts analysis.

First of all, is this a single-fitted commissioned piece? Or a generic piece? If it's fitted, do you have a cast or measurements of the person's face, or will you cast them as part of the process? Do you need it to fit perfectly against the face, such as for a custom leather Commedia mask? If so, allow appropriate time, experience, and materials. Or can you use an existing or generic cast because you will be building up with clay anyways, so it doesn't have to be skin tight? If it is oversized, do you need a cast at all?

There are time-saving measures for casting a face: these processes are listed from the more simple and rapid through more complex and time-consuming. Your results may vary, though, as simple techniques such as paper mache can be done quickly by students with little experience and can be used with great care and detail by experienced artists. Also, many mask

(A)   *Students beginning to create direct paper masks*

(B)   *Model Magic being formed over a purchased base*

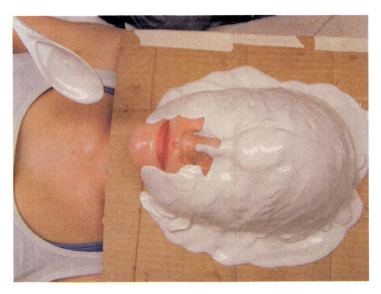

(C)   *Casting the face using a direct plaster method: the wet plaster makes a detailed cast and was then supported by plaster bandage over it. The negative cast could be used as a mold for paper mache or thin thermoplastic*

(D)   *Leather mask being formed over a wooden matrix by Giorgio Santelli*

(E)   *Oversized masks for The Water Carriers first people were built freehand without a form then attached to caps*

FIGURE 6.8   *Mask-making options*

makers combine multiple techniques and materials to create the most effective pieces.

- Direct masking: form a mask with paper or plaster bandage on your face, then decorate and finish it (Figure 6.8a).

- Use a purchased or pulled mask base, fit it to the actor, and decorate the outside.

- Fill a purchased mask base with plaster, use that positive for building mask directly over, with paper mache pulp or Model Magic. DO check that the mask you are starting with is scaled to an adult face: some cheap mask forms are scaled for children, are cast very shallow, or simply aren't as big as an adult face (Figure 6.8b).

- Use a stock base or purchased base (support it inside with plaster, clay, or tightly crumpled paper) to build clay form over, then cast a negative mold or build a positive form directly over it.

- Make a silicon or plaster direct cast of face, supported on the outside, and use it as a negative mold of the actor's face (Figure 6.8c).

- Do an alginate/plaster bandage facial cast, and plaster positive of face, clay design and Hydrocal negative mold – days of work, plus the cast in paper mache, latex, or neoprene.

- Leather mask process, including facial cast, plaster positive, clay sculpt, freeze, and work leather directly over frozen clay.[2]

- Leather mask process, including facial cast, plaster positive, clay sculpt, plaster negative, Hydrocal positive, leather shaping over positive.

- Leather mask process using a carved wood matrix instead of a Hydrocal positive to form the leather over (Figure 6.8d).

- Oversized, body, and parade masks may be constructed without a facial cast, as they are likely to be supported by a headband or helmet. Balloons, bowls, balls, crumpled paper or foil, cardboard, and masking tape can be combined to create the rough shape (Figure 6.8e).

- Foam masks that are flexible, and those worn over the head instead of on the face may not need a face to work on at all – though a helmet mask may include a fitted cap or band that integrates with the performer's face.

- Carved wooden masks do not have a time-saving method, but knowing the actor's face size is necessary, and the measurements can be transferred with calipers.

- 3D print the actor's face, and add clay to the digital life cast, or cast a mask over a 3D printed design.

PROCESS: FITTING THE ACTOR

Masks come in many sizes, shapes, weights, and materials. Regardless of the design and materials, the performer's comfort and safety must be considered. These safety issues include vision, respiration, comfort/movement, and sometimes vocalization. They should be considered in the design of the mask, and tested during the process of construction. It is important for the performer to be comfortable in the mask and to have access to it or a prototype during rehearsals.

Vision: Can they see? How big are the eyeholes? The bigger they are, the more the performer can see, but … do we want the observer to see in? The size and shape of the opening is an important design feature. If the holes are large, should there be a screen to mask them? What of? How close to the face is the mask? Closer fit allows better vision, but the eyelashes must move freely without hitting the mask, and if the mask is worn by more than one person, there is no universal perfect fit, so the mask may need to be padded to make it work. Is the mask reflective? Is there a screen to look through? If the performer's eyes are not aligned with the mask's eyes, how will their viewing aperture fit within the design? How is the mask stabilized on the head to keep the viewing area consistent? If there are several performers in one mask, as with a Chinese Dragon, who leads? How does that work?

Respiration: Can they breathe? Obviously, if the mask has nose holes and an open mouth that align with those of the performer, that helps! But if not, there needs to be space inside a closed mask for air to circulate. When using strong glues, paints, varnishes, or latex, time is needed for the materials to gas off, so chemical odors don't irritate the eyes, nose, throat, lungs, or skin. Moleskin, felt, or foam padding can hold the

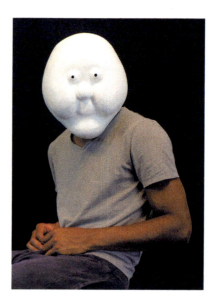

FIGURE 6.9(A) *Basel mask with very small eyeholes needs to be held securely so the holes align with the performer's eyes*

FIGURE 6.9(B)   Fitted masks by Bernardo Rey for Woyzeck were sculpted over life casts of the performers to ensure good alignment

FIGURE 6.9(C)   A Barong-inspired Ass provided vision through the mouth and below the jaw for the front performer, while the second wearer could see the floor around her and had contact with the other performer. Designed by the author for Bali Dreams at Butler University

mask away from the skin. Obtain and read the manufacturer's Material Data Safety Sheets (MSDS), following manufacturer guidelines and erring on the side of caution.

Perspiration: Breathing includes not only respiratory airflow, but also the skin's ability to perspire. Does the performer's skin have the ability to breathe also, either because there is airflow or because the mask against the face is absorbent? Leather is prized as a mask material because it absorbs moisture from and can mold to the performer's face. Wood and paper are also able to absorb moisture from perspiration and respiration. Plastics, not so much. Does the actor have any allergies? Latex allergies can be severe, so before investing in latex masks, be sure the performers are

FIGURE 6.10   This mask for Marie in Woyzeck was sculpted to match the performer's eyes and lip line by Bernardo Rey

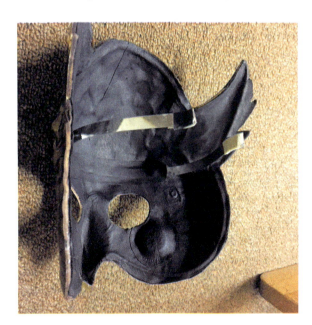

FIGURE 6.11   Pigskin lining is comfortable against the skin. Denise Wallace embedded a headband, which allows it to be worn on the face or on the top of the head

FIGURE 6.12 *Commedia masks leave the mouth free to vocalize. Arlecchino by Santelli*

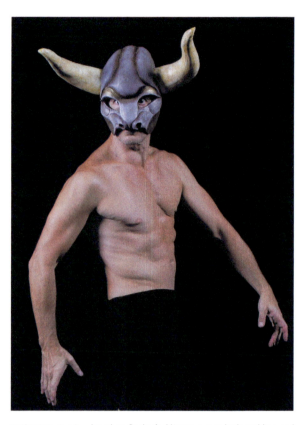

FIGURE 6.13 *Jonathan Becker's Minotaur uses both padding and elastic to secure the mask to the performer*

not allergic to latex. If using a non-absorptive material, or if (as you should) your paper mask is sealed, then a felt, fabric, or pigskin lining in the mask will improve its comfort. Pigskin is also good because it can be wiped clean.

Vocalization: Do the performers need to talk? Generally full-faced and closed-mouth masks do not speak. If the mask does talk, how open is the mouth? Will we see the performer's mouth in the opening, or cover the hole with a dark gauze? Will the mask include a hinged jaw? If using a half mask as in Commedia, does the upper lip align with the performer's mouth? How much sound projection is needed? Will there be any amplifying devices set in or built into the mask? Do you want to imitate the ancient Greek masks with a megaphone type mouth, or resonant space? Does the resonant space in the mask affect the performer's ability to hear well? Bruce Marrs also notes that if the performer is to speak, the mask should not dampen the resonators on either side of the nose by adhering to the face there.[3] Padding the outer corners of the cheek bones and forehead can lift the mask off the nose and sinuses.

Comfort: Can the performer move expressively, maintain balance, and keep the mask stable to the body as they move? How does the mask feel on – does it lay close to skin, have a small space, or large space around the face? Is there an absorption layer? Is it free from sharp or rough surfaces? Are the balance points and tension of elastic or straps comfortable? It is important that the mask be stable on the performer's head, keeping eyes and air clear, and the weight of the mask supported comfortably. Straps usually sit just above the ear (for masks attached with straps or elastic), which is also at the top of the bridge of the nose/eyeline/temples. Full and heavy masks may distribute weight across the head with additional straps, padding, addition of a wig, or an embedded hat or helmet. Masks that don't speak may include a balance point on the chin or jawline.

Movement: Are there moveable parts to the mask? Lights? Sound? How are they controlled? Can they be manipulated while worn via switches, levers, or remote control? Or only when the mask is off? Are there parts which can be added or removed for different looks? How are changes effected?

With these practical considerations in mind, there are many sizes and configurations for masks that were discussed in the design chapter. Once the design form and function are clearly understood, the building begins. First, know the fit needs and prepare the base. If it is going to be a custom fit, cast the actor's face. If it is an adapted fit, you can work from measurements or a premade form. If it is a generic fit, a premade form is adequate. Second, prepare the design matrix or sculpt. Third, cast the mask, and then fourth, fit, and fifth, finish it.

FIGURE 6.14 *Pinocchio masks with multiple noses by Candy McClernan*

PROCESS: SCULPTING THE DESIGN, CASTING AND MODELING – CREATING THE BASE FOR THE MASK

Assuming you are not just decorating an existing mask, the construction process starts with the prepared life cast or generic base.

Custom masks that need to fit a specific performer's face begin with a life cast. Available techniques include plaster bandage, alginate, silicone, and 3D printing. In each it is best to keep the subject sitting up or slightly reclined, and (except for the digital print), their face and hair must be protected with a layer of petroleum jelly (Vaseline) to keep hair from embedding in the casting agent. Most of these can be cast in about an hour – less for the model, and less as you become more skilled. It is a good practice to have two people available to facilitate the casting process and keep the subject comfortable.

Plaster bandage face cast: plaster bandages (orthopedic tape) were commonly used for making casts and are still available from a variety of health and art supply companies. Beware! Plaster is exothermic (gives of heat): it can cause burns, so be sure to use a low heat product and do a test before applying it directly to anyone. The face is coated with Vaseline, and a layer of thin tissue paper can be laid on top if desired (this is especially recommended for people with facial hair). The water-activated bandages are put directly on the face, smoothed to the performer's skin, and allowed to harden in place. Many mask artists create self-portraits in this way. Done carefully, it can create a suitable life cast that can be turned into a mask itself or reinforced to use as a base for a character sculpt. To use as a base, it needs to be sturdy enough to take the pressure of adding clay and perhaps the mask material. Reinforce it by filling it with plaster and sealing the outside. If desired, use additional plaster or sandpaper to smooth the surface before sealing.

Alginate is a casting agent that was used for dental impressions before digital scans became common. It comes as a powder (in different flavors, mind you, but don't eat it!) which is mixed by weight with water, applied to the actor's face, then immediately covered with a supporting shell of plaster bandages or plaster/cheesecloth wrap. Alginate comes in quick-set and slow-set formulas. The quick-set alginate mixed with cool or tepid water allows about 3 minutes to apply, and 3–5 more to set; it's great if you have some experience and work efficiently. The slow set allows a bit more working time and can be sped up by using warm water, which is more comfortable for the performer. Both kinds capture good detail, are non-allergenic, and are moderately easy to work with. Alginate's flexibility makes it easy to remove; small holes can be filled with Vaseline or another small batch of alginate, and then the negative alginate cast is filled with plaster to form the life cast. Once the plaster is set, the alginate cast is pulled off and discarded. The whole process takes an hour, including clean up, but only about 15–30 minutes for the performer.

Silicon is a more durable casting agent than alginate, and more expensive. Its two ingredients can be mixed and applied with a spatula, or applied with a caulk gun that mixes the two parts together as they are extruded.

BOX 6.1 THE LIFE CAST

Have the studio clean and materials prepared:

Prepare the Model

Welcome the model, explain the process, and answer any questions the model may have.

Arrange a hand signal for the model to use if they need to stop the casting process at any time.

You may wish to offer relaxing music or background soundscape.

Provide a smock or other cover to protect the model's clothing.

Cover the model's hair with plastic (a bald cap is ideal, or plastic wrap covered with tape).

Have the model add a layer of release agent (petroleum jelly/Vaseline) to their face, especially at eye brows and lashes, to avoid embedding hairs in the cast.

If the model has a moustache or beard, and the Vaseline is not enough to smooth it, you may wish to add a layer of tissue paper or plastic wrap over it (so it sticks to the Vaseline) and additional Vaseline over that.

If the performer is concerned about covering their eyes and precise lids are not required, you may add a small oval of tissue to the eye also.

Paper straws or a rolled piece of paper should be on hand for the performer to place in their nostrils just before you begin the cast if it would make them feel safer.

Place a strip of muslin around the model's face, under the chin at the neck, over the ears, and over the top of the head as a visual finish line. It is best to cast the face deeply even if the mask will not cover all of it. It is also useful to cut a piece of corrugated cardboard with an oval for the face in the center: place this around the model's face to establish the depth of the cast and the plane at which the back will set; it also helps to catch excess alginate or plaster.

Ensure the model is comfortable with their head resting back; encourage them to relax their jaw (rather than clench their teeth together).

Mix the Alginate

This takes a little practice and careful measuring. Check the manufacturer's instructions, as alginates have different set times. Cool water extends the set time, warm water speeds it up. Weight is more reliable than volume measure, as the powder is very fine and can compact or fluff, throwing off the ratio. Generally, by weight, it is one part powder to four parts water, and you need at least ¼ lb alginate (plus 1 lb water, which = 1 pint) to cover a whole face. By volume, the proportion is two parts alginate to three parts water, i.e. 1 c alginate to 1.5 c water. Add the powder to the water in a flexible rubber cup, stir quickly but without creating excess bubbles, to a thin batter (like pancake batter). It is also possible to use plaster of Paris instead of alginate to directly cast the face.

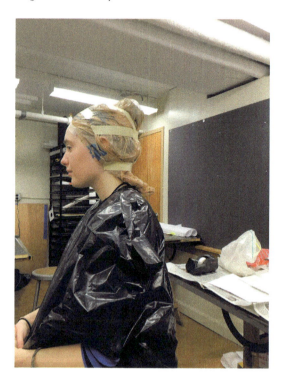

FIGURE 6.15(A1) *Model prepared with hair and clothes protected, and a layer of petroleum jelly on their skin and brows*

FIGURE 6.15(A2) *Model prepared for life cast with alginate or direct plaster method*

Mask Making 181

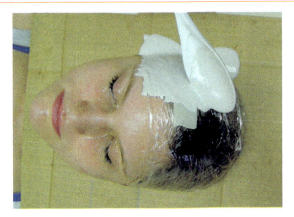

FIGURE 6.15(A3) *First layer of plaster is thin to capture detail without bubbles*

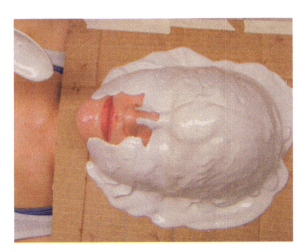

FIGURE 6.15(A4) *Working from top to bottom, leaving the nose free to breathe*

FIGURE 6.15(A5) *After the face is covered, and the plaster thickens, the form is thickened to support the face shell*

Start your Cast

Alert the model that you are about to begin, have them place the straws (if they want), close their eyes and mouth, and let them know where you are going to put the alginate as you go.

Spoon the alginate onto the model's face: forehead, brows, cheeks, eyes, chin and mouth, bridge of nose and finally around the nares and upper lip to and between the nostrils.

Use all the alginate needed to completely cover the face and under the chin/jawline.

Working times vary from 3 to 8 minutes; check your product label. Cool water slows the setting process but may be less comfortable for the performer.

Support the Alginate

As the alginate is applied, a second person should begin soaking, smoothing excess water from, and applying the plaster bandage to the alginate, gently pressing the bandage into the wet alginate. Start with the outer perimeter, then the center axis, and layering the entire alginate cast. Two-three layers are sufficient.

As the plaster cures it will warm up, then cool. When it has set (about 20 minutes total), the entire cast can be removed.

[Note: it is also possible to do a life cast without alginate by applying activated plaster bandages directly to the model's face; be sure to test the curing temperature of your brand of bandage first.]

Release the Mold

Ask the model to sit up, lean forward a little, and move their facial muscles to release the alginate. With the model holding the outside of the cast, pull the cast gently from the forehead toward the chin.

Fill any small holes with Vaseline or a small fresh batch of alginate, and wipe away or smooth out any excess. Plug the nostrils.

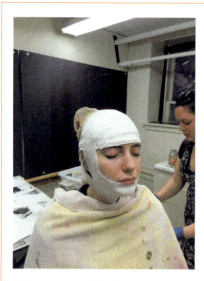

FIGURE 6.15(B) *Plaster bandages smoothed to the head and face from the outside in*

FIGURE 6.15(C) *Bandages completed leaving open area at the nostrils*

FIGURE 6.15(D) *The cured cast is removed, the nostrils plugged, and fresh plaster prepared to fill the mold*

Make a Positive Cast

Create a "nest" of crumpled newspaper or recycled bags in a box to hold the negative cast level.

Pour a fresh batch of plaster into the negative mold: begin with about a cup of liquid, and rotate the mask to ensure that all areas of the face are covered. Tap or gently pop any bubbles. Slowly add additional plaster to fill the mold, gently tapping it to allow air bubbles to rise from the edges and pop. As the plaster thickens, level the back at an angle suitable for working (you will want the base to have a flat surface against a work board). You may wish to carve the actor's name/initials for reference. It is also useful to embed a wire hanging loop in the reverse: either scoop plaster out from under the stretched wire or loop the wire up so the base still lies flat in the next process.

When the plaster positive form is cured, remove and discard the alginate casting. Allow the cast to dry thoroughly. An application of spray sealant is useful to prolong the life and usefulness of the cast.

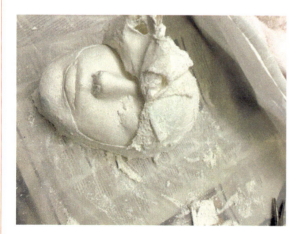

FIGURE 6.15(E) *When the plaster is hardened, the bandages are peeled away*

FIGURE 6.15(F) *The finished positive form should be cleaned of any traces of Vaseline and may be lightly sanded to erase any irregularities*

FIGURE 6.15(G) *Shellac may be used to seal the cast and protect it from moisture*

3D scan and print: Improvements in hardware and software are making it possible to scan and print the equivalent of a life cast. Scanners have varying ability to capture high resolution images, and are priced accordingly. The scan can be scaled to life size, a little larger, or with a custom design. The printing process adds layers of extruded plastic to create the form. There are a variety of plastics available in different strengths, compositions, and flexibilities.

To create the scan, an iPad can be fitted with a scanner such as Skanect Pro or The Structure by Sensor. The space for the model should be well lit, have several feet of clearance, and a fairly plain background. The model should avoid wearing shiny reflective textures. In addition to the scanner's resolution capability, a good scan is dependent on the model's ability to remain still.

FIGURE 6.16 *Dental alginate makes a flexible, detailed cast*

The digital file is uploaded into a design software program and prepared for print. You may have enough resolution to use the print as a life cast, or you may choose to adjust the file by sharpening detail, increasing the scale, or adding design features and printing it as a mask matrix. In either of these instances where you will create your mask over the 3D print, you may prefer to see the full head, but if you do not need an entire head and want to conserve resources, print only the area you need: stop the file/print at the highest level you would need to cover or fill it, or at an angle that makes it convenient to work over. Currently it is both expensive and very time-consuming to print a life-sized bust or head unless you have very high-end equipment available to you. Use the shell feature in the design software, and/or the vase feature in the print to create a hollow form. Print the file using a 3D printer.

Depending on your scanner, digital skills, printer, and plastic, you may be able to use the print directly or may need to adjust it – sanding any rough edges, or adding a smoothing layer of another material such as Sculpt-or-coat.

You can use this life cast as a base for sculpting directly (such as with paper mache) or model a design in clay over it and use that character sculpt as the base for casting. It is also possible to design a character digitally over the face scan, or digitally design a character and subtract the face scan from it. See Box 6.10 for a Case Study on using 3D printing.

MASK TECHNIQUES AND MATERIALS

There are many techniques and materials for making masks. In this section, we will look at different options for realizing masks, and consider the pros and cons, including cost, availability of materials, difficulty/ease of working, time requirements, skill/training necessary. Many techniques are suitable for use with a variety of materials. The "easier" ones are presented first, but it should be noted that this ranking in technique and materials does not suggest a similar ranking in quality. Each technique can produce beautiful, effective masks, and the patience, skill, and attention to detail of the mask maker is a critical factor in the artistry of the mask. For example, paper mache is a simple technique of laying strips of paper (or cloth) over a form with a binder and has been used successfully since ancient times. It is a technique accessible to people of all ages and abilities; in skilled hands, it can yield beautiful works of art. Mask artists should also be open to considering a variety of materials; often a successful mask requires several techniques in combination. In some situations, resources (TTT) may dictate construction techniques, in other, tradition does. For many, the mask artist is free to

FIGURE 6.17 *Multi-material mask for Oedipus el Ray inspired by images of Quetzalcoatl, designed by Anita Yavich and built by Denise Wallace-Spriggs for the Public Theatre. Denise built a base of cardboard and masking tape. Over this she made a frame of Varaform (thermoplastic mesh) covered with paper mache and painted white. She patterned, cut, and applied Fosshape for dimensional relief on the teeth and decorative borders. She also cut and added hinged feathers, then painted it to unify the elements, and again with black light-activated paints to reveal pattern under light*

select the best materials. Table 6.1 lists some properties, pros, and cons of each.

Purchase and Adapt

There are lots of masks available on the market. Purchasing a mask base can be a great option if you have limited resources. Some are super cheap, just a few dollars each, made of plastic, cloth, metal, or leather and ready to adapt and decorate for your project. Purchased masks can be adapted to fit your face by applying padding to the bridge of the nose, forehead, or other inside area as needed to keep it balanced on your face and properly aligned with your eyes. Check that the mask ties sit just above the ears/at the eyeline, which balance the tension/touch points of the forehead, cheeks, and bridge of the nose; you may prefer a second tie, and wider or stronger elastic to keep it secure; you may also want a lighter or darker color to match your hair or wig that will cover its edges. You may need to adjust the mouth, nostril, or eyeholes slightly to optimize vision and airflow. There are infinite ways to create character on top of a basic form.

FIGURE 6.18 *Adapted masks: these masks were adapted by Elizabeth Snyder for Butler Ballet's production of the Firebird suite. Design conceived by Kathleen Egan*

FIGURE 6.19 *Adapted masks: the monsters began as five-dollar shiny gold plastic vacuform masks: she cut them down, painted them, and added snug knit kerchiefs/hair made of dyed recycled T-shirts for the corps de ballet*

FIGURE 6.20 *Adapted masks: Katshei's mask is a full-head latex Halloween mask ($25): she added mesh patches to the shadowed areas of the nose, cheeks, and temples to improve air flow, painted it, added hair and beard from a variety of yarns and cording, and built a lightweight craft foam crown to balance the beard and fit the dancer*

Among ready to wear masks, domino masks and simply shaped fabric ones are light and comfortable and can support a variety of decorative treatments (you may need to strengthen the ties or elastic that hold it on). Others that are mass produced for Halloween, parties, and cosplay with specific characters might work "off the rack." These party store masks are generally not "live" masks, but decorative or fright masks. Etsy, online market places, and craft fairs have a wide range of masks in many different styles and materials. There are beautiful masks in galleries and studios that are considered (and appropriately priced as) art.

If you have the budget, there are many contemporary mask makers who make and market specific masks geared toward schools and professional theaters: these artists create neutral, larval, emotional, Commedia, character, and popular masks that are at a higher quality for study and performance. If you have the advance planning time and financial resources, many mask makers will also do custom masks for specific projects for schools, productions, and private clients. Appendix B provides a mask estimate worksheet that may be helpful in starting a conversation.

Direct Methods

It is possible to create a mask directly on the face using a strip technique and either low heat plaster bandage or paper mache. While some people are hesitant or uncomfortable with the process of casting or covering their face entirely during the

FIGURE 6.21 *Commercial masks for sale at a craft store*

FIGURE 6.22 *Jonathan Becker's studio with sample masks for commissioned sale*

FIGURE 6.23 *Decorative masks for sale to tourists in Venice*

FIGURE 6.24 *Students creating direct paper masks in studio class*

processes, for many, it is an opportunity for relaxation, meditation, and reflection. Appendix B provides instructions for a paper version of a direct mask; it is less detailed and takes more time than a plaster bandage cast but is an interesting exercise and requires no special materials. It can be difficult to maintain detail while it is drying off the face, so support the inside with crumpled paper or a small bowl or coffee can.

You can also work directly on a pulled or purchased stock base and fit it to the actor later. Paper pulp (such as celluclay), lightweight modeling compound (Crayola Model Magic), and heat-sensitive Friendly Plastic can be formed directly into a 3D character mask (reinforce the pulp or Model Magic with paper mache). This may be more accessible to beginners than doing a life cast, sculpting in clay, and then doing a mask over that.

Direct modeling is a fine choice for situations where the process is the focus of creating a mask, when creativity is being explored (as with a mask workshop or children's classroom project), when in need of a quick facial cast, and when you do not need to make multiple copies of a single design. It's not always the most successful for performance.

FIGURE 6.25 *A student's completed direct paper mask*

FIGURE 6.26 *Chinese terracotta warrior mask created with paper mache for The Children's Museum of Indianapolis*

Strip Techniques

Strip techniques use layers of torn paper, fabric, or gauze bandage along with a binder to create a mask over a positive form or into a negative mold. These are time-honored methods in many cultures and often combined with other techniques as supporting or finishing layers. Strip techniques are also employed with contemporary materials that do not require an added binding agent: Celastic and thermoplastics can be used this way, but with a chemical or heat as the agent that allows adhesion.

The form: It can be as simple as a balloon, bowl, or purchased mask base, or as detailed as a facial cast, clay sculpt, plaster or Hydrocal form. You may wish to use a sealer, saran wrap, or foil on the form to protect it from moisture.

Release agents: A release agent is applied to the form to prevent the mask from sticking to it. Vaseline, liquid soap, soap flakes + olive oil, silicone spray, and other commercial products are possibilities, depending on the material of the form and the binder. The release agent should be applied in a thin, smooth layer, and reaching all crevices and surfaces. Be aware that some mask materials such as neoprene need the plaster to remain able to "breathe" – to absorb moisture from the casting compound – in order to set properly.

FIGURE 6.27 *Release agents*

BOX 6.2 RELEASE AGENTS

Release agents are used to prevent a cast from sticking to its subject (positive or negative mold). It is important to check both the mold and the casting materials for chemical compatibility. Here are some common release agents, what they work on, and how to clean them off.

Vaseline is an oil-based product, works by creating a barrier between skin and other water-based formulas, such as plaster, alginate, wallpaper paste, and acrylics. To clean from the skin, wipe off with tissue or cloth, followed by a mild soap/warm water wash. Isopropyl alcohol (rubbing alcohol) will also help clean it off of surfaces with minimal damage (not latex, which is also dissolved by IA). Petroleum solvents, including acetone and paint thinner, will dissolve petrolatum but may also damage the item you are cleaning (such as thermoplastics), so be aware of potential interactions. All these products are flammable.

Silicone sticks to itself, but nothing else. Silicone spray will act as a release agent for other materials such as plastic but create a sticky surface for itself. Available in aerosol spray, be sure to distinguish between a silicone spray that is a release agent for other items, and a silicon mold release that is for use with silicon casting/molds.

Water if hot can be used to soften thermoplastics. It is also useful to keep fingers and tools from sticking to the warmed product.

Plastic Wrap is useful to mask a person's hair during a life cast, can be secured with tape. Also, sometimes used to cover a plaster or clay sculpt before starting a paper mache mask.

Metal Foil: Aluminum is sometimes used as a barrier to water or other liquids, for example, a plaster character cast might be covered in foil to protect the cast from the moisture of a paper mache made on it, or from a sticky Worbla mask.

Wax is also useful as a barrier to water-based and some oil-based materials. Paraffin is usually white (clear in small amounts), and harder than beeswax that has a golden color and softer hand. Either can be warmed or melted and rubbed into a surface to create a waterproof barrier layer. Some forms are spray wax – fabsil cotton fabric wax (amazon), otter wax (for cloth), and spray paraffin (beauty supply); spray furniture polish usually includes lemon or orange oil and a cleanser that leaves an odor not conducive to performance. I do not recommend car wax in any of its forms (spray, liquid, or paste) – most combine hard shiny carnauba wax with softer beeswax or oils and noxious petroleum distillates, resins, and sealers. Remember that waxes are flammable, use caution when heating them, and don't leave paper/wax masks near heat sources (including dressing room light fixtures). Paraffin and beeswax can be mixed together to achieve a softer or harder finish.

Beeswax, a naturally softer wax, can be melted and brushed or rubbed on plaster forms to seal out water for further casting or mask making. It is advisable to brush it in (for speed and ease) then rub with a soft cloth to erase any brush marks or irregularities that might show in a cast. Beeswax can also be rubbed into a mask and buffed as a finishing (i.e. on sanded paper mache).

Paraffin is a synthetic petroleum-based wax, usually white/clear, which is a bit harder than beeswax. It melts at about 99°F, so can be massaged into a surface, but it is more difficult to get a smooth surface. Try a hairdryer to soften the paraffin after applied to the mask or casting, then buff in small circular motion or directional pattern following the mask contours. Avoid too thick a layer as it may create more of a shell coating that can crack or scratch. Solvents include ether and benzene.

Soap Solution can be made with flakes of bar soap and a small amount of water, warmed to a thick liquid; it may be used to clean and coat the negative mold; the mold was also coated with melted beeswax before pouring the gypsum life cast.

Mold Release Agents: This term covers many products. Each is specific to a material – plastic, rubber, silicon, metal, plaster, etc. The porous quality of the mold is also a factor: some release agents work with porous, "thirsty" molds – such as the mold release put on plaster for casting neoprene. Others require a barrier for porosity – as using Vaseline or wax between layers of plaster and Hydrocal (gypsum cement). Smooth-On markets and includes information about a variety of casting products and release agents.

MSW: Mild Soap and Water is useful for cleaning most molds, and can be rinsed or wiped away easily.

IA: Isopropyl Alcohol is a useful astringent for cleaning and disinfecting plaster, neoprene, metal, and thermoplastics. It is also a solvent for latex and grease.

The strips: Newsprint, cotton rag, natural fiber, and a variety of art papers work well, including bark cloth, charcoal paper, rice paper, and handmade specialty papers. Fabric options include tissue linen, cheesecloth, gauze bandage, and lightweight buckram. Some artists use a combination, such as a layer of cheesecloth between layers of news print, and a specialty paper on top. Avoid using papers that have been chemically treated with flame retardant – they are often identifiable by their slick, shiny quality.

BOX 6.3 PAPER PROPERTIES

Papers vary based on their content, process, texture, and finishing. Paper can be made of cotton, linen, and a wide variety of plant fibers, new or recycled. Wood pulp, which is most common, is naturally acidic, so low-quality untreated papers such as newsprint deteriorate rapidly. Most are made by machine and are uniform, but there are beautiful handmade papers available at art and stationery shops. In addition to using a variety of fibers, papers can be chemically treated or dyed and given a variety of textures.

Paper content:

- Rag paper includes a high percentage of cotton or linen fiber, is generally very slow to fade or yellow, and is used for etchings and watercolor by artists. It may be recycled.
- Newsprint – if untreated with anti-inflammatory chemicals (which make it shiny), it tears well and softens well for paper mache. Note it is usually acidic though, so while cheap, it may not be the best for something you want to keep for a generation.
- Kraft paper, lunch bags, and grocery sacks – these brown staples are often great for tearing, paper mache blending, and can be recycled. They come in different weights, so can be useful to use for structural and detailed areas – I use grocery bags for the perimeter and beginning structure and extended pieces but prefer thinner lunch bags for smaller details such as eyes, nose, and lips.
- Canson paper, pastel or charcoal papers feature a high rag content, slight tooth, different colors, and are easy to tear and mold.

- Art papers include a variety of handmade papers made from all kinds of fibers. Rice paper is thin, strong, and has a grain for added strength. Bark cloth is thick, absorbent, and malleable. Mulberry, lace, marbled, and many more have beautiful decorative textures. Good art stores often carry a selection, or you can order them online from retailers such as www.dickblick.com.

Paper treatments:

- Acid free paper is treated to have a pH of 7.07 or higher, is longer lasting, and won't yellow or become brittle quickly. If you are making art, go for this quality. Also called archival paper.
- Sizing is applied to paper to prevent penetration by writing or drawing inks – so the ink won't blur, basically.
- Bond paper has more sizing: stationery and resume papers are often bond.
- Coated papers have an additional surface, smoother finish, and higher printing quality. They may crack when creased, so color-coated papers will show base (usually white) if scored or torn.
- Laid paper has a pattern of fine parallel lines, either dimensional ridges/furrows or opaque/translucent bands.
- Wove paper has a faint mesh pattern.

Paper weights:

- Weight can be listed in grams of a single sheet of paper 1-meter square (gsm).
- In United States, weight is pounds per ream (500 sheets).
- Photocopy paper 80 gsm, airmail 45 gsm, drawing 150 gsm, card stock 250 gsm and up, then measured in microns per sheet.
- Medium weight cartridge paper or card stock is a good basic weight: framing and larger structures may benefit from heavier weights; lighter ones might be better for curled and decorative details.

FIGURE 6.28 *A variety of craft paper, newsprint, specialty art papers, toweling, and paper bags are useful*

The binder: There are a variety of useful binders, including those made with cellulose wallpaper paste, wheat flour, cornstarch, plaster, and glues. They allow for varying amounts of plasticity, dry time, and breathability.

BOX 6.4 BINDERS

Cellulose wallpaper paste:

- Buy this at a hardware store, it's made of wheat and may include a mold-inhibitor.
- Mix one part of wallpaper paste powder with three parts of water.
- Whisk gently to combine without making it frothy.
- Use fingers to break up any lumps.

OR

- Fill a container with water equal to the amount of paste you will need.
- Add powder a little at a time until the consistency is like thick cream or gruel.
- If it's too thick, add a little more water. Too thin? Add powder.

Flour and water:

- This is the classic original. Cheap and easy, but doesn't keep and may attract bugs (after a long time ….), also, you need to make it fresh daily as the gluten breaks down and it gets weak after a day.
- Mix equal parts flour and water, stir well, eliminate lumps.
- If you prefer a clearer glue, boil it a while.
- Add a tablespoon of salt or some clove or cinnamon oil if you like – the salt should slow the formation of mildew, and the oil smells good, but the best thing is to dry it completely.
- Use four to six layers to build enough strength to avoid warping as it dries.

Cornstarch:

- Put 1 cup of cornstarch into a heat-safe bowl: glass and ceramic work well.
- Add enough cold water to make a paste, and thin to a batter consistency.
- Add a little less than 3 pints boiling water, and stir vigorously with a whisk; it should become translucent.
- Cool to working temperature. Add a bit of white glue to improve durability.
- Keeps in fridge about three days. Adding a little salt can help prevent mildew.

Rabbit skin glue:

- A traditional material made from animal collagen, used for sizing and as an adhesive. It comes in blocks or granules and is carefully mixed with water and heated (but not boiled, or it loses its adhesive quality). It has a quick dry time (a few minutes working time, vs. 15–20 for pva glues). It is great for oils, but not compatible with acrylic paints, which may flake off.

White glues: Elmer's, Flex Glue, Modge Podge (matte), PVA (polyvinyl acetate).

- This gets really sticky and doesn't breathe as well – some people don't like it.
- Mix one part of glue with two to three parts of water. It depends on the paper, too – stiffer paper needs more glue, but if too wet, it gets soggy without sticking. Different brands of glue are more or less wet – so go for a mixture that softens the paper and still holds the layers together. It should feel a little slick.

Wood glue: It is a yellow-colored PVA similar to white school glue.

- Is stronger than white glue, and is a little less sticky when dry, but a bit more expensive.
- Can be thinned with water or thickened with plaster of Paris. If adding plaster, make small batches because the plaster sets after about 15–20 minutes.

Plaster:

- A little harder to get the hang of mixing, relatively inexpensive when purchased in bulk, and stronger than grain-based mixes.
- Follow manufacturer's directions.
- Sand to a smooth finish surface, can also add carved or scored detail.
- Seal to support – need to eliminate water permeation and add plasticity. Cracking is a possibility when the mask is flexible.

FIGURE 6.29 *Binders*

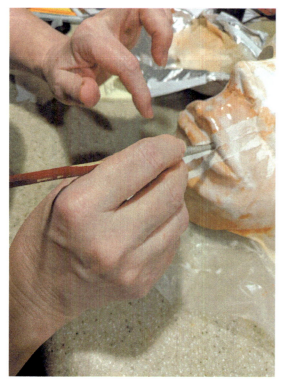

FIGURE 6.30 *Using a brush to apply glue and paper to the form*

FIGURE 6.31 *Changing colors of paper to track layers*

Mask Making 193

FIGURE 6.32 *Paper pulp added to increase dimension and covered with additional glue/paper strips*

FIGURE 6.33 *Checking for weak areas by looking for light leaks*

FIGURE 6.34 *Marking edges in a fitting*

194 Theatre Masks Out Side In

FIGURE 6.35 *Calipers are useful both to measure the performer initially and to check balance when trimming the mask*

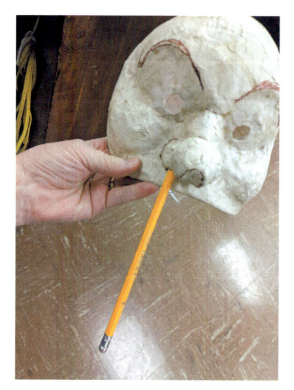

FIGURE 6.36 *A dowel or pencil is useful for reaming the nostrils if you don't have a punch; trim or cover any ragged edges*

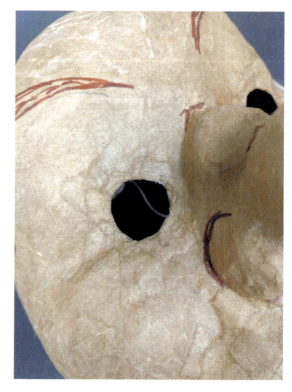

FIGURE 6.37 *Sealing the trimmed edges at the eye requires narrow strips of paper*

The process:

- Prepare a few layers worth of torn strips, in narrow and medium widths (up to an inch wide) and lengths. Tear, don't cut. The irregular edges blend smoothly.

- Saturate the strips in the binder (glue, paste, etc.), then slip the excess binder off between two fingers, and lay the strip onto the mask form, smoothing each layer of moistened paper over the former one. It is also possible to use a brush to apply layers: lay paper into the form, then use one brush to apply binder, then a dry brush to push the next layer of paper into the binder, repeat. The brush can be more effective than fingers to reach small detailed areas, as well as being less messy (Figure 6.30).

- I tend to work from the center out, beginning with a strip down the center of the nose, then outward in alternating directions to build a framework of support. Then I fill larger planes of the forehead, jawline, and cheeks, before working on the finer shapes of the nose, lips, and eyes.

- Take your time, use smaller pieces for detailed areas, and smooth the layers together to avoid air bubbles and wrinkles. If one forms, gently lift, tear, and overlap the pieces.

- It is useful to alternate colors of paper to keep track of layers – such as using paper bags of different colors, a layer of tissue paper, or newsprint in grayscale then color. Using white or light paper on the final layers can be useful if the mask is going to be painted (Figure 6.31).

- If using many layers, or limited in work sessions, you may need to dry the mask after each three to four layers. In this case, you may use a pencil to scribble on a dried layer, ensuring that the next layer covers it entirely.

- Depending on the artist and project, you may want to lay in anywhere from three to ten layers, until the mask is sturdy enough at 1/8–1/4 in. thick. A total of six layers make a fairly sturdy mask. Pulped areas may be a little thicker for some features or designs (Figure 6.32).

- When you take the dried mask off the form, check for thin areas by holding the face of the mask to the light. If you can see light seeping through any areas, reinforce them with additional layers of paper (Figure 6.33).

- You can add on to the dried mask in stages, to add features, thickness, or detail, pattern, or texture.

- It's ok to air dry the mask. If you wish to speed the drying process, set it in sunlight, or use a hairdryer on low heat. It's possible to create a drying space with a sturdy box and hairdryer, with a fabric section to allow moist air out. You might consider warmed oven, but remember the materials are flammable, and may emit unwanted fumes from chemicals in the process. Forced heating may increase shrinkage or warping if overdone or unevenly applied.

Next the mask should be trimmed, wired, decorated, sealed, and fit.

- Remove the mask from the form, and wipe any Vaseline from the inside. If the mask seems greasy, you may wish to add a layer of paper to the inside of the mask.

- Mark and trim the eyes – start with the hole a little smaller than you expect to finish it. It is easier to make the eye-hole bigger than to add back in layers of paper. Ensure that the mask will sit comfortably on the face at the nose and align with the eyes, mouth, and cheeks (especially for half masks) (Figure 6.34).

- Mark the perimeter, checking that it is even (assuming the design is symmetrical). Trim the rough edges away, again leaving a margin outside the perimeter line to allow for corrections. When satisfied with the final perimeter line, trim it even (Figure 6.35).

- Open the mouth and nostrils with an exacto knife or hole punch (a pencil is useful for reaming them and rounding the edges) (Figure 6.36).

- All edges need to be sealed so the layers do not separate. Use overlapping tabs of paper to wrap each cut edge at eyes and mouth, ensure that the nostril openings are smooth inside and out; a small donut-shaped piece of paper can be useful to apply over the reamed edges. If the mask is flexible, enclose a wire in the perimeter as you seal the outer edges (Figure 6.37 eye detail).

FIGURE 6.38 *Encasing a wire at the mask edge with paper tabs adds strength and some ability to maintain and finesse its shape*

Wiring the masks: To strengthen your mask, and to prevent curling, splitting, or loss of shape, wire the edge of your mask. Millinery wire comes in several weights; its fiber wrapping helps grip the mask material. I have also had success with aluminum wire or baling wire. Clothes hanger wire is usually too hard; florists wire is too thin. It should be soft enough to model with your hands, but strong enough to keep its shape and to adjust the paper form.

- Mark and trim the perimeter it to the desired shape, using calipers to check balance.
- Have some clothes pins, binder clips, or masking tape pieces ready.
- Cut a piece of wire about 3″ longer that the perimeter –part of the extra is to overlap at the top or the chin, the other may be used to attach elastic or ties to the finished mask.
- I prefer to start at the center of the chin with the center of the wire, and work in both directions, checking as I go for evenness.
- Begin shaping the wire to the edge of the mask, holding it in place as you go with the binder or clothespins, and (if desired) letting a small loop of wire loose just above the eyeline at the top of the ear. Fine tune the wire to fit the full outline of the mask. Overlap the extra and tape or clip in place.
- Use tabs of paper mache to encase the wire and the edges of the paper mache mask, or wrap the seam allowance of the mask over the wire. Ideally, the wire should sit at the edge of the mask (not inside or outside). Add a second layer of tabs, and finish with a smooth strip across the tabs ends inside and out.
- If you have left loops or a little bump out for attaching elastic, do not cover it, but instead slide the paper tab under the wire at those two spots.

Finishing:

- For a more consistent appearance, apply Gesso, Spackle, Sculpt or Coat, or wood filler to smooth the paper texture. The surface of the mask is then lightly sanded to remove brush or sponge marks. Wipe away the dust before continuing.
- Alternately, if a deliberate texture is desired, these fillers or other items may be applied to create a specific texture or decorative element.

FIGURE 6.39 *Masks with a base coat, lip, and eye detail ready for highlight and shadow. Courtesy of Jonathan Becker's studio*

Mask Making **197**

FIGURE 6.40 *An assistant adds highlight and shadow to the primed and painted mask. Courtesy of Jonathan Becker's studio*

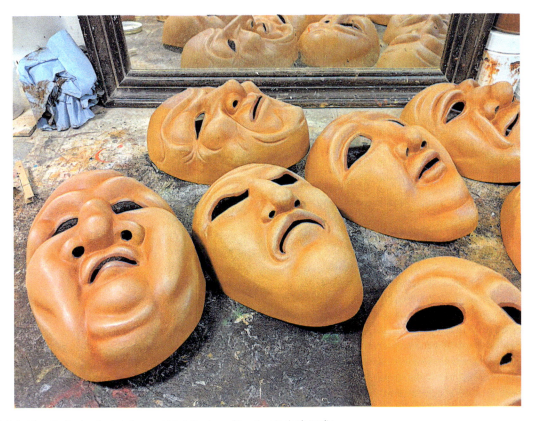

FIGURE 6.41 *Masks showing painting completed. Courtesy of Jonathan Becker's studio*

- The mask is then painted: a primer/sealer is a useful first layer, then decorative paint or stain to highlight/shadow the features, and/or add decorative elements.

- Most artists paint the interior of the mask as well, often a uniform black, though Benda used gold leaf and lacquer. The dark color minimizes bounce light that helps the performer see better. Also, when the mask is removed, it has a neutral, finished interior.

- Finally, the mask may be sealed with shellac, polyurethane, Modge Podge, or another sealer to protect it. Use smooth synthetic bristled brushes for water-based products, and natural bristles for oil-based substances. Cotton rags are used to apply and to even out or wipe off sealers of both types. Stir rather than shake these to avoid excess air bubbles. If bubbles appear, try applying thinner coats or wipe gently with a rag. Use steel wool or fine (220) grit sandpaper to rough the surface lightly between layers, wiping away any residue each time. Two or three coats are sufficient.

Fitting

If the mask was custom made on a life cast, it should fit the face well with minimal adjustment. Review the fitting information to ensure the actor is safe and comfortable. A thin piece of moleskin or felt may be glued to the interior for comfort. You may also provide the actor with an absorbent fabric hood to cover the forehead and hair.

MODELING TECHNIQUES

Direct Modeling

This technique uses lightweight three-dimensional formation on an existing base to develop the mask design over an individual or generic face cast. Paper pulp, Activa's CelluClay, and Crayola's Model Magic are materials suited to this process. Friendly Plastic can also be used to create a three-dimensional mask directly.

The form: These are best made over an existing mask base or facial cast.

Release agents: Use a thin layer of Vaseline on the plaster facial cast, or none if intending to leave the base in the mask.

The paper: Pulp allows you to build up thickness faster than layering torn paper. It can be purchased as fiber, or made by tearing or shredding paper, soaking it overnight and then simmering for 20 minutes, chopping in a blender or food processor (with plenty of water – you can strain it off later), then straining and mixing with a binder, plus a little salt or fungicide to keep from spoiling, and a few drops of clove or peppermint oil to inhibit mold. Pulp often has a slightly lumpy/rough/pebbled texture-like some egg cartons. Pulp is smoother when pressed into a negative mold.

BOX 6.5 SEALERS

Acrylic sealers come in matte and gloss finish, adhere to a variety of surfaces, are in convenient spray options, and provide some protection from moisture and wear.

Wax can be used on the outside of a mask as a moisture barrier.

Urethane-polyurethane is a liquid plastic, available in water- or oil-based forms, and with a variety of textural finishes from glossy to satin. It's available as a liquid or spray.

- Water-based versions have lower odor and toxicity, dry faster, and do not add the amber color of oil-based products. Like shellac, they may discolor with heat extremes or chemicals, but care of the masks should prevent problems.
- Fortified water-based polyurethanes such as Minwax Polycrylic are a bit more durable and can be used over both oil- and water-based finishes using synthetic bristles or cotton cloth. This form in a satin finish often works well.
- Oil-based polyurethane is more durable and should be applied with a natural bristle brush or rag. It adds a slight tone but handles heat well. It takes much longer to dry and cure and should be applied in a well-ventilated area using a respirator.
- Allow time for gas-off.

Shellac is a natural alcohol-based finish, available in liquid or solid form, applied with a natural bristle brush or cotton rag: shellac creates a protective coat, adds a slightly amber tone, is suitable for wood and other porous surfaces, but can be negatively affected by heat and chemicals. The finish is fairly shiny.

Varnish is a generic term for a top coat or finish; it is applied with a natural bristle brush, protects wood from moisture, light, and UV.

Lacquer is an exceptionally hard, shiny finish applied in several coats with a sprayer in a well-ventilated workspace. It is damage resistant but can discolor with time. For performance masks, the gloss may interfere with perception of expression because of the lacquer's reflectivity.

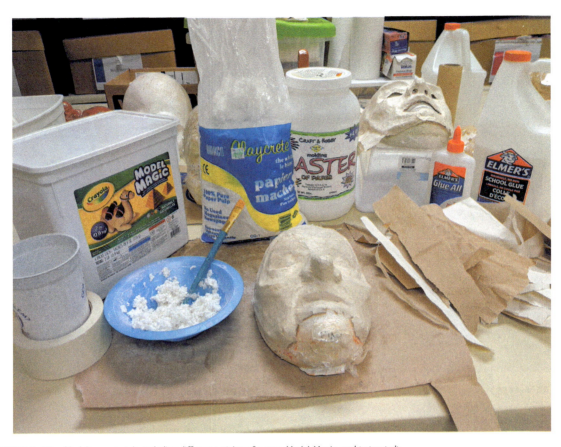

FIGURE 6.42 *Modeling materials, including different weights of paper, Model Magic, and paper pulp*

FIGURE 6.43 *Paper pulp can be used to increase the dimension of a paper mache form*

The binder: Cornstarch, wheat paste, wallpaper pastes, wood glue or white glue all work well. Plaster can be added to strengthen any of these binders but needs to be mixed in smaller batches and used before it sets. See Box 6.4, Binders.

The process is explained below.

Wiring the edge uses a similar process to strip techniques but may use lighter wire and embed it into the pulp or modeling compound. It will be more secure with a layer of strips added over it.

Finishing techniques are the same as for paper mache.

Fitting is also the same, but be more aware of the weight distribution, especially if the mask is oversized or flattened.

Laura Morelli's *Venice: A Travel Guide*[4] describes contemporary artists who make affordable tourist market masks with paper pulp over a plaster base, then trim, buff, paint, and wax or polish the surface … other methods/materials also vary by artisan. Painted Chinese opera masks for the tourist trade are also made this way.

Celluclay or other paper mache mix is a mix of paper fiber and binder, which you can just add water to and model the mask directly on a positive form – either a life cast, or a purchased base.

FIGURE 6.44(A) *Venetian tourist mask made of paper with an acrylic coating*

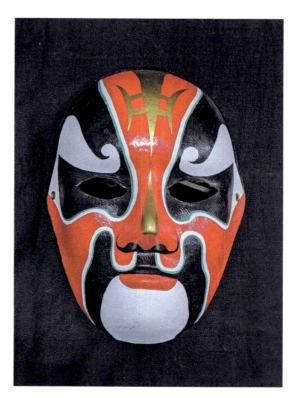

FIGURE 6.44(B) *Chinese opera tourist mask made of paper pulp pressed into a form*

Start with 1 cup of Celluclay and ¼ cup water to make moist pulp. If water pools out at the bottom, it's too wet, add more pulp or wallpaper paste. If it doesn't stick to itself, add more binder. Eli Simon in *Masking Unmasked*[6] shares a plan for doing this to make Libby Appel style[6] masks:

- Start with an old or neutral plastic mask base, cardboard, crumpled paper, and tape it all together into a rough asymmetrical design somewhat larger than your head.
- Cover the rough with aluminum foil, all the way to the base and wrap or tape it to the cardboard base.
- Mix and lay on ¼–½ in. layer of Celluclay, leaving holes for eyes and mouth. Let the mask dry, then peel away the foil.
- [At this point, I would check the fit/vision, thin spots, and balance.]
- Build up details if desired to emphasize features.
- Dry completely, sand any sharp edges, and smooth the inside.
- Cover the open mouth (inside) with black gauze or mesh, anchoring the edges of the screen with strong cement.
- Paint simply [a neutral color, perhaps some minimal highlights and shadows, though Libby describes hers as having a "highly textured effect which combines with a subtle and rich mixture of colors[7]"].

- If desired, spray with clear matte protective varnish.
- Sew, staple, or tie elastic bands to holes in the mask or with fishing line.

Model Magic™ My students have had success sculpting with Model Magic™, Crayola's exceptionally lightweight, non-toxic modeling compound, and a light paper mache cover. It works well for individual Libby Appel style and characters' masks that can be created in just a couple of sessions. See Appendix B for step-by-step instructions.

- Work on either a facial cast or a generic base mask.
- You may wish to extend the mask beyond the edges of the face with cardboard for some projects.
- Build up features in Model Magic, using a little water or water + white glue to smooth features. Model Magic can crack a little as it dries/shrinks (~5%); fill the cracks with glue.
- Cover the dried Model Magic with two or three layers of light paper mache, being sure to wrap the paper edges around to encase base mask and/or cardboard extensions.
- Use small torn pieces to ensure the smoothest possible surface, and sand lightly.
- Paint, fit, and finish … artists' acrylics work well, are inexpensive, and resist flaking, but make the mask less breathable.

Mask Making **201**

FIGURE 6.45 *Selection of emotional masks made with Model Magic and paper mache on a prepurchased form*

FIGURE 6.46 *Model Magic formed over a trimmed paper pulp base, and bound with paper mache (in progress)*

Friendly Plastic comes in beads or sheets at craft stores and online. It's also sold as InstaMorph® and Adapt-it® pellets. Benefits include that it's non-toxic, easy to use, recyclable/reusable, very sturdy, and requires little equipment. However, it has minimal flexibility and can get heavy in larger masks. It's not as easy to perfect detail (unless you do fine-tuning with a Dremel tool), but you can embed objects, glue on trims, dye it, and paint with acrylic or enamel. There is no need to seal it. Friendly Plastic is the same as the plastic in Wonderflex, but in pellet form for modeling rather than embedded in a textile sheet. A Wonderflex base is ideal for building up with Friendly Plastic. This material is also available in solid or perforated sheets under the name of Protoplast. Note that you will probably sacrifice a bowl to the melting process unless it has a silicon coating, but you can reuse the bowl to reclaim the remainder.

- Work over a solid facial cast with a smooth surface and limited undercuts: it is rigid when cool and will not come off complex forms easily. Foil and Vaseline are helpful release agents; the Vaseline can be washed off the plastic when cool.

- Working onto a negative mold is a little easier for capturing detail as long as there are no significant undercuts.

- Friendly Plastic melts at 150–170°F, so can cause burns if not handled carefully.

- Pellets can be melted in a glass bowl of hot water, and sheets can be softened with hot water or a heat gun.

- Tools and wet hands can be used to shape the pellets into free forms; if they become stiff, use a hairdryer or heat gun to resoften.

- Additional material can be added, removed, or recycled by softening and reshaping.

MOLDING AND SHAPING

Leather, buckram, and a variety of thermoplastic products are useful for mask making. These can be formed into a mold or cast, have good shape retention, and may be flexible. The materials are a little more expensive, may need to be ordered from a specialty supplier, and take more time to master.

Thermoplastics

Thermoplastics are popular and useful options for mask making. The popularity of cosplay has resulted in many online tutorials about working with these materials, both from the manufacturers and by individuals. Available in a variety of weights, colors, and transparencies, these materials are softened with heat and can be molded and remolded using a combination of heat and pressure. They are certainly more expensive than working in paper mache, and take a little practice to use effectively. They are a bit heavier and less flexible than paper or leather. As they are not at all absorbent, a bit of lining or padding is desirable for comfortable wear. On the other hand, because they are waterproof, they are useful for outside work and humid conditions, though they should not be left in a hot car or place where they could soften and warp. They are sturdy, relatively easy to work, and if properly stored last a long time. Latex free and unlikely to cause allergic reactions, thermoplastics are more user-friendly. Many of these materials are compatible, so can be mixed: for example, you might use a Sintra base form with Worbla trim pieces. Sturdy craft scissors, leather shears, box cutters, or other sharp blades work well to cut these. For lighter materials, it is also possible to use die cut machines and laser cutters.

Most thermoplastics can be activated by wet or dry heat – including a hot water bath, steamer, 1000-watt hairdryer, heat gun, or iron. Teflon sheets are useful to protect the iron and ironing table; oven safe "turkey bags" or crockpot liners can be used to protect a hat block or other form. Be careful not to overheat the material or it can bubble (Worbla and Teraflex) or shrink (Fosshape) or burn

FIGURE 6.47(A) *Using a heat gun to soften Wonderflex onto a form*

(Wonderflex or others). Keep the heat gun a few inches away from the material, and move it back and forth as it softens. Use rounded items such as a spoon, paintbrush handle, popsicle stick, or clay modeling tools to press layers together, form indentations, smooth the surface, and/or create surface textures. Tweezers can be used to pull or tear the material, or stretch areas. Small detail irons used by quilters and dolls' clothes makers are great for warming small areas and smoothing surfaces. Thermoplastics can be free formed, but it is more efficient to work over

FIGURE 6.47(B) *Beginning to mold details of the form underneath*

Mask Making **203**

FIGURE 6.47(C) *Smoothing the texture and creasing the intersection of planes with a wood tool*

FIGURE 6.47(D) *Adding an extension to lower the jawline is accomplished by pressing two warmed areas together firmly*

FIGURE 6.47(E) *Smoothing a warm seam*

a form, and helps to avoid accidental stretching, shrinking, or warping. Both positive and negative molds are suitable for thermoplastics. If your material is sticking to the form, try wrapping the form in plastic wrap or aluminum foil and misting it with cooking spray (such as Pam). Do not work thermoplastics directly on clay, as they are likely to soften it. In general, you can warm up the material, work it for a few minutes, then reheat to work on smaller areas. It is wise to set the general shape of the piece as a whole first, then clarify features and edges, finish the textures, and then focus on smaller details after the form is set. For domino masks, make a paper pattern to check size and shape first, then trace it onto the material. You may choose to cut to finish, or add a seam allowance to strengthen the edge. For larger dimensional items, consider using foam, a plastic ball, crumpled foil, or another lightweight filler to support a "skin" of thermoplastic material.

Use caution to avoid burning your fingers as you work. Smooth wooden tools such as clay modeling tools can be helpful, and for prolonged work, tight fitting insulated gloves are appropriate. It is not safe or appropriate to put hot thermoplastics directly on the face to shape – this can burn your skin. Use a cold pack or bowl of ice water to cool the work quickly before trying it on.

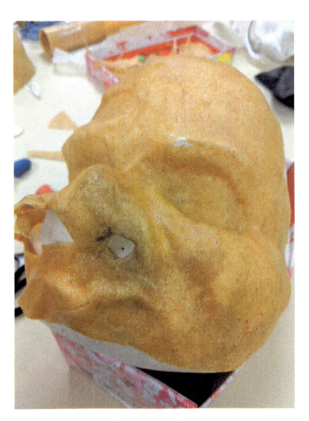

FIGURE 6.47(F) *Adding more detail*

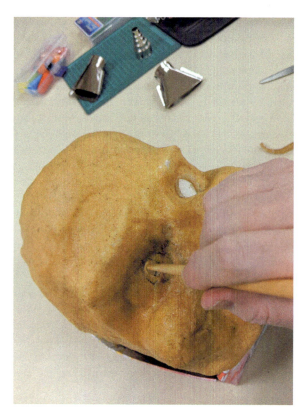

FIGURE 6.47(G) *Opening the eyes on the form helps prevent distorting the mask. They could also be cut when it is cool*

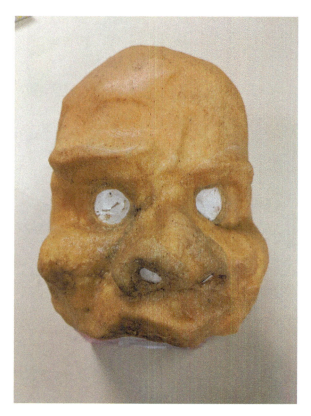

FIGURE 6.47(I) *Ready to remove from the form*

FIGURE 6.47(H) *Adding a layer to reinforce the brows*

For detail work, consider clay techniques: blend or smooth layers with a rolling pin, roll balls, cones, tubes for decoration, cut strips, scales, or intricate shapes to apply, or press softened material with stamp or tool for surface texture. Water helps to minimize stickiness on tools and fingers.

If the edges are rough, sand them or lightly warm and smooth them with a tool. For extra strength, lightly heat the edges and roll the seam to the inside, pressing the material back on itself and smoothing it from the inside with a curved tool such as a spoon or glass bottle. If there are sharp curves, notch the seam allowance (cut v shapes out of it) to avoid a bumpy overlap. Eye and nose holes should also be smooth and allow for comfortable vision and breathing.

For finishing and decorating, you can sand to smooth, or add gesso, plaster, Bondo, Sculpt or Coat, and other flexible plastic-friendly surface treatments. Most latex acrylic paints work well, whether artist or house grade. Fabric, gems, feathers, and other decorations can be embedded or applied with spray adhesive (for a full fabric cover), milliners glue, or hot glue.

Fosshape is a felt-like thermoplastic sheet, available by the yard in white or black and in different weights/sizes: 300 is lightweight, 600 is heavy. It is non-toxic, paintable, and compatible with other thermoplastics. Fosshape can be sewn easily, especially before excessive heating. It is usually worked over

Mask Making **205**

FIGURE 6.47(J) *Marking and trimming a margin on the edge*

FIGURE 6.47(K) *Turning the edge for reinforcement and comfort*

FIGURE 6.48 *Mask-making materials (from left side, clockwise): fosshape, buckram in two weights, Worbla (tan), Wonderflex (with gauze embedded), and Sintra (dull and shiny sides)*

a form to take advantage of its ability to stretch and mold. Be aware that stretching too much will thin and weaken it. A good hairdryer or heat gun is best for softening, you can use a steamer or iron but the heat is less consistent. Fosshape takes a little getting used to, especially in controlling the shrinkage (which may be up to 25%) and uneven texture. There is a point at which it will stop shrinking and become quite hard and (with pressure) smooth. It will not expand again once shrunken but remains slightly flexible unless completely shrunk. If the cast you are working over has strong undercuts, consider cutting a slit in the Fosshape form to release it from the mold, and sewing it closed. The lightest of these thermoplastics, and most flexible, it benefits from having a milliners' wire or other light wire support sewn or embedded in the edge. Once set, it can be sanded or coated with gesso, painted, and sealed. Fosshape can be pricey, with a high cost per yard, but you can make many masks from a yard of 45" Fosshape. Now available as **FuzzForm** as well. It's also used in millinery.

Wonderflex, also sold as **Altraform**, has a loosely woven fabric embedded on each side of a thermoplastic sheet, which has a built-in adhesive to help pieces stick to each other. One side has a slightly heavier fabric, so is less sticky. The fabric support allows some stretching but prevents excessive warping: use the flexibility of the bias appropriately when laying out. It features a heavier weight, less shrinkage, high amount of stickiness, and can be reworked. Because it is rigid when cool, it is not suited to deep undercuts. It softens from 150 to 170°F, getting softer and stickier with higher heat. Wonderflex can be heated and pressed into/over a form to mold, or cut and melted just at the seams based on a pattern. Detail and surface texture can be built up with strips, patches, or small forms of additional Wonderflex, or molded from Friendly Plastic and attached while both surfaces are warm. Available in 44" × 54" sheets, or in half, quarter, eighth, and sixteenth pieces, about 1/16th in. thick; for thicker pieces, heat both sheets and press together. You can also fuse Wonderflex to fabric, wood, paper, foam, and Fosshape. A full sheet weighs about 3–4 lb; it can be stapled, screwed, bolted, drilled, or heat fused. One side is smooth for easier coating/painting. Originally a light blue-green color, now it is also available in white. Beginners get successful results, but it takes some practice to get outstanding results. It's often more expensive than Fosshape, but there is less waste.

FIGURE 6.49 *Fosshape Pinocchio masks with interchangeable noses designed and created by Candy McClernan for the North Carolina Ballet*

Worbla/Terra Flex: Worbla original and Terra Flex (Tandy Leather's trademark name for a similar product) are made of wood pulp and plastic, so have excellent modeling properties that work better for some sculpted detail, such as scrollwork, scales, horns, etc. Worbla works at a higher temperature (194°F), but scraps can be melted together and reused so there is no waste. Pale tan, and a little granular, Worbla darkens as it heats but returns to its natural tan as it cools. Remember it sticks to itself, so keep it flat on a Teflon sheet or foil as you heat it. Use water on forms and fingers to work without sticking. Worbla is very popular with cosplayers and comes in a variety of forms. As of this writing, there are seven Worbla products, including original, clear, black, extra strength, fire retardant, flexible embedded mesh, and pellet formats. KobraCast, the type with an embedded mesh,

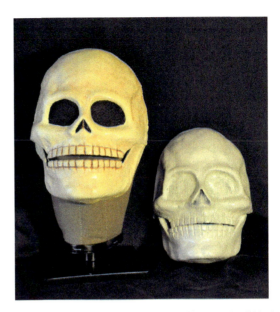

FIGURE 6.50(C) *Skull with hinged moveable jaw made of Wonderflex formed on a clay matrix. The matrix is next to the mask. Created by Candace McClernan and Rachel Pollock for* No Hiding Results: Evaluating mask-making methods to find the optimal build. *(Stage Directions, March 2016: 14–17)*

remains somewhat flexible even when cool and is the thinnest product – about the same as cardstock – so it is possible to form it on mask sculpts that include undercuts. The transparent is also lovely and paintable with acrylic. These are more expensive than most other thermoplastic sheets.

FIGURE 6.50(A) *Two black ravens by Candy McClernan: The bases were created with Fosshape and an added layer of Wonderflex to give the masks substance. The Wonderflex has inherent glue to hold the attached Fosshaped feathers. The beaks are made of Wonderflex Pro on the left and Wonderflex on the right*

FIGURE 6.50(B) *Bluebird masks for Ballet West in Utah by Candy McClernan. Fosshape base covered in Wonderflex and fashion fabrics provided by the designer*

FIGURE 6.51 *Worbla noses and brows combine with fake fur and purchased glasses for the tailors in Lafcadio at Butler Theatre*

FIGURE 6.52 *Anubis carved in blue foam and covered with tin foil, then used to construct a Varaform base and paper mache ears. The mask form was then painted and fabric added. Note that the performer can see out through the mesh of the Varaform*

Varaform/Hexcelite Thermoplastic Mesh: Hexcelite was developed in the 1980s by Hexcel Corporation and used in the medical profession for making casts to set broken bones. Originally packaged as orthopedic tape, it also can be purchased in large sheets. While the term Hexcelite is still used by people who work with it, the new trade name is Varaform. This product is a coarse cotton mesh embedded with thermoplastic, in gauze, lightweight, or heavy mesh. It can be heated with water or air, softening in about 30 seconds at 160°F, and giving 2–4 minutes working times before needing to be reheated. Pieces can be free formed, put over a mold, or patterned, taking the grain into consideration for how it can stretch or compact. The open grid makes this lightweight, more breathable than solid forms, and marginally flexible, but it does not take fine detail. Scraps can be melted together to reuse several times, and a more solid appearance and increased strength achieved by layering the grid to offset the holes, and using pressure to spread the plastic. Varaform can be tinted by adding dye to the hot water bath and accepts a variety of coatings and paints.

Sintra is an expanded closed cell PVC, or PVC Foam Board. It's pretty expensive, but quite light in weight. It is available from manufacturers, at plastics and cosplay stores, and online. Originally used for outdoor signs, it is very durable, rigid, lightweight. It can be cut with a knife, shaped with a heat gun, glued or stuck to other heated thermoplastics, and sanded/painted with a variety of finishes. It takes less detail, so may not work as well for detailed character faces. But it is a good material to consider for large-scale items, shield-shaped masks, or if you are good with intricate patterning.

FIGURE 6.53 *Completed Anubis mask by Candy McClernan*

Leather

Leather is the gold standard for mask making, and the traditional material used in masks of the Commedia dell'Arte. It is light, breathable, flexible, natural, able to hold a form, and beautiful. Fava declares it "an irreplaceable material … best for shaping, contact with actor's face, continuity of skin to skin, light, adaptable, functional, symbolic …"[8] Many mask artists and performers use leather exclusively. It offers the best breathability by absorbing and releasing moisture from both the actor and the atmosphere. It will mold to the actor's face, especially if designed over a life cast to fit the performer individually. It is flexible enough to move with the performer's facial expression, and lighter in weight than most cast or thermoplastic materials. Its uniform surface is comfortable against the skin, so often requires no additional padding for the actor's comfort. Leather is long-lasting and ages well. However, it takes more time and skill to create a leather mask – many days or weeks, in addition to creating the mold over which it will be formed. It is a skill that one can begin to learn in a few weeks, but which takes years to master. Leathers must be selected carefully and prepared in specific chemical process in order to work for the masks. A few specific tools are needed, so advance planning is important to acquire materials, prepare the forms, and then make the masks. Leather is suitable for domino masks, both simple and ornately pierced or decorated, and is popular with cosplay and LARP fans. There are a number of YouTube videos and pages that show simple techniques for cutting, lightly shaping, staining and painting leather. Decorative or "party" masks may make use of colored or textured leathers. For a living character mask, plain leather is appropriate, and a more developed technique is necessary to set the planes of the face effectively.

The design of the mask should incorporate strong, realistic planes and integrated features and will ideally be sculpted over a life cast of the performer.

Leather shaping must be done on a sturdy positive form. The Sartoris reintroduced the Commedia dell'Arte method of shaping the mask over a carved wooden form such as pine, fir, or cembra pine.[9] This has the advantage of absorbing and releasing moisture, remaining firm in all climates, being reusable and repairable, and therefore useful for many copies of a mask design. However, mastering the art of wood carving is not easily or quickly developed. A Hydrocal (gypsum cement) cast can be used a few times, as in the Woyzeck case study.

Seal any plaster cast with spray on shellac or wax to minimize moisture damage. Newman uses frozen Plastilina #4 clay successfully, eliminating the second casting process and lacing the leather to the form rather than tacking it.[10]

Choose vegetable-tanned cow or buffalo leather from the belly for maximum shapeability, or flank.[11] Top grain (unsplit) is better than split grain that has had the skin layer removed, so is sueded (rough) on both sides. The top grain texture is more skin like, has better shape memory, and is more durable. Lighter weights and thicknesses can take more detail in shaping; heavier ones can be better for projecting features and durability. 3 oz (thin)–8 oz (thick) are a reasonable range of weights.

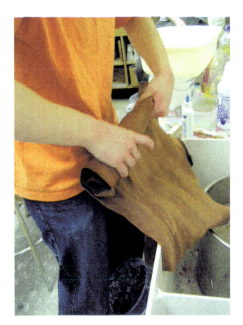

(A)   Wringing the soaked leather

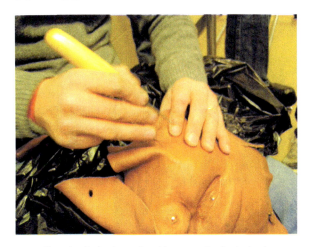

(B)   Centering the leather and working outward to begin shaping

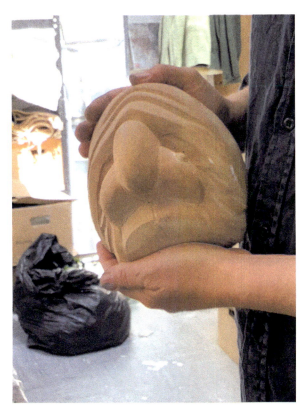

FIGURE 6.54   Wooden matrix by Russell Dean

FIGURE 6.55   Leather mask process (Woyzeck) (Continued)

This is one process for creating leather masks with a 3-mm vegetable-tanned cow belly leather

- Ensure your leather piece is ample enough to cover the mask area plus an inch or two of margin at each edge.
- Soak the leather in water for 10–20 minutes to relax the fibers.
- Wring and squeeze with your hands to remove excess water (Figure 6.55a).
- Drape the leather over the mask form, ensuring all edges are covered.
- Begin working the leather from the eyes/nose outward, over all features (Figure 6.55b).
- Plan where any seam/splice may be needed (often under the nose on a half mask, and the center back if a full mask with hair).
- It is helpful to tack the leather to the form where it will not show: eyes, nostrils, and outer perimeter beyond the edge of the mask design. An alternative to tacking is to lace the edges across the back of the form (Figure 6.55c).

(C) Tacking the leather at eyes, nostrils, and hidden seams

(D) Blunt tools to shape the leather to the planes of the form

(E1) Hammering the formed leather condenses and sets the shape

(E2) Mask showing hammer marks

FIGURE 6.55 *Leather mask process (Woyzeck)* *(Continued)*

- Using blunt tools (we used buffalo horn hammers and ebony tools) to press and hammer the leather, pressing and compressing it into the shape of each mask. This may be done in a couple of stages if necessary. Keep the changing planes of the mask clearly articulated (Figure 6.55d).
- If the leather dries out as you work, use a damp sponge to keep it moist.
- Once the form is set, a horn-tipped hammer is used to tap the mask all over, further compressing the leather and reinforcing the shape of the mask (Figure 6.55e).
- When dry, the edges of the mask are trimmed, skived to a thin edge, notched, and glued over a wire to set the finished edge of the mask (Figure 6.55f). The seams were also skived, glued, and covered with a thin strip of leather for neat reinforcement. On full head masks (that cover the skull as well as the face), a center slit is left in back to ease putting the mask on and off.

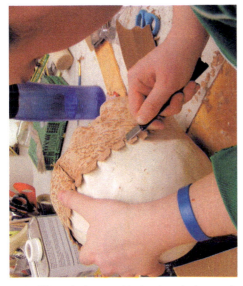

(F1) Trimmed edges are skived and notched to turn in over a wire

(F2) The inside edge of the mask is prepared with contact cement

(F3) Thin strips of leather with contact cement to cover the notched edge and seams

FIGURE 6.55 Leather mask process (Woyzeck) (Continued)

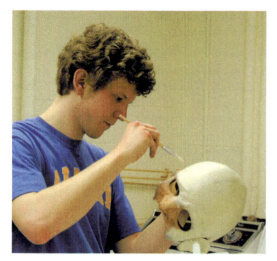

(G1) Base coat to texture before painting

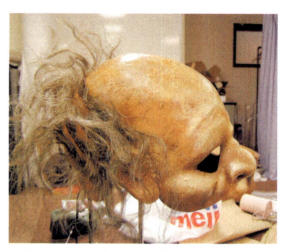

(G2) Texture and color were added to these masks to continue the grotesque style of the production

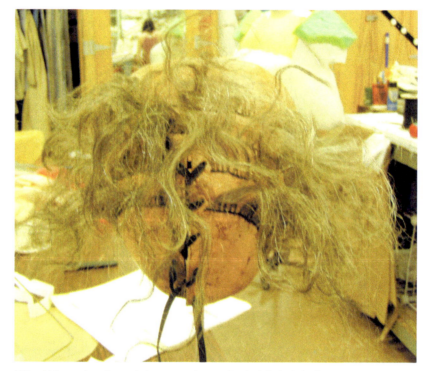

(H) Hair completes the mask character and covers the elastic lacing in back

FIGURE 6.55 Leather mask process (Woyzeck) (Continued)

- If desired, the exterior of the mask can be given a textural coating, paint, or dye to suit the design.
- To finish the masks, each was crafted a pair of leather ears which were sewn on (before the texture and paint), and moustaches, brows, and hair were selected and applied. The hair was then dressed (distressed, really), thinned, or grayed as appropriate (Figure 6.55g).
- Each mask has a wide elastic inside to secure the mask against the face from the temples, and an elastic in the center back slit to hold it gently around the skull so that it moves seamlessly with the performer's body (Figure 6.55h).

Mask Making   213

(1)   *A selection of leather masks designed and created by Bernardo Rey, with Wendy Meaden, and students at Butler University for* Woyzeck

FIGURE 6.55   *Leather mask process (Woyzeck)*

BOX 6.6 ARTIST PROFILE: BERNARDO REY, MASK ARTIST AND THEATRE CREATOR

Bernardo Rey Rengifo is a Colombian director, designer, and creator of masks. The Centre for Theatre Research – CENIT – was created in Bogotá in 1992 by Bernardo Rey and Nube Sandoval. Since its inception, the Centre has developed an interdisciplinary approach to research, generating a continuous dialogue between performing and visual arts, creating unconventional theatrical spaces and deepening the study of the mask, its construction and use. Theatre CENIT has worked extensively within social care sectors using theater as a privileged instrument to develop resilience and empowerment in vulnerable social contexts. In collaboration with the CIR-Italian Council for Refugees based in Rome, CENIT spent ten years developing the theatrical project of psycho-social rehabilitation with refugees and victims of torture. Their experience of more than 30 years consolidates the basis of their methodology: "Theatre as Bridge." Together they have created works in South and North America, Africa, and Europe. They have earned recognition for the importance and quality of their work, including the "Ellen Stewart International Award" (New York 2016).

Here are some excerpts from our conversations about his work in mask theater.

TB 6.6   *Image of the artist Bernardo Rey*

TB 6.6(A)   *Nube Sandoval as Antigone in mask by Bernardo Rey*

TB 6.6(B)   *Leather mask in Commedia style*

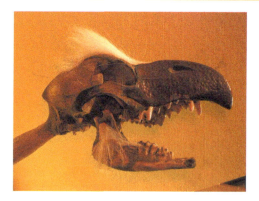

TB 6.6(C)   *Phoenix,* Conference of the Birds, *leather and bone*

How did you begin as a theater artist?

When I was young, 17, I studied architecture for three years, and painting with a master painter in Colombia. I saw an exhibition of Jean-Marie Binoche – father of the French actress Juliette Binoche – he lived in Colombia and was a mask maker, director, and educator. I like working with my hands, so began mask work after that, and scenography for theater.

There is no tradition of masks in Colombia, so I started to invent them with wood powder and glue. I did more and more theater. Later Donato Sartori came to Bogota and I did a workshop with him. Donato liked my work, so I went to Italy for a one-month workshop with him. He invited me to stay after that, where I was collaborating and learning, little by little, how to use the mask.

Next, I went to study performance and met Jerzy Grotowski, Eugenio Barba, and others. Although they did not use masks, I was learning to act and continued to mix acting and masks. I also continued to practice scenography, which like architecture considered how to use space. My methodology is founded on that.

What drew you to making masks initially?

I like to work with my hands. I like sculpture. The mask is the first sculpture in movement, an object in action. That idea inspired me a lot. The mask has an essence only if he is active; it is not enough just to look in his eyes on the wall. A mask is a human being: she laughs and cries. The first mistake of the new mask maker is to have only one expression. You may laugh for 3 minutes, then ok you get it, and then you are done: too soon we understand the mask is dead if it does not do more. The form of the mask is very important: we must be able to see from fifty, a hundred feet distance, that it laughs, cries, changes – without the performer's action, how can an object that doesn't move do these things? The mask must be more than an aesthetic object like a sculpture.

What circumstances make masks effective in performance?

Because the mask is used well with the body, there are codes of communication. It is extra-quotidian. You cannot be natural, like in common life. The mask will be dead. When you use a mask and it's working, you are a new being, and very strange: it requires your attention. It is like a little animal; it demands your attention. But it must be used right – it needs precise bodywork.

Masks have a rhythm. This is the most important thing I found out. It dies without that. It is not mental, it must be felt, must be done, action, action, action, you never just express emotion, you must do action. React. Don't show you are angry, be angry. Do something. Not shake your fist, but throw something. Do not gesture a cliché to show you are angry with your fist. Do be angry.

Do you make new masks for each project? Do you ever reuse masks?

Always new masks for a new project. For example, in the new Woyzeck, we will focus again on hospital scenography and objects. We will research again, for new actors, and a new performance. The mask is an exact object.

What were some key elements you learned from the Sartoris?

Donato Sartori was a real master. He was one of the artists who learned generation by generation; they developed the knowledge of how to do one thing completely.

All his tools were handmade – quality is important, and there was no buying cheaper tools from someplace else. I had to learn the craft by hand first, to know the process and materials, before I could do any other way. I could not use electric tools.

I developed the very best techniques, from paper to wood to leather. I was very fortunate to work with him, and he became like a friend and father and mentor. I learned not only craft, but the ethic of work and perfectionism – no cheating yourself or the art. Sartori also explored the contemporary mask – so I learned not only the craft, but also the concept and growth.

When making masks, what do you focus on? What makes a live mask?

The mask is an instrument, not an aesthetic. To help the actor, it must not bother the actor. First, the measurements have to be perfect both to fit the face and to carry to the audience. You must be able to see it from far away, a hundred feet. The lines and the form must be clear. This is especially true for Commedia masks: they are a single color, so they rely on form which must catch the light – it is a game of light and shadow. Also, the mask is human, so must be able to cry, to laugh, be angry. How to help him change moods? The technique of the actor is necessary, and the line as expression of the mask works with the action.

In the sculptures of Michelangelo, there is opposition in direction, such as someone looking in one direction but the body is facing the other way. Synthesis then brings the opposing elements together, so, for example, the *Pieta* has an apparently relaxed pose but is actually very difficult to enact; or Rodin in whose *Thinker* the elbow rests on the opposite knee – now it is in opposition – the artist thinks with the whole body – the spine is active, a spiral, not actual natural rest.

In a mask, there are four oppositions: lines that go down with gravity, lines that go up, from outside to center or center to outside. With these four, you can make oppositions. Without them, the mask will be dead in 2 minutes. We can think of Pantalone, who is aged and has lines that go down, but also moments when for lust or money the eye should go up.

The eyes and mouth are very expressive. If the audience can't see them, the actor must move the body even more, and must be very well trained to make it work.

How does the costume work with the mask?

The mask is a whole look, not just a face piece. The costume continues and complements the mask. Charlie Chaplin, for example, has a little jacket and big pants in

TB 6.6(D)   *Carved wooden head object for* Macbeth

opposition. The actor needs a partner. It can be an essential object. For Chaplin, it was the cane. The performer must be the master of that object/partner. It is with you for the whole performance, he must do incredible things with it. It is part of the costume. The mask and costume are the same – ready to move.

What considerations are there in lighting the mask?

Normally we light a mask at 45-degree inclination. Light should be from the top, there needs to be a geometric plane, so the light and shadow change. If light is all over, there is no shadow and we don't see the form. If the mask is painted, the color can create the highlight and shadow, so if I want a lot of light, I suggest a painted mask.

What advice do you have for people starting out in mask making?

First know what you want to do. Who is the character? How does he act? What words are said about him? Then you must be a hunter, looking for concepts how to get to a concrete form and material. So maybe the character is a lawyer; how does he act? Think of an animal – perhaps he is a dog, always looking, sniffing out things – ah, so perhaps a bloodhound. For the action, the nose is important! So perhaps it becomes the beginning of the form, and the dog/lawyer has eyes that droop down; then I know the brows, and the nose where the energy is. The mistake with thinking of an animal is to make a mask of it – you should not see the animal, it should be hidden. Do not make a mask of a dog. But use the qualities to help with the body, the action, the voice, the energy, and the expression of the mouth.

What are some particularly effective masked projects you have done that have had impact on the world?

I like masks that don't just make us laugh. Life is more than that. I do work that is more human; I want to mirror

TB 6.6(E)   *Production photo, Exodus, 2012*

life for people. We react to real situations in the world, we cannot do nothing, we must react and say and do something in response.

Our change is not only in the message of the play, not only the performance, but in the doing. The group has a responsibility to forge community, so the relationships we create with people, in action and reaction, are important. We must change the world by pointing out the rules that are good to everybody.

For example, the work we did in Italy with refugees and victims of torture, it allowed the people from many places to develop a new sense of self and community together, it brought their stories to the public, and it made better awareness of the plight of displaced peoples. This can influence people to make policy and laws that help people. These ten years with refugees developed our work of "Theatre as Bridge," to heal and empower people. This was just part of our work.

What are you working on now?

We continue with building the Cenit Arte Natura – the Center for Art and Nature – in Colombia. It is a place for people from all over the world to collaborate on projects. CENIT dedicates its work to the continuous dialogue between the arts and the use of theater as an instrument for resilience in vulnerable areas. We work with local populations using theater to develop community. We always start with the village people in charge of culture, then ask for suggestions on who to work with, and explain our project. We find what the people have for materials and interests and build on that. For example, in one place where they had abundant balsa wood, the kids are already expert with machetes, so they cut three trees, and made masks building on their abilities. Another project engaged children in making paper mache carnival masks. At another village, I worked to make masks in leather with a local group of already very accomplished artists. Their interest is in presenting political comedy – like a tropical Commedia dell'Arte – all with professional university-educated people, who have decided to make theater; it is very popular. Another project is spending one month in each village in an abandoned area of Colombia's Pacific Coast: a group of people are travelling and creating a performance centered on the traditional songs of African cultures there. We took that performance to a festival with the goal to maintain the peoples' tradition. Also, we are working with the Truth Commission and many people to create *Develaciones: un canto a los cuatro vientos*, which is to promote understanding, healing, and reconciliation in Colombia.

TB 6.6(F)   *Teatro Cenit Arte y Natura, Colombia*

Buckram

Buckram is a woven textile impregnated with sizing; it comes in a variety of weights and can be purchased from millinery suppliers. It can be cut and sewn from a pattern, or draped and darted into a form using steam. For greater flexibility and detailed shaping, it can be dipped in water for a few seconds and then stretched/compressed to a mask form and left to dry. If used, the edges should be wired for stability. Edges can be turned over the wire or encased with bias tape. It can be painted and can be seen through, so is sometimes used with little or no eyehole, or as an inset in the eye area of a mask.

Wire

Wire Mesh or coil can also be formed into masks using pressure over a sturdy form, and wired and painted for a mask the wearer can see out of. Be sure to encase the edge of the wire

FIGURE 6.56(A)   *Buckram in two weights*

for comfort and safety: metal foils and strips are available to use in this way as well as for decoration.

Foam

Craft foam or closed cell foam can also be used in a variety of ways. It is useful for patterning, can be stitched or glued,

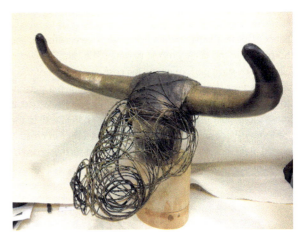

FIGURE 6.57   *Bull helmet mask made by Denise Wallace-Spriggs for Yerma, designed by Olivera Gajic for the Huntington Theatre Company*

responds to some shaping with heat, and takes paints and glues well. It is very lightweight and flexible, but sturdy enough to hold its shape. It can be used for a whole mask, in combination with other materials, or to add dimensional details to other masks.

CAST MATERIALS

Cast masks are created by pouring a liquid into a negative mold and allowing it to cure (solidify).

Latex, foam latex, neoprene, and silicon products are available for casting. Some, such as cold foam, require both a positive face cast and the negative of the design to be fitted together.

FIGURE 6.56(B)   *Lego Batman helmet mask constructed of Olefin foam, covered in Wonderflex, and spray painted black. The actor sees through the mouth area, which is made of buckram. Created by Candace McClernan*

FIGURE 6.58(A) *Latex Halloween mask from the author's kids' closet*

Latex

Latex masks are familiar to us from Halloween costumes and horror, sci-fi, and fantasy movie makeup. They are not generally used by stage performers, as the costumey nature of them as masks feels unrealistic and does not play well in a person-to-person live performance. This type of flexible latex mask is more successfully used in film and makeup when fit well to the performer's face and character. Latex is also useful in creating a solid, flexible surface over another material such as foam or fabric.

Latex is a natural product made from the sap of the rubber tree. Liquid latex is mixed with ammonia, so should be used with good ventilation. Also, some people are allergic to latex, so do ask before using or asking some to wear a latex mask. If unsure, try a small dab of it on the inner forearm, to gauge their sensitivity to it. I strongly recommend erring on the side of caution. Even for those who are not allergic to latex, prolonged contact can be irritating as it is not porous and does not "breathe" well.

Latex is capable of taking very good detail, and as it is flexible can manage undercuts.

Its flexibility is helpful in following the curves of the face and stretching to put on a variety of people, but these same properties make it quite soft, so it does not hold its shape well, unless supported by a face or other embedded structure. Latex can be made stronger by embedding gauze in the layers. Another helpful property of latex is that wet will adhere to dry, so additional layers can be added to bolster a thin area, patch small tears, and embed hair.

Latex requires compatible paints – acrylic/latex – or if used as an appliance, the appropriate makeups (PAX or RMG).

Latex rubber masks such as one might purchase at a Halloween or costume store are made by sculpting a three-dimensional full head mask design, casting the front and back negatives in plaster (generally two pieces, with keys to ensure proper alignment of the mold halves), applying a release agent to the mold, then pouring layers of liquid latex into the negative mold (which will be like a vase). The form and latex must be gently rotated to ensure that the latex coats all the interior surfaces with enough rubber to make an evenly sturdy mask. When the latex is cured, the inside is powdered, the mold is

FIGURE 6.58(B) *Latex masks; surface treatment with acrylic paint, mesh inserts, and cotton cords for Katshei in Butler Ballet production of* The Firebird. *Design by Kathleen Egan. Created by Elizabeth Snider*

opened, and the mask is gently pulled from the mold. Airbrush is most commonly used for painting latex, but brushes and sponges are also useful.

In Cheralyn Lambeth's book *Creating the Character Costume*,[12] SFX artist Spat Oktan shares a mask-making process for cosplay and LARP (live action role play) fans: starting with a hard hat base, he builds a 10–12 ga wire armature, adds foam shapes (with duct tape), covers the form with pantyhose to create a consistent textured surface, and applies layers of Mold Builder latex over that all with a chip brush. Acrylic paints flex with the latex. Note that latex takes longer to cure in humid environments and look for low ammonia latex if you are allergic or have poor ventilation – fans help both to diffuse the ammonia smell and help the latex cure faster (so does a dehumidifier).

Neoprene

Neoprene is a synthetic latex-vinyl that, purchased in liquid form, is poured into a negative mold, allowed to sit overnight, then poured off, leaving a fairly rigid mask. Neoprene comes in different formulas with varying flexibility, although the thickness of the mask also affects rigidity. The casts should be

FIGURE 6.59(A)   *Plaster mold brushed with a release agent*

BOX 6.7 ARTIST PROFILE: JONATHAN BECKER

Jonathan Becker, a mask artist, performer, educator, and collaborative creator, has been making masks for over 35 years. He received a bachelor's degree in theater, earned two master's degrees in acting, directing, and theater pedagogy, and studied performance at International Theatre School Jacques Lecoq. He has performed with and without masks in Europe, Asia, and North America. In addition to his work as a master mask maker, Jonathan is the Artistic Director of The North American Laboratory of the Performing Arts, an ongoing project intended to develop new works and to increase our understanding of what makes work successful and why. When he is not teaching, he makes and sells both stock and commissioned masks to schools, professional theaters, collectors, and individual artists. Currently he is settled in a historic home in Indiana where he has his mask studio and business, TheatreMasks.com.

Jonathan works primarily in neoprene, a non-allergenic synthetic latex that is an extremely durable cast material. His mask designs are characterized by clear, clean planes which have strength in performance. He acknowledges the impact of Commedia dell'Arte on many of his masks and describes them as having "extremely high energy and style"; the frequently exposed eyes and mouths of the performer "encourage the actor to use his eyes to convey expression, and to move his head so that the audience can see different angles of the mask." He uses masks for actor training and designs and provides masks for theatrical performance. In a recent conversation, we asked Jonathan when it is appropriate to use masks. He promptly replied, "When you can't do without them." He went on to explain:

> Masks heighten, and are extraordinary. Greek theatre needed them for scale, but now the masks allow the students to stand and be present, and allow us to believe the profundity of the story and the higher level of the tragedy. In Juan Darien, they are necessary to impart the style that drives the event. The top hat masks of Crow and Weasel are useful because they allow both the animal aspect of indigenous storytelling and the actors' vocalizing. By contrast, Shakespeare is about text, so masks compete with the language. When we need to say things humans can't say, masks fill that space.

Jonathan also reminded us that "Masks are not costumes: you can't just put them on. Masks have to be there from the beginning. They are how the actors communicate. A mask is like a violin; the performer must learn to play it."

FIGURE 6.59(B) *Jonathan Becker pours neoprene into molds at his studio*

made larger than the finished product because neoprene shrinks as it dries, by about 10%. Some performers using neoprene masks appreciate a bit of lining or padding at contact points to absorb sweat and to assist with airflow. Large masks can get heavy and need additional securing to the head. Neoprene is great for classroom masks that will be worn by a variety of students, as they can be quickly wiped with alcohol to disinfect them. In addition to being cleaned easily, they are durable in a variety of conditions, take detail reasonably well, are slightly flexible, and very long-lasting. Preparing the design and negative mold are time-consuming and resource heavy, but once a successful mold is cast, many masks can be made from that mold.

Create positive sculpt of mask in water-based clay, allowing extra for shrinkage (you may want to do a paper mache version now to check the liveliness of the mask: if so, make any corrections to the sculpt then …).

- Cover the clay sculpt with a non-oily release agent, such as liquid soap. Neoprene does not cure well if in contact with oil.

- Make a sturdy plaster or Hydrocal negative mold of the mask design, being sure to cast beyond the edge of the mask: you will need to fill the mask with neoprene, so the edges must come up as a bowl. As the Hydrocal sets, create a flat base parallel to the edges of the cast.

- When the plaster is set, clean the clay from the mold. Pull as much as you can out, and wipe the interior well. Additional residue can be removed with a swab of acetone; Bruce Marrs also recommends pouring a quick layer of liquid latex into the mold, then pulling it out to get any remaining matter.[13] Let it dry for a day.

- Add a release agent to the inside of the negative mold. Chicago latex sells one that can be brushed on. The plaster must still be able to breathe, so is not sealed.

- Nest the negative mold in a box of crumpled paper or packing material so the edges will be level.

- Pour neoprene into the mold gently; you may want to pour a little, rotate the mold to ensure a good outer layer (no bubbles), then fill the mold so all areas are covered. Tap a bit to raise bubbles from the edges to the surface. As the mold absorbs some moisture, the level will drop; add more neoprene if it nears the mask edge (in the first 20 minutes or so).

- Let set for 1.5–2.5 hours, then pour off the remaining neoprene for reuse. The longer it sets, the thicker it will become.

- I like to rotate the mask a little after the pour off to ensure even distribution of the neoprene; it will pool and thicken low points of the cast (tip of the nose, lips, brows, chin).

- Let the mask cure an additional 10–24 hours, until it is no longer sticky to the touch.

- Trim out the eyes, nostrils, mouth opening, and edges per your design when you remove it from the mold.

- It is helpful to lightly sand the surface before priming or painting to help the paint stick.

- Complete gas-off before finishing with acrylic paints and adding ties (rivets work well).

- Additional neoprene, contact cement, goop, and E6000 are useful for adding hair, brows, and other items.

- The interior may be more comfortable with foam or felt padding at key contact points, especially on larger/heavier masks.

FIGURE 6.60 *Untrimmed, trimmed, and painted versions of the mask*

PATTERNING AND FORMING

Some masks are formed from a pattern – several flat shapes that fit together to create the planes of the mask face. Patterns are the starting place for masks made of cardboard, buckram, or foam. A sheet of card stock, brown craft paper, or paper plate can be turned into a rudimentary mask. As an opening to creativity, technique building, and sense of other, they are useful and entertaining. Folding, curling, piercing, crumpling, and layering paper provide a variety of ways to add features, texture, and dimension to simple masks.

BOX 6.8 PAPER TECHNIQUES

Paper grain:

- Bends more easily with the grain (lengthwise) than across it (so can roll finer tubes).
- Folds more cleanly with the grain than across (for crisp detailed creases).
- Tears more smoothly with the grain.
- Folds at angles to the grain can cause uneven tension and buckling – consider this in making scored folds.
- These properties are more pronounced in heavy papers.

Folding, scoring, creasing:

- Fold by hand on a flat surface with edges away and bottom/fold toward you.
- Score with sharp blade along metal edge 2/3 way through thick paper – on mountain (outer) side – weakens paper.
- Crease/indent with dull tool on inside of form, supported by gully underneath paper.
- Mountain folds go up (convex), valley folds go down (concave); accordion pleats alternate, knife pleats go to one side, box pleats alternate left-right, radiating Pleats come from a center point.

Other techniques:

- Origami, the Japanese art of paper folding, presents great architectural forms and whimsical shapes and figures.
- Pop-up – familiar with holiday cards and children's books – introduces some moving parts and interesting depth from simple cuts and folds.
- Quilling, invented as a cheap substitute for metal filigree, uses narrow strips of paper curled into circles, hearts, leaves, ovals, spirals, and other shapes, and can offer a wonderful textural decoration.
- Sculpture is useful in adding dimension and features with folded and scored segments
    - cones, cylinders, boxes, pyramids, steps
    - undulating variations of all these with alternating mountain and valley folds
    - fluid forms such as spirals, leaves, ogees, from curled papers
- Texture can be increased by weaving, braiding, twisting, pleating, scrunching, stitching, cutting, or perforating.

TB 6.8(A) *Paper Techniques can be used for texture and structure*

TB 6.8(B) *Paper cranes: origami mask by Hannah Martin*

Paper masks can be incredible works of craftsmanship and engineering. Michael Grater's *Paper Maskmaking* includes a variety of patterns for simple but effective animal masks that can be cut and assembled to present the structural essence of each animal and decorated to develop its character. Jackson[14] uses a variety of cut, scored, and folded cards to create lively faces. American artist Wladyslaw T. Benda used four different techniques for paper mask making with which he created many beautiful quality masks.

Simple paper masks are a great place to begin creative exploration. They are also useful for working out patterns and shapes before moving to expensive materials.

Foam has great potential for mask making. Foams have a wide variety of textures that result from the specific chemicals used, the size of the pores, density, flexibility, and whether the cells are open (porous) or closed. Its lightweight makes it great for large creations. It is malleable in many ways. Different forms can be cut into patterns, folded, bent, glued, stitched, and assembled. Others can be compressed to take on curved features. Some are carved to achieve intricate detail. A variety of tubular forms work well for bone and silhouette construction, and for smaller details such as claws and whiskers. Foams can often be sewn, glued, coated, and/or painted. Furniture and carpet stores may have substantial scraps of polyfoam, or your local print shop may discard foam core that you can have or purchase for much less than sewing/craft stores. With a little effort, you may find a manufacturer in your area that will sell direct to you and may provide custom sizes, shapes, and edging.

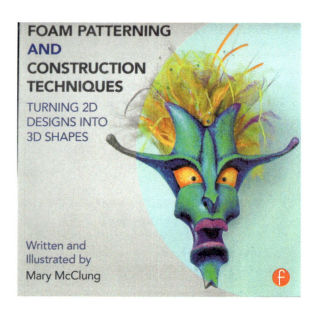

FIGURE 6.61 *Mary McClung's book is a terrific resource for foam mask work*

You can also find foam items such as Nerf Balls, coolers, and pool toys to try out some foam techniques. Designer Mary McClung creates brilliant foam masks, costumes, and puppets with many techniques: creating a surface pattern from a sculpted model, cutting away to reveal a solid form, assembling shaped pieces, and adapting existing patterns. Her book *Foam Patterning and Construction Techniques* is an excellent resource.

BOX 6.9 FOAM

Polyfoam Polyurethane or polyether foam (upholstery foam) – comes in sheets, tubes, rods, and blocks: different colors for different densities (tan, green, blue, white). It has fine pores and is very soft, compressible, lightly sewable, glueable.

Headliner foam – a thin sheet of polyfoam adhered to a layer of fabric, usually knit. ¼″ is available in many fabric/upholstery stores.

Filter foam (Scott foam) – sewable, holds a stitch. Density measured in pores per inch; the higher the ppi, the denser the foam.

Fun foam – closed-cell fine grained, also called mini-cell. Lots of colors and texture in craft stores – in 1/8–1/4″ thicknesses in sheets, rolls, and precut shapes. Easy to cut, sew, glue, can heat shape with good hot hairdryer.

Ethofoam or Ethyfoam – packing and pipe insulation also toys such as pool noodles: stiff, holds space, comes in sheets and rods. Nice for finishing rough edges, making long curves, details.

Polystyrene – rigid, available in blocks for carving, sanding, super lightweight. Cut with a serrated knife or fine saw. Don't heat it or it will release toxic fumes. Three forms include:

Styrofoam, which has a rough pebbled texture; EPS (Expanded polystyrene, or Beadboard) has finer texture; extruded polystyrene is denser, comes in insulating sheets in different thicknesses. Test glues.

Rigid urethane foam – comes in various densities and forms, including a spray form that can be put into a negative mold or applied freely and carved or sanded.

Foam core – ¼″ thick sheet of fine-grained Styrofoam with paper on both sides; available in black, white, and different colors. Often used inside the mouths of puppets or for oversized masks.

Gator foam – ½″ thick foam core.

PVC pipe – rigid white pipe, used in plumbing and electrical work, in different widths, can be bent with care using a hairdryer, hot sand, or steam in a well-ventilated space.

Glues: Always test some samples first: try hot glue, low temp hot glue (less sturdy on seams), contact cement (such as 3-M and Parabond), spray glues. Work in a well-ventilated space.

Finishes: Floral spray (Design Master) or airbrush have lighter, better coverage than a brush for direct painting. Normal acrylic spray paint may harden the foam. Test materials for compatibility.

For a more solid surface, cover with fabric, latex, sculpt or coat, or acrylics.

Tools: straight single-sided razor blades, box cutters, scissors, serrated knife, hot wire, and electric knife (popular for carving meat in the second half of the 20th century! Ask an older relative or try Goodwill).

Cardboard is an inexpensive, readily available, recyclable material that can work well for large forms that need to stay light and rigid. It may not survive excessive wear and tear as it softens with moisture and can warp or degrade in hot, dry conditions.

Buckram is a sized gauze material in different weights that can be sewn and wired dry as well as draped and molded with moisture.

Wire armatures are sometimes used to create a structure, which is then filled with buckram or paper mache. Benda created some fantastic masks in this way.[15]

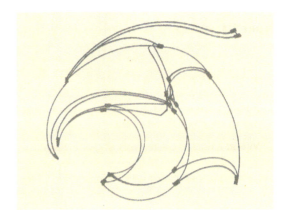

FIGURE 6.63(A) *Benda's plan for a wire armature*

FIGURE 6.62 *Cardboard First People masks by the author for* The Water Carriers

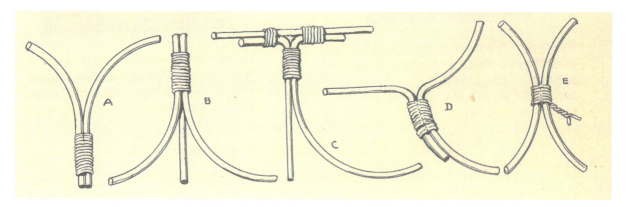

FIGURE 6.63(B) *Benda's detail for joining wires*

CARVED MATERIALS

- **Foam** comes in blocks that can be carved to shape and given a range of surface finishes.
- **Wood** is used to create masks all over the world.

Carved wood is used for masks in Topeng, Noh, Mexican carnival animal, German altemaske, Yupik and other indigenous Pacific Northwest peoples, and other cultures.

The wooden forms carved to serve as a base for leather mask forming are not worn themselves. However, carved wooden masks are a part of many social and performance traditions, including Balinese, Mexican, North American, Korean Hahoe, German altemaske, many African cultures, and Japanese Noh drama masks. The skills needed to carve wooden masks are often handed down through generations from master to apprentice. Hideta Kitazawa chose to follow in his father's footsteps, learning the art of wood carving after earning a college degree. Bidou Yamaguchi completed college study in design, and when fascinated by Noh masks, undertook learning to carve on his own; his remarkable talent led to being accepted as an apprentice to Gendou Ogawa, a living national treasure of Japan. Master Bidou earned his title after only five years of apprenticeship, about half the usual time.[16] Balinese artist I. Ketut Molog was inspired by Topeng drama and began copying established characters' masks, then developed a sense of wood's qualities, then music and dance impacted his designs. He worked ten years on his own before studying with a master for four more years; now has his own studio making both "production" masks for export and commissioned masks for professionals, as well as offering workshops to aspiring artists and educators.[17]

The learning process includes observation, copy, and practice. Artists learn by doing, combining instruction and experience with a passion and affinity for the art. There are a number of artists around the world who generously share their knowledge with aspiring mask makers willing to dedicate time and effort to learning.

Woods are selected from indigenous species, which inform the process and sometimes the style of masks. Sometimes, as in Bali, wood cut from a living tree includes ritual thanks to the tree that gives part of its life to the mask. In Mexico, mask makers only cut into living trees at the full moon, to avoid infestation by worms or termites: "it is a traditional belief that seems true by trial and error but with no scientific basis."[18] Other woods are harvested from fallen trees to preserve limited or endangered resources. The best Noh masks are carved from Hinoki, a Japanese cypress, that is a hundred or more years old.[19] Grain, softness, lightness are all important qualities. The weight of the wood is a factor in the design, as it may be worn on top of the head, tied to the face or body, or held in the teeth, and may be subject to exuberant movement. The grain and density affect the ease with which it is worked and its durability. The age may affect its likelihood of splitting either during construction or as time passes. The natural shape of the wood may inspire the artist's design, as shown in Dalio Angel Perusquia's masks.[20] And there may be traditional or spiritual reasons for selecting a particular species.

Processes are similar in many traditions. It begins with harvesting (or purchasing) the wood – by cutting a tree, excavating part of a living plant, or collecting fallen wood, then controlling the humidity through drying, storing, or restoring water. Next the artist plans the design and considers the grain, adding some guidelines to the design. The form is roughed out with saws, axes, or chisels, then the features are clarified with finer chisels, files, and drills. The surface texture is completed with fine carving or sanding. If not already created, the eyes, nostrils, and mouth will be opened, and the interior hollowed out to fit the performer.

Finishing processes vary. For some masks, the wood itself is the desired finish, with or without sanding, polishing, oil, wax, or lacquer as a protective layer. For many, the artist may dye directly on to surface of the wood or may paint on layers of gesso or other foundation for an even smoother finish, then paint details on top of the primer. The addition

FIGURE 6.64 *Mexican El Tigre helmet mask made of wood: from the collection of Richard Judy and Jane Lommel*

FIGURE 6.66 *Wooden mask courtesy of the London Clown Museum*

of hair, teeth, jewelry, or other effects may be created dimensionally or as surface representation. The interior of the mask may be left untreated to absorb perspiration, or treated to protect the wood from moisture.

FIGURE 6.65 *Japanese masks of Tengu feature a distinctive long-nosed profile*

ADVANCED MATERIALS

Epoxy Resin is a modeling compound that mixes two parts together to activate it and can be worked for several hours before it hardens. Epoxy resin is very hard and durable; finishing structural details are cut, routed, drilled, and textured with Dremel tools. Its sturdiness is useful if parts need to be screwed, riveted, or hinged. It takes enamel and latex paints as well as metallic finishes. It can be time intensive but is good for a single durable custom design. It makes great alien, helmet, robotic and apocalyptic styles. It's available at moderate cost, but must be used with good ventilation.

Vacuformed styrene masks require specialized equipment and dedicated space to store/set it up. Once setup is complete, it becomes relatively easy to produce several blanks in a row. Styrene comes in several weights. Most of us are familiar with the lightweight, somewhat flexible form, frequently used for party masks that can be purchased from costume and prop suppliers and from stores such as JoAnn, Hobby Lobby, Walmart, Amazon, and costume companies. The lighter form is not strong: it will crack or split if mishandled, but is easy to cut with craft scissors or blades, takes acrylic paint and most glues. Styrene is not at all porous, so a cloth lining or felt pads at contact points improves comfort. Some designers use a heavy weight material that is durable and is easy to wipe clean.

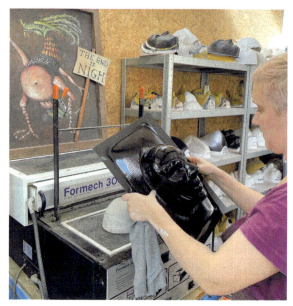

FIGURE 6.67 (A–D)   *A sheet of plastic laid over a mold in the vacuform process*

Celastic is less available on the market, but is treasured by many who learned to work with it in the 20th century, and still favored by puppeteers. Celastic is a canvas weight textile embedded with plastic (cellulose nitrate); when dipped in acetone or MEK (methyl ethyl ketone), it becomes soft and very flexible, so drapes well over forms. It can be manipulated to take on facial features either as whole cloth or in torn pieces like paper mache. Softened Celastic sticks to itself, making it easy to add pieces for support or to build a three-dimensional piece. When dry, it rehardens, retaining the manipulated shapes, and can be resoftened if adjustments or smoothing of the surface are needed. Once formed, it can be sanded and painted. It is relatively light, durable, and very strong. However, as acetone and MEK are not only flammable but also require both a skin barrier (butyl or rubber gloves) to prevent absorption into the body and a full respirator to prevent inhalation (as well as a ventilated workspace), non-toxic materials are generally preferred as they are more environmentally friendly. FormFast is another acetone-activated fabric available in light, medium, and heavy weights.

Aquaform, a casting resin by Dr. Zeller, is useful but no longer available in small quantities for individual artists. It can be poured into a negative mold, or you can vary the viscosity by adding filler to make it putty like for modeling. It is also a good binder for strip techniques. It's flexible enough to keep from being brittle, but very lightweight and strong. A wired edge and pigskin lining improve stability and comfort.[21]

Mask Making   227

FIGURE 6.68(A) *Celastic strips, which are activated by acetone, require the use of protective gloves and a respirator, as well as a well-ventilated space*

FIGURE 6.69(A) *Metal mask*

Sheet metal can make an effective mask. Thurston James provides instructions for creating a hammered metal mask using a pitch box.²² Metal masks are less flexible (though chain mail and wire could lend flexibility to sheet pieces), so must either fit the individual actor's face if close fitting, or lose

the connection to the head. Sheet metal would be challenging for a large mask but might be really interesting as a partial mask – such as brows, nose, and jaws. With advances in laser cutting technology, there are many filigree metal masks available for purchase as well: these can be minimally adjusted to

FIGURE 6.68(B) *Akiko, Celastic mask by Rob Faust*

FIGURE 6.69(B) *Metal mask*

FIGURE 6.69(C) *Purchased filigree sheet metal party mask*

fit a performer's face and can be backed with a sheer fabric if the edges are not entirely smooth. Craft stores carry a selection of thin metal sheets that can be cut with tin snips (NOT the fabric shears!) or good craft shears; E6000, JBWeld, Surebond gray metal bond, and other epoxies are useful glues if you do not have the option to weld or solder. Rivets and studs can also be used to attach pieces. Do take care to finish all sharp edges by buffing, turning, or binding. There are very effective surface treatments to simulate metal that should also be considered, such as paints, rub-n-buff, foils, and metal leaf.

3D Printing requires expensive specialized equipment, knowledge of particular computer software, and specific construction materials. Both the hardware and software are improving and expanding their ability and options. There is certainly a learning curve for mastering modeling software, but many are making well-designed, detailed forms. Currently the plastics available for 3D printing are mostly inflexible materials: their rigidity, lack of absorption, and expenses have not brought them to the forefront. For stage use, plasticity can be a barrier to effectiveness. In film and cosplay, they are gaining ground. Flexible materials and better resolution are helping.

It will be interesting to see where this technology goes. It is now possible to scan, map, and print a performer's face digitally rather than use plaster/alginate techniques. The face could be printed as a solid object or hollowed as a mask. Vicki Wright's Evolution Project used 3D prints of the skulls of ancient species as a base on which she modeled larval masks.

Digital design of the mask over the face scan presents other possibilities to replace the clay modeling process. Amy Cohen scans her performer's head, then uses Blender software to scale the scan up so there is space for resonance between the face and mask, as well as to age, impose character traits, and strengthen features to read at a distance.[23] She then prints the designs and makes a fabric mache mask over the 3D print.

You may also choose to sculpt your mask matrix in clay or other material, then scan and print it in an appropriate size. McClerman and Pollock had success with this, creating a skull-like mask for under ten dollars.[24] They note that a flat black surface is optimal for a 3D scan,[25] so if copying an existing mask or a new one, painting the matrix is recommended.

Once set up, a series of masks could be recreated fairly easily either alike, or scaled to different sizes to accommodate actor fit or a design choice. It could be a little heavy, depending on how thick and/or solid the mask is.

3D printed masks are available online, but do check the size: many of them are small decorative items, not scaled for wearing. Available plastics include a semi-flexible nylon that is fairly light and comes in a variety of paintable colors as well as a translucent version.

The industry is changing rapidly. Currently a combination of hardware (an occipital scanner) and software (such as Skanect Pro) are used to scan the head. Other programs are used to manipulate the design. Tinkercad and Fusion 360 are free online programs with some functionality, or Try Pixologic's Sculptris (free) and Zbrush (advanced) software to design a mask by pushing, pulling, twisting, and texturing form in three dimensions. Blender software is also useful to sculpt the design and adjust scale, then print. Panda 3D, Shapeways, and other sites offer printing services for your files as well as a selection of other artists' designs.

BOX 6.10 USING 3D PRINTING FOR A BASE FORM

Dr. Amy Cohen, a Classics Professor at Randolph College, directs, designs, and produces Greek plays with an approach she describes as "experimental archeology." Because her plays are performed outside in a replica of a Greek amphitheater, she is focused on creating resonant masks and takes time to introduce her students to a linen/animal glue construction process that is one of the ways scholars believe the originals may have been made. She sees the characters as real people and prefers to use the natural appearance consistent with the diversity and individuality of her cast rather than copying Greek stereotypes. She uses 3D printing in the process of making Greek-style masks to capitalize on a naturalistic style. She and her students follow these steps:

(a) Scan the performer in a characteristic open-mouthed, but relaxed expression. The audience's imagination is capable of projecting a variety of emotions on the mask face when the actor's performance supports the physical and vocal interpretation of the text.

(b) Use blender software to adjust the scan: increasing size, creating space for resonance between the face and mask (about 3/4 in.), smoothing over hair which will be under the mask, and removing the ears. The additional space also allows for air circulation and eases putting the mask on and off. She may also manipulate features to indicate the character's gender, age, or traditional appearance. Three-quarter helmet masks are consistent with many research images and allow for hair to be added continuing the illusion.

(c) 3D print the adjusted scan; this may be done in sections depending on the size of the mask and available equipment.

(d) Use a soldering iron [or glue] to assemble the printed pieces.

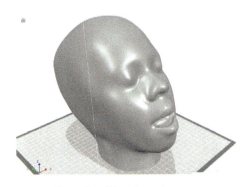

TB 6.10(B)   *Scan adjusted in scale to print*

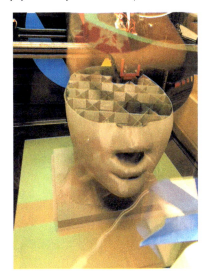

TB 6.10(C)   *3D print in progress*

TB 6.10(A)   *Digital scan of the actor*

TB 6.10(D)   *Sections of the scan being joined with a soldering iron*

TB 6.10(E) *Head coated to smooth surface before casting in plaster*

TB 6.10(F) *Bias linen being formed into the negative cast with glue binder*

TB 6.10(G) *Linen face removed from cast and integrated with helmet part of mask*

TB 6.10(H) *Interior fittings added to maintain resonant space*

(e) Cover the assembled head with smooth coat. The remaining steps are based on traditional methods:

(f) Apply Vaseline as a release agent on the 3D form, and make a plaster cast (negative mold) of the 3D Face.

Using pieces of linen on the bias and rabbit skin glue, press the pieces of fabric into the negative mold with a brush, working to achieve a smooth surface. She has had luck with using four triangular pieces with seams at the compass points, and darts if needed. She used a fine linen for the first (outer) layer, and two coarser, heavier layers to support it inside. [Extra fabric at the edges may be trimmed away or folded in to strengthen the edges from ear to chin.]

(g) Join the mask face and helmet with the overlapping pieces from the face, and add a final layer of fine linen to smooth the top/outside surface.

(h) Fit the mask for resonance, using intersecting bamboo arcs inside from ear to ear and forehead to nape, to hold the mask away from but secure to the head.

(i) Next, mark and trim the edges, puncture the pupils, and smooth the surface; these masks are ready for addition of color and hair (beards and/or wigs).

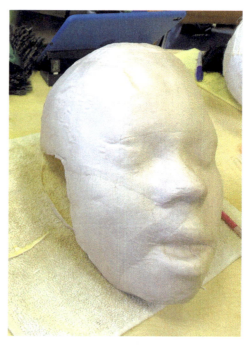

TB 6.10(I) *Mask ready for inspection and finishing*

(j) Chorus and Medea at Randolph College.
(k) Rack of finished masks.

Amy R. Cohen is Professor of Classics and Director of the Greek Play at Randolph College, Lynchburg, Virginia. Her article, "Can you Hear Me Now? – Implications of New Research in Greek Theatrical Masks" (Didaskalia: volume 7, Issue 1, Winter 2007), describes the process and results of her experience with making resonant masks.

TB 6.10(K)   *Group of masks created over adjusted 3D prints*

TB 6.10(J)   *Finished masks of Medea and chorus at Randolph College*

FIGURE 6.70(A)   *3D printed skull mask by Candy McClernan and Rachel Pollock*

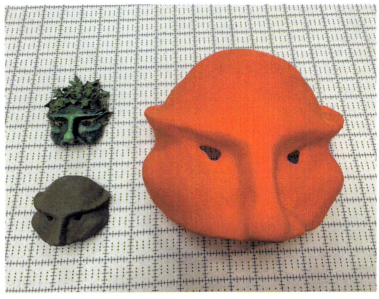

FIGURE 6.70(B)   *Maquette, model, and 3D print by Athene Wright for a class project at University of North Carolina*

BOX 6.11 ARTIST PROFILE: WERNER STRUB

Werner Strub studied at the School of Decorative Arts in Basel before earning a diploma in Directing in Geneva, where he became inspired by the mask work of Amleto Sartori. Strub began teaching himself to make leather masks in 1959, with long-distance help from Sartori. Over decades of work as a theater designer, Strub developed his affinity for mask work, collaborated with a host of colleagues throughout Europe, and created brilliantly evocative masks in a variety of styles. He earned an international reputation and represented Switzerland at the 1987 Prague Quadrennial, an international exhibition of Performance Design. His work grew from the leather forms of Commedia half masks to full head coverings. He moved from leather to other materials, including plants, hair, fur, wool, fabrics, and eventually string and fiber. These later personal creations are marked by a feeling of lightness and transience.

Matteo Soltanto, himself an artist and scenographer and longtime friend, writes of visiting Strub's studio in this tribute:

> *I was looking for the human factor. Here it is. And it's multiple: multi-ethnic, multi-generational, multicolored and monochromatic. They are all here; the alert one, the happy one, the loner who turns his back on me, the sociable one who keeps the group entertained, the other one who suddenly notices me, and now looks at me, …in the unaccustomed silence of this cavern…*
>
> *[Werner's] current work is the result of an equilibrium of minimal resistances, human frailties and delicacies. Souls and cartilages, thoughts and tendons intersected and knotted with anatomical skill. Here everything is clear. Proven. This is us. Werner has caught us. His theatrical masks, his "leathers," which used to be nailed in place in his Geneva studio and absorbed so much of the wood which shaped them, changed their skin a few years ago, caressed by the rarefied air of the hills up here. Drained of actoral necessities they have woven the finest of threads around their limbs, and drawing on the fertile space which gave them life, they have taken flight. Werner has taken flight, and the thread which now holds his humans in midair seems to prevent them not so much from falling as from ascending definitively to the heights.*[26]

The recipient of many awards and accolades for his theater artistry, Werner Strub died in 2012.

TB 6.11(B)   *Othello, leather, by Werner Strub*

TB 6.11(A)   *Papageno and Papagena in string and pigment by Werner Strub for* The Magic Flute

TB 6.11(C)   *Coal Miner, leather, by Werner Strub (photographs by Giorgio Skory)*

Mask Making   233

FIGURE 6.71(A) *Tokoloshi found object mask by the author for The Water Carriers (egg cartons, wire, string, paint)*

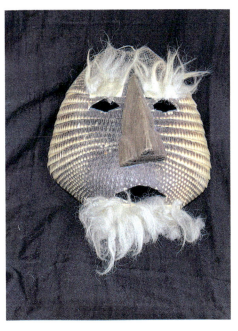

FIGURE 6.71(C) *Mask made from an armadillo shell, wood, and animal hair*

FIGURE 6.71(B) *An interesting mask could be made of found objects in a Steampunk style*

Other Materials

There are few limits to what can be used for masks – use your imagination, and try things! Found/repurposed objects may inspire a mask for a Steampunk, fantasy, or horror mask.

Decorative masks are made in many materials, as weight and comfort are not critical factors. The choices are as extensive as our imaginations, and reflect the breadth of our interest in creating masks. Terra cotta, stone, wood, metal, ivory, glass, tile, precious stones, textiles, and shells have all been used.

As a mask artist, you will have times when you can and should jump in and experiment, and let the process take you where it will. However, doing your research is also important and can save you time, money, and frustration. Understand what the mask needs to do, what environment it will be in, who will wear it, and what materials are best suited to that particular project. Enjoy the process, and don't be afraid to come up with your own unique solutions.

FIGURE 6.72 *Laiifao by Damselfrau: art mask inspired by found and manufactured items: mesh, brass findings, beads, pearls, sequins, pompoms, and rayon cording*

FIGURE 6.73 *Zebratown Mask 1 (2013) by Willie Cole: leather shoes, stainless steel wire, nylon thread, and screws. 20 × 22 × 11 in./51 × 56 × 28 cm. Photo by Joerg Lohse, courtesy of the Artist and Alexander and Bonin, New York*

PROJECTS FOR FURTHER STUDY

- Make a direct paper mask, answer the personal journal prompts, and share your mask with your class and follow the group prompts (Appendix B).

- Working in pairs, make a direct mask using plaster bandage.

- Cast a face with alginate or silicon, and make a positive plaster cast as a base for other projects.

- Explore the 3D modeling process using a prefab or cast base to create a sculpted emotional or character mask and answer the prompts (Appendix B).

- Research and recreate a mask from or inspired by a cultural or performance tradition.

NOTES

1. Fava, Antonio, *The Comic Mask in the Commedia dell'Arte*, 13–15.
2. Newman in Bell, ch. 3, 108.
3. Bell, 106.
4. Morelli, *Venice: A Travel Guide to Murano Glass, Carnival Masks, Gondolas, Lace, Paper and More*.
5. Simon, Masking Unmasked, 176–178. Bracketed comments are mine.
6. Appel, Mask Characterization, an Acting Process. Libby's actor training course used a series of Celastic masks created for her by Paul Appel: the features were "purposefully contradictory," "Slightly Grotesque," and their "fundamental characteristic … is their contrary and ambivalent qualities." 4–5.
7. Ibid, 5.
8. Fava, 13–15.
9. Ibid, 14.
10. Bell, 108.
11. Fava, 15.
12. Lambeth, 206–213.
13. Bell, 104–105.
14. Jackson, Paul, *The Encyclopedia of Origami and Papercraft Techniques. A Step-By-Step Visual Directory, with Practical Projects and a Gallery of Finished Designs* (Philadelphia, PA: Running Press, 1991).
15. Benda, Wladyslaw Theodore, *Masks* (NY: Watson Guptill, 1944).
16. Teramoto and Yamaguchi, 2018.
17. Naversen, 2004.
18. Bell, 123.
19. Kitazawa, 2018.
20. Bell, 125.
21. Wallace, interview, 2018.
22. James, The Prop Builder's Mask-Making Handbook, 30–36.
23. Cohen, interview, 2018.
24. McClernan, Candy and Rachel E. Pollock, *No Hiding Results: Evaluating Mask-Making Methods to Find the Optimal Build*. Stage Directions Magazine, March 2016, 14–17.
25. McClernan, Candy and Rachel E. Pollock. *No Hiding Results: Evaluating Mask-Making Methods to Find the Optimal Build*. Stage Directions magazine, March 2016, 14–17.
26. Soltanto, Matteo, Pagina dedicate all'amico Werner Strub, Grande Maestro Mascheraio, 26 September 2012. http://www.matteosoltanto.com/werner_strub.html. Accessed 8 July 2021.

SELECTED RESOURCES

Allison, Drew and Donald Devet. *The Foam Book: An Easy Guide to Building Polyfoam Puppets*. Charlotte, North Carolina: Grey Seal Puppets, Inc., 2002.

Appel, Libby. *Mask Characterization: An Acting Process*. Carbondale, Illinois: Southern Illinois Press, 1982.

Becker, Jonathan. Interview, Muncie, IN. November 2017.

Bell, Deborah. "The Mask Maker's Magic." *Theatre Design and Technology*. Vol. 41, No. 1 (Winter 2005), 29–43.

Bell, Deborah. *Mask Makers and Their Craft: An Illustrated Worldwide Study*. Jefferson, North Carolina: McFarland, 2010.

Benda, Wladyslaw Theodore. *Masks*. New York: Watson Guptill, 1944.

Kitazawa, 2019. Weblog. https://www.betweenthestones.com/past-events/. Accessed 2 October 2019.

Ching, Elise Dirlam and Kaleo Ching. *Faces of Your Soul: Rituals in Art, Maskmaking, and Guided Imagery with Ancestors, Spirit Guides, and Totem Animals*. Berkley, Iowa: North Atlantic Books, 2006.

Cohen, Amy. Interview. Virtual. Randolph College. 13 August 2018.

Cohen, Amy R. "Can You Hear Me Now? – Implications of New Research in Greek Theatrical Masks." *Didaskalia – The Journal for Ancient Performance*. Vol. 7, No. 1 (2007). Randolph College, n.d. Web. 29 November 2016.

Fava, Antonio. *The Comic Mask in the Commedia dell'Arte: Actor Training, Improvisation, and the Poetics of Survival*. Translated by Thomas Simpson. Evanston, Illinois: Northwestern University Press, 2007.

Grater, Michael. *Paper Mask Making*. New York: Dover, 1984.

Hart, Eric. "Celastic" Eric Hart's Prop Agenda. Blog post. 25 June 2017. http://www.props.eric-hart.com/tools/celastic/

Hill, Chris. "What's the difference Between Polyurethane, Varnish, Shellac and Lacquer?" HGTV, March 26, 2021 https://www.diynetwork.com/how-to/skills-and-know-how/painting/whats-the-difference-between-polyurethane-varnish-shellac-and-lacquer

Hunt, Deborah. *Masks and Masked Faces a Manual for the Construction of 22 Masks and Their Variations*. San Juan, Puerto Rico: Maskhunt Motions, 2013.

Jackson, Paul. *The Encyclopedia of Origami and Papercraft Techniques. A Step-By-Step Visual Directory, with Practical Projects and a Gallery of Finished Designs*. Philadelphia, Pennsylvania: Running Press, 1991.

James, Thurston. *The Prop-Builders Mask Making Handbook*. Cincinnati, Ohio: Better Way Books, 1990.

Lambeth, Cheralyn. *Creating the Character Costume. Tools, Tips, and Talks with the Top Costumers and Cosplayers*. New York: Routledge, 2017.

McClernan, Candy and Rachel E. Pollock. "No Hiding Results: Evaluating Mask-Making Methods to Find the Optimal Build." *Stage Directions*. Vol. 29 (March 2016): 14–17.

McClung, Mary. *Foam Patterning and Construction Techniques: Turning 2D Designs into 3D Shapes*. New York: Focal Press, 2016.

McClung, Mary. Interview with the Author. Virtual. 11 February 2019.

Naversen, Ronald. "The Benda Mask." *TD&T*. Vol. 46, No. 4 (Fall 2010), 34–45.

Naversen, Ronald. "Learning to Carve Masks in Bali." *TD&T*. Vol. 40, No. 1 (Winter 2004), 38–43.

Simon, Eli. *Masking Unmasked: Four Approached to Basic Acting*. New York: Palgrave MacMillan, 2003.

Yamaguchi, Bidou and Dr. John Teramoto. "Making Faces: The Remarkable Masks of Master Bidou Yamaguchi," Public Lecture. Indianapolis Museum of Art at Newfields, 7 September 2019.

Wallace, Denise. Interview with the author, Boston, Massachusetts. July 2018.

CHAPTER 7

MAKEUP, A LIVING MASK

FIGURE 7.1 *Mask like makeup*

There are great performance traditions that use makeup instead of, or in addition to, masks. The distinction between mask and makeup is sometimes blurred to describe any "process by which an actor presents a face not his own to the audience."[1] Can makeup be a mask? It is often referred to in that way. This question is debated by performers, artists, and scholars. For some, the answer is a resounding "No!" For others, their experience is an enthusiastic "Yes!" Without trying to resolve this very complicated issue, let's take a moment to compare the forms and functions of masks and makeup and learn about some of the traditions which utilize makeup in ways similar to masks. Included in these are *special effects (SFX)* makeups for stage and film, mime and clown makeups, and several Asian dramatic forms including Chinese Jingju, Japanese Kabuki, and Indian Kathakali.

FORM

We'll begin with the obvious.

Physical Form

If our definition focuses solely on a technical definition of a mask as a solid free-standing artifact, then no, makeup is not a mask. A mask is an independent object which maintains its integrity without being worn; makeup must be integrated with a living face. But other components of form can apply to either masks or makeups.

Coverage

Physically, mask and makeup can cover some, all, none of, or more than the face. For example, a clown's red nose covers very little space whether mask or makeup. Commedia dell'Arte uses half masks, so the actor's actual face is part of that composition. Other masks may be worn above the face, defining the character while preserving the performer's expressions entirely. Makeup may also cover varied amounts of the face. Natural color, highlight, and shadow may cover the face without apparent change to the features, or supply moderate effects such as aging or illness. Bold colors and patterns applied to some or all of the face (as in many Asian traditions) cover features more completely, even while emphasizing expression. False noses, brows, scars, or other dimensional effects are often used to change the landscape of the face. In the most extreme prosthetic makeups, even the actor's eyes and lips may be disguised. Chinese opera uses false beards and mustaches to identify character types. Kathakali adds beards, chutti, and chutti poove to define the features of certain characters.

Movement

While most masks are static, some masks have moving parts such as eyes or jaws that add expressiveness to the mask. The artist threadstories' masks are fluid, changing form with performance movements. (See figure 5.28.) Makeup allows for a great deal more movement, but there are extreme prosthetic makeups which are physically restrictive and static (although

FIGURE 7.2 *The white forms of chutti poove add dimension to the face*

restriction is not the goal of a makeup artist!). There are even wearable animatronic pieces.

Aesthetic

Both mask and makeup can replicate, idealize, minimize, neutralize, amplify, exaggerate, or distort features. Both can use natural, bright, or neutral coloring. Either may employ strong lines, shapes, patterns, or textures. Both can include symbolic elements.

FIGURE 7.3 *In Chinese opera, makeup and facial hair convey information about character types and temperaments, as well as specific roles. Jing roles have the most complex patterns*

FUNCTION

What if we consider the mask not as a noun, but as a verb? The presence of similarities in form between mask and makeup leads us to ask, does makeup also function like a mask? Does it disguise the performer, create character, transform identity, and suggest production style? As you will see, all of these functions of makeup echo functions we have previously identified for masks.

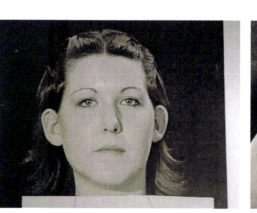  

FIGURE 7.4 (A–C) *Some naturalistic makeups can be transforming, as suggested by this actor headshot and sketch for old age makeup*

FIGURE 7.5 (A–C) *This student created makeup designs for three different characters with varying levels of disguise*

Disguise

Makeup varies in disguising the performer depending on style and the use of extreme color, line, texture, and prosthetics. Naturalistic makeup, including *straight* and *contour (corrective)*, enhances the actor's appearance but does not disguise their identity. Some *character* makeup however does disguise the wearer partially or fully. These makeups may cover the majority of the face creating an effective disguise, so that we no longer recognize the performer. In *Making Faces, Playing God,* Thomas Morawetz addresses disguise from the audience perspective considering both the actor's physical transformation and our willingness to accept the character's identity in lieu of the actor's. Successful makeup designs, Morawetz writes:

> *can be 'read' to evoke a personal history, a set of dispositions and propensities, a spectrum of feelings and expectations. We can be fooled to the extent that artifice*

FIGURE 7.6 *Jingju makeup effectively masks the performer's face*

FIGURE 7.7 *Kathakali inspired scene*

[directs] our response. Even when we may know that we are confronted with a convincing false face rather than a real one, we may experience – viscerally and emotionally – the face as real and the actor as provisionally lost within the makeup.[2]

In *Beijing Opera Costumes*, Alexandra Bonds also acknowledges that,

Paint, while not the same kind of barrier as a mask, still alters the face enough to significantly affect the normal expectation of recognition and human interaction, and so can successfully separate the jing and chou from the natural world.... In each case [jing and chou], the natural face is obscured, and the identity of the character is visualized in the external appearance of the face.[3]

Character

Masks maintain character by their physical form. It is interesting to consider the role of makeup design in defining character as it relates to permanence. In many Asian forms that use mask or complex makeup, the characters are identified by specific visual conventions that are passed down from generation to generation as part of a codified system. These groupings parallel mask types, including gods, demons, animals, clowns, and heroes. For example:

Characters in the Indian dance drama Kathakali are divided by emotional capacity and defined by corresponding makeup types. They are grouped first by a few broadly differentiated types (*satvik* = heroic, pious, and virtuous, *rajasik* = passionate, heroic, but aggressive, and *tamasik* = demonic, rude, or evil). These broad character groups are then divided into seven types which share colors and styles of makeup: *paccha*/green, *payuppu*/ripe, *katti*/knife, *thadi*/bearded, *kari*/black, *minukku*/shining, and *theppu*/special. Within each group, there are variations for different characters and situations, but the primary pattern and color scheme remain consistent. Colors hold symbolic meaning, as do many of the shaped facial features. This visual language informs the audience of each character's nature.[4]

Zhao Menglin notes in *Peking Opera Painted Faces* that the strong shapes, colors, and patterns of Chinese opera makeup serve not only to define characters, but also to "enable audiences to see clearly the distinguishing features and colors on the actor's face from a distance and to enjoy the exquisite beauty of the design when near. With the addition of appropriate signs and symbols, a painted face can reveal not only physical and psychological features (age, appearance, temperament) but also socially endowed aspects (status, skills, nicknames) and even the articles or weapons a character habitually uses."[8] Chinese opera audiences are familiar with the traditional colors, shapes, and symbols used to convey this information.

BOX 7.1 INDIAN KATHAKALI MAKEUP

[This section is condensed from an addendum to the article "An Introduction to Kathakali Costume" by the author, published in *TD&T*, Winter 2013.]

The Classical Indian dance drama Kathakali developed as a distinct art form in the state of Kerala during the mid-17th century, drawing influences from a variety of performance traditions. Kathakali can be performed in temple grounds as well as in private and public areas, and there is implicit understanding that Kathakali, like its forerunners, reinforces moral codes and glorifies the gods through dramatic representation. The epic stories come from the *Ramayana, Mahabharata, and Bhagavata Purana*. The performance integrates drumming, singing, cymbals, and dance marked by specific body stance, hand gestures, facial expressions, and eye movements. Characters are mostly superhuman archetypes: gods, demons, and humans, plus a few animals. Men traditionally played all roles, but women train and perform in some contemporary troupes. Kathakali requires skills developed through years of intensive training.

Scholars refer to four separate dramatic elements of Kathakali. *Aharyabhinaya* refers to the decorative elements of the play, particularly costume, makeup, and accessories. The others are *Vacikabhinaya* (speeches and songs), *Angikabhinaya* (dance, body positions, mudrahs/hand gestures, eye movements, etc.), and *Satvikabhinaya* (the expression of psychic states associated with emotions).[5] Costumes and makeup are an important element of Kathakali, as they identify characters, bring focus to expressive areas of the body, create an other-worldliness appropriate to the characters and stories, and provide extravagant spectacle against a minimal set.

Elements Most Indicative of Kathakali Makeup Include

Chutti or ***cutti***, a rice paste mixed with limestone powder, is traditionally used for the white parts, giving them more dimension than the flat colored paints.

Chutti is also a stiff white curved framework for the jawline, originally made by patient layering of rice paste onto the performer's face. Today, they are available in pressed paper or molded plastic forms which can be affixed with spirit gum. The shapes vary according to codified character designs, but all serve to bring attention to the facial expressions of the performer, framing and casting light onto the face. As facial expression is a key component of a fine performance, the chutti is an important component. Pandeya assigns it symbolic value as well, with the gradient ridges representative of the five rivers of India.[6]

Chutti poove, white knobs that vary from mushroom to doorknob in size, are affixed to nose tip and forehead for some characters, using rice paste (traditionally), or spirit gum and cotton (contemporary).

Chunda poovu, crushed seeds of the solanum pubescence plant are put in the eyes to bring up a bloodshot red color which brings focus to the eye movements. On paccha characters, it also contrasts the green base. Iyer describes the powerful effect this reddening has in enhancing expression.[7]

Damshtram, or ***dhumstras***, are fangs worn by demons and some animal characters. Kathi (black) roles require them, as do some other characters. They are held in the mouth and pushed forward to show when a character is revealing its fierce nature. The false canines are connected by a strip, which sets at the upper gum line. Although the teeth are flat cutouts, they are interestingly curved and resemble shapes found in artistic representations of beasts and demons.

Characters

Paccha "Green"

The heroes, good natured characters, are called paccha, after the green makeup that is the base color for their facial makeup. Refinement, heroism, and moral excellence are qualities of satvik characters. Their makeup also features, red lips, wide black eyes, and a trefoil vaisnava (devotional mark on the forehead) surrounded by the white, bow shaped, terraced cutti that frames the face.

Payuppu "Ripe"

Four specific divine characters wear this makeup that has the same basic shapes as the paccha, but with an orange base rather than green.

TB 7.1(A)   *A Paccha Vesham by FACT Jayadeva Varma*

Katti "Knife"

Demonic characters who retain some virtues or nobility are in this category. Valor, love, and grace may be retained, but their aggressive and evil tendencies are stronger. Their makeup also has a green base but is broken in several ways. A stylized red patch outlined in white "cuts" the face, running up high on the cheek bones. The knife shape can be gracefully curved or long and straight, depending on the character. White, knob-like cutti flowers appear on the nose and between the eyebrows. Fangs complete the transformation. Katti also wear the face framing cutti.

Tati "Beard"

Tati have beards instead of the cutti frame on their faces. They are less refined in nature, which is also reflected in the use of coarser fabric or fur for their jackets. There are three subgroups:

- **Cuvanna tati**, or *cokanna tadi*, refer to red savages: vicious, vile, power-crazed characters who wear the wide full red beard. The base makeup is also red, with black and white contrasts emphasizing fiendish round eyes, enlarged black lips, white bristles from the upper lip to eyebrows, and extra-large cutti knobs on the nose and forehead. Cuvanna tadi are the most visually impressive in size and fearsomeness.
- **Karutta tati**, or *karuppa tadi*, are black-bearded characters representing forest dwellers, hunters, and aboriginals. The characters are primitive schemers. The base color is black, with white bristles, bracketed eyes, flaming red lips, and a cutti flower on the nose.
- **Vella tati**, or *veluppa tadi*, are white-bearded characters from a higher form of being than their other bearded counterparts. Hanuman, the Monkey King, is one well known example: his makeup is stylized to represent the animal features.

Kari "Black"

Kari are the most grotesque Kathakali characters, including vile ogresses (*raksasis*). The face is black with white patterns (of pox or warts) and fangs.

Minukku "Radiant," "Shining," "Polished"

Minukku includes most humans (Brahmins, sages, princes, and women), including demonesses pretending to be women (but not the *raksasis*). These characters are gentle, poised, and of high moral quality. Their makeups are much more sedate. For *strivesham* characters (females), the base color of the makeup is a warm pink/gold complexion: rosy but not inhuman. The features are emphasized but not exaggerated to the point of distortion as in the

TB 7.1(B) *Katti vesham is similar to Paccha in colors but "cuts" the face with a red and white patch*

TB 7.1(C) *Kathakali Kattaalan vesham by FACT Jayadeva Varma*

TB 7.1(D) *Hanuman the Monkey King is a well-known vella tati with white beard and fur coat; this version by FACT Jayadeva Varma*

gods' and demons' makeup categories. Lips are outlined in black, filled with red; eye liner is extended on both top and bottom lid, and brows are thickened and extended. In addition, stylized black curls of (painted) hair frame the upper half of the face, and white dot decorations sit above the brows. A *bindi* completes the makeup. A dusting of mica is used to bring radiance to the face.

Theppu "Special"

Animals, clownish characters, and others that do not fit into the five regular groups are called *theppu*. Their makeups are specific to each character. Animal makeups are stylized to simulate their features, and may include artificial beaks and wings.

Masked

There are a few masked characters as well. They fall into three categories: real, symbolic, and imagined. The mask may be full face (one is of an old woman), or partial (the swan's beak). Occasionally, characters are masked to indicate a major transformation, such as from death to life.

TB 7.1(E) *Strivesham (female) minukku makeup worn by Kalamandalam Gopi*

TB 7.1(F) *The versatile Kathakali artist Sri Kalamandalam K G Vasudevan Nair as the swan, one of the Theppu categories that includes a beak*

TB 7.1(G) *A Kathakali interpretation of the Paṭṭābhiṣēkaṃ of Śrī Rāma*

FIGURE 7.8 *Jingju Stage Picture. Reprinted by permission from* Beijing Opera Costumes *courtesy of Alexandra Bonds*

BOX 7.2 CHINESE OPERA MAKEUP

Jingju is a style of Chinese opera that developed in the late 18th century in Peking (now Beijing). Like other Asian forms, Jingju elements include instrumental and vocal music, simple props used in expressive ways, highly stylized movement including acrobatics, dance, martial arts, and coded posture, movement, and gesture, and highly symbolic appearance through costume, headgear, and makeup. There are two primary divisions of Jingju. *Wen (civil)* plays were more plentiful in earlier development, with themes of love, marriage, and relations between the sexes, and frequently featured women as main characters. *Wu (Military)* operas center on themes of war and power, climax in spectacular acrobatic battles, and feature main characters who are usually, but not always, male.

Character Types are divided into four primary categories (*Dan, Sheng, Chou,* and *Jing*) which subdivide into an array of characters. While visual attributes create a vocabulary that is understood by audiences, they do not stereotype the roles into narrow interpretations. Attributes of age, class, intelligence, humor, and personality which vary from role to role are reflected in details of dress and makeup. Dan and Sheng roles wear a simpler style called *junban* (beautiful or handsome face) or *jiemian* (smart face); Jing and Chou roles wear the complicated designs called *huamian* (flowered face) or *jing* (painted). The remaining categories of minor supporting roles who serve as non-speaking soldiers, maids, and entourages wear a more natural makeup.

Dan are female characters. Except for old women, they wear *junban*: a simple pale pink/white base, strongly angled eye liner and eyebrows rising up toward the temples (silkworm shape), a strong contrast of the white bridge of the nose with the deep pink/red of the eye sockets which blends gently into the cheeks (peony blush), a strong, full red mouth (as opposed to the small bow shaped mouth of the Japanese), and an artistic frame of dark hair to create a perfect oval shape. The subtypes of Dan roles are:

- *Zhengdan/Qingyi*: leading females, young – to middle aged, wife or mother, serious, dignified, decent, demure, they act according to polite social convention and filial duty.
- *Guimendan*: young unmarried lady, immature, introverted, but slightly mischievous.

- *Huadan*: flower female, lively person, coquette, flirtatious and energetic, a bit comic/lighthearted.
- *Wudan*: military women: acrobatic, simple clothing.
- *Daomadan*: warrior female: elaborate dress.
- *Laodan*: old mother, old woman: subdued costume, natural voice, and *shuaiban* (old makeup) natural or warmer tone, hair gray or white in bun, 3 lines of crow's feet drawn in.

For centuries, Dan roles have been played by men, but in the modern era women also perform. There is still high respect culturally for famous Dan performers such as Mei Lanfang.

TB 7.2(B) *Sheng role (left)*

TB 7.2(A) *Dan role*

Sheng are the leading male roles, in both *wu* and *wen* operas. They are primarily typed as young, warrior, and old men, and there are subtypes in each class by personality and status. All are stately, decent, dignified people who act honorably despite challenges presented in the plot.

Male leads also wear *junban*: a pale ivory/pink/natural base color (lighter for younger characters), strong dark slanted brows and eyeliner, warm peachy-red above the eye, and natural color on the cheeks and lips. Shen makeup also features an arch or angular shaped blush between the brows. Less intense or contrasting than the makeup of the Dan roles, these are described as "simple rouge and powder." The overall appearance is relatively natural but heightened to carry from stage. Mature characters wear a variety of beard shapes, sizes, and colors.

- *Xiaosheng*: young males, handsome, unmarried or recently wed, beardless; high pitched voice; scholars or warriors.
- *Wusheng*: warrior males, acrobatics and martial arts expert, natural voice. Usually bearded, skin toned faces, and the rouge between the brows is arrow shaped, pointing upward.
- *Laosheng*: old males: dignity of bearing, gentle polished manners, generals, high ranking officers, cultivated disposition of scholar, also officials and landowners. Bearded. May use *shuaiban* with white beard for feebler characters.

Chou ("choh") are the clowns in Jingju. The character for chou also means ugly so makes a humorous homophone. These roles are also referred to as *doufu* = "bean curd" (tofu) or *xiao hualian* (little painted/flower face). The characters can be of any rank or social position, male or female, servant, warrior, or official. They are frequently funny, foolish, awkward, simple, and sincere; occasionally they are villains or traitors. Usually, these characters have minor roles but occasionally take lead roles in comedies.

All chou designs include a shaped white patch in the center of the face. Some sources suggest this came from a joke about a bird flying overhead… White signifies craftiness or disloyalty: the bigger the patch, the more wicked or untrustworthy the character. Chou can be complex designs as well as simple ones – the complexity of the makeup is related to the complexity of character. Roles are considered "smaller than life,"[9] so designs are within the smaller area of the inner face, as well as

TB 7.2(C) *Chou role*

TB 7.2(D) *Jing role*

showing small eyes, mouth, and brows. There are three subcategories of Chou:

- *wenchou*: civil – white covers eye area
- *wuchou*: martial – narrow white zone – down nose
- *choudan* or *caidan*: female

Jing (painted face) roles, also called *Hualian* (flower face) roles, are the most recognizable images from Chinese opera. They belong to bold leading males, with positive or negative characteristics, forceful personalities, swaggering, self-assertive manners, and high social positions. In addition to striking looks, these roles feature deep, robust voices. They can be *wujing*, or *wenjing*, as well as good luck spirits and gods. The style is attributed to three main sources: one is the historic mask traditions of Nuo folk dramas and ceremonial dances of south China. Several popular sources credit the origin to 7th century dancers who used makeup to imitate the mask which the brave warrior king Lan Lin wore in battle to appear more fearsome.[10] A practical explanation is that painting symbols on performers' faces indicated supernatural beings who would not be realistically portrayed.[11]

Jing includes a complex system using color, shape, and symbols to convey information about each role. Characteristics are exaggerated, and "larger than life," so the makeup, too, expands past the normal parameters of the face.[12] Artistry trumps realism in creating the ideal look for the character. "Though the Chinese social norm prefers that one's inner nature be concealed; the Jing wear their personalities on their faces. Through precise conventional patterns, the unique facial design for each character conveys information about their inner feelings and morals."[13]

Color, line, and shape are symbolic indicators of character traits: "Although these symbolic meanings are fairly well established, they are not hard and fast. Great flexibility is allowed in the use of color [which] symbolize[s] human nature in Peking opera. The choice of colors, largely empirical, is based on the experience of many generations of veteran dramatic artists, through whom a fairly complete set of Peking opera facial patterns has been created."[14]

For simple designs, the primary color is the one with the most coverage. For complex designs, the dominant color is on the forehead. Usually, face color contrasts with costume for better visibility, and the makeup colors do not share the ranking or meaning of costume colors.[15]

Shapes: In addition to color symbolism, divisions of the face/design patterns are significant. The shape of the brows is most important as it is so expressive and extends onto the forehead. Some styles include:

- straight (wide at top, narrow & slightly rounded at bottom) = dignity
- curved = restless
- triangular = sinister
- elderly = hang down at outer ends
- saw-toothed, serrated, spiked, wolf's teeth = thugs
- ladle shaped = thoughtful/troubled
- thin = composed
- wicked (inside ends turned up like hooks) = fierce, unruly
- mantis = wicked, fiendish

TABLE 7.1 *Chinese Opera Color Symbolism*

Color	Qualities	Roles
Red	Courage, loyalty, warm hearted, resolute	Good and heroic characters
Dark red	Strong willed	Time tested warrior, lower half of face
Maroon		full face, barbarian
Purple	Bravery, wisdom, steadfastness	Sometime a red-faced character at a later stage in play showing he has aged or mellowed
Black	Loyalty, integrity, wisdom, seriousness, strength; B. also temperamental, choleric	May be rough in education or manners but good in nature
Pink	Aged (for jing; different from *junban*)	Old people and stubborn arrogant high officials
Gray	Extreme age or frailty	Old scoundrel or bandit, some mythological (like silver)
White	Untrustworthy, crafty	Clowns and villains
Watery white (fenbai)	Treachery, cruelty, intolerance, lack of sympathy	Villains
Oily white (youbai)	Inflated, domineering	Villains
Blue	Fierce, crafty, rough; fierce bold, and loyal, as well as calculating	Characters with valor and resolution, Robin Hood like
Green	Chivalrous, but excitable, impulsive, and violent, tending towards being evil and wicked	Formidable bandits, heroes, generals, minor spiritual
Light green	Virtue, honesty, fairness	Specific to role of Parn Kuan, a judge of the Tang Dynasty (Lu, 15 plate 183)
Gold	Supernatural	High ranking Immortal deities and other supernatural
Silver	Supernatural	Lower ranked immortal deities, Buddhas, spirits, demons
Yellow	Craftiness, brutality, ferocity, cunning – hidden strength and mystery	Clever brave warriors, outlaw bandits

- staring (one brow up, one down) = neither fierce nor peaceful
- club and duck egg = fierce monks

Willow leaf brows have several applications and meanings, and butterfly brows are part of multi-colored and broken face patterns. There are many that are descriptive such as the one stroke (connected in center, as the Chinese character for one), swastika, and bottle gourd brows. Some are used for just one specific character, such as silkworm and spoon brows.

Next in importance are the eye sockets, which are always fully painted and have many variations. In general, smaller eyes suggest a gentle, peaceful nature, while larger, open sockets indicate rough, crude, or strong nature. Angles suggest a scheming character, and square corners imply obstinacy. Slender may be reserved, and narrow villainous.[16]

The forehead may indicate information about the character through colors, shape, characters, or symbols. One group includes symbols from mythology or legend. A second group signifies particular characteristics or abilities, and the third category is "other" which doesn't fit in the first two.[17] For example, the flame forehead is used only on gods and immortals and signifies dignity. The moon on Pao Cheng's forehead indicates his ability to travel to the nether world, and the golden forehead shows a character's immortal status.

Mouth patterns can indicate character by simulating an expression or the mouth of an animal. Beards also provide clues. "The length and color of a beard – red, black, brown, blue, or white – betoken the wearer's official rank, social importance, and masculinity, as well as his age. The hero never has a moustache, the villain sports a lengthy one."[18] Nose patterns are not named specifically, as they vary widely and are often part of a larger face pattern.

Facial shapes combine to form over a dozen pattern groups, with subtypes based on the role's physical and mental characteristics. As each character is different, so the makeup is individualized from the vocabulary of color and pattern. Simple, honest, and straightforward characters have simpler patterns. The more complex or unschooled emotional characters tend to have more complex patterns. Steve Lu lists the three-tile, multi-colored, and broken faces as the main forms. Full face, rubbed, dyed, and perfect faces have a single dominant color. Three tile/pit faces and their subsets have a wide-eyed socket and brow leaving the forehead and cheeks the same color. Broken flower or scattered faces show more detailed variation and complexity. Many subgroups reflect character groups of elders, monks, eunuchs, villains, gods, demons, and animals.

Kabuki theatre of Japan also uses conventions of color and style to define character types. *Kumadori*, the stylized face makeup of the Aragoto characters, uses colored lines on a white background to reflect the musculature and blood flow of the face; it is perceived as an exquisite reinforcement of the character's emotions as projected by the performer. Beni (red) is used for protagonists with righteous anger, while Ai (indigo) is for souls with characteristics inappropriate to human behavior. Kabuki artists and scholars are particular about separating Kumadori makeup from the term mask. Kabuki master Shozo Sato explains that while the designs are passed down from generations of artists, the makeup is just a suggestion: 60–70% of characterization is created by makeup; the actor must supply the remaining expression.[19]

FIGURE 7.9 *Date Kurabe Okuni Kabuki, by Toyokuni Utagawa III: three Kabuki scenes by Utagawa Kunisada*

BOX 7.3 JAPANESE KABUKI MAKEUP

Kabuki theatre takes its name from the characters *Ka* = song + *Bu* = Dance + *Ki* = acting. It developed as a secular theatre tradition in 16th century Japan and remains popular over four hundred years later. It is often touted as combining the best elements of opera, ballet, and drama. Over three thousand scripts are known; about a tenth of them are still performed. Stories tell of swaggering heroes, eloping lovers, treacherous villains, brothel assignations, and choreographed fights between a hero and his opponents. Character types include:

- *Tachiyaku*: loyal, good, courageous men
- *Katakiyaku*: villainous men
- *Wakashukata*: young men
- *Dokekata*: comic roles, including comic villains
- *Koyaku*: children's role
- *Onnagata*: women's roles (traditionally played by men)
- Demons and animals

A musician narrates, often singing the actor's part as well as setting the scene, commenting on the action, and reciting dialogue. Music replaces speaking as emotion builds, fills effects of clashing swords or battles, and focuses audience attention. Movement includes expressive dances, choreographed fighting, and codified styles of both walking and posture for each type of character. Visual effects include ornate two-dimensional settings, traditional props, extravagant costumes and wigs, and traditionally styled makeup.

Kabuki makeup colors the entire face and strongly accentuates the features. Normal human characters have clear simple makeup. Regular male roles utilize a strong white or flesh colored base, and strong dark brows, lined eyes, and darkened upper lip. Female roles have a white face, red at the outer corner of the eyes, and red lips. Young women also feature small, high, dark brows, while married women are browless and may darken their teeth.[20]

Within the Kabuki tradition, Aragoto roles, including heroic, superhuman, demonic and animal, are characterized by a more dramatic makeup called *kumadori* (kuma = lines, wrinkles + dori, from toru, to take, follow, draw).[21] Kumadori falls primarily into two categories: *Beni* (red) are for Aragoto protagonists, and *Ai* (indigo) for souls with characteristics inappropriate to human behavior such as vengeful spirits, demons, and villains. Rui Tsuda explains that the essence of Aragoto is in the expression of anger. *Beni* indicates *Yang*, a positive, extroverted, righteous anger, marked by aggressiveness, quick tempers, hot bloodedness, and other qualities usually assigned to youth. "You could then say that the anger of an Aragoto hero is represented in red to symbolize hot-bloodedness and the righteousness associated with youth."[22] In contrast, *Ai* types demonstrate *Yin* anger, which is negative and introverted. "Yin anger is found more often among mature adults, who through experience have become accustomed to all of the mechanisms and conventions that comprise this world. Even if they felt vexed by the inconsistencies of real life, they would not [allow] anger

TB 7.3(A) *A Japanese actress in onnagata makeup and wig*

[to] explode straightforwardly. Instead, the anger is held back within, where it builds up. Inevitably, this casts a dark shadow on the personality, with evil clouding the heart. … In effect, the Aragoto drama revolves around a simple basic theme in which the positive anger vanquishes the power of negative anger."[23]

TB 7.3(B) *Illustration of Kumadori makeup designs*

The red and blue that define the character's essential nature are set on a white face; additional colors are used to add nuanced information to the representation. The colors represent the character's emotional composition and status. The makeup patterns emphasize the performer's facial structure and signify specific characters.

TABLE 7.2 *Kumadori Color Symbolism (after Shaver, 342)*

Name	Color	Meanings
Beni	Deep red	Anger, indignation, forcefulness, obstinacy
		Aragoto protagonists
Beni	Red	Activeness, eagerness, passion, vigor
		Aragoto protagonists heroic roles
Usuaka	Pink or pale red	Cheerfulness, youthfulness, gaiety; used for only a few characters, including a charming or amorous fox
Asagi	Light blue	Calmness, coolness, composure
Ai	Indigo	Melancholy, gloominess; second most common hue, used for villains and ghosts
Midori	Very light green	Tranquility; limited use, [sometimes ghosts]
Murasaki	Purple	Sublimity nobility, loftiness; limited use
Taisha	Brown or burnt sienna	Selfishness, egoism, dejection; worn by villains among court nobles and by Gods
Usuzumi	Gray	On chin, dreariness, cheerlessness
Sumi	Black	Fear, terror, fright, gloom
	Gold	Rare, but used for lion, tiger makeups
Oshiroi	White shades	Makeup base layer

TB 7.3(C) *Kabuki images on a souvenir board game*

Similarly, there are many characters in Western literature and culture which have been represented on stage, in film, and in costumes with specific visual traits that identify them. First, we have many general types: the sweet-lipped dimpled little girl, the pale-skinned slender vampire, pointy-eared elf, white-faced clown, or wrinkled and grizzled grandfather, all of whom have various interpretations based on a few key traits. Additionally, makeup can define a specific identifiable character, regardless of who wears it. Just as we recognize Arlecchino's round cheeks and forehead wart, or Pantalone's hooked nose and beard in several forms of masks, we recognize Hanuman the Monkey King, Frankenstein's monster, or an Egyptian mummy in several makeup designs. Finally, makeup has defined some very specific characters, including the film horror characters Pinhead, Leatherface, and Freddy Kruger, as well as science fiction and fantasy creatures from *Star Trek*, *Star Wars*, DC and Marvel comics, *The Wizard of Oz*, and *The Lord of the Rings* series. These have become iconic images for many in the United States. In this sense, the functions of mask and makeup to create a character are similar. When a makeup design becomes codified and repeatable, more identifiable than the actor, it takes on additional permanence, and like a mask, it invites a performer to inhabit a specific "other." As the visual elements of character achieve stand-alone recognition, they share some permanence with Asian theatrical forms and masks.

Transformation

Does the actor also experience the effect of disguise? Does he see himself, or some "other," in the mirror? Do makeups provide transformation to a character with its own sense of movement, gesture, sound, or ideas? This phenomenon of other is nearly always present in masks. Regarding transformation, Commedia dell'Arte master Antonio Fava flatly denies that makeup is equivalent to mask, insisting that the performer must see another, not himself. *"A mask is a mask only if it forces the actor to reimagine himself with a whole different face. No matter how elaborate, a painted mask maintains intact in the actor the perception of his own visage and, in the audience, the sense of the individuality of the performing artist."*[24] Actor Kane Hodder might agree: he differentiates the effects of makeup and mask when becoming Jason Voorhees in *Friday 13th Part VII – The New Blood*. Makeup Designer and Director John Buechler designed special effects (SFX) makeup to be worn under a distressed, partial hockey mask. Hodder describes the mirror moment:

> *I tell you, it was the strangest thing. I felt so perfectly natural, sitting there. When I just have the prosthetics on, it just is a rotted, horrible-looking corpse. The real moment of transformation came when I put the hockey mask over it for the first time. I said, 'Oh, shit!' and I started doing things in the mirror. … Even now, I change totally once I put the hockey*

FIGURE 7.10 *Jingju character Sun Wukong, with monkey features that are common in color and shape to other Asian performance makeups*

FIGURE 7.11 *Mummy makeup and costume shows wrapped, distressed fabric, and darkened features that suggest a skeleton*

mask on. If I have just the makeup on and the mask is next to me, I'm just me sitting around on the set, but once that mask goes on, I'm not joking around with people anymore.[25]

Tadashi Inumaru, who writes of the indispensable role of Kumadori makeup as it contributes to the beauty of Japanese Kabuki, shares a similar perspective. He notes that Kumadori allows for a greater power of expression since it closely follows the actual facial features and expressions of the actor.[26] He argues that the use of makeup to enhance the performer's features is distinctly different from a mask which supplants the performer's identity with the persona of the mask.

However, there is a transformative function of makeup, too, a sense of "me, but not me" when taking on a character. We see this acutely in children at Halloween and grown-ups at cosplay conventions. Commonly, performance training starts with physical and vocal work, and many actors study to "become" their character by understanding the character's background, circumstances, objectives, emotions, and personality long before taking on visual trappings. They often view the later donning of makeup as "an integral part of getting into character and/or as a way of hiding themselves from an audience so they are psychologically free to do whatever the role demands of them."[27] Keith Johnstone's *Improv!* confirms, "Actors can be possessed by the character they play just as they can be possessed by Masks. Many actors have been unable to really 'find' a character until they put on the make-up, or until they try on the wig, or the costume."[28]

Many examples of this transformation pepper the theatre tradition. Russian theatre pioneer Konstantin Stanislavsky describes a "Mask state" in *Building a Character*. A drama student struggled to design an effective character makeup, so began to remove the makeup in frustration. As the smeared makeup distorted his features, he exaggerated the effect. Of the result he raved: "I glanced in the mirror and did not recognize myself. Since I had looked into it the last time a fresh transformation had taken place in me. 'It is he, it is he!' I exclaimed." The student then found himself inspired to take on a specific character – a critic – and a different way of moving and gesturing, and sustaining this new character. "Can I really say that this creature is not part of me? I derived him from my own nature. I divided myself, as it were, into two personalities. One continued as an actor, the other as an observer."[29]

Keith Johnstone contributes his opinion that Charlie Chaplin's Tramp is a mask, since its sense of self, identity, and movement came from the clothes, makeup, and mustache. Chaplin's autobiography shares:

On the way to wardrobe I thought I would dress in baggy pants, big shoes, and a cane and a derby hat. I wanted everything to be a contradiction… I added a small mustache which, I reasoned, would add age without hiding my expression… I had no idea of the character. But the moment I was dressed, the clothes and make-up made me feel the kind of person he was… he ignited all sorts of crazy ideas that I would never have dreamt of until I was dressed and made-up as the Tramp.[30]

Mask artist Bari Rolfe noted that director and teacher Michael Chekhov advised actors to put on a face as though it were

FIGURE 7.12 *Kumadori styled makeup on a student*

FIGURE 7.13 *Charlie Chaplin in a 1915 studio photo by P.D. Jankens*

makeup. "The more you can imagine your face as resembling that of the person you have under scrutiny, … the more you will be able to experience what this person experiences."[31] She found that by adopting an expression, "the physical configuration of the body creates a pathway into the interior of a characterization suggested by the mask. Make-up, acting as a mask, can have a similar effect."[32]

In *Behind the Mask of the Horror Actor*, Doug Bradley shares several performers' experiences in adopting special effects makeups[33]: for many, adding extreme makeup creates a sense of being another person altogether. Bradley reflects on his own experience as Pinhead in the *Hellraiser* film series: journalists frequently asked about his life as a "mild-mannered family man" in contrast to the "sado-masochistic Lord of Hell." He notes that "the makeup creates the fascination …. But the transformation is so total that the contrast with the human being beneath is absolute."[34] In addition to the audience perspective, he describes the "mirror moment" of seeing himself in Geoff Portass' completed makeup for the first time:

> I asked - politely - if everyone would leave the room. I sat and stared at the mirror, letting a flood of sensations and emotions wash over me. After all the preparation that had gone before most of my real decisions about the character and how I wanted to play him were probably made in about twenty minutes right there. On the one hand it is a genuinely unsettling experience. Where was I? Left behind somewhere, an identity in my head, but according to the mirror not here anymore. On the other, it was thrillingly exciting: this idea, sketch, description was now three dimensional and real.

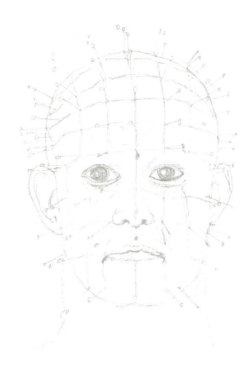

FIGURE 7.14 *Sketch of Doug Bradley in Pinhead Makeup by Geoff Portass (Hellraiser)*

> I moved my head a little this way, that way: I went close to the mirror, moved back from it. Then I began to tentatively move my mouth and face. A frown, A sneer,

FIGURE 7.15 *A Kathakali artist adding makeup for a performance*

Raise an eyebrow. Smile. Laugh. Scream. Then words... I'll tear your soul apart... Angels to some, demons to others... To put no finer point on it, I fell in love! I bathed in the sense of power and majesty that the makeup gave me.[35]

Kathakali performers also experience transformation. A long preparation period for each performance includes lighting symbolic lamps, praying to the gods, applying complicated makeup, donning dozens of costume pieces, and contemplating the character. The importance of makeup and costume is indicated in the level of transformation from performer to character; several sources report that once a performer is in makeup and costume, he is no longer addressed by his own name.[36] Makeup is "not merely to cover or beautify the face, but rather to transform the actor into a demon or a god."[37]

Professional Clowns with developed visual identities also perceive transformation to a separate persona. They register their makeup designs as a specific signifier of their clown character's identity. Emmet Kelley, a famous clown hobo in the United States is often quoted for saying "A clown's makeup and character, that's all he has to sell …. He loves and believes in that character. 'Weary Willie' is very real to me." This separation of character and performer is also evident in that clowns do not appear in public half dressed, or doing normal

FIGURE 7.17 *White-faced clown makeup of Mattie Feint's registry egg*

FIGURE 7.16 *Here, Weary Willie's clown character is immortalized in a carving at a Clown Museum in Peru, Indiana*

things such as eating lunch.[38] In the case of clowns, the makeup defines the character, includes a set of visual and performance expectations, and transforms the actor's appearance and behavior. Clown Mattie Faint defines the makeup as a mask, "absolutely, because it is everything: the face, the nose, the costume, the movement and action, the whole character."[39] While a person may be identifiable under the makeup, many clowns express the transformative experience of becoming their clown character.

Style

Mask genres are defined by codes of stories, language, music, characters, movement, and appearance (as discussed in Chapter 2). Style markers include not only these areas, but also the influence of particular countries, cultures, artists, and materials. They have in common the audience's reaction to masks: we are alerted by our limbic response to the specific otherness of the masked face, our imaginations are engaged, and we are prepared for a heightened level of presentation. What types of makeup elicit this response? What triggers that sense of otherness? How does makeup efficiently tell us what kind of world to place the character in?

Let's examine some styles of makeup.

Natural Makeup

In a realistic production, actors are made up as characters but remain clearly recognizable, even if the performers feel they have undergone a transformation. Naturalistic makeup suggests that the story, characters, and experience of the performance will likely mimic real life and invites the audience to empathize with human characters. Transformations based on life – such as old age, imitations of historical or famous people, or scarring effects – derive power from the illusion of reality. Even as we effectively perceive characters, naturalistic makeup is unlikely to fully disguise the performer, define a new archetype, surprise the audience, or transform the actor's sense of identity. While consistent with the style of realism, it does not create a leap to a significant mask state.

Character Makeup

Subtle makeup is easy to overlook, but non-realistic makeups really get our attention. Morawetz points out that, "While there is very little shock value in comparing an empty canvas with a painting, … there is a world of wonder in comparing the model with the wholly new being he or she has become."[40] Character makeup provides a more complete disguise of the performer. It also gives information to the viewer about the character in the same way a mask does: telegraphing age, health, temperament, and suggesting a physicality, voice, attitude, and behavior unique to the character. This can be done realistically, or symbolically. Historic or dystopian makeup designs that maintain the actors' faces (*Marie Antoinette, The Hunger Games*) can take us to a place long ago or into the future. When the visual aspects move away from naturalism, makeup is more likely to trigger the audience's expectations for a more theatrical presentation.

Many of Robert Wilson's works (including *Shakespeare Sonata* and *The Makropulos Case*) include highly stylized makeup that maintains the recognizability of the human performer but stretches the level of reality. These productions reveal a visually controlled, physically precise choreographed world in which characters are often cast cross-gender, with whitened faces, strong sculpted shadows, and a nearly colorless palette. This renders the performers somewhat less human, less connected, less overtly emotional, despite the strong mime-like use of expression. Even though faces are visible, the makeup instantly signifies the heightened theatricality of the production. "Wilson's aim… is to by-pass realistic acting and the psycho-emotional characterization that goes with it."[41] Junk opera such as the Tiger Lillies' *Shockheaded Peter* uses even more extreme, almost clown-like character makeups to indicate the macabre nature of the story. Makeup for Alfred Jarry's *Ubu Roi* often carries us into the world of the grotesque. The fantastic makeups of Cirque du Soleil's productions draw

FIGURE 7.18(A) Fox makeup for a production of The Little Prince

FIGURE 7.18(B) Student character makeup for the Cheshire cat as represented in cartoon form

us into worlds of fantasy and wonder. The Broadway musical CATS and Theatre for children often presents animal or other non-human characters through the use of makeup, with varying degrees of disguise.

Japanese Kabuki, Indian Kathakali, and Chinese Jingju are especially striking, commanding our attention with makeup that defines character through the use of color, shape, line, and culturally specific symbols. In each of these traditions, standardized patterns and colors are mapped to the performers' faces to define specific characters and groups, and seem to fully transform the actors' appearances. People unfamiliar with these genres often describe the makeup as mask-like, because the non-realistic style incorporates bright colors and strong divisions of the face. For those familiar with these styles, the knowledge of how to read them provides a wealth of information about the character's temperament, type, age, gender, status, and more. The patterns are codified and repeated on many generations of performers with minimal variation. Each of these performance traditions adheres to codified forms of music, movement, gesture, character, costume, and makeup.

These heightened makeups take us to worlds of gods and demons, fairies and aliens, animals and nature spirits, as well as places of extreme emotion and social distortion and other historic periods. They grab our attention, provide an opportunity for the actor to have a heightened sense of transformation; at their most extreme, they create a whole new world.

Special effects makeup (SFX) greatly increases the potential for character makeup to be mask-like. Both work from an understanding of anatomy and design elements and principles. Both frequently use a process of facial casting, mold making, and casting of tangible artifacts (prosthetics) that are worn on the face. Both strive for a "live" aesthetic that can take on apparent changes of expression. SFX makeup includes a wide range of two- and three-dimensional techniques and materials. "Painted" effects include modeling with highlight/shadow, manipulating color, and representing texture. Simple dimensional effects can be created with putty wax, latex, tissue, cotton, gelatin, or small appliances. Advanced casting techniques can be used to create latex, silicon, or gelatin prosthetic appliances. Both makeup artists and actors develop skills in using makeup: in film, professional staff oversee every element, while in stage performance actors often do their own makeup with initial guidance from a designer or makeup artist. Ideally, these designed pieces are created, applied and able to move with facial muscles, creating lifelike expressions. Morawetz assures us that fully disguised by makeup and costume, "the actor's identity is wholly, if temporarily, in limbo; recognition by others is wholly a response to what he creates rather than who he is. He has, in a sense, disappeared from the interpersonal world and been superseded."[42]

Other categories of performance with distinctive makeup deserve consideration.

FIGURE 7.19 *Dimensional SFX makeup*

Mime is an easily recognized genre using non-verbal storytelling, controlled physical gesture and movement, a body emphasized by fitted clothing, and the face painted with a single uniform color accented by strong brows, eye liner, and mouth. Faces may be white with simply reinforced features, or for many buskers, the bronze, marble, or verdigris patina of statuary. When we see this makeup style, particularly in stillness, it grabs our attention the same way a mask does. It signifies that something special is about to happen. Of the makeup used by many mimes, Marcel Marceau explained, "the white face was created not to pay attention to the face and facial expressions of the actor, but to shift it to the whole body."[43] This statement clearly suggests a parallel function of the painted face to the solid mask. In fact, scholars often use "mask" in the title of their mime articles, and many refer to the oft-employed white face as a mask. In performance, a mime's face is often still and mask-like. However, facial expression is clearly projected and necessary to punctuate and contribute to the story arc, as the mime responds to both the imagined situation, and the audience. We can always see his eyes, and both subtle and significant changes of expression. These attributes are definitely unlike masks. Without makeup, the physical performance would still be impressive, but it would lack the engagement generated by the made-up face as a stylistic cue and communication tool. Mime makeup definitely contributes to the form: it heralds a theatrical event, shifts focus to the body, and may disguise the actor, but does not create the character,[44] and could not be replaced by a mask. Mime makeup is icing on the cake. Incidentally, many mask performers study mime and clown techniques and use similar physical skills.

Clowns are a category of performers identified by makeup, or by the red nose mask worn by many. They exist in the circus realm, where they share some attributes with zanni, chou, and other comic theatre characters. They also exist in the real world, performing independently at parties, parades, fairs, hospitals, in commercials, and more. In addition to bridging the real and performance worlds, they exhibit several dualities: they are both human and not-quite human. They combine the silliness of childhood and slyness of ridicule, can be manic and exuberant or self-defeating, and maintain tension between surface and subliminal meaning.[45] Like masked figures, clowns are met with fascination by some, and fear or misgivings by others. The fixed emotions caricatured on their painted faces give no clue to whatever human feelings lie beneath. "Unlike characters in plays and movies, clowns are not bound by scripts … they extemporize. In the guise of play, they seem licensed to taunt, embarrass, and coerce."[46] Frequently nonverbal, the performance genre relies on training for excellent physicality, including movement, posture, gesture, and timing to create character and story. They share with masks the sense

FIGURE 7.20 *A street performer in detailed makeup and costume*

of something hidden and an improvisatory possibility. Clowns develop their own individual makeup and costume; their signature look considers their given or constructed body type, energy, emotional attitude, themes, and personal preferences for color and pattern.[47]

CONCLUSION

We have examined the overlap between the form and function of makeup and masks.

Clearly, some makeups are able to physically transform a performer's appearance, making it difficult if not impossible to recognize the actor. This is true for some decorative, SFX, and many Asian forms and is effective for both performers and audiences.

All but the most naturalistic makeups define character. Whether an individual interpretation or a traditional representation, the designer emphasizes essential physical and emotional qualities which provide information about the character. Some makeups define a recognizable character regardless of who wears them. This lends them a sense of permanence, like a mask, to have lives of their own.

There is always an element of "me, not me" in taking on a performance role; adding costume and makeup completes that transformation from individual to character. In both Eastern and Western practices, some actors do lose sight of themselves in the makeup and experience the same sense of becoming someone else that masked performers feel.

Visual styles direct the audience to expect a particular genre of performance, with its defining elements. Makeup completes the aesthetic of the world of the play.

So, is makeup a mask? We feel strongly that makeup may serve functions that a mask does. We acknowledge the strong feelings on both sides and are content to rest in ambiguity. Try some and see what you discover.

PROJECTS FOR FURTHER STUDY

- Research the makeup styles of an Asian performance tradition.

- Attend a performance that features stylized makeup; respond to the design effects.

- Compare several versions of designs for a single character such as Dracula, Werewolf, or Frankenstein's monster. How do the design choices affect the impact of the character?

- Research a cultural tradition that includes face painting.

NOTES

1. Bradley, Douglas. *Behind the Mask of the Horror Actor*, 14.
2. Morawetz, Thomas. *Making Faces, Playing God*, 6.
3. Bonds, Alexandra. *Chinese Opera Costumes*, 204.
4. Kalamandalam Govinda Warriar's essay on costume and makeup in Nair and Paniker's *Kathakali, Art of the Non-Worldly* offers more detailed information on interpreting the features of each makeup style.
5. K. Bharatha Iyer, *Kathakali: Sacred Dance-Drama of Malabar* (London: Luzac Co., 1955), 42.
6. Avinash C. Pandeya, *The Art of Kathakali* (New Delhi: Munshiram Manoharlal, 1943. Reprinted 1999), 122.
7. Iyer, 52.
8. Menglin, Zhou & Yan Jiqing. *Peking Opera Painted Faces*, 25.
9. Alexandra B. Bonds, *Beijing Opera Costumes* (Honolulu: University of Hawai'i Press, 2008), 207.
10. Steve Lu, *Face Painting in Chinese Opera*. (Singapore: M.P.H. Printers Sdn. Bhd, 1968), 9.
11. Zhao Menglin and Yan Jiqing. *Peking Opera Painted Faces* (Beijing: Morning Glory Pubs, 1996).
12. Bonds, 207.
13. Bonds, 14.
14. Menglin, 14.
15. Bonds, 207.
16. Lu, 19 and Bonds, 213.
17. Lu, 20.
18. Freund, 141.
19. *Kabuki Makeup/Japanese Culture* with Shozo Sato. (PBS Learning Media. 6:40).
20. Oscar G Brockett, *History of the Theatre* (Boston: Allyn & Bacon, 1982), 301.
21. Ruth M. Shaver, *Kabuki Costume* (Rutland, VT: Charles E. Tuttle, 1966), 337.
22. Rui Tsuda, in Morita, *Kumadori* (Tokyo: JICC Co, Ltd., 1985), 10.
23. Tsuda, 10.
24. Fava, Antonio. *The Comic Mask in the Commedia dell'Arte*, 16.
25. Bradley, 238.
26. In Toshiro Morita. *Kumadori*, 5.
27. Sartor, David and John Pivovarnick. *Theatrical FX Makeup*, 23.
28. Johnstone, Keith. *Improv*, 148.
29. Johnstone, 146.
30. Johnstone, 145.
31. Rolfe, Bari. *Behind the Mask*, 10.
32. Rolfe, 10.
33. Bradley, 53, 62, 151, 168, 184, 204, 228, 238
34. Bradley, 12.
35. Bradley, 224.
36. Iyer 53, Singha 101, Pandeya 133.
37. Balakrishnan, Sadana. *Kathakali*, 50.
38. Granfield, Linda. *Circus: an album*, 79.
39. Mattie Faint, interview, London. 28 May 2019.
40. Morawetz, xii.
41. Shevtsova, 123.
42. Morawetz, 30.
43. Pichlikova, 6.
44. *Marcel Marceau: Life and Work*. Horizons (video) Characters may have a specific costume, but mime does not define specific characters. Marceau noted that even as Bip, he "is a character playing a character that the audience must imagine…" Marceau clarified that mime is the art of portraying the human being. Mime makeup is not transformative for the actor or the audience. Rather, it presents the universal human element of the performer.
45. Morawetz, 203–4.
46. Morawetz, 203–4.
47. "So, you want to be a clown?" Ringling Brothers Circus Clown College, np.

SELECTED RESOURCES

Agostino, Christopher. *Transformations*. Berlin: Kryolan GmbH, 2006.

Barnes, John et al., directors. The Art of Silence: Pantomimes with Marcel Marceau and his Partner Pierre Verry. Illinois: Encyclopedia Britannica Educational Corporation, 1975.

Balikrishnan, Sadanam. *Kathakali*. New Delhi: Wisdom Tree, 2004.

Bonds, Alexandra B. *Beijing Opera Costumes*. Honolulu: University of Hawai'I Press, 2008.

Brady, Tara. "No Laughing Matter: Why Are We So Terrified of Clowns?" *The Irish Times*. 9 September 2017. https://www.irishtimes.com/culture/film/no-laughing-matter-why-are-we-so-terrified-of-clowns-1.3209215

Bradley, Doug. *Behind the Mask of the Horror Actor*. London: Titan Books, 2004.

Brandon, James R. *The Cambridge Guide to Asian Theatre*. Cambridge: Cambridge UP, 1997 (2009 printing).

Corey, Irene. *The Mask of Reality: An Approach to Design for Theatre*. Anchorage, Kentucky: Anchorage Press, 1968.

Corson, Richard. *Fashions in Makeup*. London: Peter Owen, 2003.

Corson, Richard, Beverly Gore Norcross and James Glavan. *Stage Makeup*, 10th ed. Boston, Massachusetts: Allyn & Bacon, 2010.

Debreceni, Todd. *Special Makeup Effects*, 2nd ed. New York: Focal Press, 2013.

Fagundes, Dave and Aaron Perzanowski. *The Fascinating Reason Why Clowns Paint Their Faces on Eggs* (bbc.com, 6 December 2017). http://www.bbc.com/future/story/20171206-the-fascinating-reason-why-clowns-paint-their-faces-on-eggs

Feint, Maddie. Interview with the author. London, 28 May 2019.

Freund, Philip. *Stage by Stage. Oriental Theatre: Drama, Opera, Dance and Puppetry in the Far East*. London: Peter Owen, 2005.

Gener, Randy. *Moved to Silence.* Interview with Marcel Marceau. American Theatre. January 2011. New York: TCG, 2011. https://www.americantheatre.org/2011/01/01/moved-to-silence/ accessed March 15, 2019.

Granfield, Linda. *Circus: An Album*. New York: DK, 1998.

Iyer, K. Bharatha. *Kathakali: Sacred Dance-Drama of Malabar*. London: Luzac Co, 1955.

Johnstone, Keith. *Impro*. New York: Routledge, 1992.

Kabuki Makeup/Japanese Culture with Shozo Sato. PBS Learning Media. 6:40. n.d. https://www.pbslearningmedia.org/resource/jacult.arts.drama.makeup/japanese-culture-kabuki-makeup/#.XHW7uJNKiAw

Lu, Steve. *Face Painting in Chinese Opera*. Singapore: M.P.H. Printers Sdn. Bhd, 1968.

Marceau, Marcel. "The Poetic Halo." [Lecture Presented in 1956]; transcribed in *The Mime*, Dorcy, Jean, ed. New York: Robert Speller, 1961. 103–105.

Marcel Marceau: Life and Work. Horizons (video). 1984. https://www.youtube.com/watch?v=uAZLDn8or3M

Meaden, Wendy. "An Introduction to Kathakali Costume." *TD&T, Winter 2013, NY: USITT*, 2013.

Menglin, Zhao and Yan Jiqing. *Peking Opera Painted Faces*. Beijing: Morning Glory Pubs, 1996.

Morawetz, Thomas. *Making Faces, Playing God: Identity and the Art of Transformational Makeup*. Austin: University of Texas Press, 2001.

Nair, Appukuttan D. and Ayyappa K. Paniker, eds. *Kathakali: The Art of the Non-Worldly*. Mumbai: Marg Foundation, 2009.

Pandeya, Avinash C. *The Art of Kathakali*. New Delhi: Munshiram Manoharlal, 1943. Reprinted 1999.

Pichlikova, Lenka. "Performing in Mask: Michael Chekhov's Pedagogy, Commedia and Mime." *Critical Stages*, #15. 19 April 2017. http://www.critical-stages.org/15/performing-in-mask-michael-chekhovs-pedagogy-commedia-and-mime/

Price, Vincent and V.B. Price. *Monsters*. New York: Grosset and Dunlap, 1981.

"So, You Want to be a Clown?" Ringling Brothers Circus Clown College: International Video Entertainment, 1987. np https://www.youtube.com/watch?v=KbSn5mKFWps. Accessed 3 October 2019.

Sartor, David and John Pivovarnick. *Theatrical FX Makeup*. Portsmouth, New Hampshire: Heinemann, 2001.

Shaver, Ruth M. *Kabuki Costume*. Tokyo: Charles E. Tuttle, 1966.

Shevtsova, Maria. "Robert Wilson." *Designers' Shakespeare*. Stephen Di Benedetto, ed. New York: Routledge, 2016. 118–136.

Tokyo SFX Makeup Workshop. *A Complete Guide to Special Effects Makeup*. London: Titan Books, 2012.

Toshiro Morita. *Kumadori*. Tokyo: JICC Co, Ltd, 1985.

APPENDIX A: GLOSSARY

MASK

n: a covering for part, all, or more than the face worn to hide, decorate, protect, or transform the wearer

v: to put on or wear a disguise or mask

CHAPTER 1: FIRST ENCOUNTERS WITH MASKS

Anti-Masking Laws: sumptuary laws prohibiting the use of masks

Cosplay: the practice of dressing up as a character, often from comics, games, films, or other popular arts, with a goal to be as visually proficient as possible, but not necessarily including role play

Form: the physical properties of a mask, including scale, style, size, and aesthetics

Function: the purpose of using a mask, which may be sociocultural, religious, practical, decorative, or for entertainment; masks also call attention to a presentational style, act as transformative agents, give character information to the audience, and disguise the wearers

LARP: live action role play, usually with character specific costumes and props

Maskaphobia, Masklophobia: fear of masks or masked characters

Pareidolia: tendency to see faces in non-face objects or configurations

Rite of Passage: an official ceremony or formal event, which marks a person's transition in life or a momentous occasion; these may be public or private

Transformation: a dramatic change in form, substance, or appearance

CHAPTER 2: FACING THE STAGE

Agum: static pose (Bali)

Angsel: fluid transitional movement (Bali)

Alus: refined quality of high-status characters (Bali)

Atellan Farce: vulgar comedies popular in Rome from about 300 BCE through the 2nd century CE

Barong: Balinese High Spirit, a benevolent Lord of the Jungle in animal form

Bian Lian: a form of Chinese performance that features a rapid succession of mask changes

Bondres: low status clown characters in Balinese Dance Drama

Bugaku: collective term for a body of ancient Japanese masked dance forms

Calonarang: one of a collection of ritual ceremonies, dances, and stories about powerful demonesses (Bali)

Carnivale: a festive pre-Lenten season frequently celebrated with masked events

Code, Codified: "A code is a system of meaning common to the members of a culture or subculture. It consists both of signs (i.e., physical signals that stand for something other than themselves) and of rules or conventions that determine how and in what contexts these signs are used" (Fiske, 1990, pp. 19–20)

Commedia dell'Arte: an improvised comedic form using masks for many characters, developed in Italy and popular throughout Europe from the Middle Ages through the 18th century

Costume: "All the body garments worn by actors, all the accessories they carry as part of their characters, all the items related to hairdressing, and everything associated with face and body makeup, including masks if they substitute for facial makeup" (Russell, 1985, p. 5)

Co-Opt: to use in a way different from the original intent; to adopt for one's own use

Cultural Appropriation: the use of cultural elements by an outside entity without permission from, understanding of, or benefit to the source group; in contrast, *cultural appreciation* encompasses learning about others, respecting their traditional ideas and behaviors, as well as deriving aesthetic pleasure from their arts; *Cultural Exchange* describes sharing where cultural appreciation is mutual, and both groups contribute and benefit equally

Cultural Blending: overgeneralizing and/or combining incongruous elements, such as a teepee (of the Plains tribes) with decoration in a Kwakiutl style (pacific Northwest)

Cuda Manik: devotional mark between the eyebrows (Bali)

Durga: Balinese witch character

Farce: style of low comedy marked by physical humor

Gara: Sri Lankan Demon

Gigaku: a Japanese performance tradition including a liturgical procession, staged vignettes and musical interludes, incorporating Buddhist dogma with humorous secular elements

Gyodo: tradition of Buddhist rites and ceremonies performed by and for monks (Japan)

Hahoe: wooden mask style native to Korea

Honmen: original Noh masterpiece masks, from which new masks are copied

Jauk: Balinese masked dance dramas presenting stories from the Ramayana and Mahabharata

Kanmuri: hairline on Japanese Noh masks specific to particular character types

Keras: unrefined traits of low-status characters (Bali)

Kolam: Sri Lankan performance cycle that uses a variety of intricate masks

Kumoru, Kumorasu: the "clouded" expression of sadness seen when a Noh mask tilts downward

Kurai: the persona, mood, details, and essence unique to a Noh mask

Kyogen: comic interludes between Noh plays

Rangda: Balinese low spirit – a witch – who battles the Barong

Tokenism: inclusion of an item, person, or other effect in order to create the appearance of inclusiveness and equality

Lazzi: established comic routines, usually physical and specific to the stock character as well as the actor who developed them, utilized in the Commedia dell'Arte

Masques: lavish court spectacles, including music, dancing, and allegorical presentations

Miracle Plays: Medieval European dramas presenting the lives of Christian saints

Morality Plays: Medieval plays that taught Christian ethical behavior by presenting an 'Everyman' seeking spiritual redemption

Mumming: folk tradition of disguising as characters and processing from house to house as entertainment and seasonal celebration

Mystery Plays: Liturgical dramas of the European Middle Ages

Noh: formal Japanese drama that combines music, poetry, and movement

Pantomime: performance featuring an actor or dancer who uses exaggerated facial expression and body gesture to convey meaning

Punch and Judy: puppet show with characters and conventions inspired by Commedia dell'Arte

Sanni: Sinhalese term for disease, and the curative masked rites associated with them

Shite: leading character in Noh drama

Sokari: folk opera of Sri Lanka

Taksu: Balinese term for spiritual charisma that ancestors bestow on performers

Tapel: Balinese word for mask

Telek: refined masked dance of Bali

Teru, Terasu: "brightening" of a Noh mask as it is tilted up, creating a joyous expression

Topeng: Balinese dance drama

Tovil: Sri Lankan religious ritual

Trestle Stage: temporary stage set up in public space either as a platform on trestles, or on a wagon (medieval Europe)

Tsuina: Japanese ritual to drive out evil spirits before the New Year, or the long-nosed mask used in such rituals

Undagi Tapel: mask maker (Bali)

Usobuki: whistling mask used in Japanese Kyogen comedies

Utsushi: faithful copies of Noh masks

Waki: sidekick in a Noh drama

Wayang Wong: a performance presenting tales from the Ramayana, dramatizing the triumph of virtue over vice and reinforcing moral codes of behavior (Bali)

Wayang Orang Parwa: Balinese performance in which unmasked dancers and masked clowns enact scenes from the Mahabharata

Yugen: quality of beauty encompassing intensity and ambiguity in a Noh mask

CHAPTER 3: THE DIRECTOR'S PERSPECTIVE

Costume Design: the creation of clothing, including accessories such as hats and scarves, and makeup that helps to define the characters within a theatrical production, as well as the style and time period of the production itself

Devised Theatre: a process in which a theatrical production is created collaboratively, in difference to productions that begin with a previously completed script

Distortion: alteration or contortion of something away from its natural or realistic appearance to an extent that its original identity remains recognizable

Essentialize: to distill or express the essential qualities of something, i.e., a gesture, action, or character

Framing: to enclose, set apart, or introduce an action or event by creating a distinction between it and the surrounding action

Lighting Design: the creation of lighting for a theatrical production; the use of lighting to illuminate performers, direct audience attention, create mood, establish time and place, and enhance the work of other designers

Live Mask: a mask that seems animated in performance, creating the illusion of multiple expressions

Naturalism: an extreme form of *realism*, aiming for a greater reproduction of "real life," including adherence to the Aristotelian unities of time, place, and action; stories often concern characters who are victims of their social circumstances

Parody: imitation of a style or person with the intent to satirize or lampoon

Physical Theatre: a form of theatre, or those elements of any theatrical production, which emphasize the use of movement for the expression of character, action, or story

Production: in theatrical parlance, a play is the textual script or performance score, a production is the unique realization of the play, and a show is a specific performance of the production

Production Concept: the creative idea or ideas that unify the various theatrical elements – designs, performance style, etc, of a particular production

Prototype: the first model, from which others are copied

Raked Stage: stage that slopes upward, so that it is raised at the upstage end; also referred to simply as a rake

Realism: a style of production and performance which attempts to create an illusion of reality, through accurate representation of physical, psychological, and social reality; stories often focus on the psychology, motives, and actions of characters

Set Design: the creation of the scenic elements of a theatrical production, the physical surroundings in which the action will take place, including the background, furniture, and properties; as with other areas of design, set design will also help establish the style of the production

Sound Design: the creation of the sonic elements of a theatrical production, including music and sound effects, and the amplification and treatment of sounds made on stage by the actors; sound design is very important in establishing production style and creating time, place, and mood

Stage Manager: person responsible for practical and organizational support of a production during rehearsals and performance, and overseeing the show as well as calling the cues during performances

Suspension of Disbelief: temporarily allowing oneself to believe something to be true, even though you know it isn't, as when we accept an actor as a character or accept the events in a play

Transformation: in acting, this refers to the physical, vocal, and imaginative changes that an actor undertakes in order to allow the audience to identify them with the character

Uplighting: light from a source below the actor, often a light source on the stage floor

CHAPTER 4: THE ACTOR'S PERSPECTIVE

Articulation (in movement): movement of separate parts at a joint or place of connection, as in moving the head separately from the neck or the shoulders separately from the head

Blocking: setting of stage positions, movement, and action, including entrances and exits, as well as the location of props and set elements such as furniture

Character: sum of the qualities that make one individual distinct from another; the personality; in mask theatre, characters are often (though not always) derived from *types* or *stock characters*

Clocking: when an actor looks directly at or toward the audience, allowing the audience a chance to observe their thought or reaction, and to focus their attention on that particular character in that moment; particularly useful – though easily overdone – in mask performance

Codified: "A code is a system of meaning common to the members of a culture or subculture. It consists both of signs (i.e., physical signals that stand for something other than themselves) and of rules or conventions that determine how and in what contexts these signs are used" (Fiske, 1990, pp. 19–20)

Counter-Mask: alternate personalities or qualities of a character expressed in the design and or performance of a mask

Distortion: alteration or contortion of something away from its natural or realistic appearance to an extent that its original identity remains recognizable

Entrance: the action of a character appearing in the performance space; can also be used to describe the place where this happens (i.e., stage left entrance)

Exit: the action of a character leaving the performance space; can also be used to describe the place where this happens (i.e., stage left exit)

Exposition: the introduction of background information an audience needs in order to understand the characters, follow the story, and enjoy the unfolding action on stage

Exaggeration: the magnification or intensification of something truthful beyond its normal scale, as in physical features or everyday behavior, usually done for emphasis or to call attention

Focus: in the context of staging a performance, this is the place the audience is meant to be giving their attention to the action on stage at any particular moment

Framing: to enclose, set apart, or introduce an action or event by creating a distinction between it and the surrounding action

Full-Face Mask: a mask designed to cover the entire face of the actor; quite often these masks do not allow for speech, though some are specially designed so that they do

Grotesque: a figure with extremely exaggerated or distorted features, creating tension between attractive and repellent qualities and often highlighting qualities through exaggeration

Half-Face Mask: a mask designed to cover half (or less) of the face of the actor; usually these masks allow the actor to speak and allow for better sight and more mobility for the actor

Improvisation: the act of creating characters, story, conflict, and action in the moment; quite often a tool for creating mask performances, the improvisations can later be set as a script or performance score

Inner Monologue: the series of thoughts that the actor builds as a tool to experience and express the moment-to-moment intentions, actions, and discoveries in the life of a mask character

Isolation: the separation of one movement or action from those that precede or follow it

Larval Mask: a mask that has roots in the Carnivale masks of Basel, Switzerland; it is a naïve, semi-formed character first used in actor training by Jacques Lecoq

Lazzi: established comic routines, usually physical and specific to the stock character as well as the actor who developed them, utilized in the Commedia dell'Arte

Naturalism: an extreme form of *realism*, aiming for a greater reproduction of "real life," including adherence to the Aristotelian unities of time, place, and action; stories often concern characters who are victims of their social circumstances

Neutral Mask: a mask developed to aid in training actors toward a greater physical awareness and experience of the state of calm which precedes and follows action

Objective: what the character wants or needs; the goal of a character in any given moment

Obstacle: the person or thing that stands in the way of a character achieving their objective

Presentational: in this instance, a style of performance that overtly acknowledges the presence of the audience and may even include a direct relationship between character and audience

Realism: a style of production and performance that attempts to create an illusion of reality through accurate representation of physical, psychological, and social reality; stories often focus on the psychology, motives, and actions of characters

Status: the power relationship between two characters; good acting requires an awareness of the character's status in any given moment

Stock Character: a stereotypical character that has repeated use across different plays within a genre; in difference to a *type*, this is usually a named character with consistent qualities

Suspension of Disbelief: temporarily allowing oneself to believe something to be true, even though you know it isn't, as when we accept an actor as a character or accept the events in a play

Stereotype: portrayal of a character using oversimplified and possibly exaggerated but commonly recognized characteristics, for instance, characteristics often ascribed to a particular social group

Tempo-Rhythm: the speed and timing of a character's movement, speech, actions and reactions, and the sense in which that speed and timing helps to define the character

Three-Quarters Mask: a mask designed to cover a substantial portion of the face, but which still allows for speech; usually this means the mask covers the forehead, eyes, and nose and extends down the sides of the face but leaves the mouth and chin exposed

Upstage: as a verb, the act of placing or moving yourself further back on the stage (upstage) from the audience, so that another actor must turn their back to the audience to see you

CHAPTER 5: MASKS BY DESIGN

Caricature: representation with exaggerated features for comic effect

Cultural Appropriation: the use of cultural elements by an outside entity without permission from, understanding of, or benefit to the source group

Elements of Design: the building blocks of design, including line, shape, form, texture, color, and value (light/dark)

Form: the physical and aesthetic attributes of a mask

Grotesque: a figure with extremely exaggerated or distorted features, creating tension between attractive and repellent qualities and often highlighting qualities through exaggeration

Maquette: three-dimensional scale model

Negative Space: space between objects or focal points in a composition, such as the area between two performers or the space between a mask profile and the blank wall behind it

Physiognomy: the practice of ascribing character traits to physical features

Principles of Composition: ways of combining the elements of design to achieve specific effects

Rendering: picture of a designed product, usually two-dimensional

Rhythmic Coordination: W.T. Benda's term for a design process that utilizes repeated shapes and forms to direct the eye and unify the whole

Undercut: a property of a feature that creates an overhang, such as a beak that curves down and back leaving a concave area between it and the face

Zoomorphism: giving animal characteristics to human images and attributing the animal behavior to their personality

CHAPTER 6: MASK MAKING

Alginate: quick setting, flexible, hypoallergenic dental casting material

Binder: agent that holds things together, such as glue, flour paste, or plaster

Cast: to take an impression

Celastic: a canvas weight textile embedded with plastic; requires a chemical softener and protective gear to use; not health or environmentally friendly

Life Cast: 3D copy of a performer's face

MSDS: Material Safety Data Sheet, the manufacturer's information about a product's safe use

Negative Cast: a concave impression, like the inside of a bowl

Positive Cast: a three-dimensional convex form; it reads forward, like your actual face

Release Agent: substance that prevents two surfaces from sticking to each other

Thermoplastics: set of materials that soften when heated

Undercut: shape that curves back on itself creating a concave recess or overhang, such as forming a nose that hangs lower at the tip than at the columella

CHAPTER 7: MAKEUP, A LIVING MASK

Character Makeup: application that serves to change the performer's appearance and present a specific role

Codified: defined by a system of cultural expectations

Corrective: makeup style that idealizes the face

Coulrophobia: fear of clowns

Jingju: Chinese opera that features four categories of makeup: jing, sheng, dan, and chou

Kathakali: dance drama of Southern India, which includes codified makeup patterns

Kumadori: traditional makeup style of Japanese Kabuki theatre

Prosthetics: three-dimensional forms that are adhered to the face to change its shape

Semiotics: the study of signs and symbols, including visual, aural, and movement patterns that communicate information or ideas

SFX: special effects makeup including significant elements of disguise or change in appearance

Straight: realistic makeup style that uses highlight, shadow, and color to reinforce a performer's natural features

APPENDIX B: PROJECT WORKSHEETS

Mask Documentation Checklist

Performance Response

Mask Construction Worksheet

Mask Performer Measurement Sheet

Mask Estimate (Worksheet)

Direct Paper Strip Mask (Project)

Emotional Sculpted Mask (Project)

MASK DOCUMENTATION CHECKLIST

Use this form as a guideline for collecting information.

Culture

Country, ethnic group, and subgroup or society that makes/uses the mask
Tradition
Text, story, or concept associated with use

Function (theatrical, social, religious, ritual, entertainment, protective, decorative)

Character (specific)

Name
Type
Roles (good, evil, comic, heroic, ruler, citizen, servant, general, animal, ancestor?)

Visual form

Materials
Scale/size
Features
Colors
Textures
Variations in category
Costume worn with it?
Symbolism of mask, design, or features

Makers (Who makes them? How does one learn? Associated rites? Storage?)

Movement

Formal/informal, set/improvised,
Interaction with other players, masks, audience, gods

Performance

Wearers (gender, social rank, ownership of mask, family tradition, training?)
Audience (public, private, family, social group, gods?)
Locations (public, private, theater, temple, court, field?)

Other?

Sources (include a one to two sentence annotation for each)

PERFORMANCE RESPONSE

Discuss how the masks functioned in the performance you saw.

- Note the title of play or name of ritual, the tradition or style of production, who produced/presented this performance, where/when you viewed it, and in what format (live, filmed, streamed, etc.). If known, include the playwright's, director's, and mask designers' names.

- What was your initial response to seeing the masks? Did it change as the performance progressed?

- What was the overall mood and style of the presentation? Were the masks styled to be realistic, exaggerated, grotesque, or fantastic? How were the elements and principles of design used to support the mood and style of the production?

- How did masks specifically define characters? Groups? Relationships? Were there mask changes? What did they signify? Were all characters masked? Why? How was your response to masked and unmasked characters the same or different? How do you think the masks and costumes might have helped (or hindered) the performers?

- What country and culture developed this tradition? Was this presentation in a historical tradition or a contemporary version of a tradition? Identify any ways in which collaborators chose to diverge from tradition in selecting time, location, language, or other elements of presentation.

- Why did the creators choose to use masks in this context? How did the use of masks impact the production?

- Give your overall impression of the masked performance, using specific examples from the production to support/illustrate your analysis.

MASK CONSTRUCTION WORKSHEET

Character

Production/event

Venue/scale for viewer

Designed by

Due dates

Purpose: define character, stock training, decorative accessory

Kind: helmet, full-face, 3/4, half, domino, feature, parade

Scale/size

Worn by

Fit: custom   adjustable   NA

Life cast? Measure?

Flexibility

Integration: helmet, headband, fixed strap, elastic, ribbon, teeth, hand, rod

Weight

Balance

Quick change

Durability (length of run, classroom stock)

Moving parts?

Materials/techniques

Surface treatment

Decoration

MASK PERFORMER MEASUREMENT SHEET

Character

Production/event

Designed by

Type (full, half, feature, etc.)

Fit points

Vertical Measures

Top of head to chin

Forehead (hairline) to chin

Forehead to nose pit

Forehead to nose tip

Forehead to mouth

Horizontal Measures

Width of forehead

Width at eyeline

Width at cheekbone

Width at jawline

Eye span

Breadth nose

Breadth mouth

Depth

Forehead to ear line

Brow ridge to ear line

Nose pit to ear line

Nose tip to ear line

Chin to ear line (perpendicular)

Additional Notes

MASK ESTIMATE

Character   Production

Date   Venue

	Notes	Materials	Cost	Prep	Fit	Complete
Design						
Actor cast						
Character sculpt						
Character cast						
Prototype						
Base						
Dimensional work						
Surface prep						
Surface decoration						
Interior						

MASK PROJECT – DIRECT PAPER STRIP MASK

Goals

Each student will create an undecorated neutral mask directly on their own face using the direct method and working in a mirror.

Materials

- Plastic or thin cloth to cover hair
- Brown paper grocery and lunch bags, torn into strips
- White glue
- Q-tips to apply glue (optional)
- Small container of warm water to soften paper and degum fingers (margarine tub is fine)
- Washcloth or rag to keep fingers clean
- Scissors to trim eyes, mouth, and edges
- Pencil
- Elastic cord for strap
- Felt or foam for padding if needed for air flow

Time

- 45 minutes – initial mask (in class) *smaller pieces take longer but create finer features*
- 45–60 minutes to trim and reinforce (in class)
- 30 minutes sand, wipe, and seal
- 15 minutes fit and finish

Procedure

- Gather supplies, and cover your hair as much as possible with a plastic bag or bandanna.
- Tear ~1 dozen long 1″–2″ strips and some medium and small bits and strips of paper.
- Tape 2 long strips at one end into headband, and tape around forehead securely (seam in back).
- Add strip ear to ear over top to anchor; add strips to fit face temple to temple under chin; remembering at this stage to glue ends only (keep your jaw relaxed to enable breathing).
- Glue additional strips to frame to outline and fill entire face, leaving openings for eyes and nose, and a small slit for the mouth (optional). A Q-tip is useful to apply glue as you hold the strips to your face to dry.
  - long narrow strips are useful for establishing forehead, jaw, and nose centerline
  - medium pieces fit the major planes of the face
  - small pieces work best in detailed areas and curvy parts, including the eye sockets, lips, and chin

*I recommend this order: forehead, temple to jaw line, centerline down nose to chin, upper lip, nose (bridge to nares), cheeks, eyes, chin, and mouth. More glue adheres the paper better for a stronger mask, but too much will seep onto your face and create a soggy mask that doesn't breathe as well.

- Apply two layers to the whole face, then remove mask and dry over crumpled paper for support.
- Hold the mask to the light and reinforce any weak spots or irregular edges, then add a third layer of small (1″ or less) pieces over all.
- Try the mask on again, and mark eyes, mouth and edges while checking in the mirror.
- Take off the mask, even and trim as marked, and check again for vision and airflow.
- If mask is flimsy, add fourth or fifth layer as needed. Bind the edges with folded glued paper. It is common to add a shaped wire edge for support, encasing it in overlapping tabs of brown paper.
- Sand rough edges and seams, and all over lightly.
- Brush dust off well and seal with shellac or glue (Modge Podge).
- Punch holes in mask sides just above ear, string elastic, or cord through to fit and finish off inside with squares of paper or felt over the ends of the elastic.

Studio Work

Reading the mask
Bringing the mask to life
Using the body to communicate

Journal Prompts

After the first day of mask making:

- How did you feel before starting? Excited? Nervous? Reluctant? What made you feel this way?

- As you began the mask, what did you feel?

- When your face was covered? As the covering continued, how did you respond emotionally?

- What was your level of awareness of yourself? Of the mask? Of what was going on around you? How did that awareness change during the process?

- Did you feel the mask is yourself, or someone else? Do you know who?

- How did you feel coming out of the mask today?

- As you work on the next layers at home, what are your thoughts?

After the class shares masks:

- Now that your mask is finished, how do you feel looking at it?

- Is that different from how you feel wearing it?

- Do you sense a character in the mask?

- How did others perceive you in the mask?

MASK PROJECT – LIBBY APPEL STYLE EMOTIONAL MASK

Goals

To explore sculptural methods of creating features on an emotional mask in the style of Libby Appel's teaching masks. These masks have full faces, larger than life features, open mouths (backed with gauze), and an emphasis on contrary and ambivalent qualities. For example, one side of the mouth may droop, while the other moves upward, or a worried brow opposes a defiant chin. They have a primitive, slightly grotesque style and expression, but complex color and texture.

Materials

- Research pictures of Libby Appel style masks and emotional faces
- Neutral mask for base
- Plastic film/cling wrap and/or gallon ziplock baggie (for storage)
- White glue
- Crayola model magic
- Dish of warm water
- Paper bag, torn for top layers
- 12″ of 1/2″ braided elastic
- Acrylic paints, neutral tones
- Sponges and brushes for painting
- Felt or foam padding

Time

- 10 minutes base prep (elastic, preliminary fitting)
- 30–60 minutes sculpt (dry overnight)
- 30–40 minutes paper mache layers (dry overnight)
- 15–30 minutes paint and seal with Modge Podge (matte finish)
- 10 minutes final fit

Process

Base prep (skip first two steps if using a preformed mask as base):

- Cover cast or clay form with a light layer of Vaseline, then a sheet of saran wrap.
- Using fabric soaked and squeezed in flex glue, lay strips/pieces to create base layer: it may extend beyond the size of your base. Dry with hairdryer to establish face shaped mask base.
- Punch two holes in base at temple and 1″ below temple (each side) thread elastic braid and fit to face, applying interior padding as needed. Make sure you can see and breathe comfortably.

Character:

- Trim base edges and check fit for comfort (label inside with your name now if part of a class!).
- Pencil the major features of your design onto the mask base, and trim eyes, nose, and mouth to approximate size/shape.
- Press a half-inch thick layer of model magic into the base to form the desired head size and shape. Leave open holes for eyes, mouth, and nostrils. Check air and visibility as you work by holding mask up to face.
- Keeping base Model Magic layer damp with water, build up features (asymmetrically) to suggest emotion(s) as per your design. Work to blend the planes of the face and features. Check the side views and other angles of your mask as you go.
- When satisfied with the liveliness of your mask, smooth a layer of flex glue thinned with water over the entire front of the mask with your fingers.
- Dry overnight.

Finishing:

- *Model magic shrinks ~ 5% when it dries, which may cause cracks. These may be filled with white glue before painting.*
- Cover the mask with two to three layers of paper mache using brown paper lunch bags or paper towels and white glue or Modge Podge. Be sure to wrap the paper mache layers around the outer edges and features also, to keep it from separating from the base mask.
- Sponge or brush a neutral base color over entire mask.
- Stipple highlights with a sponge to elevations: brows, nose, cheeks, chin, lips, as needed.
- Stipple shadow as desired under brows, nose, jaw, temples, and recesses as desired.
- Seal dried paint with flex glue, modge podge, or white glue.
- Adjust fit using felt or foam padding. Tie elastic into temple holes, and glue elastic ends inside temple of mask, covering ends with squares of felt or paper.

APPENDIX C: RESOURCES FOR BUYING MASKS AND SUPPLIES

This is a small selection of resources available for purchasing mask materials at the time of printing this book. It is certainly not exhaustive and is subject to change. Fortunately, online sourcing is a valuable tool available to many of us.

PRODUCTS AND SUPPLIERS

Active Foam Products, Chicago www.activefoam.com

Armor Venue www.armorvenue.com (visored helmets)

Cheap Joe's Art Supplies www.cheapjoes.com

Chicago Latex www.spartancompany.com/chicago-latex-products.html (neoprene)

Clark Foam Products www.clarkfoam.net (diverse line of foam products, including custom cuts)

Critical Coatings www.criticalcoatings.com (neoprene)

Dharma Trading Post www.dharmatrading.com (fiber art supplies and tutorials)

Dick Blick Art supplies www.dickblick.com

Douglas and Sturgess, Inc. www.artstuf.com
730 Bryant St. San Francisco, CA 94107
800-992-5540

The Foam Board Source www.foamboards.com (Sintra – a thermoplastic board)

The Foam Factory www.thefoamfactory.com

Grainger, Inc. www.grainger.com (adhesives, tools)

Industrial Plastic Supply, Inc. www.iplasticsupply.com (sheeting and ABS for vacuform)

Landwerlen Leather Co. https://landwerlen-leather-co.business.site/
365 S Illinois Street, Indianapolis, IN 46225 (317) 636-8300 (great selection and service by knowledgeable staff in family-owned business)

Plasti-Dip. PDC-7
3760 Flowerfield Rd., PO Box 130, Circle Pines, MN 55014
800-969-5432

RIT dyes www.ritstudio.com (dyes and tutorials)

Southeastern Foam Rubber Company, P.O. Box 7183, 1409 Progress Avenue High Point NC 27264. 336-882-6881 Polyfoam (rolls)

Studio Creations www.studiocreations.com (vacuform tutorials, including building a simple table)

Tandy Leather www.tandyleather.com (various leather and supplies)

Torb and Reiner Australia https://www.hattersmillinery-supplies.com.au/torb-and-reiner/ (millinery supply, thermoplastics, and tutorials)

Worbla www.worbla.com (selection of thermoplastic products)

MAKEUP AND SFX SUPPLIERS

Alcone Co. www.alconeco.com 5-49 49th Avenue, Long Island City, New York 11101

Ben Nye www.bennye.com 5935 Bowcroft St. Los Angeles, CA 90016

FX Warehouse, Inc. www.fxwarehouse.info

Kryolan Corp. www.kryolan.com 132 Ninth St, San Francisco, CA 94103-2603 also Chicago, Germany, & more

Makeup Designory www.mud.edu/ Burbank, CA and New York

Monster Makers. www.monstermakers.com 7305 Detroit Avenue, Cleveland, OH 44102

Stan Winston School www.stanwinstonschool.com (online courses)

ASSOCIATIONS

ALI – Association of Lifecasters International
CITT – Canadian Institute of Theatre Technology
CSA – Costume Society of America
IATSE – International Alliance of Theatrical Stage Employees
IMACO – International Mask Arts and Culture Organization
OISTAT – International Organization of Scenographers, Theatre Architects and Technicians
OSHA – Occupational Safety and Health Administration
SPAM – Society of Props Artists and Makers
USA – United Scenic Artists
USITT – United States Institute for Theatre Technology

APPENDIX D: ARTISTS AND THEATER COMPANIES THAT WORK WITH MASKS (A SELECTION)

These individual artists and companies have done significant mask work as performers, directors, and mask makers in recent decades, mostly in Europe and North America. While this list is not intended to be exhaustive, it should serve as a good starting point for those who wish to research mask styles or inspiration from the many ways that masks have been employed in contemporary theater. For additional information on mask makers outside Europe and North America, we recommend Deborah Bell's excellent book, *Mask Makers and Their Craft: An Illustrated Worldwide Study*.

INDIVIDUALS (MASK MAKERS AND THEATER ARTISTS)

- Torbjorn Alstrom
- Jonathan Becker
- Peter Brook
- Mike Chase
- Carlo Clementi
- Jacques Copeau
- Russell Dean
- Matteo Destro
- Joe Dieffenbacher
- Rob Faust
- Antonio Fava
- Dario Fo
- Zarco Guerrero
- Peter Hall
- Craig Jacobrown
- Hideta Kitazawa
- David Knezz
- Jacques Lecoq
- Marco Luly
- Bruce Marrs
- Ariane Mnouchkine
- Newman
- Omar Porras
- Bernardo Rey Rengifo
- Amleto Sartori
- Donato Sartori
- Joan Schirle
- Jeff Semmerling
- Stanley Allan Sherman
- Anna Shishkina
- Werner Strub
- Julie Taymor
- Toby Wilsher
- Robert Wilson
- Larry Wood
- John Wright

COMPANIES

- Animacy Theatre Collective
- Boxtales Theatre Company
- Bread and Puppet Theatre
- Complicité
- The Dell'Arte Company

Familie Flöz
Grafted Cede Theatre
The Mask Center, Gateway Performance Productions
Habbe und Meik
Horse and Bamboo Theatre
In the Heart of the Beast Puppet and Mask Theatre
Mr. Pejo's Wandering Dolls
Mummenschanz Theatre
Punchdrunk
San Francisco Mime Troupe

Strangeface Theatre Company
El Teatro Campesino
Teatro Cenit
Théâtre du Soleil
Theatre Grottesco
Theatre Nohgaku
Theatre Temoin
Trestle Theatre Company
Vamos Theatre
Yuyachkani

APPENDIX E: PLAYS THAT USE MASKS (A SELECTION)

There have been many wonderful productions that have employed masks – whether the playwright called for masks or not. In some cases, these plays come from a theatrical tradition in which the artists and audience would have expected the use of masks. In other cases, the plays were written outside an existing genre, and the author was seeking an innovative use of masks. And finally, we have included some plays that do not explicitly call for the use of masks, but which have been successfully produced using masks. While this list is by no means exhaustive, it should provide an indication of the rich and varied tradition of mask use and serve as a starting point for those who wish to experiment with the use of masks in a production. There are many wonderful mask shows created by the companies listed in Appendix D. Many of these shows are available for production.

TRADITIONS THAT HISTORICALLY USE MASKS

Here are some theatrical traditions in which masks would have originally been used, along with some representative plays and playwrights in each. Many of these plays have since been adapted for use with and without masks.

Greek

Sophocles. *Oedipus Rex; Antigone.*

Aristophanes. *The Birds.*

Aeschylus. *The Oresteia Trilogy.*

Euripides. *The Bacchae.*

Roman

Terence. *The Brothers; The Mother-in-Law.*

Plautus. *The Brothers Menaechmi (Twins); Bacchis (twin sisters); Miles Gloriosus.*

Seneca. *Phaedra; Medea; Women of Troy.*

Medieval

Mystery plays (biblical stories) of Chester, Coventry, Wakefield, and York.

Morality plays: *Everyman, The Seven Deadly Sins, The Castle of Perseverance.*

Miracle plays: *St. George and the Dragon, St. John the Hairy.*

Commedia dell'Arte

Goldoni, Carlo. *Servant of Two Masters.*

Gozzi, Carlo. *The Stag King; The Green Bird; The Love of Three Oranges.*

Moliere, Jean-Baptiste. *Sganarelle, or the Imaginary Cuckold; Les Fourberies de Scapin.*

PLAYS THAT INCORPORATE MASKS

These authors and works have been presented with the use of masks. In some cases masks were called for in the original script, and in other cases the use of masks is a result of successful choices by the creative team.

Anouilh, Jean. *Thieves' Carnival.*

Brecht, Bertolt. *The Good Person of Szechwan; Caucasian Chalk Circle; The Measures Taken; Antigone; The Life of Galileo.*

Beerbohm, Max. *The Happy Hypocrite*.

Čapek, Karel. *R.U.R.*

Camus, Albert. *Caligula*.

Cocteau, Jean. *Antigone; Orpheus*.

Durrenmatt, F. *The Visit*.

Fugard, Athol. *The Cell*.

Gogol, Nikolai. *The Inspector General*.

Garcia Lorca, Federico. *Yerma; Blood Wedding*.

Genet, Jean. *The Blacks: A Clown Show; The Balcony; The Screens*.

Gerstenberg, Alice. *Overtones*.

de Ghelderode, Michel. *Pantagleize*.

Handke, Peter. *Kaspar*.

Howe, Tina. *Birth and After Birth*.

Ionesco, Eugene. *Jack, or the Submission; The Future is in Eggs*.

Jarry, Alfred. *Ubu Roi*.

Müller, Heiner. *Slaughter*.

O'Neill, Eugene. *The Great God Brown; Lazarus; The Hairy Ape*.

Pirandello, Luigi. *Fable of the Transformed Son; Right You Are, If You Think So*.

Shakespeare, William. *Romeo and Juliet; The Tempest; Comedy of Errors; Midsummer Night's Dream*.

Shange, Ntozake. *Spell #7*.

Stephens, Simon. *The Curious Incident of the Dog in the Night-Time*.

Still, James. *Appoggiatura*.

Washburn, Anne. *Mr. Burns: A Post-Electric Play*.

Wilson, August. *Gem of the Ocean*.

Yeats, William Butler. *The Dreaming of the Bones; At the Hawk's Well; The Only Jealousy of Emer; the Player Queen*.

OTHER WORKS

Many works, including animal and fantasy characters, are suited for mask work, for instance:

Aesop's *Fables*.

Kipling, Rudyard. *The Jungle Book*.

Leonard, Jim. *Crow and Weasel*.

Dahl, Roald. *James and the Giant Peach; Fantastic Mr. Fox*.

Rumplestiltskin; Jack and the Beanstalk.

APPENDIX F: MUSEUMS WITH MASK COLLECTIONS (A SELECTION)

Many museums around the world include mask collections. Some images are accessible digitally on the museum website. This is just a small sampling of collections we have used.

Virtual Museums
Masks of the World
https://masksoftheworld.com/

Second Face Museum of Cultural Masks
https://www.maskmuseum.org/

Australia
The Australian Museum
https://australian.museum/

Museums Victoria
https://museumsvictoria.com.au/

National Museum of Australia
https://www.nma.gov.au/

Western Australia Museum
http://museum.wa.gov.au/

Canada
Museum of Anthropology, University of British Columbia, Vancouver
http://collection-online.moa.ubc.ca/search?category%5Bobjecttype%5D%5B%5D=1496239

Museum of Civilization, Ottawa
https://www.historymuseum.ca/search/?q=mask

Egypt
The Egyptian Museum, Cairo
https://egymonuments.gov.eg/en/collections/masks-of-yuya-and-thuya-6

Ghana
The National Museum of Ghana, Accra
https://www.ghanamuseums.org/

Greece
National Archaeological Museum, Athens
https://www.namuseum.gr/en/

India
Kerala – Kottarakkara Kathakali Museum – https://kerala.me/destinations/museums/kottarakkarakathakali_museum

Indonesia
Museum Negeri Propinsi Bali ("Bali Museum")
Jl. Mayor Wisnu No.1, Dangin Puri, Kec. Denpasar Tim., Kota Denpasar, Bali 80232

Iran
National Museum of Iran
http://irannationalmuseum.ir/en/

Israel
The Israel Museum, Jerusalem
https://www.imj.org.il/en/search/site/masks

Italy
Sartori Mask Museum, Padua
http://www.sartorimaskmuseum.it/

Japan
Kanazawa Noh Museum
https://www.kanazawa-noh-museum.gr.jp/english/index.html

Tokyo National Museum
https://www.tnm.jp/?lang=en

Korea
Hahoe Mask Museum
http://www.mask.kr/default.htm

Mexico
Museo Nacional de la Mascara
Villerías No. 2, 78000 San Luis Potosí
www.museodelamascara.com

The Mask Museum of San Miguel de Allende
https://www.maskmuseumsma.com

Thailand
Bangkok National Museum
https://www.museumthailand.com/en/museum/National-Museum-Bangkok-Phranakorn

United Kingdom
British Museum
https://www.britishmuseum.org/

Victoria and Albert Museum
https://collections.vam.ac.uk/search/?q=masks

Wellcome Museum
https://wellcomecollection.org/works?query=mask

United States
Brooklyn Museum, New York
https://www.brooklynmuseum.org/opencollection/search?keyword=mask

Eiteljorg Museum, Indianapolis
https://eiteljorg.org/

Getty Museum, California
https://www.getty.edu/search/?qt=mask&pg=1

Indianapolis Museum of Art at Newfields, Indianapolis
https://discovernewfields.org/

Metropolitan Museum of Art, New York
https://www.metmuseum.org/search-results#!/search?q=mask

Museum of Fine Arts, Boston
https://collections.mfa.org/search/objects/*/masks

St. Louis Art Museum, Missouri
https://www.slam.org/collection/objects/?se=mask&show_on_view=true&featured_objects=false

Seattle Art Museum
https://www.seattleartmuseum.org/

Smithsonian Museums, Washington, D.C.; National Museum of the American Indian
https://americanindian.si.edu/

University of Oregon Museum of Natural and Cultural History
https://mnch.uoregon.edu/collections-galleries/native-american-masks-northwest-coast-and-alaska

APPENDIX G: FILMS AND VIDEOS THAT FEATURE MASKS (A SELECTION)

This is not intended to be an exhaustive list, but rather an inspiring place to continue research for those who are interested in masks and their possible uses.

I. Anthropology and Cultural Masking

Bali, Masks of Rangda
Bellin, Harvey F., Elda Hartley, and Peter Henry. Bali Mask of Rangda. Cos Cob, CT: Hartley Film Foundation, 1980.

Beauty and the Beast: Two Igbo Masquerades
Cole, Herbert M. Beauty and the Beast: Two Igbo Masquerades. Seattle, WA: African Studies Program in the Jackson School of International Studies, University of Washington, 1985.

The Celestial Dance of Bhutan
Catteau, Manuel, and Florence Tran. The Celestial Dance of Bhutan. Paris, France: ZED, 2006.

The Drum and the Mask Time of the Tubuan
Yocoe, Caroline, Charles Chess, and William Takaku. The Drum and the Mask Time of the Tubuan. Honolulu, HI: Pacific Pathways, 1999.

Endangered Civilization. Dancing with Masks: The Bolon People of Burkina Faso
Bourrillon, Alain, Redo Porgo, Pascal Bensoussan, and Gary Granville. Endangered Civilizations. Dancing with Masks: the Bolon People of Burkina Faso. Paris: 10 Francs, 2007.

The Human Face: Emotions, Identities and Masks
Archer, Dane, and Jon Silver. The Human Face: Emotions, Identities and Masks. Berkeley, CA: Berkeley Media, 1995.

Kwagh Hir
Harper, Peggy, and Francis Speed. Kwagh Hir. London, UK: Royal Anthropological Institute, 1975.

Masks from Many Cultures
Masks from Many Cultures. DVD Glenview, IL: Crystal Productions, 1993.

Masks of Arcadia
Dunlop, Geoff. Masks of Arcadia. London, England: British Broadcasting Corporation BBC, 1989.

Masks of Mexico
Masks of Mexico. Albuquerque: KNME-TV, 1998.

Music and Society. Island of Temples
Bhattacharya, Deben. Music and Society. Island of Temples. Montpelier, VT: Multicultural Media, 2003.

Northern Edo Masking Traditions with Jean M. Borgatti
Morell, Karen L., and Jean Borgatti. Northern Edo Masking Traditions with Jean M. Borgatti. Seattle, WA: University of Washington, Instructional Media Services, 1992.

Rasinah the Enchanted Mask
Grauer, Rhoda, and Harmayn Shanty. Rasinah the Enchanted Mask. New York, NY: Filmakers Library, 2006.

Singsing Tumbuan (Mask Dance)
Berman, Marsha. Singsing Tumbuan (Mask Dance). Boroko, Papua New Guinea: Asples Productions, 1995.

The Spirit of the Mask
von Puttkamer, Peter. The Spirit of the Mask. San Francisco, CA, USA: Kanopy Streaming, 2015.

The Tribal Eye: Behind the Mask
The Tribal Eye: Behind the Mask. BBC: David Attenborough, 1975 50:35.

Yaaba Soore, the Path of the Ancestors
Roy, Christopher D. Yaaba Soore, the Path of the Ancestors. Iowa City, IA: University of Iowa, 1986.

II. Theater Traditions and Interviews

Acting Techniques of Topeng: The Masked Theatre of Bali
McMullen, Larry, and John Emigh. Acting Techniques of Topeng: The Masked Theatre of Bali. East Lansing, MI: Michigan State University, 1980.

Adapting Topeng: The Masked Theater of Bali. An Interview with John Emigh, and Excerpts from the Little Red Riding Shawl
McMullen, Larry, John Emigh, and Farley P. Richmond. Adapting Topeng: The Masked Theater of Bali. East Lansing, MI: Michigan State University, 1980.

Ancient Theatres of Greece and Rome
Films for the Humanities & Sciences (Firm), Infobase, and King's College London. 2006. Ancient theatres of Greece and Rome. New York, NY: Infobase. https://fod.infobase.com/PortalPlaylists.aspx?wID=152898&xtid=34695.

Behind the Mask: A Study of Masks and How to Use Them
Shepherd, Cheryl. Behind the Mask: A Study of Masks and How to Use Them. Melbourne, Victoria: Appleseed Media Group, 1990.

Behind the Mask
Heaven, Simon, and Hewish, Saul. Behind The Mask. London: British Broadcasting Corporation, 2013.

Butoh: Body on the Edge of Crisis
Butoh: Body on the Edge of Crisis. San Francisco, CA, USA: Kanopy Streaming, 2014.

Commedia by Fava
Fava, Antonio. Commedia by Fava. Reggio Emilia, Italy: ArscomicA, 2014.

Commedia dell'Arte
Poli, Giovanni, and John Dietrich Mitchell. Commedia dell'Arte. New York, NY: IASTA, 1980.

Commedia dell'Arte: The Story, the Style
Films on Demand, and Films Media Group. 2010. Commedia dell'Arte: The Story, the Style. Lawrenceville, NJ: Films Media Group. http://digital.films.com/PortalPlaylists.aspx?aid=8601&xtid=37626.

In Order to Innovate You Must Play with Fire. Interview with Julie Taymor
Taymor, Julie. In Order to Innovate You Must Play with Fire. The Nantucket Project, 2014. https://www.youtube.com/watch?v=5aFoWU_JYHo.

Kabuki Makeup
Shozo Sato PBS Learning Media, 2011. https://illinois.pbslearningmedia.org/resource/jacult.arts.drama.makeup/japanese-culture-kabuki-makeup/.

Les deux voyages de Jaques Lecoq
Lecoq, Jacques, Jean-Noël Roy, Jean-Gabriel Carasso, and Jean-Claude Lallias. Les deux voyages de Jacques Lecoq. France: On Line Productions, 2006.

Man and Mask: [Oskar Schlemmer and the Bauhaus Stage]
Man and Mask: [Oscar Schlemmer and the Bauhaus Stage]. San Francisco, CA, USA: Kanopy Streaming, 2014.

Medieval Drama: From Sanctuary to Stage
Films for the Humanities and Sciences, Films on Demand, and Films Media Group.
2010. *Medieval Drama: From Sanctuary to Stage*. Lawrenceville, NJ: Films Media Group.
http://digital.films.com/PortalPlaylists.aspx?aid=8601&xtid=10819.

Mummenschanz Swiss Mime and Mask Theater
Mummenschanz Swiss Mime Mask Theater. Kent, CT: Creative Arts Television, 1976.

My Commedia dell'Arte
Luly, Marco. Online course through Theatre Practitioners Online. https://theatrepractitioners.online/course/my-commedia-dellarte-marco-lully/.

Noh Masks: The Spirit of Noh Theatre
https://www.youtube.com/watch?v=qsMnyrxqe6w&ab_channel=DymSensei.

Theater in Japan: Yesterday and Today
Films for the Humanities & Sciences (Firm), Films Media Group, and Arts Council of England. 2006. *Theater in Japan: Yesterday and Today*. New York, NY: Films Media Group. http://digital.films.com/PortalPlaylists.aspx?aid=8751&xtid=10986.

III. Mask Making

African Carving a Dogon Kanaga Mask
Blakely, Thomas D., Eliot Elisofon, and Robert Gardner. African Carving a Dogon Kanaga Mask. Watertown, MA: Documentary Educational Resources, 2008.

Bidou Yamaguchi in Conversation with Dr. Kendall Brown
https://www.youtube.com/watch?v=VySTpAc5Y40&ab_channel=AsiaSocietyTexasCenter.

Noh Masks: The Spirit of Noh Theatre
https://www.youtube.com/watch?v=qsMnyrxqe6w&ab_channel=DymSensei.

Kwa'nu'te Micmac and Maliseer Artists
Kwa'nu'te' Micmac and Maliseet Artists. New York: National Film Board of Canada, 1991.

IV. Theatrical Performances with Masks

A Commedia dell'Arte Hamlet
Alaimo, Michael, Michael Dannenberg, Martin David, Norman David, Nick Havinga, Allan Mann, Sig Moglen, and James Morrison. A Commedia dell'Arte Hamlet. Kent, CT: Creative Arts Television, 2000.

Oedipus Rex. Julie Taymor
Stravinsky, Igor, Emi Wada, Igor Stravinsky, George Tsypin, Jean Cocteau, Jean Daniélou, Julie Taymor, et al. 2012. Oedipus Rex. Berlin: C Major Entertainment. http://www.aspresolver.com/aspresolver.asp?DAIV;2088493.

Oedipus Rex. Tyrone Guthrie
Guthrie, Tyrone, Leonid Kipnis, W. B. Yeats, Douglas Campbell, Eleanor Stuart, Robert Goodier, William Hut, et al. 2017. Oedipus Rex. https://library.usu.edu/catlog/url856.php?url=http://www.kaltura.com/tiny/52pjr.

Oresteia
Hall, Peter, Tony Harrison, Aeschylus, and Aeschylus. 1983. Oresteia. v. 1, v. 1. Princeton, N.J.: Films for the Humanities.

The Taming of the Shrew. Commedia-style production
Ball, William and American Conservatory Theatre of San Francisco, 1976. https://www.youtube.com/watch?v=rAPF5SIYj88.

V. Feature Films/Television Programs with Masks

Many performances use masks as decoration, to visualize (or hide) an alien or monster, or to create tension through anonymity. The vast genres of fantasy, horror, comic books, and science fiction include many such films. We have not listed those here but do include films where mask is part of defining a world or demonstrating a tradition. These may be of particular interest.

Fools Fire
Taymor, Julie. American Playhouse Productions, PBS. 1992. https://www.youtube.com/watch?v=C8Iqzlz-dNE.

Frank
Abrahamson, Lenny, Domhnall Gleeson, Maggie Gyllenhaal, and Michael Fassbender. 2020. Frank. https://torontopl.kanopy.com/node/10206752.

The King of Masks
Wei, Minglun, Tianming Wu, Xu Zhu, Yim Yin Chao, and Wengui Chen. 2015.

Mirror Mask
By Neil Gaiman and Dave McKean with Iain Ballamy, Tony Shearn, Stephanie Leonidas, Jason Barry, and Rob Brydon. 2008. Škofljica: Blitz Film & Video Distribution.

VI. Databases and Sources for Video

Additional ways to search for recorded materials include many performances available on YouTube and other video platforms, which also feature excerpts of productions from many of the artists and companies we have discussed in the book.

Check with your library for access to these databases that list streaming video resources:

AVON – Academic Video Online (Alexander Street Press)
AVON: Academic Video Online is a comprehensive multidisciplinary streaming video resource.

Digital Theatre +
Digital Theatre + contains streaming videos of a variety of theater productions and includes study materials and interviews with practitioners.

Films on Demand
Films on Demand is a state-of-the-art streaming video platform for a variety of educational media content.

Second Face Museum of Cultural Masks hosts documentary films of Asian, Latin American, European, and North American mask traditions. https://www.maskmuseum.org/videos/.

TED Talks have some wonderful presentations about masks by artists, including:

Russell Dean. "Puppets and Perception." TEDx Talk, 2017. https://www.youtube.com/watch?v=X_MoIj8L6nM.

Rob Faust. "Behind the Mask/Beneath the Ego." TEDx Talk, 2014. https://www.youtube.com/watch?v=eaInFD4uVm0.

Amanda Mattes. "Kabuki: The People's Dramatic Art." TED Talk, 2013. https://www.ted.com/talks/amanda_mattes_kabuki_the_people_s_dramatic_art.

Julie Taymor. "Spider-Man, the Lion King, and Life on the Creative Edge." TED Talk, 2011. https://www.ted.com/talks/julie_taymor_spider_man_the_lion_king_and_life_on_the_creative_edge.

Melissa Walker. "Art Can Heal PTSD's Invisible Wounds." TEDMED Talk, 2015. https://www.ted.com/talks/melissa_walker_art_can_heal_ptsd_s_invisible_wounds.

BIBLIOGRAPHY

Agostino, Christopher. *Transformations.* Berlin, Germany: Kryolan GmbH, 2006.

Alene, Anne Geismann, Bidou Yamaguchi, Kendall H. Brown and California State University, Long Beach. *Traditions Transfigured: The Noh Masks of Bidou Yamaguchi.* Long Beach, California: University Art Museum, California State University, 2014.

Allison, Drew and Donald Devet. *The Foam Book: An Easy Guide to Building Polyfoam Puppets.* Charlotte, North Carolina: Grey Seal Puppets, Inc., 1997.

Appel, Libby. *Mask Characterization: An Acting Process.* Carbondale, Illinois: Southern Illinois Press, 1982.

Appukuttan Nair D., K. Ayyappa Paniker, Pankaj Shah and Sangeet Natak Akademi. *Kathakali, the Art of the Non-Worldly.* Mumbai, India: Marg Publications, 1993.

Arrighi, Gillian. *The Neutral Mask: Its Origins and Its Applications to the Creative Processes of the Actor.* Saarbrucken, Germany: Verlag Dr. Muller, 2010.

Ashton, Geoffrey. *Catalogue of Paintings at the Theatre Museum, London.* London: Victoria and Albert Museum & The Society for Theatre Research, 1992.

Bailey, Mark S. and H. Janaka de Silve. "Sri Lankan Sanni Masks: An Ancient Classification of Disease." *BMJ: British Medical Journal.* Vol. 333, No. 7582 (2006), 1327–1328.

Balikrishnan, Sadanam. *Kathakali.* New Delhi, India: Wisdom Tree, 2004.

Barba, Eugenio and Nicola Savarese. *A Dictionary of Theatre Anthropology: The Secret Art of the Performer.* Translated by Richard Fowler. New York: Routledge, 2006.

Barone, Rose Sage. *Neoprene: Where to Buy, How to Use.* The Puppetry Home Page. Accessed February 12, 2019, https://www.sagecraft.com/puppetry/building/neoprene.html

Becker, Jonathan. Interview with the authors. Muncie, Indiana. November 2017.

Bell, Deborah. "The Mask Maker's Magic." *Theatre Design and Technology.* Vol. 41, No. 1 (2005), 29–43.

———. *Mask Makers and Their Craft: An Illustrated Worldwide Study.* Jefferson, North Carolina: McFarland, 2010.

Bell, John, ed. *Puppets, Masks, and Performing Objects.* Cambridge, Massachusetts: MIT Press, 2001.

Benda, Wladyslaw Theodore. *Masks.* New York: Watson Guptill, 1944.

Belting, Hans S. *Face and Mask: A Double History.* Translated by Thomas S. Hansen and Abby J. Hansen. New Jersey: Princeton University Press, 2017.

"Bidou Yamaguchi In Conversation with Dr. Kendall Brown" YouTube. Asia Society Texas Center, November 24, 2014. https://www.youtube.com/watch?v=VySTpAc5Y40.

Blumenthal, Eileen and Julie Taymor. *Julie Taymor, Playing with Fire: Theater, Opera, Film.* New York: H.N. Abrams, 1995.

Bolton, Andrew. *Superheroes: Fashion and Fantasy.* New York: The Metropolitan Museum of Art, 2008.

Bonds, Alexandra B. *Beijing Opera Costumes: The Visual Communication of Character and Culture.* Honolulu, Hawaii: University of Hawai'i Press, 2008.

Brady, Tara. "No laughing matter: why are we so terrified of clowns?" *The Irish Times.* September 9, 2017. https://www.irishtimes.com/culture/film/no-laughing-matter-why-are-we-so-terrified-of-clowns-1.3209215.

Bradley, Doug. *Behind the Mask of the Horror Actor.* London: Titan Books, 2004.

Brandon, James R. *The Cambridge Guide to Asian Theatre.* Cambridge, Massachusetts: Cambridge University Press, 2009.

———. *Theatre in Southeast Asia.* Cambridge, Massachusetts: Harvard University Press, 1967.

Brockett, Oscar. *History of the Theatre.* 4th ed. Boston, Massachusetts: Allyn & Bacon, 1982.

Brecht, Stefan. *Peter Schumann's Bread and Puppet Theater.* London: Methuen, 1988.

Brown, Betty Ann and Ewing Museum of Nations. *Máscaras: Dance Masks of Mexico and Guatemala*. Bloomington, Illinois: Illinois State University, 1978.

Brown, John Russell. *The Oxford Illustrated History of the Theatre*. Oxford: Oxford University Press, 1995.

Brown, Kendall H., ed. *Traditions Transfigured: The Noh Masks of Bidou Yamaguchi*. Long Beach, California: University Art Museum, 2014.

Campbell, Joseph. *Primitive Mythology: The Masks of God*. New York: Viking Penguin, 1991.

Cavaye, Ronald, Paul Griffith and Akihiko Senda. *A Guide to the Japanese Stage: From Traditional to Cutting Edge*. Tokyo, Japan: Kodansha International, 2004.

Chaffee, Judith and Olly Crick, eds. *The Routledge Companion to Commedia dell'Arte*. Routledge Companions, 2017: 4. London: Routledge, Taylor and Francis Group, 2017.

Chandavij, Natthapatra and Prompom Pramualratana. *Thai Puppets and Khon Masks*. London: Thames and Hudson, 1998.

Chase, Mike. *Mask: Making, Using and Performing*. Gloucestershire: Hawthorn Press, 2017.

Cheong, Jannette and Richard Emmert. "Hideta Kitazawa." Between the Stones, 2019. https://www.betweenthestones.com/past-events/.

Ching, Elise Dirlam and Kaleo Ching. *Faces of Your Soul: Rituals in Art, Maskmaking, and Guided Imagery with Ancestors, Spirit Guides, and Totem Animals*. Berkley, California: North Atlantic Books, 2006.

Cohen, Amy R. "Can You Hear Me Now? – Implications of New Research in Greek Theatrical Masks." *Didaskalia – The Journal for Ancient Performance*. Randolph College, n.d. Web. November 29, 2016.

Cohen, Amy R. Interview with the author. Virtual via Randolph College, Lynchburg, Virginia. August 13, 2018.

Congdon-Martin, Douglas, Jim Pieper and California Heritage Museum. *Masks of the World*. Atglen, Pennsylvania: Schiffer, 1999.

Cordry, Donald. *Mexican Masks*. Austin, Texas: University of Texas Press, 1980.

Corey, Irene. *The Mask of Reality: An Approach to Design for Theatre*. Anchorage, Kentucky: Anchorage Press, 1968.

Corson, Richard. *Fashions in Makeup from Ancient to Modern Times*. London: Peter Owen, 2003.

Corson, Richard, Beverly Gore Norcross and James Glavan. *Stage Makeup*. 10th ed. Boston, Massachusetts: Allyn & Bacon/Pearson, 2010.

Craig, Edward Gordon. *The Art of the Theatre*. New York: Theatre Arts Books, 1956.

Daniel, Ana. *Bali Behind the Mask*. New York: Alfred A. Knopf, 1981.

Daugherty, Diane. "The Pendulum of Intercultural Performance: 'Kathakali King Lear' at Shakespeare's Globe." *Asian Theatre Journal*. Vol. 22, No. 1 (Spring 2005), 52–72.

Dean, Russell. "Mask Artistry." Interview with the author. Kent, England. May 2019.

———. "Puppets and Perception." Tedx Guildford: April 2017.

Debreceni, Todd. *Special Makeup Effects*. 2nd ed. New York: Focal Press, 2013.

Dibia, Wayan I. and Rucina Ballinger. *Balinese Dance, Drama and Music*. North Clarendon, Vermont: Tuttle Publishing, 2004.

Duchartre, Pierre Louis. *The Italian Comedy*. Translated by R.T. Weaver. New York: Dover, 1966.

Etcoff, Nancy L. *Survival of the Prettiest: The Science of Beauty*. New York: Anchor Books, 2000.

Eldredge, Sears A. and Huston, Hollis W. "Actor Training in the Neutral Mask." *The Drama Review*. Vol. 22, No. 4 (1978), 19–28.

Eldredge, Sears A. *Mask Improvisation for Actor Training and Performance: The Compelling Image*. Evanston, Illinois: Northwestern University Press, 1996.

Emigh, John. *Masked Performance: The Play of Self and Other in Ritual and Theatre*. Philadelphia, Pennsylvania: University of Pennsylvania Press, 1996.

Evans, Mark and Kemp, Rick. *The Routledge Companion to Jacques Lecoq*. London: Routledge, Taylor & Francis Group, 2016.

Fagundes, Dave and Aaron Perzanowski. "*The Fascinating Reason Why Clowns Paint Their Faces on Eggs*" BBC.com. BBC, December. 6, 2017. http://www.bbc.com/future/story/20171206-the-fascinating-reason-why-clowns-paint-their-faces-on-eggs.

Faust, Rob. "Behind the Mask/Beneath the Ego." Tedx Reset: 2014.

———. Interview with the author. Indianapolis, 2019.

Fava, Antonio. *Commedia by Fava: The Commedia dell'Arte, Step by Step – Part 1*. Fremantle, Australia: Contemporary Arts Media. 2006. https://search.alexanderstreet.com/view/work/bibliographic_entity%7Cvideo_work%7C3925215.

———. *The Comic Mask in the Commedia dell'Arte: Actor Training, Improvisation, and the Poetics of Survival*. Translated by Thomas Simpson. Evanston, Illinois: Northwestern University Press, 2007.

Fienup-Riordan, Ann. *The Living Tradition of Yup'ik Masks: Agayuliyaraput, Our Way of Making Prayer*. Seattle, Washington: University of Washington Press and Anchorage Museum of History and Art, 1996.

Films for the Humanities & Sciences. *Commedia dell'Arte: The Story, the Style*. New York: Films Media Group, 2007.

Foreman, Jennifer. *Maskwork*. Portsmouth, New Hampshire: Heinemann, 1999.

Freund, Philip. *Stage by Stage. Oriental Theatre: Drama, Opera, Dance and Puppetry in the Far East*. London: Peter Owen, 2005.

Gelber, Carol. *Masks Tell Stories. Beyond Museum Walls*. Brookfield, Connecticut: Millbrook Press, 1993.

Gontard, Denis. *Nô-Kyôgen: Le Masque Et Le Rir = Mask and Laughter = Maske Und Lachen*. Marburg, Germany: Hitzeroth, 1987.

Goonatilleka, M.H. *Masks and Mask Systems of Sri Lanka*. Colombo, Sri Lanka: Tamarind Books, 1978.

———. *Masks of Sri Lanka*. Colombo, Sri Lanka: Department of Cultural Affairs, 1976.

Granfield, Linda. *Circus: An Album*. New York: DK Ink, 1998.

Grantham, Barry. *Playing Commedia: A Training Guide to Commedia Techniques*. Portsmouth, New Hampshire: Heinemann, 2000.

Grater, Michael. *Paper Mask Making*. New York: Dover, 1984.

Griffiths, David. *Mask: The Training of Noh Actors*. New York: Routlege, 2005.

Gregor, Joseph. *Masks of the World: An Historical and Pictorial Survey of Many Types and Times*. New York: Benjamin Blom, 1937 and 1968.

Hall, Peter. *Exposed by the Mask: Form and Language in Drama*. New York: Theatre Communications Group, 2000.

Hart, Eric. *Eric Hart's Prop Agenda: "Celastic."* Eric Hart, June 25, 2017. http://www.props.eric-hart.com/tools/celastic/.

Hill, Chris. "What's the Difference Between Polyurethane, Varnish, Shellac and Lacquer?" HGTV, March 26, 2021. https://www.diynetwork.com/how-to/skills-and-know-how/painting/whats-the-difference-between-polyurethane-varnish-shellac-and-lacquer.

Hunt, Deborah. *Masks and Masked Faces: A Manual for the Construction of 22 Masks and Their Variations*. San Juan, Puerto Rico: Maskhunt Motions, 2013.

Iyer, K. Bharatha. *Kathakali: Sacred Dance-Drama of Malabar*. London: Luzac Co., 1955.

JoongAng Broadcasting Corp, dir. *Beijing Opera Masks: Face of Chinese Tradition*. New York: Films Media Group, 2006.

Image and Identity; the Role of the Mask in Various Cultures, An Exhibition Organized by the UCLA Museum of Cultural History. April 11–June 3, 1972.

International Festival of Masks. Los Angeles, California: Craft and Folk Art Museum, 1984.

Introduction to Mold Making and Casting. Workshop. Reynolds Advanced Materials. Chicago, Illinois: February 21, 2019.

Jablon, Sarah. "Historical Accuracy in Costume Design." PhD diss., Iowa State University, 2016.

Jackson, Paul. *The Encyclopedia of Origami and Papercraft Techniques. A Step-by-Step Visual Directory, with Practical Projects and a Gallery of Finished Designs*. Philadelphia, Pennsylvania: Running Press, 1991.

James, Thurston. *The Prop-Builders Mask Making Handbook*. Cincinnati, Ohio: Better Way Books, 1990.

Johnstone, Keith. *IMPRO*. New York: Routledge, 1992.

Johnstone, Keith. *Improvisation and the Theatre*. New York: Routledge, 1987.

Jones, Clifford R. and Betty Jones. *Kathakali: An Introduction to the Dance Drama of Kerala*. New York: Theatre Arts Books, 1970.

Lambeth, Cheralyn. *Creating the Character Costume: Tools, Tips, and Talks with the Top Costumers and Cosplayers*. New York: Routledge, 2017.

Lecoq, Jacques, Jean-Gabriel Carasso and Jean-Claude Lallais. *The Moving Body: Teaching Creative Theatre*. Translated by David Bradby. New York: Routledge, 2001.

Lévi-Strauss, Claude. *The Way of the Masks: Swaihwe Mask Traditions of American Northwest Coast*. Translated by Sylvia Modelski. Seattle, Washington: University of Washington Press, 1982.

Lindahl, Carl and Carolyn Ware. *Cajun Mardi Gras Masks*. Jackson, Mississippi: University Press of Mississippi, 1997.

Lu, Steve. *Face Painting in Chinese Opera*. Singapore: MPH Publications, 1968.

MacGowan, Kenneth and Herman Ross. *Masks and Demons*. New York: Harcourt, Brace, and Co., 1923. Reprint: Kraus Reprint Co., 1972.

Mack, John, ed. *Masks and the Art of Expression*. New York: Abrams, 1994.

Mackerras, Colin. *Peking Opera: Images of Asia Series*. Hong Kong: Oxford University Press, 1997.

Marceau, Marcel. *The Art of Silence: Pantomimes with Marcel Marceau*. Chicago, Illinois: Encyclopedia Britannica Educational Corp.

———. "Moved to Silence. Interview with Marcel Marceau." *American Theatre*. By Randy Gener. New York: Theatre Communications Group, January 2011. https://www.americantheatre.org/2011/01/01/moved-to-silence/.

———. "The Poetic Halo." [lecture presented in 1956]; Transcription presented in *The Mime* by Jean Dorcy. New York: Robert Speller, 1961.

Masks from Many Cultures, DVD Glenview, IL: Crystal Productions, 1993.

Marcel Marceau: Life and Work. YouTube. Horizons, June 14, 2016. https://www.youtube.com/watch?v=uAZLDn8or3M.

Marcia, Alberto and Centro Maschere e Strutture Gestuali. *The Commedia dell'Arte and the Masks of Amleto and Donato Sartori: Centro Maschere E Strutture Gestuali*. Florence, Italy: Casa Usher, 1980.

Marvin, Stephen E. *Heaven Has a Face, So Does Hell*. Warren, Connecticut: Floating World Editions, 2010.

Mauldin, Barbara. *Masks of Mexico: Tigers, Devils, and the Dance of Life*. Santa Fe, New Mexico: Museum of New Mexico Press, 1999.

McCleman, Candy and Rachel E. Pollock. "No Hiding Results: Evaluating Mask-Making Methods to Find the Optimal Build." *Stage Directions*. Vol. 29 (March 2016): 14–17.

McClung, Mary. *Foam Patterning and Construction Techniques: Turning 2D Designs into 3D Shapes*. New York: Focal Press, 2016.

McClung, Mary. Interview with the author. Virtual. February 11, 2019.

McDonald, Marianne and J. Michael Walton. *The Cambridge Companion to Greek and Roman Theatre*. Cambridge: Cambridge University Press, 2007.

McPharlin, Paul. *Masks, Occult and Utilitarian*. Bloomfield Hills, Michigan: Cranbrook Institute of Science, 1940.

Meaden, Wendy. "An Introduction to Kathakali Costume." *Theatre Design & Technology*. Vol. 49, No. 1 (Winter 2013), 58–69.

Menglin, Zhao and Yan Jiqing. *Peking Opera Painted Faces*. Beijing, China: Morning Glory Pubs, 1996.

Miettinen, Jukka O. "Kolam, Masked Folk Theatre" Asian Traditional Theatre and Dance. Theatre Academy, University of the Arts, Helsinki, 2018. Accessed April 1, 2021, https://disco.teak.fi/asia/kolam-masked-folk-theatre/.

Morawetz, Thomas. *Making Faces, Playing God: Identity and the Art of Transformational Makeup*. Austin, Texas: University of Texas Press, 2001.

Morelli, Laura. *Venice: A Travel Guide to Murano Glass, Carnival Masks, Gondolas, Lace, Paper & More*. Sea Island, Georgia: Authentic Arts Publishing, 2015.

Morita Toshirō. *Kumadori*. Tokyo, Japan: JICC, 1985.

Naversen, Ronald. "The Benda Mask." *Theatre Design & Technology*. Vol. 46, No. 4 (Fall 2010), 34–45.

———. "Learning to Carve Masks in Bali." *Theatre Design & Technology*. Vol. 40, No. 1 (Winter 2004), 38–43.

Nicoll, Allardyce. *Masks, Mimes and Miracles: Studies in the Popular Theatre*. New York: Cooper Square, 1963a.

Nicoll, Allardyce. *The World of Harlequin*. Cambridge, Massachusetts: Cambridge University Press and Company, 1963.

Nunley, John and Cara McCarty. *Masks: Faces of Culture*. New York: Harry Abrams, 1999.

O'Neill, Eugene. Preface to *The Great God Brown*. Cited in Valgemae, Mardi, "Eugene O'Neill's Preface to the Great God Brown." *The Yale University Gazette*. Vol. 43, No. 1 (July 1968), 24–29. New Haven, Connecticut: Yale University. https://www.jstor.org/stable/40859471.

Pallardy, Richard. "Makeup: Performing Arts." Britannica. Encyclopaedia Britannica Online. Accessed March 19, 2019. https://www.britannica.com/art/makeup-performing-arts.

Pandeya, Avinash C. *The Art of Kathakali*. New Delhi, India: Munshiram Manoharlal, 1999.

Pennick, Nigel. *Crossing the Borderlines: Guising, Masking, and Ritual Animal Disguises in the European Tradition*. Berks: Capall Bann Publishing, 1998.

Perez, Carlos Rodriguez. "Transformation in Drama Therapy." *Behind the Masks*. Carbondale, Illinois: Southern Illinois University Museum, 2005.

Perzynski, Friedrich. *Japanese No Masks*. Translated by Stanley Appelbaum. New York: Dover, 2005.

Pichlikova, Lenka. "Performing in Mask: Michael Chekhov's Pedagogy, Commedia and Mime." *Critical Stages*. April 19, 2017. http://www.critical-stages.org/15/performing-in-mask-michael-chekhovs-pedagogy-commedia-and-mime/.

Pieper, Jim. *Guatemala's Masks and Drama*. Torrance, California: Pieper and Associates, 2006.

Porras, Omar, Villegas Jiménez Benjamín, García Urrego Luz María, Stella de Feferbaum and López Villagómez Ernesto. *Teatro Malandro*. Bogotá, Colombia: Villegas Editores, 2007.

Price, Vincent and V.B. Price. *Monsters*. New York: Grosset and Dunlap, 1981.

Raymond, Dave. *The Power of Fun*. West Grove, Pennsylvania: SDR Consulting, 2019.

Reato, Danilo. *Le Maschere Veneziane*. Verona, Italy: Arsenale Editrice, 1988.

Rickenbach, Judith. *Alte Masken aus der Innerschweiz; Fastnachtsmasken aus der Sammlung des Rietbergmusuems*. Zurich, Germany: Museum Reitberg, 1996.

Robertson, Mary Lou. *Khon Masks of Thailand*. Seasitte.niu.edu, n.d. Accessed April 23, 2019, http://www.seasite.niu.edu/Thai/literature/ramakian/khonmasksofthailand/khonkhon.htm.

Rolfe, Bari. *Behind the Mask*. Berkeley, California: Persona Books, 1992.

Rubin, Leon, and I Nyoman Sedana. *Performance in Bali*. New York: Routledge, 2007.

Rudlin, John. *Commedia dell'Arte: An Actor's Handbook*. London: Routledge, 1994.

Rudlin, John and Olly Crick. *Commedia dell'Arte: A Handbook for Troupes*. London: Routledge, 2001.

Saint-Denis, Michel. *Theatre: The Rediscovery of Style and Other Writings*. London: Routledge, 2009.

Sand, Maurice. *History of the Harlequinade*. London: Martin Secker, 1915.

Sartor, David and John Pivovarnick. *Theatrical FX Makeup*. Portsmouth, New Hampshire: Heinemann, 2001.

Savarese, Nicola. *In Scaena: il Teatro di Roma Antica*. Rome, Italy: Electa, 2007.

Schüler, Hajo. Interview with the author. Berlin, Germany. June 2019.

Shank, Theodore. *Beyond the Boundaries: American Alternative Theatre*. Ann Arbor, Michigan: University of Michigan Press, 2002.

Shaver, Ruth M. *Kabuki Costume*. Illustrations by Soma Akira and Ota Gako. Rutland, Vermont: Charles E. Tuttle, 1966 and 1990.

Sheppard, W. Anthony. *Revealing Masks: Exotic Influences and Ritualized Performance in Modernist Music Theater*. Berkeley, California: University of California Press, 2001.

Shevtsova, Maria. "Robert Wilson." *Designers' Shakespeare*. John Russell Brown and Stephen Di Benedetto, eds. New York: Routledge, 2016, 118–136.

Shozo Sato. "Kabuki Makeup | Japanese Culture." PBS Learning Media, 2011. https://www.pbslearningmedia.org/resource/jacult.arts.drama.makeup/japanese-culture-kabuki-makeup/#.XHW7uJNKiAw.

Simon, Eli. *Masking Unmasked: Four Approaches to Basic Acting*. New York: Palgrave Macmillan, 2004.

Sivin, Carol. *Maskmaking*. Worcester, Massachusetts: Davis Publications, 1986.

Slattum, Judy and Paul Schraub. *Balinese Masks: Spirits of an Ancient Drama*. Hong Kong: Periplus Editions, 2003.

———. *Masks of Bali: Spirits of an Ancient Drama*. San Francisco, California: Chronicle Books, 1997.

Slivka, Martin. *L'udove' masky*. Bratislave: Tatran, 1990.

Smith, Susan Harris. *Masks in Modern Drama*. Berkeley, California: University of California Press, 1984.

"So you want to be a clown?" YouTube. Ringling Brothers Circus Clown College: International Video Entertainment, 1987. https://www.youtube.com/watch?v=KbSn5mKFWps.

Smith, Corey. Interview with the author. Chicago, Illinois. September 2019.

Stepan, Peter and Iris Hahner-Herzog. *Spirits Speak: A Celebration of African Masks*. Munich, Germany: Prestel, 2005.

Stephens, Michael, Moya Rubio and Victor José. *Mexican Festival and Ceremonial Masks: An Exhibition Catalogue*. Berkeley, California: Lowie Museum of Anthropology UCLA, 1976.

Steward, James Christen, George Knox and Berkeley Art Museum and Pacific Film Archive. *The Mask of Venice: Masking, Theater & Identity in the Art of Tiepolo & His Time*. Berkeley, California: University of California, Berkeley Art Museum and the University of Washington Press, 1996.

Taplin, Oliver. *Greek Tragedy in Action*. London: Routledge, 2003.

Taymor, Julie. *The Lion King: Pride Rock on Broadway*. New York: Disney Editions, 1997.

Terry, Ellen and Lynne Anderson. *The Theatre Student: Makeup and Masks*. New York: Richards Rosen Press, Inc., 1971.

Tokyo SFX Makeup Workshop. *A Complete Guide to Special Effects Makeup*. London: Titan Books, 2012.

Toshiro Morita. *Kumadori*. Tokyo, Japan: JICC Co, Ltd., 1985.

"Tovil and Sanni, Powerful Exorcism Rituals." Asian Traditional Theater & Dance. Theatre Academy, University of the Arts Helsinki. #71, 2018. Accessed April 1, 2021. https://disco.teak.fi/asia/tovil-and-sanni-powerful-exorcism-rituals/.

Trendall, A.D. and T.B.L. Webster. *Illustrations of Greek Drama*. London: Phaidon, 1971.

Twycross, Meg and Sarah Carpenter. "Mask and Masking in Medieval and Early Tudor England." *Studies in Performance and Early Modern Drama*. Burlington, Vermont: Ashgate Publishing Co., 2002.

Udaka, Michishige. *The Secrets of Noh Masks*. Tokyo, Japan: Kodansha, 2010.

Vaught, Louis Allen. *Vaught's Practical Character Reader*. Chicago, Illinois: L.A. Vaught, 1902.

Vidal, Teodoro. *Las Caretas de Carton del Carnaval de Ponce*. Puerto Rico: Ediciones Alba, 1983.

Wallace, Denise. "Mask Collaborations." Interview with the author. Boston, Massachusetts. July 2018.

Westlake, E.J. *World Theatre: The Basics*. New York: Routledge, 2017.

Wilsher, Toby. *The Mask Handbook*. New York: Routledge, 2007.

Wright, John. *Why Is That So Funny? A Practical Exploration of Physical Comedy*. New York: Limelight Editions, 2007.

———. *Playing the Mask: Acting Without Bullshit*. London: Nick Hern Books, 2017.

Wright, Vicky. Interview with author. London, United Kingdom. April 25, 2019.

———. Making Faces Theatre website. 2019. https://making-facestheatre.co.uk/2019/04/05/the-journey-so-far/.

Wyles, Rosie. *Costume in Greek Tragedy*. London: Bloomsbury, 2011.

Yamaguchi, Bidou. Interview by Dr. John Teramoto. "Making Faces: The Remarkable Masks of Master Bidou Yamaguchi." Indianapolis Museum of Art at Newfields, September 7, 2019.

Yamaguchi, Bidou. "Masks." Personal website. 2022. http://bidou-yamaguchi.com/index2.html.

Zarrilli, Phillip B. *Kathakali Dance-Drama: Where Gods and Demons Come to Play*. London: Routledge, 2000.

FIGURE CREDITS

COVER AND FRONT MATTER

Figure	Description	Credit
Center Cover	Mask by Mike Oleon for Rough House Theatre's *Invitation to a Beheading*	Author
Left Cover	The Fool by Bernardo Rey Rengifo for *Woyzeck* at Butler University	Steve Nyktas
Right Cover	Interior of Balinese Sidakarya Mask	Steve Nyktas
Back Cover	Neutral Mask by Alfredo Iriarte	Author
Contents	Paper Masks by WJ Meaden	Author
Acknowledgments	Roman Tragic Female Mask	Metropolitan Museum of Art, NY
Introduction	Larval Mask by Jonathan Becker	Author

CHAPTER 1

FIRST ENCOUNTERS WITH MASKS

Figure	Description	Credit
1.1	Neolithic stone mask, Musée Bible et Terre Sainte	Photo by Gryffindor
1.2 A	Expressive faces	Author
1.2 B	Daumier, *Masks of 1831, plate 143, La Caricature*	The Art Institute of Chicago
1.3 A	Pareidolia allows us to see faces in non-human objects	Author
1.3 B	Larval mask by Jonathan Becker	Jonathan Becker
1.4	Sketch of Archimboldo's *The Vegetable Gardener*	Author
1.4 A	*Sole Brother Number One* by Willie Cole (2007)	Photo by Jason Mandella, courtesy of the artist and Alexander and Bonin, New York
1.4 B	*Sole Brother Number Two* by Willie Cole (2007)	Photo by Jason Mandella, courtesy of the artist and Alexander and Bonin, New York
1.5 A	"The Sorcerer" sketch, Trois Frères, France	Author
1.5 B	"Bull Sorcerer" sketch, Trois Frères, France	Author
1.5 C	Aztec people, Ritual Impersonator of the deity Xipe Totec	The Art Institute of Chicago
1.5 D	Shell Mosaic Ritual Mask, Teotihuacan Culture, Mexico	The Art Institute of Chicago
1.5 E	"Mask of Agamemnon," gold, Mycenae	Xuan Che, CC 2.0, https://commons.wikimedia.org/w/index.php?curid=15165017
1.6	Russell Dean and Mike at the office	Author
1.7	Vamos Theatre Company walkabout	Graeme Braidwood Photography
1.8	EMPATIA Stocking mask created for a protest in Brazil	Arianne Vitale Cardoso
1.9	Hockey Mask for Boston Bruin goaltender Tuukka Rask	Jai Agnish for Shutterstock
1.10	Sande Society Mask, Gola People, 20th C.	Indianapolis Museum of Art
1.11 A	Wax Death mask of Benjamin Disraeli	Wellcome Museum, London
1.11 B	Egyptian Mummy mask: 332–30 BCE	Indianapolis Museum of Art
1.11 C	Funeral mask for a Peruvian Ruler, Lambayeque (Sicán) culture	Metropolitan Museum of Art, NY
1.12 A1	An elaborate beaded Kuker mask	Belish for Shutterstock
1.12 A2	Kukeri in procession to drive out evil spirits	GEORGID for Shutterstock

Figure Credits

1.12 A3	Kuker masks. XIX International Festival of Masquerade Games Pernik, 2010	aladjov. CC 3.0 https://commons.wikimedia.org/wiki/File:Kukeri-Surva-festival-Pernik-2010--06.jpg
1.12 B	A Halloween mask	Author
1.13 A	Executioner's mask made of steel	Wellcome Museum, London
1.13 B	Scold's Bridle, Europe	Wellcome Museum, London
1.14	Balinese Mask of Rangda	The Children's Museum of Indianapolis
1.15 A	Practical splatter mask for a soldier, Britain, WWI	Wellcome Museum, London
1.15 B	Practical mask for a beekeeper	Author
1.15 C	Practical mask for an astronaut	Vadim Sadovski for Shutterstock
1.15 D	Copy of a Plague Doctor's mask	Claudio Stocco for Shutterstock
1.16 A	Japanese mask armor intended to intimidate	Stephen Bluto for the Metropolitan Museum of Art, NY
1.16 B	Close Helmet with Mask Visor in form of a human face, attributed to Kolman Helmschmid ca. 1515, German	Metropolitan Museum of Art, NY
1.17 A	Sporting masks for Kendo, a Japanese martial art	Wellcome Museum, London
1.17 B	Wrestling mask	The Children's Museum of Indianapolis
1.17 C	A utilitarian catcher's mask	The Children's Museum of Indianapolis
1.18	*Gulma Sanniya*, demon of Parasitic worms and stomach ailments	Author
1.19 A	Zorro's black fabric mask	Author
1.19 B	Bauta masks, Pietro Longhi, *Colloquy Between Masks*	Didier Descouens
1.20	Decorative mask from the author's collection	Author
1.21	Architectural tragic mask by Carl Milles	Holger Ellgaard
1.22 A	Duckbilled domino party mask by Newman	Author
1.22 B	A Helmet mask, worn for the fun of it	Author
1.23	A collection of theater masks	Author
1.24	Dance masks for *The Firebird* adapted by Elizabeth Snider	A J Mast courtesy of Butler Ballet
1.25 A and B	Latex Fright masks for Halloween	Author
1.26	Sketch of mask forms	Author
1.27 A	W.T. Benda, lifelike mask	Public Domain
1.27 B	Idealized Masks: Igbo Maiden Spirit	Indianapolis Museum of Art
1.27 C	Idealized Masks: Apollo in black figure vase style	Author
1.27 D	Emotional Masks by Todd Espeland	Author
1.27 E	Sketch of W.T. Benda's satiric mask, *The Old Wag*	Author
1.27 F1	Grotesque mask by Werner Strub	Giorgio Skory
1.27 F2	Grotesque mask in leather with stucco by Bernardo Rey	Bernardo Rey
1.27 G	"Gasp" Abstract Mask designs by Rob Faust	Faustworks
1.27 H	Larval Masks by Craig Jacob-Brown	Author
1.27 I	A pair of neutral masks by David Knezz	Author
1.27 J	*Knowledge* allegorical mask by student Kait Lamansky	Author
1.28	Design concept cartoon	Author
1.29 A	Fiber helmet mask, Maninka people	Indianapolis Museum of Art
1.29 B	Leather mask of Hermes by Werner Strub	Giorgio Skory
1.29 C	Paper masks by the author	Author
1.29 D	Wooden masks from Zaire, from the private collection of Richard W. Judy and Jane Lommel	Author
1.29 E	Neoprene mask by Jonathan Becker	Jonathan Becker
1.29 F	A stitched fabric mask: Mayor, *Dr. Festus* by Werner Strub	Giorgio Skory

1.29 G	Found objects incorporated into a mask by the We people	Indianapolis Museum of Art
1.29 H	Terra-cotta mask, ChupÃ-Cuaro	Indianapolis Museum of Art
1.29 I	Tin mask from Mexico	The Children's Museum of Indianapolis
1.30	Leather mask by Werner Strub	Giorgio Skory
Box 1.1	Many of Our Idiomatic Expressions Relate to Faces	https://www.wordclouds.com
Box 1.2	Masks in Action	Arianne Vitale Cardoso

CHAPTER 2
FACING THE STAGE

Figure	Description	Credit
2.1	The ancient Greek theater at Taormina, Italy	Photo by CH Munro
2.2	Folk theater celebration of Jonkonnu in Jamaica	WikiPedant/wikimedia commons
2.3 A	Plain masks in *The Curious Incident of the Dog in the Night-Time*	Zach Rosing, courtesy of Indiana Repertory Theatre
2.3 B	Moon mask by Kaleb Loosbrock for Lorca's *Blood Wedding*	Glen Thoreson for Butler University Theatre
2.4	Mudras indicate words and ideas	Author
2.5	Navarasas show nine basic human emotions	Jean-Pierre Dalbéra
2.6	Japanese patterns of footsteps for warrior, gentleman, and maiden	Author
2.7	*The Two Pantaloons, Etching on paper (1616),* Jacques Callot	The Art Institute of Chicago
2.8	Greek masks: Relief of Menander	By Dave & Margie Hill / Kleerup - Princeton University Art Museum, Public Domain
2.9 A	Balinese Alus (high status) characters	Author
2.9 B	Conquistador mask showing European features	The Children's Museum of Indianapolis
2.10	Balinese bondres mask	Author
2.11	American Hillbilly Halloween mask	The Children's Museum of Indianapolis
2.12	Mike Chase's Commedia mask of Flautino	Mike Chase
2.13	Bian Lian performer	Paisan Pangjunan for Shutterstock #1319795399
2.14	Japanese woodblock print of a mask carver	The Art Institute of Chicago
2.15	Japanese Bugaku mask	Metropolitan Museum of Art, NY
2.16 A	Japanese Noh mask: Asakurajo	The Art Institute of Chicago
2.16 B	Hakushiji-jo (Okina), mask by Hideta Kitazawa	Courtesy of the artist and Sohta Kitazawa, photographer
2.17	Japanese Noh mask: Kojo	Metropolitan Museum of Art, NY
2.18 A and B	Japanese Noh mask: two views of a Ko-Omote	Metropolitan Museum of Art, NY
2.19	Japanese Noh mask: Chūjō i- young male aristocrat	Metropolitan Museum of Art, NY
2.20	Hannya, mask by Hideta Kitazawa, private collection, 2013	Courtesy of the artist and Sohta Kitazawa, photographer
2.21	Japanese Noh mask: Mikazuki	The Art Institute of Chicago
2.22	Usofuki mask by Hideta Kitazawa, photo by Sohta Kitazawa, Department of Theatre and Dance, University of Hawai'i at Mānoa	Courtesy of the artist and Sohta Kitazawa, photographer
2.23	Balinese Topeng mask of Sidha Karya	Author
2.24	Balinese Topeng masks	Author
2.25	Balinese Topeng bondres mask	Author
2.26 A–D	Korean painted masks	The Children's Museum of Indianapolis
2.27	Korean Hahoe masks of Kaksi, Yangban, and Sonpi	©¯mers
2.28 and 2.29	Thai Khon masks	The Children's Museum of Indianapolis

Figure	Description	Credit
2.30 A	Sri Lankan Maha Kola mask, encompassing the 18 sanni demons	Wellcome Museum, London
2.30 B	Naga Raksha Demon mask from Sri Lanka	The Children's Museum of Indianapolis
2.30 C	Demon mask from Sri Lanka	Wellcome Museum, London
2.31 A	Sri Lankan theatre mask	Wellcome Museum, London
2.31 B	Sri Lankan Kolam mask of a soldier	Wellcome Museum, London
2.31 C	Sri Lankan theatre mask	Wellcome Museum, London
2.32	A mosaic depicting Ancient Greek masks	© Ad Meskens / Wikimedia Commons
2.33 A and B	Ancient Greek actor statuettes in comic mask	Metropolitan Museum of Art
2.33 C	Satyr with mask of Silenos	The Art Institute of Chicago
2.34 A	Ancient Greek vase depicting actor with mask	Metropolitan Museum of Art, NY
2.34 B	Silver Denarius (coin) depicting a mask of Pan, Roman, 48 BCE	The Art Institute of Chicago
2.35 A	A female Roman tragic mask	Metropolitan Museum of Art, NY
2.35 B	Masks from the Paris Opera collection	The Art Institute of Chicago
2.36	Masked mummers by Robert Seymour	Robert Seymour (1798–1836), Public Domain, via Wikimedia Commons
2.37 A	A medieval farce	Public Domain, via Wikimedia Commons
2.37 B	Devil mask made for a Carnivale celebration	Alejandro Linares Garcia
2.38	Commedia dell'Arte performance	Unknown, French School, Public Domain, via Wikimedia Commons
2.39	Pulcinella and a musician	Cooper Hewitt, Smithsonian Design Museum, Public Domain, via Wikimedia Commons
2.40	Commedia player sketch by Jacque Callot	The Art Institute of Chicago
2.41	Masks made for Four Plays for Dancers by W. B. Yeats	Photo by Davy Ellis, reprinted with permission, all rights reserved
2.42	Bread and Puppet Theatre, photographed by Walter S. Wantman	Pilar Aymerich i Puig, via Wikimedia Commons
2.43	El Teatro Campesino's production of Bernabe	Courtesy of El Teatro Campesino
Box 2.3 A	Mask artist Hideta Kitazawa	Courtesy of the artist and Sohta Kitazawa, photographer
Box 2.3 B	Refining the carving of a mask in progress	Courtesy of the artist and Sohta Kitazawa, photographer
Box 2.3 C	Crazy Jane. Mask by Hideta Kitazawa. Photo by Sohta Kitazawa. Property of David Crandall. Created for Theatre Nohgaku's 2010 production of Crazy Jane	Courtesy of the artist and Sohta Kitazawa, photographer
Box 2.3 D	Cordelia. Mask by Hideta Kitazawa. Photo by Sohta Kitazawa. Property of Jubilith Moore. Created for Theatre of Yugen's 2011 production of Erik Ehn's Cordelia	Courtesy of the artist and Sohta Kitazawa, photographer
Box 2.3 E	Armistead. Mask by Hideta Kitazawa. Photo by Sohta Kitazawa. Property of Elizabeth Dowd. Created for Theatre Nohgaku's 2017 production of Gettysburg	Courtesy of the artist and Sohta Kitazawa, photographer
Box 2.5 A–H	Commedia character sketches from Masques et Bouffons by Maurice Sand	British Library, Public Domain

CHAPTER 3
THE DIRECTOR'S PERSPECTIVE

Figure	Description	Credit
3.1	Theatre Temoin's production of The Marked	Courtesy of Theatre Temoin, photography by Idil Sukan
3.2	El Teatro Campesino's 2018 production of La Carpa de los Rasquachis	Courtesy of El Teatro Campesino, photography by Robert Eliason

3.3	*Dead Good* by Vamos Theatre	Courtesy of Vamos Theatre and Graeme Braidwood Photography
3.4	Goddess Hera in *Jason and the Argonauts*	Courtesy of The Absolutely Fabulous Theatre Connection, Hong Kong, China
3.5	A Vamos Theatre character from their Walkabout experience	Courtesy of Vamos Theatre and Graeme Braidwood Photography
3.6	"Gasp" by Rob Faust	Courtesy of Rob Faust/Faustworks
3.7	*Finding Joy* by Vamos Theatre	Courtesy of Vamos Theatre and Graeme Braidwood Photography
3.8	Grafted Cede and Theatre Temoin's *Nobody's Home*	Courtesy of Grafted Cede/Theatre Temoin, masks by Will Pinchin and Dorie Pinchin, photo by Jet Sun
3.9	Two characters in *Invitation to a Beheading*	Courtesy of Rough House Theatre, photo by Evan Barr Photography
3.10	*Infinita* by Familie Flöz	Courtesy of Familie Flöz
3.11 A and B	A character mask by Jonathan Becker	Courtesy of Jonathan Becker
3.12	A production of *Woyzeck* at Butler University	Author
3.13	*Dr. Nest* by Familie Flöz	Courtesy of Familie Flöz
3.14	*Soldier's Song* by Strangeface Theatre	Courtesy of Strangeface Theatre, photography by Mark Dean
3.15	*Nursing Lives* by Vamos Theatre	Courtesy of Vamos Theatre and Graeme Braidwood Photography
Box 3.2 A–C	Mask concept drawings by Mike Oleon	Courtesy of Mike Oleon and Rough House Theatre

CHAPTER 4

THE ACTOR'S PERSPECTIVE

Figure	Description	Credit
4.1	Rough House Theatre's *Invitation to a Beheading*	Mask created by Mike Oleon, photo by Evan Barr Photography
4.2	*Dr. Nest* by Familie Flöz	Courtesy of Familie Flöz
4.3	*Teatro Delusio* by Familie Flöz	Courtesy of Familie Flöz and Simona Boccedi, photographer
4.4	*Tonight We Fly* by Trestle Theatre Company	Courtesy of Trestle Theatre Company and Keith Pattison, photographer
4.5	Larval mask by Jonathan Becker	Courtesy of Jonathan Becker
4.6	Vamos Theatre's *A Brave Face*	Courtesy of Vamos Theatre and Graeme Braidwood Photography
4.7	Larval mask by Jonathan Becker	Courtesy of Jonathan Becker
4.8	A creature mask by Rob Faust/Faustworks	Courtesy of Rob Faust/Faustworks
4.9	*A Rake's Progress* by Strangeface Theatre	Courtesy of Strangeface Theatre, photography by Mark Dean, masks by Strangeface Masks
4.10	Rough House Theatre's *Invitation to a Beheading*	Mask created by Mike Oleon, photo by Evan Barr Photography
4.11	*A Rake's Progress* by Strangeface Theatre	Courtesy of Strangeface Theatre, photography by Mark Dean, masks by Strangeface Masks
Box 4.1 A	Neutral mask by Alfredo Iriarte	Author
Box 4.1 B	Neutral masks by Donato Sartori	Author
Box 4.1 C	Neutral mask by Russell Dean	Author

Box 4.2 A and B	Masks by Russell Dean and Strangeface	Courtesy of Russell Dean and Strangeface
Box 4.3 A–E	Character mask by Russell Dean and Strangeface	Photography by Jenni Carroll
Box 4.4 A–I	Character mask by Russell Dean and Strangeface	Photography by Jenni Carroll
Box 4.5 A–C	Arlecchino mask by Antonio Fava	Photography by Jenni Carroll

CHAPTER 5
MASKS BY DESIGN

Figure	Description	Credit
5.1 A	Giancarlo Santelli in studio	Estate of Giancarlo Santelli
5.1 B	Jonathan Becker	Courtesy of Jonathan Becker
5.1 C	Bernardo Rey	Bernardo Rey
5.2 A	Arlecchino Mask by Bernardo Rey	Bernardo Rey
5.2 B	Arlecchino Mask by Giancarlo Santelli	Author
5.2 C	Arlecchino Mask by Antonio Fava	Author
5.2 D	Arlecchino Mask by Benjamin Gould	Photo by Ben Craig, courtesy of Commedia of Errors
5.2 E	Arlecchino Mask by Jonathan Becker	Author
5.3 A	Mascot Statues outside the Mascot Hall of Fame	Author
5.3 B	Elvis, *Blue Moon over Memphis* by Hideta Kitazawa	Courtesy of Hideta Kitazawa, Theatre Nohgaku, and Sohta Kitazawa
5.4	Dionysus by Georgio de Marchi	Author
5.5 A	Animal-inspired mask by Werner Strub	Giorgio Skory
5.5 B	Indonesian Frog Mask	The Children's Museum of Indianapolis
5.5 C	Bird masks for Yeats' *Dreaming of the Bones*	Author
5.5 D	Ancestor Mask by Bernardo Rey	Bernardo Rey
5.6 A–C	Zoomorphic faces by LeBrun	Wellcome Museum, London
5.7	Drawing of mask forms	Author
5.8	Larval masks by Strangeface Masks	Russell Dean
5.9 A and B	Color comparison of neutral masks	Author
5.10	Benda's rhythmic coordination	Public Domain
5.11 A–D	Four Temperaments	Mike Chase
5.12 A	Rosie, who cheerfully leads with her nose	Author
5.12 B	Energetic yellow mask	Author
5.12 C	The mouth breather	Author
5.13 A	Mask sketch by Bernardo Rey for *Puntilla* (Brecht)	Bernardo Rey
5.13 B	Group study by Bernardo Rey for *Puntilla* (Brecht)	Bernardo Rey
5.13 C	Clay sculpt for *Puntilla* (Brecht) by Bernardo Rey	Bernardo Rey
5.14	Maquettes by Russell Dean	Author
5.15	Rough sculpt in clay by Bernardo Rey	Bernardo Rey
5.16	Mask sculpt prepared for casting	Author
5.17	Rob Faust performs with an alternate mask placement	Gary Gunderson, courtesy of Faustworks
5.18	Strong profiles: *Pipifaxen* by Mike Aufenfehld	Courtesy of Mike Aufenfehld
5.19	Character masks from *Hotel Paradiso* by Familie Flöz	Michaell Vogel for Familie Flöz
5.20 A	Blind "Tiresius aux antennae" by Werner Strub	Photo by Giorgio Skory
5.20 B	Apollo masks with screened eyes	Author
5.21	Mask set by Strangeface Masks for Vamos Theatre	Russell Dean
5.22 A	Round-cheeked Columbina mask by Russell Dean	Author

5.22 B	A hollow-cheeked Streha by Russell Dean	Author
5.23 A	Half smirk by Rob Faust	Photo courtesy of Rob Faust
5.23 B	Commedia dell'Arte half mask by Giancarlo Santelli	Author
5.23 C	Greek Comic Slave by David Knezz	Author
5.24 A	Prominent nosed mask by Rey	Author
5.24 B	Prominent nosed mask by Becker	Author
5.24 C	Prominent nosed mask by DeMarchi	Caterina Zanardo
5.25	Profile of a mask by Russell Dean	Author
5.26 A	Eared helmet mask	Author
5.26 B	Phra Ram mask from Khon drama of Thailand	Shutterstock
5.27 A	A receding chin on "Charles" by Craig Jacob-Brown	Author
5.27 B	Hahoe mask of Yangban with hinged jaw	Author
5.27 C	Mexican Day of the Dead Mask; carved and painted wood	The Children's Museum of Indianapolis
5.28 A	Dimensional texture carved into the sculpt	Jonathan Becker
5.28 B	Painted texture on a clown mask	Author
5.28 C	*Breath,* textile object, 2020, video still	threadstories
5.28 D	*Persona 1*, threadstories, 2021	threadstories
5.28 E	*The Watchers and the Watched,* textile object, 2020	threadstories
5.28 F	*Persona 9*, threadstories, 2021	threadstories
5.28 G	A stitched fabric mask for Faustus by Werner Strub	Giorgio Skory
5.29	Toby Wilsher's starter set	Trestle Theatre Company
5.30	*Habbe und Meik*	Michael Aufenfehld
5.31 A–D	Mask/countermask by David Knezz	Author
5.32	Strong curves create undercuts	Author
5.33	Neutral masks by Donato Sartori (leather)	Thomas Prattki
5.34	Neutral mask by Alfredo Iriarte (leather)	Author
5.35	Universal masks by David Knezz (Neoprene)	Author
5.36	Larval masks by Craig Jacob Brown	Author
5.37	Emotional masks in the Libby Appel style	Author
5.38 A	Character masks by Jonathan Becker	Author
5.38 B	Character masks by Russell Dean for Vamos Theatre	Graeme Braidwood Photography
5.38 C	Character mask old man falling by Rob Faust	Courtesy of Faustworks
5.39	Marco Luly in half mask of Arlecchino by Santelli	Photo by kalyedoscope, courtesy of Marco Luly
5.40	Grotesque Mask of Leather with a stucco texture	Bernardo Rey
5.41	Mask character supported by wig, hat, and costume	Jonathan Becker
Box 5.1 A	Bondres Masks for Villagers	Glen Thoreson for Butler Theatre
Box 5.1 B	Rendering of Barong style mask for Bottom as an Ass	Author
Box 5.1 C	The Court watches the "death" of Pyramus and Thisbe	Glen Thoreson for Butler Theatre
Box 5.1 D	Oberon and Puck in Sida Karya masks	Glen Thoreson for Butler Theatre
Box 5.1 E	Theseus and Hippolyta in Alus masks	Glen Thoreson for Butler Theatre
Box 5.2	Donato Sartori at work in his studio	Bernardo Rey
Box 5.3 A	Physiognomy in *Vaught's Practical Character Reader*	Author
Box 5.3 B	Prototype of Old Man	Metropolitan Museum of Art, NY
Box 5.3 C	Archetype: Pantalone by Santelli	Author
Box 5.3 D	Stereotype: Nurses by Russell Dean	Courtesy of Vamos Theatre and Graeme Braidwood Photography
Box 5.3 E	Caricature: The Old Wag	Author

Box 5.3 F	Parody: Elvis by Rob Faust	Photo by Timothy Latta, courtesy of Faustworks
Box 5.3 G	Allegory: Knowledge by Kait Lamansky	Author
Box 5.3 H	Countermasks: Habbe und Meik	Michael Aufenfehn
Box 5.3 I	Grotesque: The Captain, *Woyzek*	Author
Box 5.3 J	Ideal: Beauty by WT Benda	Public Domain
Box 5.4	Elements and Principles Vocabulary	Author
Box 5.5 A	Benda's lifelike renditions of beautiful women	Public Domain
Box 5.5 B	Book cover featuring sketches of several of Benda's masks	Public Domain
Box 5.5 C	Rhythmic coordination	Public Domain
Box 5.5 D	A complex pattern for a mask to be cut and assembled	Public Domain
Box 5.5 E	Image from a *Life* magazine cover	Public Domain
Box 5.7	Rob Faust	Photo courtesy of Rob Faust
Box 5.8 A–D	Vicky Wright	Photos courtesy of Vicky Wright

CHAPTER 6

MASK MAKING

Figure	Description	Credit
6.1	Big head sculpts Rob	Timothy Latta, courtesy of Rob Faust
6.2 A	Commedia masks in leather (Santelli)	Author
6.2 B	Commedia masks in neoprene (Becker)	Author
6.2 C	Commedia masks in leather and paper mache	Author
6.3 A	Oedipus, Werner Strub	Giorgio Skory
6.3 B	Amy Cohen's Linen masks	Dr. Amy Cohen
6.3 C	Leather masks by Giancarlo Santelli	Author
6.3 D	Neoprene mask, *Hecuba*	Jonathan Becker
6.4 A	Clay character sculpted on a cast of the performer's face	Author
6.4 B	Mouse Queen by Elizabeth Flauto for Butler Ballet's production of *The Nutcracker* (2020)	Author
6.4 C1 and C2	A purchased mask base for a Greek inspired class project	Author
6.4 D	Masks with adjustable straps and interior padding	Author
6.5	Skull mask with a moveable jaw	Jonathan Becker
6.6	Mask with undercuts	Author
6.7	Sequential drawing: casting and molding	Author
6.8 A	Students beginning to create direct paper masks	Author
6.8 B	Model Magic being formed over a purchased base	Author
6.8 C	Casting the face using a direct plaster method	Author
6.8 D	Leather mask over a wooden matrix by Giorgio Santelli	Author
6.8 E	Oversized masks for *The Water Carriers* first people	R. Brent Smith for Butler University
6.9 A	Basel mask with very small eyeholes	Jonathan Becker
6.9 B	Fitted masks by Bernardo Rey for *Woyzeck*	Bernardo Rey
6.9 C	A Barong-inspired Ass	Glen Thoreson for Butler Theatre
6.10	Marie (*Woyzeck*) sculpted to match the performer's eyes and lip line	Glen Thoreson for Butler Theatre
6.11	Pigskin lining	Denise Wallace-Spriggs
6.12	Commedia masks leave the mouth free to vocalize (Santelli)	Author
6.13	Jonathan Becker's Minotaur	Jonathan Becker
6.14	Pinocchio masks with multiple noses	Candy McClernan

6.15 A1	Model prepared for life cast	Denise Wallace-Spriggs
6.15 A2–5	Life cast process images	Author
6.15 B–G	Life cast process images	Denise Wallace-Spriggs
6.16	Dental alginate	Author
6.17	Multi-material mask for *Oedipus el Rey*	Denise Wallace-Spriggs
6.18–6.20	Adapted masks	Author
6.21	Commercial masks for sale at a craft store	Author
6.22	Jonathan Becker's studio: masks for sale	Author
6.23	Decorative masks for sale to tourists in Venice	Author
6.24	Students creating direct paper masks in studio class	Author
6.25	A student's completed direct paper mask	Author
6.26	Chinese terracotta warrior mask of paper mache	The Children's Museum of Indianapolis
6.27	Release agents	Author
6.28	Papers	Author
6.29	Binders	Author
6.30–6.38	Image sequence: paper mache strip process	Author
6.39	Masks ready for highlight and shadow (Jonathan Becker's studio)	Author
6.40	An assistant adds highlight and shadow (Jonathan Becker's studio)	Author
6.41	Masks showing painting completed (Jonathan Becker's studio)	Author
6.42	Modeling materials	Author
6.43	Paper pulp	Author
6.44 A	Venetian tourist mask made of paper with an acrylic coating	Author
6.44 B	Chinese opera tourist mask made of paper pulp	Author
6.45	Emotional masks of Model Magic and paper mache	Author
6.46	Model Magic over a paper base bound with paper mache	Author
6.47 A–K	Forming a mask with Thermoplastic	Author
6.48	Thermoplastic mask-making materials	Author
6.49	Fosshape Pinocchio masks with interchangeable noses	Candace McClernan
6.50 A	Two black ravens by Candy McClernan	Candace McClernan
6.50 B	Bluebird masks for Ballet West in Utah by Candy McClernan	Candace McClernan
6.50 C	Skull with hinged moveable jaw made of Wonderflex	Candace McClernan and Rachel Pollock for No Hiding Results: Evaluating mask-making methods to find the optimal build (Stage Directions, March 2016: 14–17)
6.51	Tailors: Worbla noses, fake fur and purchased glasses	Author
6.52	Anubis: Varaform base, paper mache ears, fabric	Candace McClernan
6.53	Completed Anubis mask by Candy McClernan	Candace McClernan
6.54	Wooden matrix by Russell Dean	Author
6.55 A–I	Leather mask process (*Woyzeck*)	Author
6.56 A	Buckram in two weights	Author
6.56 B	Lego Batman helmet mask	Candace McClernan
6.57	Bull helmet mask	Denise Wallace-Spriggs
6.58 A	Latex Halloween mask	Author
6.58 B	Latex masks adapted for Katshei in *The Firebird*	Author
6.59 A	Plaster mold brushed with a release agent	Author
6.59 B	Jonathan Becker pours neoprene into molds at his studio	Author
6.60	Untrimmed, trimmed, and painted versions of the mask	Author
6.61	Mary McClung's book is a terrific resource for foam mask work	Author

6.62	Cardboard First People masks	R. Brent Smith for Butler University
6.63 A	Benda's plan for a wire armature	Public Domain
6.63 B	Benda's detail for joining wires	Public Domain
6.64	Mexican El Tigre helmet mask made of wood: from the collection of Richard Judy and Jane Lommel	Author
6.65	Japanese mask of Tengu	The Children's Museum of Indianapolis
6.66	Wooden mask courtesy of the London Clown Museum	Author
6.67 A–D	Vacuform process	Russell Dean
6.68 A	Celastic strips	Author
6.68 B	Akiko, Celastic mask by Rob Faust	Rob Faust
6.69 A	Metal mask	The Children's Museum of Indianapolis
6.69 B	Metal mask	The Children's Museum of Indianapolis
6.69 C	Purchased filigree sheet metal party mask	Author
6.70 A	3D printed skull mask by Candy McClernan and Rachel Pollock	Rachel Pollock
6.70 B	Maquette, model, and 3D print by Athene Wright	Rachel Pollock
6.71 A	Tokoloshi found object mask by the author for *The Water Carriers*	Author
6.71 B	Steampunk styled tourist masks	Author
6.71 C	Armadillo shell mask	Author
6.72	Laiifao by Damselfrau	Damselfrau
6.73	*Zebratown Mask 1* (2013) by Willie Cole	Photo by Joerg Lohse, courtesy of the artist and Alexander and Bonin, New York
Box 6.6 A–F	Artist Profile, Bernardo Rey	Images courtesy of Bernardo Rey
Box 6.8 A	Paper Techniques can be used for texture and structure	Author
Box 6.8 B	Paper cranes: origami mask by Hannah Martin	Author
Box 6.10 A–K	3D digital printing	Images courtesy of Dr. Amy Cohen
Box 6.11 A	Papageno and Papagena in string and pigment by Werner Strub for *The Magic Flute*	Giorgio Skory
Box 6.11 B	Othello, leather, by Werner Strub	Giorgio Skory
Box 6.11 C	Coal Miner, leather, by Werner Strub	Giorgio Skory

CHAPTER 7

MAKEUP AS MASK

Figure	Description	Credit
7.1	Mask like makeup	Matt Hahnewald for Shutterstock #1077349709
7.2	The white forms of chutti poove	R. Brent Smith for Butler University
7.3	Chinese opera, makeup and facial hair	Reprinted by permission from Beijing Opera Costumes, courtesy of Alexandra Bonds
7.4 A–C	Actor headshot and sketch for old age makeup	Author
7.5 A–C	Student makeup designs for different characters	Author
7.6	Jingju makeup	Reprinted by permission from Beijing Opera Costumes, courtesy of Alexandra Bonds
7.7	Kathakali inspired scene	R. Brent Smith for Butler University
7.8	Jingju Stage Picture	Reprinted by permission from Beijing Opera Costumes, courtesy of Alexandra Bonds
7.9	Date Kurabe Okuni Kabuki, by Toyokuni Utagawa III: three Kabuki scenes by Utagawa Kunisada	https://commons.wikimedia.org/wiki/File:Date_Kurabe_Okuni_Kabuki.jpg

7.10	Jingju character Sun Wukong, with monkey features	Reprinted by permission from Beijing Opera Costumes, courtesy of Alexandra Bonds
7.11	Mummy makeup and costume	Lynne Ann Mitchell for Shutterstock 1536720560
7.12	Kumadori styled makeup on a student	Author
7.13	Charlie Chaplin in a 1915 studio photo by P.D. Jankens	https://en.wikipedia.org/wiki/File:Charlie_Chaplin.jpg
7.14	Sketch of Doug Bradley as Pinhead	Author
7.15	A Kathakali artist adding makeup for a performance	Santhosh Varghese for Shutterstock 1062942563
7.16	Weary Willie, Clown Museum, Peru, Indiana	Author
7.17	Mattie Feint's registry egg	Author
7.18 A	Fox makeup for a production of *The Little Prince*	R. Brent Smith for Butler University
7.18 B	Student character makeup for the Cheshire cat	Author
7.19	Dimensional SFX makeup	Kiselev Andrey Valerevich for Shutterstock 1166294866
7.20	A street performer in detailed makeup and costume	Shanti Hesse for Shutterstock 292406132
Box 7.1 A	A Paccha Vesham by FACT Jayadeva Varma	Gokul Krishna Raja
Box 7.1 B	Katti vesham "cuts" the face	Pratheep P S, www.pratheep.com
Box 7.1 C	Kathakali Kattaalan vesham by FACT Jayadeva Varma	Gokul Krishna Raja
Box 7.1 D	Hanuman the Monkey King is a well-known vella tati	Gokul Krishna Raja
Box 7.1 E	Strivesham (female) minukku makeup	Shagil Kannur
Box 7.1 F	Theppu category swan	Kathakalifans
Box 7.1 G	A Kathakali interpretation of the Paṭṭābhiṣēkaṃ of Śrī Rāma	AdvaithNair
Box 7.2 A	Dan role	Reprinted by permission from Beijing Opera Costumes, courtesy of Alexandra Bonds
Box 7.2 B	Sheng role (left)	Reprinted by permission from Beijing Opera Costumes, courtesy of Alexandra Bonds
Box 7.2 C	Chou role	Reprinted by permission from Beijing Opera Costumes, courtesy of Alexandra Bonds
Box 7.2 D	Jing role	Reprinted by permission from Beijing Opera Costumes, courtesy of Alexandra Bonds
Box 7.3 A	A Japanese actress in onnagata makeup and wig	Reinhold Möller
Box 7.3 B	Illustration of Kumadori makeup designs	AC Illustrations
Box 7.3 C	Kabuki images on a souvenir board game	Metropolitan Museum of New York

END MATTER

Figure	Description	Credit
Appendix A: Glossary	Eyeglass mask for the Tailor in *Lafcadio* at Butler University	Author
Appendix C: Resources	Domino Duck mask by Newman	Author
Appendix D: Artists and Theater Companies	First People masks for *The Water Carriers*	Glen Thoreson for Butler University
Appendix E: Plays	Brighella by Antonio Fava	Author
Appendix F: Museums	Tigre mask of Mexico from the private collection of Richard Judy and Jane Lommel	Author
Appendix G: Films	Sidakarya mask	Steve Nyktas
Bibliography	Crab mask, Mexico	The Children's Museum of Indianapolis
Index	Interior of Neutral Mask by Alfredo Iriarte	Author

INDEX

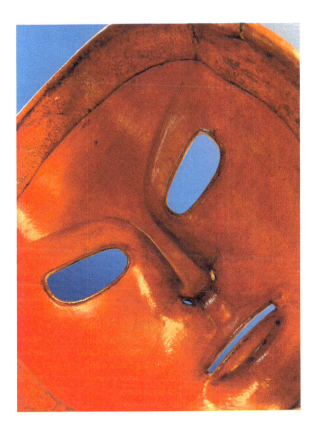

Note: Locators in *italics* represent figures in the text.

abstract masks 26, *26*, 106, 111
acrylic sealers 198
actor training with masks 101–102
adapted masks 184–185, *184*, *185*
aesthetics 26–29, 131
Agostino, Christopher 19
Ahk-Hak-Kwoe-Bum 35
alginate 179–181, *180*, 183
allegory 27, 30, 134
alternate mask placement *147*
Altraform 206
alus characters 40, 52–53, 124–125
ancestors 7, 9–11, 15, 20, 44, 51, *131*, 262
animal masks 52, 62, *129*, *207*, 217
anti-masking laws 8, 18
apollo masks 24, *149*
Appel, Libby 157, 163, 200, 274
Aquaform 226
archetypes 131, 132
architectural masks 20
Arlecchino 71–72, *120*, 126–127, *165*, *178*
articulations 112–113
Atellan farces 65, 67, 69
Aufenfehn, Michael *134*, *147*, *157*

balance 51, 138, 178
Bali Dreams (case study) 124–125
Balinese Masks: categories, 52–54;
    conventions, *40*; performance
    traditions, 51–52; Rangda, *16*
Barba, Eugenio 103
Barong (Bali) 18, 34, 51–52, 125, *125*, *177*
Basel mask 26, *160*, *176*, 264; see *also* larval
    masks
Bauta masks 19
Becker, Jonathan 4, 28, *85*, 92, *108*, *111*,
    123, *127*, *152*, *164*, *170*, *172*, *178*,
    186, 219, 220
Benda, Wladyslaw T. 134, 139, *140*,
    140–142, 147, 198, 223, 224
Bian Lian (Chinese) 35, 41, *41*
binder 191
Binoche, Jean-Marie *214*
blocking 95
Blue Moon Over Memphis *50*, 127, *128*
bondres 37, 40, 54, *124*
Bonds, Alexandra 240
Bradley, Doug 253
A Brave Face (Vamos Theatre) 86, *110*

Bread and Puppet Theatre 23, 77, 78
Brevoort, Deborah 127
Brighella 36, 71, 74
buckram 216, 223
Buechler, John 251
Bugaku 42
Bune 57
Butha 52

calipers 146, 155, *194*
Calonarang (Balinese) 51–54
camauro 165
Campbell, Joseph 10
Capitano 37, 71, 72–73
cardboard 223, *223*
caricatures 24–25, 133
Carnivale 13, 18, 23, 34, 67–69
casting 146, 174, 217; latex, 218–219;
    neoprene, 219–220; Celastic, 226, 227
Celluclay 199–200
Chaplin, Charlie 215, 252, *252*
character makeup 239, 255–258
character masks 30, *148*, 163–164

303

character types 65, 244, 248
Chase, Mike 18, 143, 156
Chinese opera: color symbolism, 246–247; makeup, 244–247; tourist mask, 200
Chinese terracotta warrior mask 187
Ch'oraengi 56
chou 240, 244, 245–246, 246, 257
Chuji 57
Chūjo 46
chunda poovu 241
chung 56
chutti 238, 241
clay sculpt by Bernardo Rey 145
clocking 110
closed cell foam 217
closed-mouth masks 178
clowns 8, 23, 37, 39, 40, 54, 125, 155, 245, 251, 254, 257
codes, codified 36–39, 102, 214, 241, 248, 251, 254, 256
Cohen, Amy 170, 228
cokanna tadi see cuvanna tati
Cole, Willie 5, 234
Colombina 71, 73–74, 150
color 138
comfort (fit) 178
Commedia dell'Arte 69–76, 70, 75, 126, 151, 169, 170, 171, 178
commercial masks 185
conquistador mask 40
Copeau, Jacques 76, 102
costumes 91
coulrophobia 265
countermask 109, 131, 134, 155, 157, 158
craft foam 217
cuda manik 52, 53
cultural appropriation 128
cuvanna tati 242

Dalem masks 53
Damselfrau 234
Damshtram 241
Dan 244–245, 245
dance dramas 59
dance masks 21
Dead Good (Vamos Theatre) 83
Dean, Russell 6, 8, 23, 96, 103, 109, 112, 115, 117, 118, 121, 132, 133, 139, 145, 149, 150, 151, 153, 155, 164, 209
death masks 7, 12, 12, 24, 26, 34, 52, 69
decorative masks 19–20, 19, 186, 233
demons 18, 29, 34, 37, 39, 42–44, 47, 51–52, 54, 57–59, 60, 61–62, 68–69, 71, 240–241, 243, 247–249, 254, 256
dental alginate 183
devil see demons
Devon Painter 35
dhumstras 241
digital design of mask 183, 228
Di Marchi, Giorgio 23, 128
dimensional SFX makeup 256
dimensional texture 155
direct masking and modeling 175, 176, 187, 198–202, 272–273

disguise 18, 68
domino masks 19, 20, 23, 136, 185, 203, 209
Dottore 37, 71, 72, 75
Doug Bradley in Pinhead Makeup 253
drama therapy 30, 124
drawing of mask forms 136
Dr. Nest (Familie Flöz) 93, 106
dual nature of masks 6

Egyptian mask 5, 12
Ehrenfeld, Hartmut 134, 144, 157
Eldredge, Sears 10, 15, 21, 36, 82, 84, 102, 103
elements of design 136, 137–139
Elvis mask 24, 50, 128, 128, 133
Emmert, Richard 48–51
emotional engagement with masks 8–9
emotional masks 25, 157, 163, 163, 201
entertainment, masks for 10–11, 20–22, 36, 59, 67–68, 140
epoxy resin 225
ethofoam 222
European medieval theater 67–69
executioner's mask 14
exercises for working with masks: articulations and isolations, 112; body, discovering, 104–105; developing material, 121; finding the body of the mask, 113–114; finding the face and finding the body, 119; finding the voice, 119; first encounters, 111–112; interacting with other masks, 116–117; interacting with the world, 114; mask, discovering, 104; playing multiple characters, 117; world, discovering, 105

Faint, Mattie 254
Familie Flöz 23, 39, 76, 90, 91, 93–95, 106, 107, 148
Faust, Rob 26, 87, 114, 133, 147, 150, 159, 164, 227
Fava, Antonio 76, 84, 120, 126, 169, 208, 251
fiber helmet mask (Maninka people) 27
Finding Joy (Vamos Theatre) 87
fitting 176–178, 177, 198
foam 176, 217, 222, 224
folk masks and theater 33, 34, 42
Fool's Fire (Julie Taymor) 164
forms of masks 10, 22–30, 137
Fosshape 204–206, 206
found object masks 15, 27, 28, 29, 233
framing effect of masks 82
framing the moment 107
Friendly Plastic 187, 201, 206
fright masks 22, 185
Fukai (Fukai-onna), shakumia 45
full-face masks 88, 92, 102, 105, 118, 119, 178; actor's role, 106–111; how the mask works, 106
full head masks 23; see also helmet masks
functions of mask 10, 84; decorative masks, 19–20; entertainment, masks for, 20–22; practical masks, 16–19;

religious masks, 15; socio-cultural masks, 11–14
funeral mask 1, 12, 24
FuzzForm 206

Gendou Ogawa 224
Gigaku 5, 42, 262
glues 223
Gould, Benjamin 127
Greek masks 39, 62–65, 63, 64, 151, 171, 178
Greek Theater 33, 33, 65, 88
grotesque 25–26, 30, 118, 134, 164, 165
Gulma Sanniya 18
Gyōdō 42

Habbe & Meik 134, 144, 157
Hahoe (Korean) 35–36, 54–57, 56, 154, 224
Hakushiji-jo (Okina) 44
half masks 23, 88, 102, 117–119, 164
Halloween mask 13, 14, 22, 34, 218, 252
Halmi 57
Hannya 46
Hanuman the Monkey King 58, 242, 242, 251
healing masks 16, 18
helmet masks 20, 23, 64, 124, 133, 136, 153, 171, 176, 217, 225, 230
hockey mask 11, 16, 124, 251
Hodder, Kane 251
hualian 246
human transformation 6, 9–10, 21, 30, 35–36, 45, 62, 84, 108, 238–239, 251, 253–254
Hunt, Deborah 151

idealized masks 12, 24, 24, 39, 43, 45, 134
Imae 56
Infinita (Familie Flöz) 91
"inner life," of mask 107
inner monologue 97, 108
intellectual understanding of masks 9–10
Inumaru, Tadashi 252
Invitation to a Beheading (Vladimir Nabokov) 88, 89
Iriarte, Alfredo, cover 103, 160, 160
isolations 112

Japanese mask traditions 38, 42–53, 225
jauk 54
jing 246, 246
Jingju 237, 239, 244, 244, 251
Johnstone, Keith 252
Jō mask 43, 45
Jo-men 45
Jung 56
Jung, Carl 30

Kabuki (Japanese) 248–250, 256
kaduru wood 61

Kaksi 57
kanmuri hairstyle/crown 45–46
kari "black" 242
karuppa tadi see karutta tati
karutta tati 242
Kathakali (Indian) 237, 240, 241–243, 253, 254
katti "knife" 242
Kelley, Emmet 254
keras characters 53
Khon (Thai) 36, 38–39, 57–59, 57, 58, 59, 154
Kijin 44
Kishin mask 43, 44
Kitazawa, Hideta 44, 47, 48, 48–51, 50, 128, 224
Knezz, David 26, 151, 158, 161
Kolam (Sri Lankan) 59–61
ko-omote 45
Korean Hahoe, sandae guk 54–57
Kuker masks 13
Ku Klux Klan 14
Kumadori makeup 249, 250, 252
kurai 43
Kyogen (Japanese) 39, 43, 47–48, 262

La Carpa de los Rasquachis (El Teatro Campesino) 82
lacquer 198
Lambeth, Cheralyn 219
language 37
larval masks 5, 21, 26, 30, 108, 109, 111, 114, 139, 160, 161
latex masks 28, 217, 218–219, 218
lazzi 121
leather mask 27, 28, 29, 170, 175, 176, 208–212, 212, 213, 214
Lecoq, Jacques 76, 102
life cast 174
life masks 24
lighting designers 91
linen mask 170
The Lion King (Julie Taymor) 78
live mask 131, 134, 156
Luly, Marco 84, 118, 165

Magojirō 45
maquette 123, 145, 231
Marceau, Marcel 257
Mascots 8, 22, 23, 126, 127, 172
maskaphobia 8
mask-making options 175
mask-making traditions 61
Mask of Agamemnon 7
Masques 68
McCarty, Cara 6
McClernan, Candace 206, 207, 208, 217, 231
McClung, Mary 23, 222
McKean, Dave 21, 159
medieval theater (European) 36, 67–69
Menglin, Zhao 240

metal masks 29, 189, 216–217, 227, 227, 228
Mexican Mask 7, 22, 29, 154, 224, 225
Meyerhold, Vsevolod 76
mime 67, 76, 257
minukku 242–243
miracle plays 68
Mirror Mask (Dave McKean) 21, 159
Mnouchkine, Ariane 78
modeling materials 199
Model Magic 175, 187, 200, 201
mold release agents 189
monotheism 34
morality plays 34, 68
Morawetz, Thomas 9, 239, 255, 256
Mouse Queen 171
movement 104–105, 112–114, 119, 178
mudras 37
Mummenshanz 76, 84
mummers 67–68
music 37, 54–55, 92
mystery plays 34, 68

Navarasas 37, 37
negative cast 174
neoprene mask 28, 28, 170, 217, 219–220
neutral masks 26, 30, 102–105, 130, 139, 151, 159–166
New Comedy 62, 65
Newman 20, 209, 277
Nobody's Home (Grafted Cede and Theatre Temoin) 88
Noh masks (Japanese) 42, 43, 44, 45, 46, 47, 127, 146, 224; categories, 44–47; construction, 43–44
Nowo masked figure 11
Nunley, John 6, 11, 36
Nursing Lives (Vamos Theatre) 98

occupational masks 10, 16–19
Oedipus Rex 76, 128
Ogwangdae 54
Okina 42, 44–45
Oktan, Spat 219
Old Comedy 63, 65
Oleon, Mike 89–90, 101, 119
onna men 45
Onryō 46–47
otoko 46
oversized body and parade masks 23, 175, 176

Paccha Vesham 241, 241
Paekchong 56
Paekjung 56
painted effects 197, 256
Pantalone 36, 37, 71, 73, 75, 84, 132, 215
paper masks 27, 28, 222
paper pulp 187, 193, 199
paper techniques 221
parade masks 23, 30, 34, 176
paraffin 188–189
Pareidolia 4, 4

parody 133
partial masks 23, 164
patih 53
patterning and forming masks 221–223
payuppu "ripe" 241
Penasar brothers 53
perspiration 177–178
Phra Ram mask 154
physical response to masks 6–8
physiognomy 131
pigskin lining 177
Plague Doctor's mask 17
plaster bandages 179, 182
plaster mold 218
plastic wrap 188
Pollock, Rachel 207, 231
polyurethane 222
Porras, Omar 164, 277
positive cast 174
potlatch 11
practical masks 11, 16–19
Prattki, Thomas 116
presentational form, mask as 106
principles of composition 136
principles of design 138–139
production concept 87, 90
proportion/scale 50, 138, 147, 160
prototypes 131
Pulcinella 70, 71, 74
Punae 57
Punch and Judy puppet shows 75
purchased masks 171, 176, 184, 185, 186, 187
pyolsandae 54

Raja Putri (topeng putri) masks 53
raked stages 91
A Rake's Progress (Strangeface Theatre) 117, 121
realistic masks 24
release agents 188, 188
religious and cultural rites 33
religious masks 11, 15
representational style of masks 23–26
resource analysis 174–176
respiration 176–177
Rey Rengifo, Bernardo 26, 123, 126, 131, 134, 144, 145, 146, 147, 152, 153, 177, 209–216
rhythmic coordination 139–142
rites of passage 11, 14, 23
ritual performance 7, 10, 11, 14, 21, 24, 30, 33, 36, 43, 51, 52, 54, 59, 62, 159, 224
Rolfe, Bari 156, 160, 163, 252
Roman theatre 12, 24, 65–67
Rude Mechanical Theatre Company 78
Ryō-no-Otoko 46

Saint-Denis, Michel 101, 102
sandae guk (Korean) 54–57
sandae nori 54
Sande Society Mask 11
San Francisco Mime Troupe 78
Sanni (Sri Lankan) 59–62

Santelli, Giancarlo *123, 126, 132, 151, 165, 170, 175, 178*
Sartori, Amleto *34, 76, 102, 130–131, 142, 160, 164, 232*
Sartori, Donato *75–76, 102, 103, 129–131, 214–215, 160*
satiric masks *25*
Savage, Rachael *86*
scale of masks *22–23*
scenic designers *90*
Schüler, Hajo *23, 94–95*
Schumann, Peter *78*
scold's bridles *14*
sealers *198*
seasonal cycles *13–14, 33–34, 67*
Sedana, I Nyoman *124*
sequential casting drawing *174*
SFX see special effects makeup
shellac *183, 198*
Shell Mosaic Ritual Mask *7*
sheng *244–245, 245*
Sherman, Stanley Allen *78*
Shockheaded Peter (Tiger Lillies) *255*
Sidakarya *52–54*
silicone *179, 188, 217*
Sintra *208*
skull masks *35, 172, 207, 231*
soap solution *189*
social control *14*
socio-cultural masks *10–14*
socio-political systems *34*
Soldier's Song (Strangeface Theatre) *96*
Soltanto, Matteo *232*
Sonbi, Sonpi *56*
sound designers *92*
special effects makeup (SFX) *251, 256, 256*
spiritual masks *15*
spiritual protections in cultures *18*
sports masks *16, 17, 18*
Sri Lankan masks *59–62, 60, 61*
Stanislavsky, Konstantin *252*
Stanley Allan Sherman *78*
St Denis, Michel *76*
stereotypes *131, 132*
stitched fabric mask (Werner Strub) *28, 156*
stock characters *118, 133*
stocking mask *9, 19*
stories *36–37*
Strangeface Theatre (Russell Dean) *39, 96, 109, 117, 121, 139, 145, 149*
Streha (Russell Dean) *150*
Strehler, Giorgio *76*
strip techniques *188*; binder, *191*; finishing, *196–198*; fitting, *198*; form, *188*; process, *195*; release agents, *188*; strips, *189*; wiring the masks, *196*

strivesham (female) minukku makeup *242*
Strub, Werner *25, 28, 29, 34, 129, 149, 156, 170, 232, 232*
Sun Wukong *251*
supernatural characters *62*
suspension of disbelief *84*
symbolic masks *18, 26, 39, 55, 69, 109, 243*
symmetry *138, 155*

taksu *51*
t'al *54*
t'al chum *54*
t'al nori *54*
tapel *51*
tati beard *242*
Taymor, Julie *78, 128, 164*
Teatro Campesino *78*
Teatro Cenit *213*
Teatro Delusio (Familie Flöz) *107*
telek *54*
temporary masks *29*
terra-cotta mask, ChupÃ-Cuaro *29*
Terra Flex *207*
Thai Khon masks *57–59, 57, 58, 59*
Theatre Nohgaku *48, 127*
theppu "special" *243*
thermoplastics *202–208*
threadstories *156*
3D printing *179, 183, 228–231, 229, 230, 231*
three-quarter masks *23, 88*
Tiger Lillies *255*
Tonight We Fly (Trestle Theatre Company) *108*
Topeng (Balinese) *51*; mask categories, *52–54*; performance traditions, *51–52*
Topeng panca *52*
Topeng Tua *53*
Tovil (Sri Lankan) *59–62*
traditions that historically use masks *279*
transformation *6, 9, 10–11, 21, 30, 35–36, 45, 62, 84, 102, 108, 239, 242, 251, 253–254*
trestle stages *69*
Trestle Theatre Company *76, 108*
A Trip to the Moon (Georges Méliès) *21*
Tsuda, Rui *249*
Tsuina *42*

Uba, rōjā, and wa *45*
Ubu Roi (Alfred Jarry) *255*
Undagi tapel *51*
undercuts *157, 172*
universal masks see neutral masks
uplighting *92*
urethane-polyurethane *198*

usofuki mask (Hideta Kitazawa) *47*
utilitarian catcher's mask *18*

vacuform *225, 226*
Vamos Theatre *8, 23, 39, 76, 83, 85, 86, 87, 98, 110, 132, 145, 149, 164*
varaform/hexcelite thermoplastic mesh *208*
varnish *198*
The Vegetable Gardener (Giuseppe Arcimboldo) *5*
vella tati *242*
veluppa tadi see Vella tati
venetian tourist mask *200*
V for Vendetta *14*
vision in the mask *176*
vocalization *178*
voice, finding *119–120*

waka–onna *45*
Wallace, Denise *184, 217*
water-activated bandages *179*
wax *188–189, 198*
Wax Death mask (Benjamin Disraeli) *12*
Wayang (orang) parwa *54*
Wayang Wong *52*
Weary Willie *254*
wenjing *246*
whistling masks *47*
white-faced clown makeup *254*
Wilsher, Toby *97, 146, 157*
Wilson, Robert *255*
wire *196, 216–217, 223*
wonderflex *206*
wooden masks *20, 28, 43, 51, 54, 56, 176, 224, 225*
wooden matrix *175, 209*
Worbla/Terra Flex *207, 207*
world, discovering *105*
Woyzeck *93*
wrestling masks *17*
Wright, Vicky *18, 162*
W.T. Benda's satiric mask *24, 25*
wujing *246*

Yamaguchi, Master Bidou *224*
Yangban *56, 56–57*
Yaryu *54*
Yeats, William Butler *76*
young lovers *71, 73*

zoomorphism *131, 135*
Zō-onna *44*
Zorro *19, 78*

9781138084186